THIS THING OF OURS:
INVESTIGATING *THE SOPRANOS*

THIS THING OF OURS:
INVESTIGATING *THE SOPRANOS*

edited by David Lavery

Columbia University Press
Publishers Since 1893
New York   Chichester, West Sussex

Wallflower Press
5 Pond Street, London NW3 2PN
www.wallflowerpress.co.uk

Copublished in North America in 2002 by Columbia University Press
and in Great Britain in 2002 by Wallflower Press

Columbia University Press
Library of Congress Cataloging-in-Publication Data

This thing of ours : investigating the Sopranos / edited by David Lavery
     p. cm.
     ISBN 0–231–12780–4 (cloth : alk. paper) — ISBN 0–231–12781–2 (paper : alk. paper)
     1. Sopranos (Television program)   I. Lavery, David, 1949–

     PN1992.77.S66 T49 2002
     791.45'72—dc21

                                                      2002073962

Wallflower Press
A catalogue for this book is available from the British Library

     ISBN 1-903364-44-2 pbk
     ISBN 1-903364-45-0 hbk

c 10 9 8 7 6 5 4 3 2 1
p 10 9 8 7 6 5 4 3 2 1

Printed in Great Britain by Antony Rowe Ltd, Chippenham, Wiltshire

CONTENTS

ACKNOWLEDGMENTS

It goes without saying in a book of this kind that many people have contributed to it. I want to thank all of the authors – Ellen Willis, Albert Auster, Robert J. Thompson, Paul Levinson, Dawn Elizabeth B. Johnston, Mark C. Rogers, Michael Epstein, Jimmie L. Reeves, Cindy Donatelli, Sharon Alward, Avi Santo, Joanne Lacey, Joseph S. Walker, Glen Creeber, David Pattie, Kim Akass, Janet McCabe, Kevin Fellezs, Lance Strate, Douglas L. Howard, Steven Hayward, Andrew Biro, and Sarah Lewis Dunne – for their wonderful contributions.

Special thanks to Jimmie Cain: our many conversations about *The Sopranos* have added a great deal to my own understanding of the series. Thanks as well to Yoram Allon of Wallflower Press for his encouragement and support.

And thanks, of course, to David Chase, for giving us such a rich television series. The final two years of *The Sopranos* will no doubt surprise us. Here, for what it is worth, is my predicted ending. FBI efforts to put Tony in jail for his organized crime activities come to nothing. When Tony finally learns of Dr. Melfi's rape, he avenges the crime, killing Jesus Rossi with his bare hands, becoming in reality the Rottweiler of Melfi's "Employee of the Month" (3004) dream, and it is this felonious act which does him in. As the series ends, Tony is in prison not for his real crimes but for his good deed on behalf of the woman who has tried to heal him. Such would be an ending which the always ironic Chase might find appropriate.

This book is dedicated to my wife, as tough as Carmela, even more understanding of the proclivities of a difficult husband, and the most authentic human being I will ever know.

LIST OF CONTRIBUTORS

Kim Akass is Visiting Lecturer in Film Studies at Royal Holloway University of London. She has researched female narrative authority in cinema and is currently developing a project on narrative developments in children's media.

Sharon Alward is Associate Professor in the School of Art at the University of Manitoba.

Albert Auster teaches in the Department of Communication and Media Studies at Fordham University. With Leonard Quart, he is the co-author of *American Film and Society Since 1945* (1991).

Andrew Biro holds a post-doctoral fellowship in Political Science at the University of Toronto.

Glen Creeber is Research Fellow in the School of Journalism, Media & Cultural Studies at Cardiff University, Wales. He is the author of *Dennis Potter: Between Two Worlds, A Critical Reassessment* (1998) and editor of *The Television Genre Book* (2001). Among other projects he is currently working on *Serial Fictions: Television Drama in the Age of the Mini-Series*.

Cindy Donatelli is Associate Professor of English and Women's Studies at the University of Manitoba. Her most recent work includes "The Statue of Liberty:

Genderbendering the Technobody" and "Driving the Suburbs: Minivans, Gender, and Family Values."

Sara Lewis Dunne is Associate Professor of English at Middle Tennessee State University. She is the co-editor of the journal *Studies in Popular Culture.*

Michael Epstein is Associate Professor at the Southwestern University College of Law, where he teaches courses on media and entertainment law.

Kevin Fellezs is a doctoral candidate in the History of Consciousness program at the University of California, Santa Cruz.

Steven Hayward is Assistant Professor of English at John Carroll University.

Douglas L. Howard is Writing Center Coordinator and Honours Program Professor at SUNY Suffolk. His work has appeared in *Literature and Theology*, *The Chronicle of Higher Education*, and *PopPolitics*. He is currently co-editing and contributing to a forthcoming volume on racial and social representations of the Gothic Other.

Dawn Elizabeth B. Johnston is a doctoral candidate in Communication and Culture at the University of Calgary.

Joanne Lacey is Senior Lecturer in Visual Culture at the University of Brighton.

David Lavery is Professor of English at Middle Tennessee State University. The author of over forty essays and author/editor/co-editor of *Late for the Sky: The Mentality of the Space Age* (1992), *Full of Secrets: Critical Approaches to Twin Peaks* (1994), *"Deny All Knowledge": Reading The X-Files* (1996), *Fighting the Forces: What's at Stake in Buffy the Vampire Slayer* (2002), *Teleparody: Predicting/Preventing the TV Discourse of Tomorrow* (2002), and *Twin Peaks in the Rearview Mirror: Appraisals and Reappraisals of the Show that was Supposed to Change TV* (forthcoming).

Paul Levinson is Professor of Communication and Media Studies at Fordham University. He is the author of such non-fiction books as *Mind at Large: Knowing in the Technological Age* (1988), *The Soft Edge: A Natural History and Future of the Information Revolution* (1997), *Digital McLuhan: A Guide to the Information Millennium* (1999), and the science fiction novels *The Silk Code* (1999), *Borrowed Tides* (2001), and *The Consciousness Plague* (forthcoming).

Janet McCabe is a Lecturer in Film Studies at Trinity College Dublin. She has written on American quality television in the British context, including a contribution to *Frames and Fictions on Television: The Politics of Identity within Drama* (2000). She has just completed her Ph.D. in early German cinema and feminist film theory.

David Pattie is Senior Lecturer in Performing Arts at Chester College, UK.

Jimmie L. Reeves is Associate Professor of Mass Communication at Texas Tech University. In addition to articles on subjects ranging from Mr. T to *The X-Files,* he is the co-author of *Cracked Coverage: Television News, the Anti-Cocaine Crusade, and the Reagan Legacy* (1994).

Mark C. Rogers is Assistant Professor of Communication at Walsh University. His previous publications include collaborative pieces on *Twin Peaks* and *The X-Files.*

Avi Santo is a graduate student at the University of Texas.

Lance Strate is Associate Professor of Communication and Media Studies at Fordham University. President of the Media Ecology Association, he is the author of *Understanding Media Ecology* (forthcoming), and primary editor of *Communication and Cyberspace: Social Interaction in an Electronic Environment* (1996, 2002), and *Cybertheory and the Ecology of Digital Media* (forthcoming).

Robert J. Thompson is Professor of Television, Film, and Popular Culture at Syracuse University, where he directs the Center for the Study of Popular Television. He has written or edited five books on American television, including *Television's Second Golden Age* (1997) and *Prime Time, Prime Movers* (1997). He is currently completing a major study of *St. Elsewhere.*

Joseph S. Walker teaches at Auburn University. His work has appeared in *Modern Fiction Studies, The Centennial Review, Colby Quarterly,* and forthcoming collections on *The Blair Witch Project* and *The Catcher in the Rye.*

Ellen Willis directs the Cultural Journalism program at New York University and is a fellow of the *Nation* Institute. Her latest book is *Don't Think, Smile! Notes on a Decade of Denial* (2000).

"COMING HEAVY":
THE SIGNIFICANCE OF *THE SOPRANOS*[1]

David Lavery

> Well, it would help me not to see anything more, for what's good, and what's bad. Because, you see, on this earth there is one thing which is terrible, and that is that everyone has their own reasons.
>
> Octave in Jean Renoir's *The Rules of the Game* (1939)

In "Meadowlands" (1004) in *The Sopranos*' first season, Tony Soprano visits the Sit Tite Loungenette to make his displeasure known to his uncle, Carrado "Junior" Soprano, concerning a recent mock-hit on Christopher Moltisanti, one of Tony's soldiers. Having just attacked Mikey Palmice, Junior's right-hand man, on the street outside with a staple gun (stolen during a visit to the hospital), Tony is in no mood for conciliation, but neither is Junior, who warns his nephew not to return again unless he is armed: "Come heavy," he insists, "or not at all." As a work of popular culture, a path-breaking television series, and a media phenomenon, *The Sopranos* itself "comes heavy," if you will, in every episode, not just with weaponry but with significance. The cultures of the United States, Great Britain, and Canada (see the essays in this volume by Johnston and Lacey), Australia, and even Italy (where it premiered in the spring of 2001) have come under its influence and contributed to the cultural conversation about it. Talk, discourse, about *The Sopranos* has migrated far beyond the water cooler.

Vanity Fair (December 1999) offers an Annie Leibovitz photograph of the cast of *The Sopranos* reenacting da Vinci's *The Last Supper*, with James Gandolfini, of course, in the role of Christ (and Big Pussy as Judas).

On National Public Radio's *Car Talk*, Tom and Ray Magliozzi, discussing the new "Eddie Bauer Edition Ford Expedition," propose other possible signature cars: first on their list is a "Tony Soprano Suburban" (which should come complete with a baseball bat mounted in the rear window).[2]

A Nashville, Tennessee furniture store, promoting a 50 per cent off sale on Italian leather upholstery, claims that they offer "Italian leather savings without the Mob." As an enticement to shoppers, they offer a prize drawing for a gift card to Romano's Macaroni Grill, a vacation to Rome, and a "Soprano's [sic] DVD collectors set."

On ESPN's Sports Center a visiting player who has hit a home run over Fenway Park's Green Monster is said to have "disrespected the Bing!" – just like Ralph Cifaretto did in "University" (3006). (The catchphrase begins to appear everywhere.)

Congresswoman Marge Roukema (R-New Jersey) introduces a resolution to condemn HBO, David Chase, and *The Sopranos* for propagating offensive Italian stereotypes. (Interviewed by the press, she admits that she has never watched the show.)

An advertisement for Season Three of *The Sopranos* (running on HBO and other networks) advises us that "Christmas will be a little late this year,"[3] as a moving camera pans across the front of Satriale's Pork Store – one of the series' primary locations – and around to the side, where it discovers the body of a whacked Santa Claus, disposed of in a dumpster.

A May 2001 panel discussion (later broadcast on C-Span), sponsored by the National Italian-American Foundation and featuring cultural critics Camile Paglia and James Wolcott but not a single advocate, doesn't have a kind word to say about *The Sopranos*.

The real Donnie Brasco (former FBI agent Joseph Pistone – Mike Newell's 1997 film was based on his six years undercover with the mob) praises the authenticity of *The Sopranos* in *Time*.

Lexicographer Jesse Sheidlower predicts that the next *Oxford English Dictionary* will contain numerous *Sopranos* citations (DeCaro, "From Jersey" 22, 26).

A man loudly seeking a late night entry to James Gandolfini's apartment building flees in terror when met at the door by none other than the "real" Tony Soprano. "Tony, man, I'm so sorry. I am so sorry!" ("James Gandolfini" 72).

The Italian-American One Voice Committee gives its first "Pasta-tute of the Year" award to *Sopranos'* creator David Chase for having sold-out his Italian heritage. In the fall of 2001 the American Italian Defense Association's denunciations of Dominic Chianese (Uncle Junior on *The Sopranos*) prevent the veteran actor and singer from touring to promote his new CD *Hits*.

Arch-conservative William F. Buckley overcomes his compunctions ("I swore I'd shoot myself if I didn't write about it, 'it' being *The Sopranos*") and castigates the series in a brief review of "University" (3006) in *National Review*. The most interesting thing about *The Sopranos*, he insists, is "its confirmation of the psychological depravity of the viewing audience." "The wonder," Buckley opines, "isn't that *The Sopranos* is so marvelously conceived and executed, but that it is so widely viewed and enjoyed without any hint of concern over the depravity it relies upon." Tony Soprano is compared to Heinrich Himmler. (In a mere 700 words Buckley manages to make several glaring errors about what actually transpires in the episode.[4])

George Anastasia, a *Philadelphia Inquirer* crime reporter who has covered the dysfunctional Philadelphia and South Jersey mob for fifteen years, tells Terry Gross on WHYY's *Fresh Air* that he watches *The Sopranos* religiously and praises David Chase's third season decision to completely deglamorize the mob. (Any ethnic group, he comments, that can give the world Antonin Scalia and Camille Paglia need not fear that Tony Soprano will become its role model.)

While at work on a collection of academic essays on *The Sopranos* a college professor receives abusive e-mails and voice-mails demanding abandonment of the project long before the book is ever published. One e-mail, from a Pittsburgh physician, calls him a "despicable human being" for doing such a book. The professor responds by asking whether the doctor routinely makes diagnoses before ever examining his patients.

"In certain kinds of writing, particularly in art criticism and literary criticism," George Orwell observed half a century ago in "Politics and the English Language," "it is normal to come across long passages which are almost completely lacking in meaning. . . . When one critic writes, 'The outstanding feature of Mr. X's work is its living quality,' while another writes, 'The immediately striking thing about Mr. X's work is its peculiar deadness,' the reader accepts this as a simple difference of opinion. If words like black and white were involved, instead of the jargon words dead and living, he would see at once that language was being used in an improper way. Many political words are similarly abused."

As a recent incarnation of "X", David Chase's *The Sopranos* has produced blatantly contradictory assessments that might make Orwell roll over in his grave. In the eyes of Ellen Willis, for example, (whose seminal essay in *The Nation* is reprinted in this volume) the HBO series is "The richest and most compelling piece of television – no, of popular culture – that I've encountered in the past twenty years . . . a meditation on the nature of morality, the possibility of redemption, and the legacy of Freud." For the always provocative Camille Paglia, however, *The Sopranos* is a contemptible "ethnic minstrel show – Amos and Andy for a TV industry that can no longer get away with demeaning stereotypes of blacks and Jews" and a "buffoonish caricature of my people" ("Feinstein").

> I have yet to watch a single entire episode of that show, which I find vulgar and boring as well as rife with offensive clichés about Italian-Americans that would never be tolerated were they about Jews or blacks.
>
> What I find especially repugnant about *The Sopranos* is its elitist condescension toward working-class life, which it distorts with formulas that are 30 years out of date. Manners and mores have subtly evolved in the ethnic world that *The Sopranos* purports to depict and that extends from South Philadelphia to central New Jersey and metropolitan New York. ("Energy Mess")[5]

Willis' and Paglia's black and white discrepancy tells us more, however, than Orwell's characteristic naïve realist view would have us believe. Might it not be that they disagree because *The Sopranos* as a text is like the body of the famous "elephant in the dark" in the Sufi story, whose nature reveals itself in entirely different ways depending on which part of its complex being is currently being examined?

Allen Coulter, the most-often-utilized of the series' stable of directors, has called *The Sopranos* "David's poem to New Jersey. I do believe that New Jersey is to David Chase what a part of Italy was to Fellini" (quoted by DeCaro, "Mob Squad" 24). In its richness Sopranoland reminds us not just of Fellini but of Faulkner, who wrote on a map of his own fictional universe, Yoknapatawpha County in Mississippi, "William Faulkner, Owner and Proprietor." Owner and proprietor David Chase's teleuniverse is filled to overflowing with rich detail and wonderful imagination. When Paglia, or the Italian-American One Voice committee, or James Wolcott (a *Vanity Fair* culture critic who first praised and then denounced the series), or L. Brent Bozell feel about the *Sopranos* elephant, discovering negative images of Italians, or excessive violence, or over-the-top profanity to be its defining features, are they blind to its thousand other moments of wit and brilliance? Why is it not the marvelous flashbacks, astonishing dream sequences, *Godfather*-quality montages, wicked, profane, often very black sense of humor, stereotype-defying idiosyncratic major and minor characters, superb cinematography, memorable set-pieces, playful, argot-laced language, real-as-it-gets dialogue, intertextual complexity,[6] and rich textual geography that they decide to notice in the series?

Let us imagine a compilation tape presented in court at *The Sopranos'* public trial – an incomplete but representative video record of quality moments meant to show its accusers (especially those who have condemned it without even watching it) the elephant in all its complexity. We might see:

Tony Soprano crying in Dr. Melfi's office when he realizes the meaning of his infatuation with the ducks visiting his swimming pool ("The Sopranos"/1001).

Cut to Tony taking his Prozac while staring into the bathroom mirror as Grace Slick sings "One pill makes you smaller/and one pill makes you tall/and the ones that mother gives you/don't do anything at all . . ." before his flashbacks to 1967 begin ("Down Neck"/1007).

Cut to Tony spraying whipped cream down AJ's throat in a father-son late-night raid on the freezer ("Down Neck"/1007).

Cut to Christopher Moltisanti's grotesque recurring nightmare in which a waste management rival he had earlier whacked returns to torture him and feed sausage to his girl friend Adriana – and then to Carmela ("The Legend of Tennessee Molisanti"/1008).

Cut to Tony using his Mafia power to force an ill-mannered young man to remove his hat in a restaurant ("Boca"/1009).

Cut to Paulie Walnuts admitting that he has seen a therapist because he lacked "coping skills" ("I Dream of Jeannie Cusamano"/1013).

Cut to a young Asian man answering "Here" when Christopher Moltisanti's name is called at a stockbroker's exam ("Guy Walks into a Psychiatrist's Office"/2001).

Cut to Junior Soprano's lament that "The federal marshalls are so far up my ass I can taste Brylcream" ("Toodle-Fucking-oo"/2003).

Cut to Richie Aprile, a violent, loathsome gangster, doing the Downward Facing Dog in yoga class ("Toodle-Fucking-oo"/2003).

Cut to Dr. Melfi's bizarre dream, in which Tony dies in a horrible head-on collision with a huge truck to the tune of a munchkin song ("Out of the Woods") from *The Wizard of Oz* (1939) ("Toodle-Fucking-oo" /2003).

Cut to a Soprano-commissioned car-jacking by two young African Americans that arouses the victim's misplaced racism; "Fucking niggers," he exclaims, shocking his family ("Commendatori"/2004).

Cut to Tony, appalled by his son's newfound nihilism and atheism, rebuking him with perhaps the most blasphemous line ever uttered on television: "She [Carmela] knows that even if God is dead, you're still gonna kiss his ass" ("D-Girl"/2007).

Cut to Christopher Moltisanti explaining his Near Death Experience vision of hell as an Irish bar where it's always Saint Patrick's Day ("From Where to Eternity"/2009).

Cut to Tony teaching AJ how to pilot *The Stugots*, completely oblivious to the small boat they swamp in their wake ("Bust Out"/2010).

Cut to Tony's food-poison-induced dreams in which (a) he self-immolates at Asbury Park to preempt death from cancer, (b) drives off with Adriana, Chris, and Furio in a tiny clown car, and (c) listens to Pussy's confession of betrayal through the words of an on-ice talking fish ("Funhouse"/2013).

Cut to Patsy Parisi urinating in Tony's pool, payback for Tony having had his brother whacked and, later, Tony inviting Patsy and his son over for a swim ("Mr. Ruggerio's Neighborhood"/3001).

Cut to Dr. Melfi's vivid dream in which she is again attacked by her rapist Jesus Rossi while her hand is caught in a soft drink vending machine and saved by a savage Rottweiller, who she later realizes (in dialogue with Dr. Kupferberg) represents Tony: "big head, massive shoulders, direct descendent of the dog used by the Roman armies to guard their camps" ("Employee of the Month"/3004).

Cut to dying-from-lung cancer hit man Bobby Baccilieri, Sr. dispatching with great difficulty Mustang Sally while coughing up blood ("Another Toothpick"/3005).

Cut to a blow-by-blow meeting of a "tumor board" called to assess Junior Soprano's treatment for stomach cancer ("Second Opinion"/3007).

Cut to Carmela, deeply depressed, crying over a Pedigree dog food commercial ("Second Opinion"/3007).

Cut to Tony and "Mr. Williams" (Furio) paying a visit to Dr. Kennedy on the golf course in order to persuade him to care for Uncle Junior – "There are worse things than cancer," Furio reminds the good doctor ("Second Opinion"/3007).

Cut to a born-again narcoleptic repeatedly inquiring "Have you heard the good news?" ("The Telltale Moozadell"/3009).

Cut to a montage of Tony's malapropisms: "Hannibal lecture" instead of Hannibal Lechter ("The Sopranos"/1001), "Prince Matchabelli" instead of Machiavelli's *The Prince* ("University"/3006), "Goyim" insead of Goya ("Amour Fou"/3012), "cathode tube" instead of catheter ("House Arrest" /2011).[7]

Cut to Tony nearly succumbing to an anxiety attack from his first encounter with "Big Mouth Billy Bass," whose rendition of "Take Me to the River" ("... drop me in the water") induces a flashback to murdering and dumping-at-sea his former friend Big Pussy ("Second Opinion"/3007).

Cut to Tony crossing "Janice's Russian" off his Christmas to-do list – he and Furio beat him senseless in payback for abusing his sister ("To Save Us All From Satan's Power"/3010).

Cut to a scrabble game between Meadow and Jackie Aprile, Jr. in which her last word is "oblique" and his is "ass" ("Pine Barrens"/3011).

Cut to Paulie and Christopher voraciously consuming packets of ketchup, mayonnaise, and relish during their night lost in the Pine Barrens ("Pine Barrens"/3011).

Cut to Paulie reporting to Christopher his confused understanding – "He killed sixteen Czechoslovakians. He was an interior decorator" – of Tony's cell phone-conveyed garbled information about their adversary Valery (Tony had told him that the Russian had been a commando, "some kind of Green Beret," who had fought in Chechnya for the interior ministry). "His house looked like shit," Christopher responds in disbelief ("Pine Barrens"/3011).

Such evidence – and a hundred more moments like these might be brought into court – should prove overwhelmingly convincing except, perhaps, to those predisposed to condemn *The Sopranos*. As *The Sopranos'* lawyer, however, I would seek to remove the biased, intolerant, and narrow-minded with my preemptory challenges. How, otherwise, would a fair trial be possible? But my advocacy would not convince anyone that *The Sopranos* is not profane – for it is; or that it is not blasphemous – for it is; or that it is not scatological – for it is; or that it is not full of wicked humor – for it is; or that it is not deeply disturbing – for it is; or that it is not brutal – for it is; or that it is moralistic – for it is not; or that it is political correct – for it is not; or that it is free of racism, homophobia, and sexism – for it is not; or that it is monological (in Mikhail Bakhtin's sense of the term) – for it is not.[8]

It has long been a commonplace of Marxist and neo-Marxist theory that cultural texts tend to repress contradiction in order to impose, or at least invite, ideologically simplistic readings, to (in the words of John Fiske) "propose a unitary, final 'truth' of the text work by resolving contradictions and thus deny the force for social change, or at least social interrogation, that is embedded in them" (88). In the terminology of the Russian theorist Bakhtin, cultural texts thus tend toward the monological (Bakhtin's favorite example is Tolstoy) not the dialogical (as exemplified by Dostoevsky).[9] They tend to speak with one voice rather than many. Deciding whether *The Sopranos* is monological or dialogical would seem to be as easy as determining whether something is black or white . . .

The Sopranos, not surprisingly, does not need protectors; it can take care of itself. In a famous episode of *The Simpsons* following President Bush's attack on the show in the 1992 State of the Union Address ("We need a nation closer to *The Waltons* than to *The Simpsons*"), Matt Groening and company responded by including Bush's actual comments in the show itself and having Bart sarcastically comment that the characters of both shows had one thing in common: "Hey, we're like the Waltons. We're praying for the end of the depression, too" ("Stark Raving Dad," Season Three). *The Sopranos*, too, has responded to its critics, staging on-screen debates, for example, about the charges of Italian-American groups that it demeans Italians,[10] portraying Columbia University administrators in a less than favorable light after the school forbid *The Sopranos* to film on location, etc. As Ellen Willis notes, the "continual reflection of [*Sopranos'*] characters in their media mirrors is also a running commentary on the show itself."

Needless to say the editor of this volume and the authors who have contributed to it assume that the reader's final judgment of its merits will be based on a careful reading of it. Like most academic critics, *This Thing of Ours'* authors' primary objective has not been summary judgment of *The Sopranos*, not the gesturing of thumbs up or down, but an understanding of the text in all its complexity. We have sought to investigate the whole elephant. To assume such a stance, we are convinced, is to view *The Sopranos* in much the same way that Chase and company view their characters and their world. We both acknowledge the truth of the line from Renoir's *The Rules of the Game* which appears as an epigraph to this prologue (and which David Chase cites in the Bogdanovich interview as his own *raison d'etre*): everyone has their own reasons.

ABOUT THIS BOOK

The essays in this volume, with the exception of those by Willis and Auster, were all written expressly for this book.

This Thing of Ours is divided into five sections. Two essays by Ellen Willis and Albert Auster offer an INTRODUCTORY overview of the series.

The second section, THE MEDIA CONTEXT, presents David Lavery & Robert J. Thompson on the creative achievement of David Chase; Paul Levinson on *"The Sopranos* as a Nuts-and-Bolts Triumph of Non-Network TV"; Dawn Elizabeth B. Johnston on the reception of *The Sopranos* in Canada; and Mark C. Rogers, Michael Epstein, & Jimmie L. Reeves on *The Sopranos*, HBO, and contemporary television.

The third section, MEN AND WOMEN, includes four essays: Cindy Donatelli & Sharon Alward on the great differences between *Sopranos* women and those in the great gangster films of the 1970s and 1980s; Avi Santo on male body image; Joanne Lacey on the way British men have responded to *The Sopranos*; and Joseph S. Walker on the clash of male and female in the first season of *The Sopranos*.

GENRE AND NARRATIVE TECHNIQUE, the fourth section, gathers essays by Glen Creeber on "Television, Tarantino, and the Intimate World of *The Sopranos*"; David Pattie on the modern gangster film and *The Sopranos*; Kim Akass & Janet McCabe on the role of women in the series' narrative structure; and Kevin Fellezs on the place of music in *The Sopranos*.

The final section, CULTURAL CONTEXTS, includes Lance Strate on *The Sopranos* and New Jersey; Douglas L. Howard on language in the series; Steven Hayward & Andrew Biro's Marxist reading; and Sara Lewis Dunne's meditation on the role of food in *The Sopranos*.

Four appendices – (a) A *Sopranos* Episode Guide, (b) The *Sopranos* Cast of Characters, (c) Intertextual Moments and Allusions in *The Sopranos*, and (d) *The Sopranos*: A Family History – a comprehensive bibliography and an index complete the volume.

INTRODUCTORY

ONE

OUR MOBSTERS, OURSELVES[1]

Ellen Willis

Midway through the first season of *The Sopranos*, the protagonist's psycho-therapist, Jennifer Melfi, has a not-exactly-traditional family dinner with her middle-class Italian parents, son, and ex-husband Richard La Penna ["The Legend of Tennessee Moltisanti"/1008]. She lets slip (hmm!) that one of her patients is a mobster, much to Richard's consternation. An activist in Italian anti-defamation politics, he is incensed at the opprobrium the Mafia has brought on all Italians. What is the point, he protests, of trying to help such a person? In a subsequent scene he contemptuously dismisses Jennifer and her profession for purveying "cheesy moral relativism" in the face of evil. His challenge boldly proclaims what until then has been implicit: the richest and most compelling piece of television – no, of popular culture – that I've encountered in the past twenty years is a meditation on the nature of morality, the possibility of redemption, and the legacy of Freud.

To be sure, *The Sopranos* is much else as well. For two years (the third season began 4 March 2001) David Chase's HBO series has served up a hybrid genre of post-*Godfather* decline-of-the-mob movie and soap opera, with plenty of sex, violence, domestic melodrama, and comic irony; a portrait of a suburban landscape that does for northern New Jersey what *film noir* did for Los Angeles, with soundtrack to match; a deft depiction of class and cultural relations among various subgroups and generations of Italian-Americans; a gloss on the manners and mores of the *fin-de-siècle* American middle-class family; and perfect-pitch acting, especially by James Gandolfini as Tony Soprano; Edie Falco as his complicated wife, Carmela; Lorraine Bracco as Dr. Melfi; and the late Nancy Marchand as the Sopranos' terrifying matriarch, Livia.

Cumulatively, these episodes have the feel of an as yet unfinished nineteenth-century novel. While the sheer entertainment and suspense of the plot twists are reminiscent of Dickens and his early serials, the underlying themes evoke George Eliot: the world of Tony Soprano is a kind of postmodern *Middlemarch*, whose inhabitants' moral and spiritual development (or devolution) unfolds within and against the norms of a parochial social milieu. This era being what it is, however, the Sopranos' milieu has porous boundaries, and the norms that govern it are a moving target. In one scene, the family is in mid-breakfast when Tony and Carmela's teenage daughter, Meadow, apropos a recent scandal brought on by a high school classmate's affair with her soccer coach, declaims about the importance of talking openly about sex. Yes, Tony agrees, but not during breakfast. "Dad, this is the 1990s," Meadow protests. "Outside it may be the 1990s," Tony retorts, "but in this house it's 1954" ["Nobody Knows Anything"/1011]. It's wishful thinking, and Tony knows it. What 1950s gangster would take Prozac and make weekly visits to a shrink – or, for that matter, have a daughter named Meadow?

In fact, contemporary reality pervades the Sopranos' suburban manse. A school counselor tries to persuade them that their son, Anthony Jr., has attention deficit disorder ["Down Neck"/1007]. Meadow hosts a clandestine party in her grandmother's empty house that gets busted for drugs and alcohol ["Toodle-Fucking-oo"/2003]. Tony's sister Janice, who years ago decamped to Seattle, became a Buddhist, and changed her name to Parvati, shows up at his door flaunting her postcounterculture reinvented self ["Guy Walks into a Psychiatrist's Office"/2001]. And while Tony displays some of the trappings of the stereotypical Italian patriarch – he is proud of supporting his family in style, comes and goes as he pleases, leaves the running of the household to Carmela, and cheats on her with the obligatory goomah – his persona as fear-inspiring gangster does not translate to his home life. Carmela is his emotional equal; she does what she likes, tells him off without hesitation and, unlike old-style mob wives, knows plenty about the business. Nor, despite periodic outbursts of temper, is Tony an intimidating father. Caught between empathy for their children and the urge to whip them into line, the Sopranos share the dirty little secret of nineties middle-class parenthood: you can't control teenagers' behavior without becoming full-time prison guards. "Let's not overplay our hand," Tony cautions after Meadow's party caper, "'cause if she knows we're powerless, we're fucked" ["Toodle-Fucking-oo"/2003].

In Tony's other "house" – represented by his office in the Bada Bing! strip club – 1954 is also under siege. Under pressure of the RICO laws, longtime associates turn government witness. Neophytes chafe at their lowly status in the hierarchy, disobey their bosses, take drugs, commit gratuitous freelance crimes, and in general fail to understand that organized crime is a business, not a vehicle for self-expression or self-promotion. The line between reality and media image has become as tenuous here as elsewhere: Tony and his men love *GoodFellas* and the first two *Godfathers* (by general agreement *Part III* sucks) and at the same time are objects of fantasy for civilians steeped in the same movies. Tony accepts an invitation to play golf with his neighbor Dr. Cusamano, who referred him to Melfi, and finds that his function is to titillate the doctor's friends ["A Hit is a Hit"/1010]; during a falling out with

Jennifer he tries to connect with another therapist, who demurs, explaining that he has seen *Analyze This!* ("It's a fucking comedy," Tony protests) ["Guy Walks into a Psychiatrist's Office"/2001]. Tony's fractious nephew Christopher, pissed because press coverage of impending mob indictments doesn't mention him, reprises *GoodFellas* by shooting an insufficiently servile clerk in the foot ["Toodle-Fucking-oo"/2003]. He aspires to write screenplays about mob life, and in pursuit of this dream is used for material and kicks by a Hollywood film director and his classy female assistant ["D-Girl"/2007]. Meanwhile Jennifer's family debates whether wiseguy movies defame Italians or rather should be embraced as American mythology, like westerns ["The Legend of Tennessee Moltisanti"/1008]. *The Sopranos*, of course, has provoked the same argument, and its continual reflection of its characters in their media mirrors is also a running commentary on the show itself.

Self-consciousness, then, is a conspicuous feature of Tony Soprano's world even aside from therapy; in fact, it's clear that self-consciousness has provoked the anxiety attack that sends him to Jennifer Melfi. It's not just a matter of stressful circumstances. Tony's identity is fractured, part outlaw rooted in a dying tribal culture, part suburbanite enmeshed in another kind of culture altogether – a split graphically exemplified by the famous episode ["College" /1005] in which Tony, while taking Meadow on a tour of colleges in Maine, spots a mobster-turned-informer hiding in the witness protection program and manages to juggle his fatherly duties with murder. Despite his efforts at concealment, his criminal life is all too evident to his children (after all, they too have seen *The Godfather*), a source of pain and confusion on both sides. Tony's decision to seek therapy also involves an identity crisis. In his first session, which frames the first episode, he riffs on the sad fate of the strong and silent Gary Cooper: once they got him in touch with his feelings, he wouldn't shut up. "I have a semester and a half of college," he tells Dr. Melfi, "so I understand Freud. I understand therapy as a concept, but in my world it does not go down" ["The Sopranos"/1001]. In his wiseguy world, that is: Carmela thinks it's a great idea.

Richard La Penna's charge of moral relativism is highly ironic, for Jennifer finds that her task is precisely to confront the tribal relativism and cognitive dissonance that keep Tony Soprano from making sense of his life. He sees his business as the Sicilians' opportunity to get in on the American Dream, the violence that attends it as enforcement of rules known to all who choose to play the game: gangsters are soldiers, whose killing, far from being immoral, is impelled by positive virtues – loyalty, respect, friendship, willingness to put one's own life on the line. It does not strike Tony as inconsistent to expect his kids to behave or to send them to Catholic school, any more than he considers that nights with his Russian girlfriend belie his reverence for the institution of the family. Nor does he see a contradiction in his moral outrage at a sadistic, pathologically insecure associate who crushes a man with his car in fury over an inconsequential slight.

In its original literal sense, "moral relativism" is simply moral complexity. That is, anyone who agrees that stealing a loaf of bread to feed one's children is not the moral equivalent of, say, shoplifting a dress for the fun of it, is a relativist of sorts. But in recent years, conservatives bent on reinstating an essentially religious vocabulary of absolute good and evil as the only legitimate framework for discussing social values have redefined "relative" as "arbitrary." That conflation has been reinforced by social theorists and advocates of identity politics who argue that there is no universal morality, only the value systems of particular cultures and power structures. From this perspective, the psychoanalytic – and by extension the psychotherapeutic – worldview is not relativist at all. Its values are honesty, self-knowledge, assumption of responsibility for the whole of what one does, freedom from inherited codes of family, church, tribe in favor of a universal humanism: in other words, the values of the Enlightenment, as revised and expanded by Freud's critique of scientific rationalism for ignoring the power of unconscious desire. What eludes the Richard La Pennas is that the neutral, unjudging stance of the therapist is not an end in itself but a strategy for pursuing this moral agenda by eliciting hidden knowledge.

Predictably, the cultural relativists have no more use for Freud than the religious conservatives. Nor are the devotees of "rational choice" economics and of a scientism that reduces all human behavior to genes or brain chemistry eager to look below the surface of things, or even admit there's such a thing as "below the surface." Which is why, in recent years, psychoanalysis has been all but banished from the public conversation as a serious means of discussing our moral and cultural and political lives. And as the *zeitgeist* goes, so goes popular culture: though a continuing appetite for the subject might be inferred from the popularity of memoirs, in which psychotherapy is a recurring theme, it has lately been notably absent from movies and television. So it's more than a little interesting that *The Sopranos* and *Analyze This!* plucked the gangster-sees-therapist plot from the cultural unconscious at more or less the same time and apparently by coincidence. In *The Sopranos*, however, therapy is no fucking comedy, nor does it recycle old Hollywood clichés about shamanlike shrinks and sudden cathartic cures. It's a serious battle for a man's soul, carried on in sessions that look and sound a lot like the real thing (at least as I've experienced it) – full of silence, evasive chatter, lies, boredom and hostility, punctuated by outbursts of painful emotion, moments of clarity and insights that almost never sink in right away. Nor is it only the patient's drama; the therapist is right down there in the muck, sorting out her own confusions, missteps, fantasies and fears, attraction and repulsion, as she struggles to understand.

The parallels between psychotherapy and religion are reinforced by the adventures of the other *Sopranos* characters, who are all defined by their spiritual state. Some are damned, like Livia, whose nihilism is summed up in her penchant for smiling at other people's misfortunes and in her bitter remark to her grandson, "It's all a big nothing. What makes you think you're so special?" ["D-Girl"/2007]. Some are complacent, like the respectable bourgeois Italian-Americans, or the self-regarding but fatally unself-aware Father Phil, Carmela's young spiritual adviser, who feeds (literally as well as metaphorically) on the neediness of the mob wives. The older, middle-level mobsters see themselves as working stiffs who expect little from life and for whom self-questioning is a luxury that's out of their class. (One of them [Paulie] is temporarily jolted when Tony's nephew Christopher is shot and has a vision of himself in hell; but the crisis passes quickly ["From Where to Eternity"/2009].) Charmaine Bucco, a neighborhood girl and old friend of Carmela's who with her husband, Artie, owns an Italian restaurant, is the embodiment of passionate faith in the virtues of honesty, integrity, and hard work; she despises the mobsters, wishes they would stop patronizing the restaurant, and does her best to pull the ambivalent Artie away from his longtime friendship with Tony. And then there are the strugglers, like Christopher, who inchoately wants something more out of life but also wants to rise in the mob, and Big Pussy, Tony's close friend as well as crew member, who rats to the Feds to ward off a thirty-year prison term, agonizes over his betrayal, and ultimately takes refuge in identifying with his FBI handlers.

Carmela Soprano is a struggler, an ardent Catholic who feels the full weight of her sins and Tony's and lets no one off the hook. She keeps hoping Tony will change but knows he probably will not; and despite the many discontents of her marriage, anger at Tony's infidelity, and misgivings about her complicity in his crimes, she will not leave him. Though she rationalizes her choice on religious grounds ("The family is a sacred institution"), she never really deceives herself: she still loves Tony, and furthermore she likes the life his money provides. Nor does she hesitate to trade on his power in order to do what she feels is a mother's duty: she intimidates Cusamano's lawyer sister-in-law into writing Meadow a college recommendation ["Full Leather Jacket"/2008]. Guilt and frustration drive her to Father Phil, who gives her books on Buddhism, foreign movies, and mixed sexual signals, but after a while she catches on to his bullshit, and in a scene beloved of *Sopranos* fans coolly nails him: "He's a sinner, Father. You come up here and you eat his steaks and use his home entertainment center. . . . I think you have this M. O. where you manipulate spiritually thirsty women, and I think a lot of it's tied up with food somehow, as well as the sexual tension game" ["I Dream of Jeannie Cusamano"/1013]. Compromised as she is, Carmela is a moral touchstone because of her clear eye.

But Tony's encounters with Melfi are the spiritual center of the show. The short version of Tony's psychic story is this: his gangster persona provides him with constant excitement and action, a sense of power and control, a definition of masculinity. Through violence rationalized as business or impersonal soldiering he also gets to express his considerable unacknowledged rage without encroaching on his alter ego as benevolent husband and father. But when the center fails to hold, the result is panic, then – as Melfi probes the cracks – depression, self-hatred, sexual collapse, and engulfing, ungovernable anger. There are glimmers along the way, as when Tony sees the pointlessness of killing the sexually wayward soccer coach, calls off the hit and lets the cops do their job (after which he feels impelled to get so drunk he passes out ["Boca" /1009]). But the abyss always looms.

Tony's heart of darkness is personified by Livia Soprano, who at first seems peggable as a better-done-than-usual caricature of the overbearing ethnic mother but is gradually revealed as a monstrous Medea. Furious at Tony for consigning her to a fancy "retirement community," Livia passes on some well-chosen pieces of information – including the fact that he's seeing a shrink – to Tony's malleable Uncle Junior, who orders him killed. When the hit is botched, she suddenly begins to show symptoms of Alzheimer's. Jennifer Melfi puts it together; worried that Tony's life is in danger, she breaks the therapeutic rule that patients must make their own discoveries and confronts him with her knowledge. He reacts with a frightening, hate-filled, paroxysm of denial – for the first time coming close to attacking Jennifer physically – but is forced to admit the truth when he hears a damning conversation between Livia and Junior, caught on tape by the FBI ["I Dream of Jeannie Cusamano"/1013].

This is a turning point in the story, but not, as the standard psychiatric melodrama would have it, because the truth has made Tony free. The truth has knocked him flat. "What kind of person can I be," he blurts to Carmela, "where his own mother wants him dead?" ["I Dream of Jeannie Cusamano"/1013]. Afraid that Junior will go after Jennifer, he orders her to leave town; when she comes back she is angry and fearful and tells him to get out of her life. He is lost, his face a silent Munchian scream. Later Jennifer has a change of heart, but things are not the same: the trust is gone. And yet, paradoxically, her rejection has freed him to be more honest, throwing the details of his gang's brutality in her face, railing at her for making him feel like a victim, at himself for becoming the failed Gary Cooper he once mocked, at the "happy wanderers" who still seem in control.

Jennifer encourages him to feel the sadness under the rage, but what comes through is hard and bleak. He tells anyone who mentions his mother, "She's dead to me," but it's really he who feels dead. During this time ["D-Girl"/2007], Anthony Jr. shocks his mother by announcing that God is dead; "Nitch" says so. (At its most serious, the show never stops being funny.) Tony mentions this to Jennifer, who gives him a minilecture on existential angst: when some people realize they're solely responsible for their lives, and all roads lead to death, they feel "intense dread" and conclude that "the only absolute truth is death." "I think the kid's onto something," Tony says.

As if to validate Richard La Penna's contempt, he uses what he's learned in therapy – that you can't compartmentalize your life – to more fully accept his worst impulses. Against his more compassionate instincts, he allows an old friend who is the father of a classmate of Meadow's and a compulsive gambler to join his high-stakes card game. When Davey Scatino inevitably piles up a debt he can't pay, Tony moves in on his business, sucking it dry and draining his son's college fund. Amid a torrent of self-pity, David asks why Tony let him in the game. Tony answers jocularly that it's his nature – you know, as in the tale of the frog and the scorpion ["Bust Out"/2010]. In the last episode of season two Tony whacks Pussy, whose perfidy has been revealed, choosing his mob code over his love and sorrow for the man. He then walks out on Jennifer, as if to say, this is who I am and will be.

Jennifer's trip is also a rocky one. In her person, the values of Freud and the Enlightenment are filtered through the cultural radical legacy of the 1960s: she is a woman challenging a man whose relationship to both legitimate and outlaw patriarchal hierarchies is in crisis. It's a shaky and vulnerable role, the danger of physical violence an undercurrent from the beginning, but there are also bonds that make the relationship possible. Tony chooses her over a Jewish male therapist because "you're a paisan, like me" ["Pax Soprana"/1006], and she is drawn to the outlaw, no doubt in rebellion against the safe smugness of her own social milieu. Predictably, Tony loses all sexual interest in his wife and girlfriend and falls in love with his doctor (if there is any answering spark, it stays under the professional surface), but after the initial "honeymoon" of therapy, trouble, as always, begins. Tony gives Jennifer "gifts" like stealing her car and getting it fixed ["Pax Soprana"/2006]; it's his way of assuring her, and himself, that his power is benevolent, but of course she only feels violated. Wanting to find out about her life, he has her followed by a corrupt cop who harasses her boyfriend, thinking he's doing Tony a favor; she can't help but be suspicious. By inviting her family to object to her criminal patient, she gives voice to her own doubts: perhaps she is not only endangering herself but abetting evil.

Her conflict intensifies when she tells Tony she must charge for a missed session, and he throws the money at her, calling her a whore ["The Legend of Tennessee Moltisanti"/1008]. It explodes in the aftermath of the attempt on his life. But then the other side of her ambivalence reasserts itself; she feels she has irresponsibly abandoned a patient and takes him back against the advice of her own (Jewish male) therapist. Now it is Jennifer who is in crisis, treating her anxiety with heavy drinking. She is frightened and morally repulsed by Tony's graphic revelations, yet also feels an erotically tinged fascination (it's like watching a train wreck, she tells her shrink ["House Arrest"/2011]). She still cares about Tony but seems to have lost faith in her ability to exorcise the demonic by making contact with the suffering human being. In the last episode, with Tony closed as a clam, she admits that she blew it, that she stopped pushing him because she was afraid. But he can't hear her ("Funhouse"/2013).

No false optimism here. Yet it's no surprise that by the second hour of the third season premiere Tony is back in Jennifer Melfi's office. The requirements of the show's premise aside, his untenable situation has not changed. Having glimpsed the possibility of an exit from despair, it would be out of character for him simply to close that door and walk away. For the same reason, I suspect our culture's flight from psychoanalysis is not permanent. It's grandiose, perhaps, to see in one television series, however popular, a cultural trend; and after all *The Sopranos* is on HBO, not CBS or NBC. But ultimately the show is so gripping because, in the words of Elaine Showalter, it's a "cultural Rorschach test." It has been called a parable of corruption and hypocrisy in the postmodern middle class, and it is that; a critique of sexuality, the family and male-female relations in the wake of feminism, and it's that too. But at the primal level, the inkblot is the unconscious. The murderous mobster is the predatory lust and aggression in all of us; his lies and cover-ups are ours; the therapist's fear is our own collective terror of peeling away those lies. The problem is that we can't live with the lies, either. So facing down the terror, a little at a time, becomes the only route to sanity, if not salvation.

In the tumultuous last episode of *The Sopranos'* first season ["I Dream of Jeannie Cusamano"/1013], another informer is killed. Tony finds out about his mother and sends Jennifer into hiding. Uncle Junior and two of his underlings are arrested, arousing fears that one of them will flip. Artie Bucco nearly kills Tony after being told – by Livia – that Tony is responsible for the fire that destroyed his restaurant (the idea was to help the Buccos by heading off a planned mob hit in the restaurant, which would have ruined the business – this way they could get the insurance and rebuild), but Tony swears "on my mother" it isn't true. Carmela tells off Father Phil. At the end, Tony, Carmela, and the kids are caught in a violent storm in their SUV; they can't see a thing but suddenly realize they're in front of the Buccos' (rebuilt) restaurant. There's no power, but Artie graciously ushers them in, lights a candle and cooks them a meal. Tony proposes a toast: "To my family. Someday soon you're gonna have families of your own. And if you're lucky, you'll remember the little moments. Like this. That were good." The moment feels something like sanity. The storm, our storm, goes on.

TWO

THE SOPRANOS: THE GANGSTER REDUX[1]

Albert Auster

> The gangster is lonely and melancholy, and can give the impression of a
> profound worldly wisdom.
> > Robert Warshow, "Movie Chronicle: The Westerner" (136)

In 1969 the political columnist Murray Kempton wrote an article titled "The
Mafia Myth". In it he described the content of some newly released FBI
surveillance tapes of the northern New Jersey Decavalcante Mafia family. To
the FBI's chagrin, and Kempton's obvious delight, what those tapes revealed
were not grandiose criminal conspiracies but petty complaints about money,
avowals of abject poverty, and all sorts of middle management disputes.
Currently, the fictional Sopranos occupy the old northern New Jersey venue of
the Decavalcantes. However, in addition to those old complaints *The Sopranos*
also deals with family squabbles, kids' college education, and the problem of
what to do with aging and infirm parents and relatives.

The focus of so much of this domestic and professional turmoil is Mafia
everyman Tony Soprano, who in totally untypical macho-Mafioso fashion
has taken to seeing a psychiatrist (a female one to boot), and knocking back
anti-depressants by the fistful. This, of course, might have deteriorated into
a one joke farce, such as the 1999 theatrical movie *Analyze This!* in which
an anxiety-laden Mafia don played by Robert De Niro turns to shrink Billy
Crystal for help. Instead, under the aegis of executive producer David Chase
(*The Rockford Files, I'll Fly Away, Northern Exposure*), it has become the kind
of sprawling narrative that was once considered the special province of the
nineteenth-century novel.

Indeed in some quarters *The Sopranos* has been referred to as the natural
heir to Francis Ford Coppola and Mario Puzo's *Godfather* saga. This raises some

interesting and inextricably linked questions. What does *The Sopranos* retain from the original genre and what departures has it made? Why is the series so popular with the TV audience (a popularity which has resulted in higher ratings than network television programs in the same time slot – a circumstance unique for a cable TV program)?

As Robert Warshow wrote in his classic essay, "The Gangster as Tragic Hero," "for the gangster there is only the city; he must inhabit it in order to personify it" (131). And indeed from *Little Caesar* (1930) onward the gangster occupied the city, albeit an imaginary one, alternately referred to as "gangland" or "underworld USA," filled with nightclubs, speakeasies, neon lights, racing sedans, machine guns, and newspaper headlines that exploded onto the screen like shotgun blasts. Not so *The Sopranos*. Theirs is a world of suburban split levels, shopping malls, soccermoms and dads, SATs, and videogames. From time to time they do make brief forays into New York City to spend the evening at a restaurant or club; there is even a brief glimpse of some northern New Jersey urban outposts such as Lodi in the series credits, but as for a city like Newark – fuhgeddaboudit! Indeed the old urban restlessness of the gangster has been replaced in *The Sopranos* by suburban smugness.

In the old gangster genre there was also contempt for popular culture, even a sense that it was somehow effeminate. Indeed you can practically hear Rico "Little Caesar" Bandelli's teeth gnashing when his best friend Joe Messara announces that he's going straight and joining a ballroom dance team. Similarly, Don Vito Corleone braces his godson Johnny Fontaine, who has been denied a coveted part in a movie, with a slap in the face and the words, "be a man."

In contrast *The Sopranos* is equally infatuated and saturated with popular culture. As a matter of fact, hardly an episode goes by in which references and even whole scenes are not devoted to popular culture. For example Tony's nephew, the violent, impulsive Christopher Moltisanti, was so besotted with the dream of becoming a screenwriter before he became a "made" Mafioso that his most fulfilling moments (when he isn't whacking someone) are spent hanging around the set of a fictional independent film supplying Italian obscenities to the producer, played by real-life indie actor Jon Favreau (*Swingers*) and, appearing in cameo roles, Janeane Garofalo and Sandra Bernhard ("D-Girl"/2007).

More than just popular culture, however, to Tony and his crew, is *The Godfather*. It is their Norse sagas, legend of the Niebelungen, and Camelot rolled into one gloriously mythic package. As a matter of fact it touches everything from the name of Tony's strip joint and prime hangout, *Bada Bing!* (after a bit of banter between Michael and Sonny Corleone) to Tony's lieutenant Silvio's repeated mimicking of Michael Corleone in *The Godfather Part III*. This is hardly just a fictional response, no better authority than real life Mafioso and John Gotti henchman Salvatore "Sammy the Bull" Gravano wrote in his memoir, *Underboss*, that on seeing *The Godfather* he "left the movie stunned, I mean, I floated out of the theater. Maybe it was fiction, but for me, then, that was our life" (Mass 72). Indeed *The Godfather* often seems more than just myth; it is frequently treated as holy writ, and misquoting it a sacrilege.

These elements, however, aren't so much radical departures as possibly interesting accruals to the gangster genre tradition. Not so, however, the depiction of women in *The Sopranos*. Here, there is a real sea change. In this *The Godfather* too paved the way with its portrayal of a big bosomed mama, the victimized and ultimately alienated Kay, and Connie Corleone's transformation from spoiled brat kid sister to Lady Macbeth.

Though Tony and his crew have their wives and *goumadas* (mistresses) none of them would ever stand for a face full of grapefruit *à la* James Cagney. (In a kind of reversal of the famous scene from *Public Enemy*, Carmela throws a cell phone at Tony when he complains about the type of orange juice she has bought ["Second Opinion"/3007].) In fact, they, as much as Tony's conflicts with his hapless Uncle Junior, the psychopathic Richie Aprile, and his anguished betrayal by "Big Pussy" Bonpensiero, provide most of the series' dramatic tension, narrative drive and moral weight; or as Tony puts it, "They all break balls."

First and foremost of these women is Tony's mother, Livia, played by the late Nancy Marchand, who prior to *The Sopranos* was probably best remembered for playing *grand dames* such as her Emmy award-winning portrayal of publisher Margaret Pynchon in the dramatic series *Lou Grant*. For *The Sopranos*, Marchand, perhaps borrowing a leaf from the pages of Marlon Brando's portrayal of the aging Don Vito Corleone, turned her usual haughty aristocratic tones into a nasal whine and a hoarse whisper.

Livia was the woman who Tony said turned his revered father into "a squeekin' little gerbil" before he died ("The Sopranos"/1001). And after she conspires with his Uncle Junior to have Tony murdered because he put her in a nursing home, he refers to her as "dead to me." Livia's behavior was undoubtedly toxic, and for this she has been justly compared to another malevolent Livia, the mother of the mad Roman Emperor Caligula. However, perhaps there is a parallel that is less classical and more petit bourgeois: one that is far closer at hand from Marchand's own career: in 1953 she played Clara, Marty's love interest in the original TV version of Paddy Chayevsky's award-winning drama. In *Marty* there is also an overbearing Italian mother who, while urging her aging bachelor son to find a wife, at the same time fears that if he does find someone she will be shunted aside and does her best to break up the relationship.

The opening episodes of the third season saw the death of Livia. And in what was probably one of the season's most effective episodes her funeral and wake. That moment was made particularly poignant and filled with dark humor when the mourners, called upon by Tony's New Age sister Janice to offer some positive memory of Livia, either remain conspicuously silent or offer platitudes about a woman that most of them either feared or secretly despised. Indeed for Tony his only solace is watching the loving relationship between Tommy Powers (James Cagney) and his mother in a video of the 1931 gangster classic *Public Enemy*.

Hardly as ruthless as Livia but just as tough is Tony's wife Carmela. Falco, who can play anything from a tough correction officer (*Oz*), to a prim and proper lawyer (*Law & Order*), to a naïve aspiring actress in the theatrical film *Judy Berlin* (2000), gives an Emmy-winning performance as Tony's tart-tongued spouse. Carmela and Tony's marriage has long since reverted to low-intensity combat. And though she looks the other way at his frequent infidelities, she won't permit any kind of threat to her home, her children, or her status.

Nor is Carmela easily trifled with personally. For instance, when the very religious Carmela realizes that her ziti-loving confessor Father Phil has been toying with her affections, she confronts him about his manipulative behavior and need for safe flirtations. Similarly, when her daughter Meadow needs a college recommendation to Georgetown, she makes a reluctant alumnus an offer he can't refuse of a ricotta cheesecake wrapped in all the menace of the Soprano name ["Full Leather Jacket"/2008].

In the series' third season Carmela's toughness is sorely tested by a Freud-like psychoanalyst who proclaims her life a lie and everything she holds dear tainted by blood ["Second Opinion"/3007]. Equally devastating are the petty crimes and misdemeanors that result in AJ being expelled from school and, save for a panic attack à la Tony Sr., almost landing in military school.

Meadow, Tony's Mafia princess daughter, is someone who also gives Tony lots of *agita*. First there is her relationship with a half-African-American, half-Jewish, political science-film major at Columbia, whom Tony insists on referring to as "sambo" and "buckwheat," and "Jamal Ginsberg, the Hasidic homeboy." Then there is her love affair with Mafia bad seed Jackie Aprile, Jr., who leaves her smarting from his betrayals and brooding over the menacing world which causes him to be whacked at the order of his sociopath would-be step-father Ralphie Cifaretto.

In the relationship of Tony and his psychiatrist, Dr. Jennifer Melfi, both a sense of menace and the series' moral dimension are given embodiment. Dr. Melfi gets more then she bargained for when she took Tony on as a patient. Dr. Melfi, who in Tony's world would be classified as a "wonderbread wop," hardly even speaks the same language. For example, in one of their sessions Tony says, "I'm worried about RICO," to which Dr. Melfi responds, "Is he your brother?" By turns obscene, brutal, self-pitying, and enormously appealing, Tony is hardly the stuff of conventional psychoanalytic case histories. Indeed even Freud could never have predicted a transference that took the form of not just the usual dreams and fantasies about the therapist but a cop associate who Tony assigns to follow and spy on Dr. Melfi. Despite this, the real crisis in their relationship comes when Dr. Melfi begins to finally realize that her patient is not just another neurotic sufferer but also a brutal criminal and murderer. It is something her ex-husband warns her about when he says, "Finally, you're going to get beyond psychology with its cheery moral relativism. Finally, you're going to get to good and evil, and he's evil" ["The Legend of Tennessee Moltisanti"/1008].

It is the same kind of dilemma that in one form or other faces the audience. No matter how appealing Tony is, and as played by the hulking, bearlike Gandolfini, he is certainly that, there is a moral dimension to his action that can't be ignored. Indeed it's something that has had to be considered ever since the first season's fifth episode ("College"), when during a campus tour with his daughter, Tony stumbles across a Mafia informer in the witness protection program and brutally garrotes him. Thus, all of Tony's very human vulnerability can't obscure the fact that he is also a killer, and ultimately some sort of judgment has to be made about him.

However, for Dr. Melfi that judgment seems to be deferred when she is brutally raped, and the rapist is released on a legal technicality ("Employee of the Month"/3004). Then she has dreams about Tony as her avenger. And, in a moment that is fraught with unbearable tension, she successfully resists telling him of her travail, knowing full well that such a confession would provoke his most violent reaction and most certainly terminate their therapeutic relationship.

Despite all of this, Americans seem to be beguiled by what Murray Kempton so long ago referred to as the Mafia myth. Part of this comes from the Mafia's appeal as an immigrant success story and its image as an oasis of tradition where family and hierarchy are still important. Also, on a more visceral level, it provides us with the vicarious pleasure of watching men who reward their friends and swiftly, violently punish their enemies.

Nevertheless in many ways this is pure nostalgia, since the power of the Mafia, though still considerable, has long been on the wane. Recent estimates of the current membership of the Mafia calculate that there are no more than 1,000 made members of the mob, down from a high of about 5,000 in the 1950s. In fact, as someone recently put it, the number of actors who have played or are currently playing made members of the mob probably far exceeds the men who were or actually are members (Klinkenborg).

Furthermore the Mafia, by today's standards of criminal activity, seems almost a model of romantic banditry. The contemporary criminal world now consists of even more terrifying criminal groups such as Columbian narco-terrorists, who don't hesitate to massacre innocent families and whole villages, or the Russian mafiya (with whom Tony gingerly does business), which not only traffics in traditional criminal items such as drugs and prostitution but has been known to steal and sell missiles and submarines, and (if John Le Carre's recent novel *Single and Single* can be trusted) even blood plasma.

Despite this, and perhaps even because of it, the Mafia and *The Sopranos* fit in with the current *fin-de-siècle* melancholy that seems momentarily to have gripped our culture. It is the feeling that our best days are behind us that permeates books like Tom Brokaw's best selling *The Greatest Generation* and *The Greatest Generation Speaks*, James Bradley's *Flag of our Fathers*, or films such as Steven Spielberg's *Saving Private Ryan*. It's a feeling that History Channel fan Tony frequently expresses to Dr. Melfi in their sessions with comments such as, "I feel like I've come in at the end. Like I missed the best bits," or his lament about the current generation of mobsters that "Nowadays, there are no values. Guys today have no room for the penal experience." As a matter of fact there seems no greater accolade for any gangster in the series than to be referred to as "old school."

Old school is also what *The Sopranos* decidedly is, despite all its contemporary elements of suburban life, psychoanalysis, popular culture, and strong women. *The Sopranos* is at its core still a gangster story. And as so many decades of the Hollywood and TV gangster genre have taught us, the gangster is essentially a lonely, doomed, and tragic figure. This is evidenced in the mock tragic conclusion of the third season in which the mobsters gather to mourn the death of Jackie Aprile, Jr., and the cancer survivor Uncle Junior serenades them with a version of the Neapolitan *canzone "cor In'gratia"* ("Ungrateful Heart"); a scene which raises the familiar spectre of violent death as the destiny of the gangster. Indeed, though two more seasons of *The Sopranos* have been promised, it is an ultimate fate (along with imprisonment) that can no more be avoided than those of the classical Greek tragedies. Nonetheless, *The Sopranos* underscores the continued vitality and contemporary relevance of the gangster genre, which to quote Jimmy Cagney in *White Heat* (1949) is still, "Top of the world."

THE MEDIA CONTEXT

THREE

DAVID CHASE, *THE SOPRANOS*, AND TELEVISION CREATIVITY

David Lavery & Robert J. Thompson

Bonnie: Livia, ever hear the old Italian saying my aunts used: "col tempo la foglia, di gelso divena seta."
Carmela: What does that mean, Bonnie?
Bonnie: Time and patience change the mulberry leaf to silk.
"46 Long" (1002), written by David Chase

It may well be the case that the seemingly random juxtaposition of ideas produces something new. But this juxtaposition arises in one person's mind. It is he who activates the structures giving rise to the ideas in question. It is he who recognizes the fruit of the encounter and assimilates it into a newly forming structure. And it was he in the first place who assembled all these constituents in the close proximity of one person's mind, his own, so that all this might happen.
Howard E. Gruber, 'And the Bush is Not Consumed' (287)

I

"Creative work takes a long time," Howard E. Gruber, pre-eminent scholar of the creative process, reminds us. "With all due apologies to thunderbolts, creative work is not a matter of milliseconds, minutes, or even hours – but of months, years, and decades" (265). But one of the great mysteries, as Gruber has stressed, remains: how a creative individual remains productive, remains original, retaining a novel point of view, continuing to work, sometimes for an entire lifetime, even without public acceptance or acknowledgment. The historical individuals Gruber and his followers have examined have as a rule been famous writers, artists, and scientists, but does Gruber's understanding of the creative process apply to popular artists as well? Apply, say, to an individual who, after long toiling in network television, finally spins late-career silk?

David Chase's mulberry leaves were many, his patience extraordinary, his creative achievement decades in the making. A precocious child, a devotee of Freud in high school (Longworth interview 28), where he authored a blasphemous story in which "somebody spies the Apostles sneaking Jesus' body out of the tomb, right before they go 'Oh, my God, he's resurrected'" (Longworth interview 24), Chase longed as a young man to be a filmmaker or perhaps a rock and roll musician. An English major in college (first at Wake Forest, later at New York University), like contemporaries and near contemporaries Francis Ford Coppola, Martin Scorsese, and George Lucas, Chase then went on to attend film school – at Stanford. The pilot for *The Sopranos*, however, would not be written until he served twenty-seven reluctant years in television, beginning as a writer in 1971.

Despite a distaste for network television he makes no effort to hide ("I loathe and despise almost every second of it" [Rucker interview]), money had kept Chase in the industry, writing, and eventually producing, for such sundry series as *The Night Stalker* (1974–75), *The Rockford Files* (1976–80), *I'll Fly Away* (1991–92), *Northern Exposure* (1993–95), and directing an episode of *Alfred Hitchcock Presents* (1985–86), but he also turned down many other opportunities as well. Though greatly admired by bigger names like *Rockford* creator Stephen J. Cannell and Dick Wolf,[1] he remained largely anonymous in a still mostly authorless medium. *Off the Minnesota Strip* (1980), a made-for-television movie he wrote, did earn him an Emmy, and he still remembers proudly the "ambitious failure" (McNeil 33) of *Almost Grown* (November 1988 to February 1989), a short-lived series about the 1960s and 1970s making use of a rock 'n' roll soundtrack and extensive flashbacks that gave him his first opportunity to create and produce his own show. But he continued to write movie scripts that never got made and to dream of leaving television for feature filmmaking.

Chase recalls how exciting the early 1970s were to him, as an aspiring filmmaker, an era in which "movies were starting to be called 'film'" (Longworth interview 26) and were beginning to be taken seriously as art, and non-Hollywood models from Europe and Japan inspired in Chase and his generation new conceptions of the medium. A screening of Fellini's *8½* at Wake Forest in the 1960s left a lasting impression (Rucker interview).[2] The films of Polanski (Rucker interview) and Buñuel would not be forgotten (Bogdanovich interview). Chase began to dream about making "personal" films that did not seem to have been mass-produced. TV, on the other hand (as Glen Creeber shows in his essay in this volume), "ruined the movies," or so Chase believed.

Though he admits to "loving television as a kid," the affair didn't last. "I fell out of love with TV probably after *The Fugitive* went off the air [1967]. And then when I had my first network meeting, that didn't help" (Rucker interview).[3] "I hated everything that corporate America had to offer," Chase tells Rucker. "I considered network TV to be propaganda for the corporate state – the programming not only the commercials. I'm not a Marxist and I never was very radical, but that's what I considered it to be. To some extent, I still do. . ." Even a quality series like *Northern Exposure,* a show he wrote for in its final two seasons, was for Chase "propaganda for the corporate state. . . . it was ramming home every week the message that 'life is nothing but great.' 'Americans are great' and 'heartfelt emotion and sharing conquers everything.'" It should not surprise us that Chase thinks of himself as "The first counterculture person in hour drama" (Rucker interview).[4] He has remained an in-house renegade.

"I think it is a sad commentary on the last two decades of television," Stephen J. Cannell writes, "that this man, who was well known to all the networks for almost twenty-five years, could not get his fresh, totally unique ideas past the guardians of our public airwaves (read network executives here). Instead of *The Sopranos,* we more often got mindless clones of last year's semi-hits, while David made his living running other people's shows, unable to sell his own" (154–5). How he did finally manage to sell his own is a story often told.[5] Chase has again and again insisted that "luck" was perhaps the major contributing factor,[6] and a cursory cataloging of the extraordinary and diverse components that contributed to the making of *The Sopranos* would seem to confirm the observation.

II

Each and every one of the following ingredients had to be added to the mix – the "seemingly random juxtaposition of ideas" and factors that would shape a "newly forming structure" – in order for *The Sopranos*-as-we-know-it to come into existence:

The faith of Lloyd Braun of Brillstein-Grey Productions – the company that had developed *The Larry Sanders Show* for HBO – that Chase "had a great series inside," which led Chase to begin reconsidering and reconfiguring *for television* ideas that had long been on the back burner.

Chase's long-time obsession with gangster films. He was a great admirer of William Wellman's *Public Enemy* (1931) when he first saw it, terrified, at the age of eight or nine, and a fan of television's *The Untouchables* (1959–63), which he watched with his father. At Stanford he even made a student gangster film. *The Rise and Fall of Bug Manousos,* Chase recalls, "was about alienation. It was about a guy driven crazy by the cheesiness, sanctimoniousness, and fakery of American society. He was frustrated – he shotgunned his TV set. And what got to him were the commercials, the astronauts, and the fact that white bread Nixonians ruled America. . . . And he dreamed of becoming a gangster, an old-fashioned gangster in a pin-striped suit, and he got his wish. He got killed in the end, but the film was poorly thought out" (Rucker interview). The state of the post-*Godfather,* post-*GoodFellas* gangster genre at the time of *The Sopranos'* germination left Chase nowhere to go except "into the family" (Bogdanovich interview), ground which proved to be fertile indeed.

The idea, encouraged by Robin Green, a writer on *Almost Grown* (see Longworth), and others (including his wife), of telling stories about his own ultra-negative mother.

Chase's own long-running therapy. In his interview with James Longworth, Chase speaks revealingly of the great influence Alice Miller's brilliant but deeply troubling *Drama of the Gifted Child* – a book that argues that many creative adults were abused children – had on his own mindset.[7] He jokes that with *The Sopranos* all the money he has spent on therapy has finally begun to pay off (Bogdanovich interview).

The conceit of a mobster seeing a psychiatrist,[8] the series' germinal idea, as Chase explained it to Bogdanovich:

> The kernel of the joke, of the essential joke, was that life in America had gotten so savage, selfish – basically selfish, that even a mob guy couldn't take it any more. That was the essential joke, and he's in therapy because what he sees upsets him so much, what he sees every day . . . he and his guys were the ones who invented selfishness – they invented 'me first'; they invented 'it's all about me' – and now he can't take it because the rest of the country has surpassed him.

The commissioning of the pilot ("The Sopranos"/1001) for Fox, which would, of course, turn it down.

Chase's inclination never to purposely create comedy. Comedy just occurs, Chase tells Bogdanovich, naturally accruing when a writer is faithful to things as they are. (Is it too much to say that it is the funniest show since *Seinfeld*?)

The casting of virtually all the roles, mostly with New York-based actors, especially James Gandolfini as Tony – an epochal decision compared by some to having Marlon Brando play Stanley Kowalski in Elia Kazan's *A Streetcar Named Desire* (1951).

The ducks, who come to hold such meaning for Tony, flown in from *Rockford Files* TV movie producer Juanita Bartlett's own swimming pool.[9]

The family dynamics drawn from Chase's own family – minus the cursing.

The shopping-around of the series to all the networks and its complete rejection.

The opportune successful pitch to HBO, heavily committed at the time to the development of new, original series. Having the series on HBO permitted Chase to use nudity, violence, and profane language in ways that would have been impossible on network television, greatly facilitating its verisimilitude, but perhaps more importantly it enabled the uninterrupted-by-commercial construction of hour-long narratives.

HBO's commitment to on-location filming in New Jersey.

Luck was with David Chase, as well, when he and his production team decided *against* some other possibilities, all seriously considered, and all of which, in retrospect, would have been grave, if not fatal, mistakes:

Making the main character a television producer with an uneasy relationship with his mother (see Longworth interview 29).

Having the whole series be told by Tony in flashbacks in Melfi's office. About half of "The Sopranos" (1001) does make use of such a narrative technique, but the idea did not survive the pilot.

Using a new song for each episode's credit sequence. In a discussion of the opening credit sequence with Bogdanovich, Chase recalls that it had been his wish to use a different song every week and had protested unsuccessfully HBO's insistence that Tony's drive from New York to New Jersey always be choreographed to A3's "Woke Up This Morning." He admits that he originally considered a single theme song – a staple of television program for decades – "bourgeois."

Killing off Tony's mother, Livia, at the end of the first season. Nancy Marchand's superb performance convinced Chase and his collaborators to keep the character alive.

Casting Steven Van Zandt, Bruce Springsteen's guitarist, who had never acted before, as Tony. "At the time," Chase recalls, "I was seeing [*The Sopranos*] more like a live-action *Simpsons*. It would have been a gangster show, but some of the more tortured aspects of Tony would probably have gone away. With Steven, it would have been a little broad. We would have played it more for laughs" (Peyser 2001).

Not having Tony kill anyone on screen (as he does, for the first time, in "College" [1005], garroting a mob traitor), fearing – as HBO itself very strongly did – that the audience might lose all sympathy for its main character.

Though Chase is known as the "master cylinder" by the cast and crew of *The Sopranos* (Daly 24),[10] it is important to remember that, like all filmic and televisual enterprises, the series is a collaborative effort. Chase has written or co-written only eight of the thirty-nine episodes so far produced,[11] and he has directed only two episodes.[12] As Chase is the first to acknowledge, *The Sopranos* has brought together a regular team of talented writers and directors,[13] with occasional guest directors attracted by the show's prestige.[14] But, like many television producer/creators, Chase gets to do final revisions (uncredited) on almost all scripts and has participated in the editing of each and every episode.[15]

Recently it has become fashionable for the creators of more ambitious TV series to take personal control over their shows' authorship. David E. Kelley (*The Practice*, *Ally McBeal*), Aaron Sorkin (*The West Wing*), and Tom Fontana (*Oz*), for example, are sometimes given screenwriting credit for nearly every episode of the programs they produce. Although this assures a greater degree of aesthetic continuity and allows a television series to exhibit the same kind of single vision that we associate with more traditional art forms, this method also invites the burnout of the auteur and the exhaustion of the narrative premise.

David Chase, on the other hand, has returned to a more old-fashioned way of delegating authorial duty, but with only thirteen episodes per year to make, he is able to do it much more efficiently. By retaining his role as the final rewriter of every *Sopranos* script, but farming out most of his episodes to other writers, Chase has chosen a dramaturgical model that may be the most effective one for telling artistically mature stories in a continuing series. *The Sopranos* is enriched by the subtly different voices that various writers bring to the series. Chase's refusal to hog all of the scripts for himself provides a degree of multivalent complexity to the universe he has created. At the same time, Chase's stewardship assures that the show takes advantage of the unique ability of a television series to tell stories that develop character and accrete detail over long periods of real and narrative time. *The Sopranos* is not so much a television novel written by a single author, as it is a collection of short stories written by a company of authors and unified by character, theme, and the careful control of a single editor. Chase's model maximizes the potential of the serial form while protecting his show from becoming a traditional television serial.

As serendipitous as all of the above might seem, we would do well to remember that at the heart of the cultural phenomenon known as *The Sopranos* "it was [David Chase] in the first place who assembled all these constituents in the close proximity of one person's mind, his own, so that all this might happen." And it will be he who decides when (and how) *The Sopranos* will end.

III

In "The Peaks and Valleys of Serial Creativity: What Happened to/on *Twin Peaks*," Marc Dolan addresses the supreme narratological difficulties facing the makers of a continuing television serial. When the run of a narrative is indeterminate (as it was with David Lynch and Mark Frost's 1990–91 drama), Dolan shows, producers and writers must discover the means to open up the story enough to allow for future plot developments – to, in Dolan's words, "replicate itself endlessly" (43) – while still keeping the possibility of closure within view. *Twin Peaks* ended badly, of course, with its hero Dale Cooper possessed (forever, since the series was cancelled) by the evil, supernatural entity BOB, and many post-mortems of the series wondered if it had been done-in by its uncertain duration as a narrative. What if *Twin Peaks* had been a miniseries, some speculated – would it not have been more coherent if Lynch/Frost and company had known just how many episodes they had to tell their story?

A great admirer of *Twin Peaks*, David Chase has long worried about similar problems concerning *The Sopranos*. Determined from the start not to make a soap opera or a serial of any kind, he even insists to Bogdanovich that what the audience took to be cliffhangers (for example, Big Pussy's disappearance at the end of Season One) were not intended as such but resulted from "sloppy storytelling." Though HBO wanted to enhance the serialized elements, Chase, still the aspiring filmmaker, remained determined to make "a little movie every week" and sought to play them down. "College" (1005) – the episode in which Tony must kill a mob rat in the witness protection program while on a New England college visit with his daughter – is, for Chase, the perfect *Sopranos* episode because it lacks any serialized elements whatsoever (Bogdanovich interview).

After publicly threatening to end the series after only four seasons, Chase agreed in the summer of 2001 to a fifth, but he has warned from the beginning that it should have a very limited run, and for good reasons:

> The fact is, I don't know how long this thing will continue to attract viewers. There are so many pitfalls in series television. There are so many things about the structure itself that can lead you to creating shit. The

need to repeat yourself beyond the point of exhaustion, the fact that there are continuing characters and nothing really can happen to them. You're boxed in so many ways. I don't want to see the show become the walking dead, a zombie of itself. I was the one who asked for the four-year cap. (Peyser)

"The model for . . . gangster pictures," Chase is well aware, "has always been *The Rise and Fall of . . . .* Our show doesn't have a rise and fall – it's like *The Going Along of Tony Soprano*. But we do know that he's involved in a lifestyle that's dangerous, illegal and dehumanizing. How long can that go on – realistically?" (quoted by Curtis). "Sometimes I call the show the Mir space station," Chase told *Newsweek* (Peyser). "It wasn't designed to be up there for five years." That he has now agreed to a longer run would seem to suggest, however, that he has envisioned new means to maintain the proper altitude, to prevent degradation of *The Sopranos'* orbit, and incineration in the atmosphere.[16]

IV

When *Hill Street Blues* debuted in 1981, it catalyzed a widespread upgrade of the dramatic television series. The creative and commercial success of the show inspired two decades of programming that was more sophisticated, more complex – indeed *better* than what had gone before. But *Hill Street Blues* didn't have much of an act to follow. It was introduced during one of the most arid periods in the history of the dramatic series, a form that had never really matured.

Like *Hill Street Blues*, *The Sopranos* is another monumental work in the development of TV drama. While *Hill Street Blues* was responding to a television tradition that included such generic contemporaries as *CHiPS* and *T.J. Hooker*, however, *The Sopranos* attracted critical acclaim amidst a schedule rich with "quality" series like *Law & Order*, *NYPD Blue*, and *The Practice*.

Judging by the number of magazine covers they inspired, two television shows seemed to dominate the American imagination, or at least the imaginations of entertainment writers, at the turn of the century: *The Sopranos* and *Survivor*. Both shows may have succeeded for some of the same reasons. After half a century of sitcoms, and cop, lawyer, doctor, and detective dramas, viewers may have been ready for something completely different. "Reality TV" and *The Sopranos* both provided this, though in very different ways. *Survivor* and the other shows in its genre offered "reality" through the use of non-actors and the introduction of improvised and serendipitous dramatic action; *The Sopranos* offered reality through its extension of the palette of language and its break with some of the traditions of TV drama that tone down and clean up any subject matter.[17]

Perhaps it wasn't just the ways in which *The Sopranos* was different from other TV that made it work, however. David Chase made two crucial decisions early in the development of the show. The decision to place Tony Soprano into therapy allowed the viewer access to the interior psychic workings of the show's lead character, thereby co-opting the tools of written literature without resorting to the contrivances of narrators or soliloquies. More importantly, however, was Chase's decision to merge the epic of the urban frontier that had been explored in *The Godfather* and *GoodFellas* with the non-epic of the suburban family that has been one of the basic units of entertainment TV from the very start. What may have seemed a ludicrous generic oxymoron now seems to have been inevitable.

V

In his cynical and brilliant *Bonfire of the Humanities: Television, Subliteracy, and Long-Term Memory Loss*, David Marc, one of the medium's acutest scholars, observes:

> The TV industry may in fact be full of wonderfully creative folks possessing the remarkable talents necessary to bring laughter, tears, and information to the great multitudes of their fellow citizens. But so far I haven't bumped into any of that crowd, *only dangerous gangsters* who you wouldn't want to meet in a dark corridor of power. (my emphasis; 136)

Marc's dark view of the industry to which he has devoted his life's work is certainly one with which David Chase, another lifer who, in his estimation, had for three decades prior to *The Sopranos* not even risen to the rank of "street boss" in the business (Rucker interview), would concur. But Chase, one of those "wonderfully creative folks" Marc evidently never met, will, should their post-*Sopranos* paths now cross, have a thing or two to tell him about the nature of the gangster. Not all of them work to maintain television's status quo. In the right hands, gangsters may even prove useful in subverting "everything that corporate America [has] to offer."

"Genius," underground filmmaker James Broughton once said, "is not having enough talent to do it the way it has been done before" (35). Boredom, too, is a factor: "You get bored," Chase tells James Longworth, "and I don't know if you can tell it from looking at *The Sopranos*, but I had just had it up to here with all the niceties of network television. I couldn't take it any more. And I don't mean language and I don't mean violence. I just mean storytelling, inventiveness, something that really could entertain and surprise people. I just couldn't take it anymore" (34).

Now that he has had his way, now that "great television series" Lloyd Braun presciently sensed he had buried within has come out, what is to become of David Chase? Two more years of *The Sopranos* remain. Will he leverage his *Sopranos* fame in order to realize his long-held dream of leaving TV for the movies? Chase, it should be noted, no longer thinks so highly of film as he once did.[18] Or will he stay in television, despite his frequent insistence that he could never return to network TV, willing now to work in a medium transformed by his loathing of it?[19]

FOUR

NAKED BODIES, THREE SHOWINGS A WEEK, AND NO COMMERCIALS: *THE SOPRANOS* AS A NUTS-AND-BOLTS TRIUMPH OF NON-NETWORK TV

Paul Levinson

Cable television was conceived in reflections. Born in the 1950s as a means of delivering network TV to areas of the country unable to receive its signals broadcast on electro-magnetic carrier waves, cable began to take wing in the 1980s as a medium of more original content – or programming somewhat distinct from networks – with CNN's all-news and HBO's all-movies. But even though HBO featured movies much newer than those seen on network TV – fresh out of the box office (hence, "Home Box Office") – it was still, after all, a second-hand operation. The movies had already been seen by many viewers in their original box office showings – in theaters.

HBO's remedy was to field "made-for-HBO" movies. These also enabled HBO to distinguish itself from competitors now also offering cinema on cable. The best of the "made-for-HBO" movies showcased important subjects (*Murrow* [1985]; *Stalin* [1992]) and major network television and Hollywood talent (*Murrow* starred *Hill Street Blues'* Daniel J. Travanti; *Stalin* was portrayed by Robert Duvall). But though these were great television movies, they fell far short of being great movies. They were smaller, psychologically as well as culturally, than *Gone With The Wind* (1939), *The Godfather* (1972), and *Star Wars* (1977). They were less daring, less experimental, than *12 Monkeys* (1995) or *The Usual Suspects* (1995). In all respects, and even at its most original and important, the cable-TV movie was still second best.

HBO and its competitors also introduced a variety of gritty documentaries on prostitution, crime, sex, and drugs. These certainly went a lot further than network documentaries, in subject matter and explicit treatment. At their best, HBO's *Taxi-Cab Confessions* (1995–) achieve a kind of down-to-earth, noirish *vérité* unavailable in most other television and cinema. And yet when a history of the TV documentary in the past decade is written, it will undoubtedly put

Ken Burns' PBS work – on the Civil War, baseball, and jazz – in first place of importance and influence. It took an original TV dramatic series – *The Sopranos* – to put HBO and cable TV in a class by itself.

OLD WINE IN NEW BOTTLES

The TV series was a natural for network television from the very beginning. Its roots were in the Saturday movie-serial and the radio series – in some cases, radio provided the entire tree (*Gunsmoke* was uprooted from radio and planted in TV). Available in the home, free of charge (the advantages of TV over motion picture theaters) and with pictures as well as sound (the advantage over radio), the 30-minute and then 60-minute weekly television series became enormously popular. Its ultimate impact on cinema was the end of the neighborhood theater and motion picture cathedrals like the Loews Paradise in favor of multiplexes in shopping malls. Radio was forced to scramble for new content, and in a master stroke (courtesy of Alan Freed) discovered rock 'n' roll.

But the television series inherited a necklace of flaws from radio. Punctuated by commercials, viewable only once and then you were out of luck, sharply limited in its language and showing of flesh, the network TV series carved a niche for itself in a mostly sanitized, superficial never-never-land. In contrast, motion pictures offered uninterrupted narrative and opportunities for repeat viewing (in the 1950s, I sat through many a movie twice – though, of course, seeing the same movie again on a different day required purchase of a new ticket). By the mid-1960s, the motion picture codes that in previous decades had frowned on even the word "pregnant" were gone; nudity was in. These advantages of the motion picture theater were no doubt in part responsible for its survival in any form in the age of television.

Meanwhile, network television was beginning to improve, in technology as well as content. The VCR, beginning in the mid-1970s, allowed people to watch their favorite shows as often as was wanted, without commercial interruption. Sitcoms such as *All in the Family* and *The Mary Tyler Moore Show* tackled much more serious subject matter than *I Love Lucy*. Two decades later, *NYPD Blue* even coughed up a little more realistic language – such as "asshole" – and a very occasional very quick glimpse of a naked body or two.

And yet the fixes were far from fully satisfactory. Fast-forwarding through commercials on a VCR is not the same as relaxing back in your chair and watching a program with no commercials in the first place. Much more importantly, the network television dramatic series were created – written from the very first word – with commercial interruptions in mind. It was and is a form of brief, ten-ish minute chapters, each needing to conclude with some kind of climax or hook to keep the viewer from wandering too far during the commercial break. This form of course survives the expunging of commercials in VCR replay.

And as for the language and nudity on *NYPD Blue*, it's still unrealistically tame. Is there any cop who hasn't said the word "fuck" to a colleague officer?

You never hear it on the ABC-TV series. And the nudity is mostly backsides, including Andy Sipowicz's to boot.

BADA BING! NUDITY

The female nude was the most popular subject of high Victorian photography, but no one talked about it then. Indeed, naked bodies remained under the covers in popular culture until *Playboy* in the 1950s, which in turn liberated the motion picture in the 1960s. But network television stayed recalcitrantly pure. Driven by the inexorable calculus of simply attaining the largest possible audience for its commercials, network TV's first commandment is "thou shalt not offend." HBO's subscription revenues encouraged no such restrictions. It was from the outset a medium midway between magazines and network television. Further, cable delivered its programming outside of the "public airways," which made it less vulnerable to Federal Communications Commission intimidation.

Nudity in itself, however, is not all it's cracked up to be – at least, not as an element of narrative. Like all aspects of drama, nudity in a storyline needs to be motivated to achieve its best effect. There should be a good reason in the story – a reason other than the viewer's enjoyment of the naked body – that characters are unclothed. Otherwise, the nudity may distract from, rather than help tell, the story.

Couples making love certainly is a logical place to dispense with clothing. But this puts a big burden on the storyline. We need to understand why our couples are having sex at the time and place portrayed. And unless the story can accommodate a good few minutes of attention to the couple in bed – the kind of attention you see in the soft porn on HBO, Showtime, and Cinemax – the viewer may not get to see the specific part of the body he or she is looking for.

The Sopranos' brilliant solution is to situate most of its nudity in the Bada Bing! strip joint run by Tony Soprano's aide-de-camp, Silvio Dante. The setting is an eminently logical place to frequently find Tony and his crew discussing business, and the naked women need no further motivation than that they are dancing in the club. The viewer can sit back and enjoy the show on at least two levels: plot unfolding at the bar or the tables, eyeful on the stage.

Of course, the strip club has its limitations as a vehicle of nudity. No males are seen naked; no full-scale sex occurs. (Devotees of the former can watch HBO's also superb *Six Feet Under* (2001–); and naked sex is all over cable, including HBO's *Real Sex* documentary series.) But Bada Bing! is nonetheless an ideal locale – doing for *The Sopranos* what the diner did for *Seinfeld* and the bar owned by Munch, Meldrake, and Bayliss did for *Homicide* – but with a physically illicit explicitness that gives sexual energy to whatever other story is unfolding.

Linguistic explicitness – language, as crude as it gets – is also a staple of *The Sopranos*, and heard throughout the show. To this day, the TV networks rarely if ever go into George Carlin's "Seven Dirty Words" territory (words, unlike "prick," which have no saving double meaning – their sound is always vulgar or obscene), but *The Sopranos* says them all. Speaking as a male viewer, I can't say that curse words are as pleasurable to hear as nudity is to see in Bada Bing!, but their presence in *The Sopranos* lends a reliable verisimilitude to every episode.

<small>ONCE IS NEVER ENOUGH</small>

A classic critique of television, among those who worried that it was undermining our literary values, was that its stories were gone the minute after they had been seen. Unlike the book, which offered endless retrieval of its pages already read, or even the motion picture, which permitted viewing more than once in a variety of ways, television basically gave it to you once, and that was it. Summer reruns were minor exceptions. Extended reruns in syndication, at first ignored, proved to be one of the most potent forces in television and popular culture, vaulting the original *Star Trek* series – which ran only three years in its first incarnation on NBC in the 1960s – into a major phenomenon that would give rise to numerous offspring series, motion pictures, and novels. And the VCR, as mentioned earlier, allowed viewers who troubled to tape the TV show the option of seeing it again.

But HBO's decision to present its original series, including *The Sopranos*, more than once a week – that is, to replay the programs – got much more directly at the human need to see again. Offering each episode on Sunday evening, and then at least two more times during the ensuing week, had two advantages over just once-a-week network TV. First, viewers could catch the episode if they missed the initial showing, and in time to pick up the very next episode the following week. Second – but in many ways even more significantly – viewers could in subsequent showings pick up and appreciate complexities and aspects of the program missed the first time around.

In all fairness to network TV, its evening programs began in the 1950s as discontinuous episodes. They had few if any ongoing storylines. The characters by and large remained static throughout the season and even across new ones. There was little if any benefit in seeing the show again. Only with *Dallas* in 1978 and *Hill Street Blues*, *St. Elsewhere*, etc. in the 1980s did prime time TV begin to indulge in continuing stories.

But even at their most complex, these night-time serials were usually paper-thin compared to *The Sopranos*, whose depth in effect expanded into a niche afforded by multiple viewings. The result is an intensity and an intricacy seldom attained even in motion pictures. Indeed, *The Sopranos* has more in common with *The Godfather* saga and *GoodFellas* than either does to its respective genres of television and motion pictures, and this is not just because they all are Mafia stories. The unity also comes from their complexity and the rewards obtained from their viewing more than once. (A very few movies are so complex that they almost cannot be appreciated until seen at least more than once. *The Usual Suspects* is an outstanding example.)

The resistance of network TV to multiple showings comes from its commercial structure – why would an advertiser pay top dollar to have a commercial broadcast on a rerun? HBO suffers no such pressure. But the lack of commercials frees HBO serials in a more direct and powerful way.

No Breaks

There is a tradition for just about everything – including commercial punctuation of narrative. Certainly the acts of a play are a form of punctuation, as are chapters in a book. But few plays are an hour in length. And the reader of a book is always able to move right into the next chapter, with no break at all.

It is a triumph of human creativity that anything worthwhile was able to emerge from the Procrustean bed of TV commercial interruption. But from this commercial interruptus, good, even wonderful television did proceed, ranging from *The Twilight Zone* to the best of *Hill Street Blues, St. Elsewhere, LA Law,* and *NYPD Blue* and *ER* more recently.

Yet few of these shows were as consistently gratifying, episode for episode, as *The Sopranos* (and, of course, *The Twilight Zone* was an anthology, not a continuing story). This is in part because the lack of commercial evisceration in *The Sopranos* makes each episode a short movie.

Probably the closest that commercial TV ever came to this cinematic ambience was *Homicide: Life on the Street.* And that show labored mightily, and not entirely successfully, to transcend its commercial tethers. Many was a *Homicide* episode that started off slowly – perfectly fine for a movie – but potentially deadly for a program that would break for a commercial a few minutes down the line. And many was a spectacular grilling by Pemberton in the box that lost a bit of its momentum in a commercial break. No wonder *Homicide* struggled in the ratings, and was eventually cancelled notwithstanding its critical acclaim. Undriven, unriven by commericals, *The Sopranos* is able to soar. Threads in each episode can be as long or short as called for. Nothing distracts from an intensity that beats like a nearing anvil; nothing gets in the way of our quiet contemplation of an endearing moment. There are interruptions, all right – but these are the interruptions of the rest of our lives during the week.

THE SOPRANOS AS PRELUDE TO WEB CASTING

It is no coincidence that cable TV found its narrative stride in *The Sopranos* and like series at precisely the same time as the Web was making its first serious mark on our culture. All the salient *Soprano* characteristics discussed here – the nudity, opportunity for repeat viewing, freedom from commercial interruption that distinguish cable from network TV – are also found on the Web. Naughty words and images abound on the Internet, they can be seen as often as desired, and such advertisements as are found there are usually at the beginnings, endings, and edges of documents and images – they frame rather than intrude. The Internet can thus be seen as a potential *Sopranos* writ large; or, *The Sopranos* can be seen as an incipient Internet.

Of course technology, however accommodating, is not enough for great narrative. There must be human minds creating the wine. The unique advantages of cable TV thus made *The Sopranos* possible; in the terms of science and philosophy, those characteristics were necessary but not sufficient for *The Sopranos*. The rest reside with the writers, actors, directors, producers.

But cable TV made them an offer that couldn't be refused.

·

FIVE

WAY NORTH OF NEW JERSEY: A CANADIAN EXPERIENCE OF *THE SOPRANOS*

Dawn Elizabeth B. Johnston

> Canada is a land of multiple borderlines, psychic, social and geographic. Canadians live at the interface where opposites clash. We have, therefore, no recognizable identity, and are suspicious of those who think they have.
>
> Marshall McLuhan (244)

At the end of August 2000, Canadian television viewers watched as CTV, Canada's largest private broadcaster of conventional television, began a series of promotional ads. Their message was short and simple: "Coming Soon: *The Sopranos*. Television for adults." In a publicly unfamiliar and unanticipated move, CTV announced that they would be airing Season One of the popular HBO series back-to-back for thirteen consecutive nights – against the Canadian Broadcasting Corporation's coverage of the 2000 Olympic Games. The announcement created a media buzz unlike any that had been seen by the Canadian television viewing public: this news not only dominated the entertainment reporting of most major television and print journalists, but also received a great deal of mainstream news attention. For weeks prior to the beginning of the broadcast, viewers watched and listened to commentary and debates about *The Sopranos*, all promising more violence, nudity, coarse language, and scandal than had ever been shown in Canadian prime time. There was widespread speculation on what Canadians would think of this very un-Canadian show. Since its debut in the United States in 1999, *The Sopranos* has challenged television's format, style, and audiences; the show's broader impact on popular culture beyond the American border was made evident in its debut in a Canadian context.

When the Soprano family was introduced to the Canadian audience, the media attention proved to be warranted and accurate: Canadians turned out in force for all thirteen episodes. According to Nielsen ratings across the country, CTV's *Sopranos* national viewership among viewers over the age of 18 ranged from an opening night of 2.1 million down to a mid-week 1.7 million, back over 2.0 million for the season finale (CTV Programming Department). CBC's coverage of the Olympic Games didn't fare nearly so well. For 10 nights out of the 13, *The Sopranos* went head-to-head against the Olympics on CBC. According to CTV programming executive Mike Consentino , CTV more than doubled the Olympics with a national average of 1.93 million viewers versus CBC's 901,000 viewers.

And even putting the ratings aside, viewer responses to CTV demonstrated just how much attention had been paid to *The Sopranos*. By the tenth episode, CTV had received approximately 1,100 e-mails and telephone calls from viewers; about 600 were positive responses to the program, 500 were negative (Brioux, "CTV"). According to CTV's Allison Vale, Vice President for Programming Communications, an additional person was temporarily hired in Audience Relations just to deal with the incredible volume of responses concerning the program. 138 irate viewers went one step further than the programming department at CTV and filed official complaints with the Canadian Broadcast Standards Council (CBSC). Complaints railed against many aspects of the show: the language, nudity, inadequate viewer advisory, ethnic stereotyping, and anti-Christian sentiments.

Ten of those complaints to the CBSC were filed as Ruling Requests, asking the CBSC to consider whether various aspects of CTV's programming decisions surrounding the airing of *The Sopranos* had contravened Canadian broadcast standards. The officially-filed complaints exhibited a wide range of knowledge, articulation, and point-of-view. One viewer was deeply offended by the language and nudity, saying:

> I only watched a few minutes of this show, which aired at 10:00 pm EST, and I was shocked and disgusted at the filth that this so-called drama spewed both visually and verbally. In one 5 minute stretch, I not only heard multiple uses of the F word, but I also had the great displeasure of seeing two topless women bearing [sic] their breasts to the camera. Nothing was left to the imagination. This show is violating community standards, and CTV should be prevented from showing this trash. (CBSC ruling)

Several complainants whose letters were quoted in the CBSC ruling referred to "filthy language," "profanity like we have never seen on conventional television," and "disgusting violence, profanity, degradation of women . . . and defamation of Italians." Another viewer who submitted a lengthy and detailed complaint to the Council took issue specifically with the ethnic stereotyping of Italians as being in direct contravention of the Council's standards:

Quite simply the program contravenes the Television Broadcasting Regulations, 1987. In these Regulations, Section 5(b) we read: "[A licensee shall not broadcast] any abusive comment or abusive pictorial representation that, when taken in context, tends or is likely to expose an individual or group or class of individuals to hatred or contempt on the basis of race, national or ethnic origin, colour , religion, sex, age or mental or physical disability." . . . I submit that the pictorial representations of persons of Italian origin or ethnic heritage taken in the context of this program are exposed to contempt and that this exposure contravenes both the letter and the spirit of the Television Broadcasting Regulations, 1987. The perception of Italians provided and nurtured by this program is that of a group of persons in whom any degree of moral awareness is absent. Obsessed by mindless violence they kill others and the taking of human life is regarded as unremarkable behavior; the intention to kill is formed and the act simply flows from it. This profoundly pejorative, and I would emphasize mistaken, perception of a particular group engenders contempt towards them. It also diminishes us who are not of Italian origin or heritage if we remain silent and allow the pictorial representations of the perception to pass across our television screens as unremarkable.

The CBSC considered each of the complaints in turn, and before ruling on them, also invited CTV to provide a response.

CTV's response to viewer complaints was consistent with its original announcement that it would air the show unedited. In a letter to viewers, the network said, in part:

Your reaction to the content of *The Sopranos* is understandable but we cannot censor this program because some people believe, however sincerely and strongly, that it contains messages inappropriate for television viewing. There are many viewers who have expressed that they would have been equally disappointed if we had edited the piece. . . . Although we'd regret losing you as a viewer for this show, we understand and respect your right not to watch if you find *The Sopranos* offensive. (Vale interview)

The network has remained firm in its position regarding the airing of the program. According to Vale, CTV considered its viewership very carefully in making their decision. Although the program challenged the comfort levels of many of those viewers, Vale says that the network demonstrated respect for the regulations of the Canadian television broadcasting industry, and sincerely believed that *The Sopranos* did not breach the codes.

Fortunately for CTV, the Broadcast Standards Council agreed with them. According to their ruling, decided on 8 March 2001, CTV's broadcast of *The Sopranos* was considered under five CAB private broadcaster codes: the Code of Ethics, Clause 2 (Human Rights), the Sex-Role Portrayal Code, Article 4

(Exploitation), and three articles of the Violence Code, on Gratuitous and Glamorized Violence, Scheduling, and Viewer Advisories. In summation, the Council said the following:[1]

> The Adjudicators watched each of the episodes and reviewed all of the correspondence relevant to this decision. The National Conventional Television Panel considers that . . . the series does not violate any of the program content requirements of the private broadcaster Codes.

The panel went on to consider each of the charged code breaches separately. With regards to human rights, it was determined that although the show did indeed show Italians engaging in criminal behavior, that "the series is about criminals acting as criminals, not about criminals acting as Italians." According to the ruling on this particular code, "the issue is not, in other words, whether programming deals with people of Italian nationality, but rather whether it portrays them in an abusively discriminatory way *on the basis of that nationality.*" On the issue of language, the Council determined that "there is no disputing that the language used in *The Sopranos* is exceedingly coarse. . . . There are few sentences in which one or another of the 'forbidden' words, four-letter and otherwise, is not present." However, as they went on to say, the language did not break any rules:

> In this case, the coarse, foul, indeed crude, language use by the mobsters is their vernacular. It is not employed gratuitously; it is used as one might expect that they would *really* use it. . . . While not endorsing its use, the Panel recognizes its relevance to the story being told. . . . The broadcast of the language itself, in the circumstances of this show, while not for everyone's ears, is not a sanctionable usage.

In contradiction to the complaints of "constant violence" and "excessive violence" in some of the viewer complaints, the Council determined that the violence of the show was not extreme in volume, and also complied with the broadcast standards.

> While there is an undercurrent of the *threat* of violence, the quantity of on-screen violence in each episode is not significant. Of each 60+ minute show, there are not more than two scenes of violent action. That being said, when it occurs, the violent action tends to be graphic. Graphic, true, perhaps because it is realistic in its presentation, but not excessive, and always contextual. The Panel considers that no act of violence in the episodes was dramatically unsubstantiated.

The ruling made similar judgments about nudity and sexual activity, indicating that although these scenes may be unpalatable to some audience members, they are within the bounds of dramatic context and are suitably contained within the advisory.

The network's use of advisory warnings, however, did result in the CBSC's determination that CTV had breached the Violence Code. In their decision on the use of advisories, the Council's ruling stated:

> The purpose of viewer advisories is sometimes thought to be oriented toward children. While their utility for that purpose is clear and important, they are, as a tool, media literacy based and oriented toward adults as much as children. They are intended to provide viewers with sufficient information to enable them to determine, whether for their children *or for themselves,* what will be suitable viewing fare.

There was no doubt, among either the Broadcast Standards Council or the general viewing public, that CTV's viewer advisory was as strongly worded as possible. The statement, which appeared at the beginning of the program, and again at the end of the first commercial break, was longer and more carefully worded than standard parental advisory warnings. It said:

> This program is not intended for children. It contains scenes of violence, extremely coarse language and nudity. Some adults may be offended by the content. Viewer discretion is strongly advised.

The Council was fully satisfied with the content of this warning, and specifically commended CTV's "adverbial underscoring" of the questionable content of the program, as well as its emphasis that some of the content might even be offensive to adult viewers.

They were not satisfied, however, with the frequency of the use of this advisory. According to the Violence Code, any program which requires advisories must show those advisories at the beginning of the program, as well as coming out of each and every commercial break. CTV's sporadic use of the advisory was found to breach the code, and the panel's written ruling required CTV to announce this decision during its prime-time programming several times within the following two weeks, as well as to provide written confirmation of the aired statement to the complainants who filed Ruling Requests. No further action was required.

The public and regulatory hoopla surrounding CTV's decision to air an unedited season of *The Sopranos* was very new to Canadians. As Allison Vale points out, CTV is the longest-running private, conventional television broadcaster in Canada and has become a fixture in Canadian households. From a network which brings its viewers news, children's programming, and fairly standard dramas and variety shows, most of the audience expects mainstream television. Many viewers, although fairly acclimatized to some degree of violence on American programs carried by the network, felt betrayed by CTV, which had never pushed the limits of television to this degree before.

CTV's decision to air the show unedited was not an easy one. In the United States a show like *The Sopranos* aired on HBO – a private cable network – rather than one of the mainstream networks like NBC, ABC, or CBS (these networks had, in fact, passed on the show during its development) for a number of reasons. The violence is significant. As the show's creators have pointed out, and many critics have agreed, that violence is not necessarily gratuitous, but it is more graphic, more intense, and more frequent than in most mainstream prime time television programming. The language is coarse. Almost every sentence contains an expletive simply not permissible in most television programming. And the nudity is not a familiar sight in prime time network programming. So for CTV, deciding to run the program unedited at 10:00pm every night for two weeks was also risky. According to programming executives at CTV, other options were explored, but none were acceptable. In a press conference last September, CTV's executive vice-president Trina McQueen emphasized that their decision not to edit was related entirely to the quality of the program in its intended form, saying, "Trying to remove the language or downgrade the language would have twisted the program into what it wasn't meant to be" (Tilley, "Singing"). Allison Vale agreed.

> We had absolute concerns about the mature content. We originally had intentions to air an edited version of the show, but the "international" version was too edited in our programmers' estimation, so they tried to hammer out an individual editing. It didn't work. The story is too tight, each piece connected to the other, intertwined and inseparable in order to tell the full story with the impact that it was designed to have. We felt we absolutely needed to preserve and protect the creative integrity of the show, and realized it couldn't be done with editing. In the end, we decided to take the risk and air it unedited. (Vale interview)

And a risk it was. Even though, as Vale has said, the quality of the program speaks for itself, the decision to air the HBO cut of the program was gutsy. CTV has a wide and loyal viewing audience and is responsible to a wide variety of advertisers. While making a point of distinguishing itself from the publicly-funded Canadian Broadcasting Corporation (CBC) in its effort to present news and entertainment of interest to Canadians, it has sought to avoid "unnecessarily" crude content. Several reporters pointed out this seeming incongruity in CTV's policies. In his coverage of CTV's press conference in the wake of its airing of *The Sopranos*, Steve Tilley noted the following:

> When asked why, then, CTV News recently bleeped out a much publicized derogatory remark made by U.S. presidential candidate George W. Bush towards a reporter, McQueen said the audience for a newscast has different expectations than *Sopranos* viewers. She said people tuning in to the news don't expect to hear words like the one Bush used (a common seven letter profanity beginning with the letter A), while *The Sopranos* will have explicit viewer discretion warnings at the beginning of the show and after commercial breaks. "I guess the difference, really, is whether you're interfering with a creative aspect of a program, and whether you decide if the publication of a vulgar

phrase is necessary to convey a news story," McQueen said. (Tilley, "Singing")

For CTV executives, the issue of explicitness in a creative television program was not subject to the same standards or expectations as the evening news. But even with that distinction, most viewers and critics were quick to note that CTV's programming has never included a show which challenges the boundaries of network television so aggressively. *The Sopranos* really pushed the conventions of CTV's programming, risking the alienation of viewers and corporate sponsors alike. But according to McQueen, the decision, although difficult, was firm. "Our decision was whether we were going to air this as the creator of the program intended, or otherwise forget about it" (Tilley, "Singing").

That decision provoked a surprisingly pseudo-patriotic response from some viewers. Many of the complainants who expressed their dissatisfaction to the CBSC commented specifically on how inappropriate *The Sopranos* was for Canadian television. Each of these comments appeared in the CBSC's written ruling regarding *The Sopranos*:

> It would be difficult for me to think of a clearer example of a fundamental difference between American culture and Canadian culture than the one *The Sopranos* provides. I hope you will respect your own Regulations and hold CTV responsible for its breach of public trust.

From another viewer:

> This show is violating community standards, and CTV should be prevented from showing this trash. This type of filth is usually reserved for American cable.

Another complainant spoke, apparently, for all Canadians:

> I am asking the Council to look carefully at the four codes that encompass our Broadcast Standards and ensure that such hostile bigotry towards an ethnic group, such horrific violence, sexism, vulgarity, profanity, and human degradation are not what we want to see on our Canadian televisions.

Finally – and almost comically in its vehemence – another Canadian would complain: "I don't care if *The Sopranos* won a billion awards. The show won awards in the States. This is Canada. We have a mind of our own" (CBSC ruling Appendix).

These responses, although they might appear uncharacteristically strong, are really not entirely disconnected from a general Canadian feeling about American popular culture. Canadians are famous for defining our culture, our cultural products, our lifestyles, and even our personalities as distinctly *un*American. One of the most successful and popular Canadian ad campaigns in recent memory was run in 1999/2000 by the Molson Brewing company. The concept was simple: an average Canadian "Joe" standing on a bare stage, facing an audience. He surveys the audience, taps the microphone, and begins tentatively:

> I'm not a lumberjack, or a fur trader,
> And I don't live in an igloo, or eat blubber, or own a dogsled.
> And I don't know Jimmy, Sally, or Suzy from Canada,
> Although I'm certain that they are really nice.
> I have a Prime Minister, not a President.
> I speak English and French, not American.
> And I pronounce it "abOUt", not "a bOOt".
> I can proudly sew my country's flag on my backpack.
> I believe in peace keeping, not policing;
> Diversity, not assimilation.
> And that a beaver is a truly proud and noble animal.
> A toque is a hat; a chesterfield is a couch;
> And it is pronounced "zed", not "zee". "ZED!!"
> Canada is the second largest landmass!
> The first nation of hockey!
> And the best part of North America!
> My name is Joe, and I AM CANADIAN!

At about the halfway point of this monologue, "Joe" gains momentum and enthusiasm, and by the end of the speech, he is yelling and gesturing to a screaming and supportive crowd. The structure of the piece is significant; it begins by debunking (though in some ways, simultaneously confirming) common stereotypes about Canadians, and it ends with an enthusiastic and patriotic declaration of the greatness of Canada, but it is obsessed with a cultural *comparison* of Canadians and Americans. "We" are everything that "they" are not.

But at the same time, obviously, our popular culture is hugely influenced by American popular culture. One need only look at the real numbers of Canadians watching American television programs such as *The Sopranos*. Canadian television and radio stations are required to meet minimum Can Con (Canadian Content) requirements in order to balance the overwhelming volume of American programming and music, but as Ian Austen points out in his article entitled "Culture between Commercials," many Canadian broadcasters squeak by in meeting those requirements through news, sports, and "signal substitution" of Canadian advertisements over American ones instead of actual Canadian programming. Canadian music and film, although certainly celebrated in Canada, are usually considered to be in opposition to or an alternative to "the mainstream." Our cultural consumption feeds primarily on a diet of American popular culture. So at one level, we are always resisting American pop culture, but when it comes to the straight-out numbers, we clearly embrace it.

There are many theories on the reason for those numbers. One answer is easy: it is simply more profitable to broadcast American programs. As Ian Austen suggests:

> It's not hard to see from a pure business standpoint why private Canadian TV broadcasters have become essentially pipelines for U.S. shows. It costs about $700,000 to $1 million to produce a single hour of real Canadian entertainment programming. . . . You buy a big American hit for about $90,000 a one-hour episode. (78)

The viewership is larger for American dramas and sitcoms than for their Canadian counterparts, and therefore commercial time garners more money during prime-time broadcasts of American shows. As Vale pointed out, advertising spots for CTV's broadcast of *The Sopranos* sold out quickly upon announcement that the show would air. Instead of losing advertisers for the sometimes-offensive program, the high quality of the American program and the potential ratings it might draw attracted its own enthusiastic advertisers.

Another possibility – one which is almost certainly a bi-product of the first – is that Canadians just don't know Canadian television. Accustomed to the higher production values, bigger stars, and flashier special effects of American television and film, Canadians don't seem to know quite how to watch (and certainly, how to appreciate) the smaller-budget, often better acted, but generally lower-key style of Canadian productions. As Noreen Golfman has written of Canadian film audiences, specifically, they are sometimes "utterly unfamiliar with and menaced by anything but a Hollywood product" (102).

And when Canadian television or film is the focus of Canadian attention, it is still very much in that context of "not American." Implicit in the phrases that I used above – smaller, better, lower – is an implied "than": smaller budget *than* American television, better acted *than* American television, lower-key *than* big American television. The comparison between our own cultural products and the much more recognized cultural products of the United States is constant. The influence of our neighbors to the South is undeniable in all of these areas of our popular culture, so it isn't entirely surprising to see that defensiveness among our citizens. Yet despite all of our very self-conscious efforts to define ourselves as not American, it seems that more than three quarters of Canadians claim it is our distinct and strong sense of our own history, *not* our desire to be unlike the Americans, that defines us (Wallace 56).

But if this is so, why such strong responses to the "un-Canadian-ness" of a program like *The Sopranos*? As the Canadian Broadcast Standards Council reported, the complaints weren't just about the violence, language, nudity, and ethnic stereotyping, but about those elements of mature content being shown on "our Canadian television." Part of it, perhaps, is that *The Sopranos*, although distinctly American in many ways, is also fairly distinctly un-Hollywood. And if Hollywood productions are Canada's perception of American popular culture, then *The Sopranos* is going to raise more response than most American television programs shown on Canadian networks. As numerous CTV programming executives pointed out in the weeks following the debut of the first season of *The Sopranos* in September 2000, viewer complaints are usually connected to such programming issues as Felicity cutting her hair or *General Hospital* being pre-empted. The network's proudly and frequently advertised self-declaration of "CTV: CANADIAN television" is rarely challenged by any concerns relating to things Canadian.

The Sopranos challenges conventions of Canadian television in a way that our viewers have rarely – if ever – seen before. But that challenge may be as much to our perception of television as to our perception of any particular culture. I expect that *The Sopranos* provides a comparable challenge to mainstream American viewers; as David Chase himself pointed out to Canadian journalists following the September 2000 broadcast, *The Sopranos* running uncut and uncensored on a major mainstream television network is "something that would never happen in the U.S." (Brioux). Almost immediately following the wrap of Season One on CTV, a private pay channel in Canada picked up the second and third seasons of the program, suggesting that Canadians, like Americans, would have to see their *Sopranos* on less mainstream television. But almost a year to the day after CTV announced its plans to air Season One for the first time, the network began its re-broadcast of the first season – to be immediately followed by the full second season – once again, uncensored, unedited, and uncut.

As distinctly un-Canadian as this ground-breaking show may be in terms of its aesthetics, writing, subject, and spirit, it draws Canadian viewers in a ferocious and tenacious way. Perhaps there is some point of familiarity or connection for Canadian viewers in the smart writing or convincing portrayal of family in *The Sopranos*, or perhaps it is precisely the lack of familiarity that tunes many of us in and keeps us watching, and sends quite a few others off to write letters to the CBSC. Whatever the future of *The Sopranos* on mainstream Canadian television, it seems fair to acknowledge the significance that this program has had – not just within American television viewing – but also within the Canadian popular cultural landscape. As one entertainment journalist pointed out, perhaps the arrival of *The Sopranos*, uncut, on the Canadian airwaves says that Canadians are "mature enough to know when television is meant for a specific audience and to welcome edgy programming on the general airwaves" (Tilley, "Wise Guys"). It is, at the very least, a sign that television – along with our viewing habits – is changing. *The Sopranos'* giant whack at our collective popular cultural past may very well push us into a gutsier, edgier television future.

SIX

THE SOPRANOS AS HBO BRAND EQUITY: THE ART OF COMMERCE IN THE AGE OF DIGITAL REPRODUCTION

Mark C. Rogers, Michael Epstein, and Jimmie L. Reeves

That which withers in the age of mechanical reproduction is the aura of the work of art.

Walter Benjamin (221)

There are many definitions of what a brand represents and to which audiences; the simplest is the following:

Product/service + Aura = Brand communication

The aura represents the communication of the signifying and differentiating characteristics of the proposition.

Iain Ellwood (10)

When I'm watchin' my TV,
And that man comes on to tell me
How white my shirts can be,
But he can't be a man 'cause he doesn't smoke
The same cigarettes as me . . .
I can't get no satisfaction . . .

Mick Jagger & Keith Richards (1965)

Satisfaction. Aura. The work of art in the age of mechanical reproduction. The art of commerce in the age of digital reproduction. That man on television selling detergent to the Rolling Stones. The branding of products. The branding of people. Another man on television contemplating Hawthorne's timeless admonition that "No man can wear one face to himself and another to the multitude without finally getting bewildered as to which may be true." All of these fragments speak to central issues raised in this examination of the political economy of *The Sopranos*. Although *The Sopranos* is a rich narrative that deserves, even demands, close critical analysis, our study places an emphasis not on the text but on the overlapping economic, technological, regulatory, and corporate *contexts* of this remarkable series. Together, these contexts constitute the enabling conditions that make possible the production of *The Sopranos*, *Sex and the City*, *Six Feet Under*, and the other original series that enhance the "aura" of the HBO brand. For us, then, it is important to situate these "ground-breaking/smash hit/critically-acclaimed" original series (to use the promotional language of HBO) in the history of the American television experience.

VENTURING INTO HISTORY

In many ways this study elaborates and extends our article published in a similar critical anthology on *The X-Files* (Reeves, Rogers & Epstein, 1996). In this earlier work, we consider the place of *The X-Files* in the flow of the first two eras of the American television experience: TV I (roughly 1948 to 1975) and TV II (roughly 1975 to 1995). The terms TV I and TV II were originally coined by Behrens (1986) and provided us with a shorthand way of discussing major economic and technological transformations, not only in the television industry, but in the larger American economy. We take the next step in the present examination of *The Sopranos*, arguing that American television has now entered its third stage of development: TV III (about 1995 to the present). As we hope to demonstrate, TV III is a period when the digital revolution in distribution is again transforming what it means to watch television. To make our arguments about the emergence of TV III cogent, we must briefly reconsider the major features of the first two eras in the American television experience.

TV I

Perhaps the most important thing to grasp about the first era of American television is its relationship to Fordism, a "rigid" economic order (named after Henry Ford) that drove the general prosperity of the great postwar boom through an expansive manufacturing economy of assembly-line production and mass consumption. As one of the chief products and major producers of the Fordist economic order, TV I's most important ideological function was promoting the ethic of consumption. It also can be said to have played decisive roles in naturalizing the nuclear family ideal, selling suburbanization, sustaining Cold War paranoia, publicizing the Civil Rights movement, maintaining the Liberal Pluralism of the New Deal coalition, demonizing radicalism, and managing social upheaval.

During the first two decades of TV I, popularity was defined in terms of brute ratings and ruled by the "lowest common denominator" or "least objectionable" programming philosophies. Dominated by westerns, situation comedies, and crime shows, the prime-time schedule of TV I evolved into a nightly showcase for the display of what Thorburn (167–8) calls "consensus narrative" (stories that attempt to speak for, and to, the core values of mainstream American culture). Though the programs of this period are certainly culturally significant and provide insight into the aspirations and frustrations of the postwar mainstream, the mundane experience of what we have termed the "casual viewer" during this period of limited program options was far from "satisfying" for many, if not most, Americans (Reeves, Rogers & Epstein 26). Mick Jagger and Keith Richards struck a responsive chord with many American teenagers when they condemned this "unsatisfying" experience in their 1965 rock anthem. But the Stones and their fans were not alone in their alienation. Soon after being appointed by President Kennedy to chair the Federal Communications Commission (FCC), Newton Minow publicly voiced his own dissatisfaction with TV I. On 9 May 1961 – only four years before the release of "(I Can't Get No) Satisfaction" – Minow delivered a famous speech to a gathering of the National Association of Broadcasters (NAB) that characterized and condemned commercial American television as a "vast wasteland."

TV II

Exhibiting and enabling the "overconsumptionism" (Davis 156) of the "post-Fordist" service economy that emerged in the 1970s, TV II was a period of steep decline for the three-network oligopoly that had commanded over 90 per cent of the prime-time audience during TV I. As an expression of the post-Fordist economic order, TV II played a decisive part in naturalizing the grand logic of niche marketing by promoting consumerist values that (in Harvey's words) emphasized "the new, the fleeting, the ephemeral, the fugitive, and the contingent in modern life, rather than the more solid values implanted under Fordism" (171). In the latter years of TV I, an emergent programming philosophy would set the stage for the niche marketing of TV II. Reconfiguring "popularity" in terms of the quest for "quality demographics," this new philosophy promoted the development of programming that attracted segments of the population that were most valued by advertisers (most notably, eighteen-to forty-nine-year old urban dwellers). According to Feuer (152), this emergent notion of popularity was largely responsible for not only the cancellation of "hayseed" comedies like *Mayberry R.F.D.* and *Hee Haw,* but also the reinvention of the situation comedy by Norman Lear and MTM Productions in the 1970s.

As we argue in our analysis of *The X-Files*, the networks' pursuit of sophisticated viewers with money to burn would later provide economic incentive to supporting a number of narrative innovations that are often labeled "postmodern." This rewriting of popularity, combined with television's maturation as a storytelling medium and the parallel maturation of the "television generation," made TV II into an era when talented producers like Steven Bochco, James L. Brooks, Chris Carter, Mark Frost, Mike Judge, David Lynch, and Hugh Wilson were encouraged to explore and blur generic boundaries in such noteworthy and notorious programs as *Beavis & Butthead, Cop Rock, Frank's Place, Hillstreet Blues, The Simpsons,* and *Twin Peaks.* But, for us, the most telling development of this period was the advent of cult programming, like

The X-Files, that inspired what we have called "avid fanship" – a level of quasi-religious engagement with television that may involve taping and archiving episodes, purchasing ancillary merchandise, and interacting with other fans in online discussion groups (26). Indeed, the relationship between Fordism's classic consumerism and post-Fordism's overconsumptionism is roughly analogous to the relationship between TV I's casual viewing and TV II's avid fanship. Though the experience of the avid fan is certainly more "satisfying" than simply watching TV as a casual viewer, there is still a sizeable downside to the displacement of TV I's consensus narrative by TV II's cult culture: the worsening fragmentation of American society into the insiders and outsiders of special interest groups, single issue groups, and various types of racial, ethnic, sexual, generational, lifestyle, taste, and backlash formations.

Commonalities between TV I and TV II

As Timothy M. Todreas demonstrates, both TV I (what he calls the "broadcast era") and TV II (what he describes as the "cable era") were characterized by "bottlenecks" that provided distributors a privileged and profitable position in the supply chain. During TV I, the bottleneck was created by broadcasting's reliance on a limited natural/public resource – the electromagnetic spectrum. According to Todreas, the bottleneck was further tightened in 1952 by the FCC's Sixth Report and Order which ended the "freeze" on station licensing that had been enforced since 1948:

> First, the FCC allocated only a limited amount of the very-high-frequency (VHF) and ultra-high-frequency (UHF) bands to television while reserving the rest for other uses. Second, the FCC followed the principle of "localism" and assigned at least one station to each community in the country. In order to accomplish this, each community could have two or three local stations instead of six or seven regional or national stations. Third, the FCC put both the twelve-channel VHF allocation and the technologically inferior 70-channel UHF allocation in the same market. In this part of the decision, the only competition that the FCC allowed was between two very unequal services. . . . With these three decisions, the FCC limited the amount of the spectrum it would allocate for television, limited the number of stations even further in order to achieve the goal of "localism," and created an unequal playing field for what competition it did allow. (13)

In the TV I era, thanks to this bottleneck, the lion's share of operating profits in the television industry went to local stations. In 1972, for example, the operating profit split was 59 per cent ($441 million) to local stations, 25 percent to production, and 15 per cent to networks (19). TV II's combination satellite and cable distribution system, augmented by VCRs, remote controls, and personal computers would still provide more operating profits to distributors (local stations, local cable operators, and multiple system cable operators) than to networks/packagers and producers. During most of the TV II era, regulatory and economic barriers protected incumbent cable operators from competition from telephone companies, Direct Broadcast Satellite (DBS) and the cable "overbuilder" (a second wireline competitor moving into the same locality). Also during this period, most cable operations had very limited channel capacity which made it difficult for new cable networks/packagers to find a place on the shelf (37–41).

In both of the first two eras of the American television experience, then, local distribution of programming content was extremely profitable because of bottlenecks generated and sustained by technological, economic, and regulatory forces. And both eras were also underwritten, by and large, by *second-order commodity relations* which Nienhaus defines as "symbolic objects or flows producing aggregate individual time for sale to third parties" (309). During TV I, these "third parties" were primarily the mass marketers of the Fordist economic order. In other words, TV I was a period when television broadcasters profited by delivering a largely undifferentiated mass audience, in lots of a thousand, to advertisers. During TV II, these "third parties" were primarily niche marketers. While niche advertisers were willing to pay a premium for spots on programs that attracted a high concentration of their target demographic, it was still the same basic second-order commodity relation. In both periods, consumers paid only incrementally or indirectly for the costs of receiving ad-supported programming through basic cable subscriptions, the purchase of television receivers, and the portion of the price of consumer goods/services used to fund advertising budgets.

Again, in both TV I and TV II, the political economy of television programming was primarily based on developing popular entertainment meant to attract the "attention" of potential consumers – "attention" that was then commodified and sold to advertisers. This, of course, distinguished popular television from the popular book publishing and motion picture industries that enjoyed more "direct," *first-order commodity relations* with the consumer market. Defined by Nienhaus as "symbolic objects or flows actually exchanged for money or having prices attached," first-order commodity relations generate a very different angle on popularity (309). In these rival sectors of the entertainment industry, popularity is a function of satisfying the desires of the audience, rather than catering to the needs of advertisers. Clearly, HBO deserves a prominent place in the annals of American media history for its pioneering efforts in introducing first-order commodity relations to the commercial television landscape. Programming free of commercial interruption and uncontaminated by the demands of advertisers – this has been the major selling point for HBO since it was launched on the evening of 8 November 1972. And it is this commodity relation that we believe will become more and more prominent during the third era in American television history: TV III (or the digital era) – a period when, as Todreas (77–95) predicts, the distribution bottleneck will finally be broken to the mutual benefit of program producers, content packagers, and privileged segments of the audience residing on the up-side of the "digital divide."

Monthly Audience Appeal

The Sopranos, then, is at the epicenter of a shift in the economic organization of the television industry. While premium cable has long operated according to a different revenue model than ad-supported broadcast or basic cable services, HBO's successful use of *The Sopranos* to build its brand and attract new subscribers represents a new level in the development of TV III. Because audiences pay directly for programming, either via a monthly subscription fee or on a pay-per-view basis, content producers and packagers are shielded from the fear of offending nervous advertisers. As is evident to fans of *The Sopranos*, this commodity relation enables producers to exercise more creative freedom and opens the door to the exploration of more adult themes and the mining of more controversial content. The fee also helps to protect packagers from charges that viewers are inadvertently receiving offensive material.

On the other hand, the first-order commodity relations of TV III create new challenges for content producers and packagers. Unlike ad-supported services, the bottom line for premium cable networks is not ratings, or even demographics – it is, instead, the intangible of customer satisfaction that takes on tangible form in the monthly payment for services rendered. As Reiss puts it, "The lifeblood (read *daily operating revenues*) of a pay service is its direct subscriptions" [emphasis in original]:

> Pay-television services must satisfy subscribers month to month, throughout the year, forestalling disconnections. A premium's services success is not determined by audience ratings of individual programs but by the general appeal and satisfaction levels generated by its overall schedule. Insofar as quantitative measurements such as ratings reflect appeal (especially for one-time only events like boxing matches or a Madonna concert) they do help gauge viewer response. But in cable, where subscribers must be persuaded to pony up month after month, qualitative measures take on greater importance. (344)

Therefore, because of the "moment of truth" triggered by the monthly billing cycle, programmers at premium cable services are concerned, first and foremost, with putting together a diversified, balanced, but differentiated package of movies, original series, and other types of entertainment fare that provides "monthly audience appeal" to as broad a subscriber base as possible.

Of course, all premium services, even HBO, experience a certain amount of turnover, or churn. Therefore, to survive and thrive, premium services must continually add new subscribers to replace those who drop out. Because the premium programs cannot be sampled easily, the pay channels must expend substantial resources on promotion and attempt to create enough "buzz" in the media to persuade new consumers to part with their hard earned money. Put another way, pay channels must develop a strong brand identity that not only sets them apart from the clutter of ad-supported services available on less expensive cable tiers, but also from competitors in the pay-TV market.

The Branding Revolution

But strong brand identification is not only an imperative in the premium cable environment – it is also widely recognized as an indispensable marketing strategy across the various forms of commercial television services in operation during TV III's age of digital reproduction. In Blackett's estimation, the recent elevation of branding to a prominent place in the corporate strategy has been nothing less than revolutionary:

> The last ten years have seen a train of events that, to use the language of marketing, have re-positioned brands. Brands are no longer of interest because they provide their owners with a colorful way to compete; they are now recognized widely as business assets of genuine economic value and as such have attracted the attention of a much wider audience. Brands are now center stage: they drive major mergers and acquisitions; they appear frequently in the balance sheets of their owners; they have vexed legislators involved in updating archaic trademark law; their application now extends to organizations who a few years ago would never have considered themselves "brands" (charities, utilities, sport's associations, cities, etc.); and they have changed irrevocably the way in which many major companies organize and run their businesses. (xi)

Inside the television industry, the topic of branding has not only inspired several recent conferences, but also has been the subject of studies published by the NAB that "focus on the importance of branding to NAB members, along with advice on how to conduct branding studies" (Bellamy & Traudt 131; see also Ducey and McDowell & Batten). But perhaps the most visible evidence of the importance of branding in TV III is the ubiquitous "bug" that stamps the corporate logo in the corner of the screen. Overlaying the network's programming with constant brand promotion, the bug is the digital equivalent of Nike's swoosh or Tommy Hilfiger's name displayed prominently on expensive tee-shirts and other types of over-priced outerwear. Clearly, where TV I was the age of mass marketing, and TV II was the age of niche marketing, TV III, at least at this juncture, must be considered the age of brand marketing.

The Sopranos won five Emmys and two Peabody Awards during its first two seasons, and its third season garnered nominations for 22 prime-time Emmy Awards (HBO led all networks with 94 nominations). To say that the series has generated a great deal of "buzz" seems somehow inadequate – unless buzz can be deafening. The press attention paid to the series has been, and continues to be, extraordinary. Using the key words "The Sopranos," a Lexis/Nexis search of articles appearing in major newspapers during the last six months was terminated by the search engine because the number of documents exceeded 1,000. In just the month prior to 16 August 2001, the same search identified 262 documents that at least mention *The Sopranos*. That is an average of almost 9 major newspaper articles a day. Clearly, the contributions of *The Sopranos* to HBO's brand equity, though difficult to quantify, surpass any of HBO's other original series. Indeed, the corporate aura generated by *The Sopranos* may even rival the value that more widely-available and highly-rated shows like *ER* (NBC), *Survivor* (CBS), *Who Wants to be a Millionaire?* (ABC), and *The X-Files* (Fox) have added to the equity of their broadcast brands. In what follows, we set the stage for a more thorough accounting of *The Sopranos* as brand equity by considering the series in the context of the corporate history of HBO. Indeed, *The Sopranos* is only one of the latest innovations promoted by HBO. As we shall see, HBO would be a key agent of change during TV II – a role that would ultimately transform it into a major media power by the dawn of the digital age. In a history that spans less than thirty years, HBO has played a role in both the cable revolution and satellite revolutions.

"IT'S NOT TV. IT'S HBO."

The brainchild of Charles F. Dolan, brought to life by the financial backing of Time-Life Cable, HBO transmitted its first program on 8 November 1972 (Gershon & Wirth 114). The program itself, a hockey game that was distributed to about 300 homes in Wilkes-Barre, Pennsylvania, was inauspicious (Berger 23). What is significant about this long-forgotten game is that it represented a new type of programming for cable, a type of programming that would presage the meteoric rise of the cable industry in the thirty years since. From its origins in the 1940s as Community Antenna Television, cable was primarily viewed as a means to retransmit television programming to homes unable to receive clear or strong broadcast signals. In these early "common carrier" years, viewers in remote areas would turn to cable to see the popular broadcast programs that were otherwise unavailable to them. Cable companies existed to facilitate broadcast viewership, not to compete with it.

Under the leadership of Gerald M. Levin, later the CEO of Time-Warner Entertainment Co., HBO devised a strategy that helped cable emerge from the shadow of broadcasters. From a programming standpoint, HBO, at its inception, offered programming content that was simply not available on traditional television channels. In the 1970s, this meant mostly sporting events and commercial-free films, many with unedited content not suitable for broadcast (Berger 23). Provided by sports promoters and Hollywood studios, these programs proved to be an effective way to establish and expand HBO's initial subscriber base ("Pay Television" 76; "Movies" 123). Although the major broadcast networks were somewhat concerned about potential competition from HBO and others, audience erosion was negligible in the early years ("Pay Television" 76).

In 1975, operating as an agitator fomenting the satellite revolution, HBO would be the first company to build a national distribution network for television programming using satellite communications. Faced with the problem of inadequate and unreliable signal transmission for an upcoming boxing match in the Philippines between Muhammad Ali and Joe Frazier, Levin and his colleagues took a gamble that changed HBO – and cable – forever.

To allow HBO to reach local cable systems reliably and clearly, HBO entered into an agreement with RCA to distribute the title bout via satellite ("Moving Closer" 24; "Pay Television" 76). In September 1975, cable subscribers in Jackson, Mississippi and Ft. Pierce, Florida watched the "Thriller in Manila" live on HBO ("Pay Television" 76; "Movies" 123). The following year, it showed the Wimbledon semi-finals ("Movies" 123).

This innovation would have both long-term and short-term implications. In the long term, the move to satellite distribution would lay the groundwork for other satellite cable networks: most notably, those associated with the Turner media empire – the first superstation, WTBS, and the first all-news basic cable network, CNN. In the short term, HBO was able to increase its subscriber base by an astounding 47 percent in the final quarter of 1975 (Gershon & Wirth 116). HBO, which had ended 1973 with a modest 9000 subscribers, had grown to nearly 200,000 by the time of the Ali–Frazier fight. With the advent of satellite transmissions, subscribers increased to 500,000 within a year. Because of these encouraging numbers, Time, Inc., which had yet to turn a profit on its cable subsidiary, entered into a $7.5 million five-year deal with RCA to lease two satellites to assure simultaneous, high quality signal transmission ("Pay Television" 76).

Although Time lost $8.7 million before taxes on its cable ventures in 1974, the magazine publishing company was bullish on the future of HBO – and cable ("Pay Television" 76). And they were right. With added competition for viewers, broadcast networks that had once attracted 90 per cent of television households began to suffer significant audience erosion, a trend that continues into the present when the combined primetime share for the major broadcast networks regularly dips below 60 per cent (See, for example, Lowry 9). On the flip side, the number of HBO subscribers grew to 14.5 million households within the channel's first ten years of existence (S. B. Smith C18). By 1985, total revenue for HBO surpassed $529 million (Clark 3).

Although HBO had become immensely profitable as a showcase for films and sports contests, it also led another revolution that changed cable: the channel's executives made the decision to develop original programming. While the costs associated with producing original films, documentaries, and series were generally high, the venture into financing exclusive original programming was made necessary by the widespread penetration/diffusion of a popular new technology, the Video Cassette Recorder, in the early 1980s (S. B. Smith C18; Morgan 50). With VCRs, viewers could rent films from video stores and watch them at their convenience. Faced with the prospect that a movie channel would not have the mass appeal it once had, HBO saw the need to diversify (S. B. Smith C18). By 1984, 30 per cent of HBO's content was original programming shown exclusively on the network, a figure that, by 1992, had risen to 40 percent ("Brave" 54; Tornquist).

Much of this move to original programming was the initiative of Michael Fuchs. In fact, when Fuchs took over as Chairman and CEO of HBO in 1984, he made a public pledge to produce mature and provocative original programming. Fuchs's idea was to target affluent, educated males between the ages of eighteen and thirty-four, a segment of the audience that broadcast networks found difficult to attract. Fuchs decided that the best way to attract these elusive viewers would be to offer edgy, controversial programs. Since HBO, as a premium cable service, was not subject to government and industry restrictions on profanity, sexuality, and violence, Fuchs saw an opportunity to turn HBO into a purveyor of adult-oriented content (S. B. Smith C18). The result was not only the transmission of films depicting graphic violence such as *Natural Born Killers* (1994) and NC-17 films like *Showgirls* (1995), but the development of sexually-themed dramas such as *And the Band Played On* (1993) and series such as *The Larry Sanders Show* and *Dream On* (Berger 23). Although Fuchs helped turn HBO into a leading producer of original content, he fell short in his efforts to create a strong brand identity for the channel. He was fired in 1995 and replaced by Jeffrey L. Bewkes. The biggest challenge facing Bewkes was the channel's slowing subscriber growth – by 1997, new subscribers to HBO had dropped by about 50 per cent to approximately 500,000 (Stevens 77).

Under Bewkes' leadership, HBO found itself on the front lines of yet another television revolution: the development of channel branding as a means of combating audience fragmentation. In a market where the combined number of broadcast stations, cable channels, and pay-per-view outlets may exceed one hundred, it becomes increasingly difficult to maintain a profitable audience base. This is a problem that Fuchs tried to address when he pledged to change HBO's image. While Fuchs didn't succeed, it appears, as of 2001, that Jeffrey Bewkes has. The difference in approach between the two CEOs, as it turns out, seems to be one of degree. Bewkes essentially pushed the envelope when it came to developing original content. Under Bewkes, HBO produced programs that upped the ante on violence, sexuality, and the macabre.

Original programming is an integral part of HBO's branding strategy. Only 30 to 40 per cent of HBO's programming is original, but because theatrical films are largely undifferentiated on premium cable, it is the "exclusivity" of its original programming that shapes HBO's identity. The network was expected to spend roughly $1 billion on original programming in 2001 (Grillo 18).

HBO generally features four types of original programming:

- *Sports.* Once the importance of sports programming to the HBO brand was second only to movies. But, for various reasons, this importance has diminished in relation to other forms of exclusive programming that help HBO differentiate itself from its imitators. Today, HBO has largely ceded the territory of telecasting live sporting events to ESPN and regional cable sports channels.[1]

- *Original Movies.* HBO operates one of the largest and most prestigious studios among cable channels. Cable in general and HBO in particular have been able to attract top name talent by offering creative freedom, accelerated shooting schedules, and opportunities to make projects that could not be made elsewhere.[2] Ironically, HBO's continued commitment to making original movies runs counter to broadcasting trends. During the age of branding, the broadcast networks have all but abandoned made-for-TV movie production because such fare represents a drain on promotional resources that does not contribute in any significant way to brand equity. The broadcast networks in TV III have, instead, emphasized developing franchise series (like *ER*) that can help brand a night of programming (like Must See TV). HBO has successfully incorporated original movies into its branding strategy by stressing quality. It has also been easier for HBO to purchase original movies on the festival circuit because it can run them unedited. But most importantly, where the heartland for the broadcast networks has always been the weekly series, at HBO (as the name Home Box Office implies) the movie will always be king. And to make up for shortages in theatrically-released films, as well as enhance subscriber satisfaction by increasing inventory, the production of original movies and acquisition of independently-produced movies that did not receive wide distribution make solid economic sense to HBO.

• *Documentaries.* HBO airs documentary films in a number of forums. The most enduring has been the *America Undercover* series, which began in 1983, and has been a regular monthly feature on HBO. In 2001, the show was given a prime Sunday slot following *The Sopranos*.[3]

• *Original Series and Specials.* Original series have been part of HBO's programming since the early 1980s, when the network began to produce the football themed comedy *1st and 10* (1984–1991), and the children's program *Fraggle Rock* (1983–1987). These have largely mirrored the kinds of programming found on the broadcast networks – sitcoms such as *Dream On* and talk show and comedy specials.[4] Initially, HBO's original series contributed little to the brand identity – apart from greater profanity and some nudity, these programs were little different from standard network fare. A show like *Dream On* was essentially a network sitcom with bare breasts and did little to make HBO a destination for viewers.

The anthology format, like the stand-up comedy showcase, is problematic for branding; by its nature, the quality and tone of the episodes are somewhat erratic, failing to deliver the consistency that is important for strong brand identity. Even so, at one time HBO did feature the macabre anthology dramas *The Hitchhiker* and *Tales from the Crypt* (based on a comic book property owned by Time-Warner, HBO's parent).[5]

The Larry Sanders Show (1992–1998), brought to HBO by the same production company (Brillstein-Grey Entertainment) that would later produce *The Sopranos*, was the first original series that helped attract new subscribers. The show was smart and well-written, and because it satirized the entertainment industry, it became an immediate favorite of TV critics. Under the leadership of Bewkes, HBO built on the success of *The Larry Sanders Show* to make original content an essential part of the brand's identity. The result of this initiative can be seen in current hits like *Oz*, an intensely violent prison drama, *Sex and the City*, a sexually indulgent comedy, and *Autopsy*, which graphically presents coroners conducting actual post-mortems. While these shows have helped HBO develop a brand image that has increased viewership, the program that has had the greatest impact on HBO subscriber numbers, of course, has been *The Sopranos*, a potent combination of violence, sexuality, and, to a lesser degree, the macabre. In 2001, the show's third season opener averaged 11.3 million viewers. The season finale drew an estimated 9.5 million viewers (Lowry 9). Audiences of this size are astronomical considering that HBO is available in only one third of US homes with television – approximately 32 million compared to 100 million for broadcast television (Carter 7). The more telling statistic is the number of viewers who have become new subscribers to HBO as a result of *The Sopranos*. Since the show's debut, HBO has added approximately 1 million subscribers per year (Saunders 2D).

The Sopranos is perfectly positioned to help HBO build its brand identity. In many ways the show takes the threads of what had been different about HBO's previous original programming – sexuality, graphic violence, profanity – and puts them in a context where they all work together to become a unique and distinctive product. *The Sopranos* brings life to HBO's key branding slogan ("It's not TV. It's HBO.") because the show is unlike anything on network or basic cable. The show manages to take advantage of the creative freedom offered by premium cable without seeming sleazy (like *Real Sex* or *G String Divas*) or gratuitous (like *Dream On*). The mature content of *The Sopranos* flows organically out of its subject matter – the audience believes that members of the mob swear frequently and hang out in strip clubs, so these elements do not seem to be tacked on to titillate. Although some have raised concerns about the level of violence in the show, particularly after the third season episode "University" (3006), in which a stripper is brutally beaten to death, the show's critical success has largely insulated it from such concerns snowballing into an outcry. This is the essence of TV III's first-order commodity relations – rather than fret about offending advertisers (who are often far more skittish than audiences), HBO just needs to worry about not being so graphic that it drives the audience away from the network.[6]

Beyond this, there are a number of factors that contribute to *The Sopranos'* success. First, the show has strong production values, is well written, and generally features strong acting performances. It is unclear who is responsible for this quality – after all, no one sets out to make a bad show, and picking winners has always been something of a crapshoot. HBO, for its part, has certainly developed a number of shows that fall short of the standards set by *The Sopranos*.[7] Still, HBO does have an influence on *The Sopranos'* success. Series creator David Chase originally developed the show for Fox, and when Fox passed, he shopped it around to the other networks (Justin 1E). Had the show made it to the air on a broadcast network, it likely would have been very different and probably would not have succeeded as a second-order commodity. HBO has cultivated and enabled the quality of the program by giving Chase the creative freedom that only premium cable and its first-order commodity relations can offer. HBO also had the luxury of allowing the program to build an audience gradually, rather than produce ratings immediately or be cancelled. Perhaps most importantly, HBO has also been willing to fund *The Sopranos* at a relatively high level, spending roughly one to one-and-a-half million dollars for each episode.

The quality of the show is also enhanced by its finiteness of scope. The show is serial, but not too serial like *Twin Peaks*. Many of the episodes have self-contained plot lines, while other plot lines continue over the course of several episodes or even entire seasons. Each of the three seasons has focused on a macro-level issue: Tony's relationship with his mother in the first season; Tony, his sister Janice, and Richie Aprile in the second season; and Tony and Carmela's relationship with their children in the third season. This combination of serial and episodic elements forms what Marc Dolan calls a "sequential" series, but also has many aspects of an "episodic serial" (33–5). This mix is important because it rewards avid fans without alienating casual viewers. Each season lasts only thirteen episodes (half as many as a standard long-form network series), allowing the show to avoid (through three seasons) some of the weak episodes that generally creep into long-running series. Furthermore, HBO allows Chase a substantial amount of time to develop each season – the breaks between the seasons have been nine months, and eleven months, and the fourth season is expected to trail the third by more than a year.

HBO has been able to afford and even benefit from the long hiatuses of *The Sopranos* for several reasons. The network produces and licenses ancillary products (books, calendars, DVDs, soundtracks, etc.) some of which come from other branches of HBO's parent company Time-Warner. These products serve two purposes. First, they allow HBO to recoup some of the cost of producing the program. Second, they keep the program in the public mind during its breaks. HBO has also accomplished the latter purpose by rerunning *The Sopranos*. On digital and satellite systems, HBO now frequently has as many as eight separate channels. Because of this multiplexing, it can rerun *The Sopranos* frequently during the season, allowing those viewers who missed an episode to catch up. In between seasons, HBO has run marathons to allow new viewers to get involved in the show. (As we write, all thirty-nine episodes of *The Sopranos* are being shown in sequence for the first time.)

HBO has also maintained interest in *The Sopranos* through its Web presence. HBO.com features pictures, an episode guide, cast and crew bios, and the other common ingredients of a television website. In addition, the site contains bulletin boards and chat rooms that serve to build the fan community and help *The Sopranos* sustain buzz. More interestingly, the site refers to www.jeffreywernick.com, the homepage of a fictional author and Mafia buff who supposedly leaks confidential information about the Soprano/DiMeo crime family. The site includes pages of Wernick's supposed notes as well as transcripts from wiretaps, newspaper clippings, and the video diaries that Meadow Soprano keeps as part of her coursework at Columbia. The Wernick site is a well-executed example of "viral marketing." Both sites take advantage of the ability of the Internet to maintain viewer engagement (or interactivity) with programming when that programming is not being televised, a key aspect of TV III.[8] The critical and commercial success of *The Sopranos* allowed HBO to make it the cornerstone of a Sunday night original programming line-up. Because each season tends to be shorter, HBO plans to rotate its original programs through the Sunday time slots. For example, soon after a season of *The Sopranos* ends, new episodes of *Sex and the City* begin. HBO has used this strategy with *Oz*, *America Under Cover*, and *Arli$$*, along with the 2001 series *Six Feet Under*, a soapy macabre-drama that focuses on a dysfunctional family of morticians.[9] One of the only empirical studies of television branding provides evidence of HBO's success at managing its brand equity. Using a survey instrument designed to measure brand awareness, the study found HBO ranked with ESPN, CNN, and MTV as one of the four most recognized and remembered cable networks (Bellamy & Traudt 148).

BRANDING, CONSOLIDATION, AND TV III

Though others, like Todreas, refer to the same stages in the history of American television as the broadcast, cable, and digital eras, we still prefer the terms TV I, TV II, and TV III. Our preference is not simply derived from our intellectual investments in these terms. Instead, we believe these terms provide a more complicated and accurate way of thinking about both the disruptions and the continuities of the television age. It goes without saying that broadcast television continued to exist in the so-called "cable era," and that, at least in the foreseeable future, broadcast and cable television will continue to exist in the "digital era." The same could be said for mass marketing and niche marketing in the age of branding. On the other hand, avid fanship, especially of daytime dramas and sports, existed during TV I. Branding, too, was a feature of the consumer experience in the first phase of television. After all, in 1965, the Stones were commenting on the branding of products/people when they shouted "he can't be a man 'cause he doesn't smoke the same cigarettes as me." Ultimately, we see the major developments that demarcate the three eras as additive. Residual aspects of TV I, including second-order commodity relations and casual viewing, persist in the TV II and TV III eras – but these aspects become less dominant as emergent commodity relations and modes of viewing engagement become more prevalent.

Because, in matters of historical analysis, distance tends to enhance clarity, we are now able to develop more refined accounts of the political economies of TV I and TV II than that of TV III. Although not as stark as the transformation from a manufacturing to a service economy, one recent industry development seems to signal a major restructuring of post-Fordism. If one trend defines the current period in U.S. media history, it would surely be *consolidation*. The $36 billion union of CBS and Viacom, the $69 billion melding of AT&T and Media One; and, most striking of all, the $180 billion fusion of AOL and Time Warner (which, of course, subsumes HBO) – all bear witness to the scope and power of current economic pressures to consolidate. Even at the local level, in large markets and small, consolidation has literally transformed the broadcasting industry. In radio, enormous station groups, like Clear Channel's 1000-plus chain, have sacrificed localism to achieve economies of scale. And, in television, the family-owned station is rapidly becoming a rare animal as television groups venture into market after market looking for bargains, searching for opportunities to downsize, streamline, and consolidate.

Just as mass marketing was an expression of the Fordist economic order, and niche marketing an expression of early post-Fordism, brand marketing is linked to the logic of consolidation in the current stage of economic restructuring. To explain this relationship, we rely on the insights of Robert Bellamy & Paul Traudt. As they observe, the consolidation/branding linkage defies conventional wisdom. After all, branding is a form of market differentiation – and market differentiation has traditionally been associated with industries in which a relatively large number of entrants struggle to "stand out" from the competition. Why, then, would branding be relevant during the emergence of a new oligopoly – an oligopoly that spans media and is global in scope? According to Bellamy & Traudt, the answer is bound up in "the nature of the new media oligopoly":

> [The emergent oligopoly] seems likely to be one of few owners and many channels. This means that branding will be essential to differentiating the "sibling" services of one corporation, a function that may be more important than differentiating the offerings of competing corporations. (133)

In the case of the AOL/Time-Warner merger, then, it is in the best interest of the parent company to maintain the brand identity of CNN and keep it distinct from HBO's brand, though both networks are now on the same team. Therefore, in the current economic environment, branding may not be so much about product differentiation in a competitive marketplace as it is about product diversification in the less competitive structure of a global media oligopoly.

Which brings us, finally, to Walter Benjamin and his famous essay. For Benjamin, "aura" withers in the age of mechanical reproduction because "the technique of reproduction detaches the reproduced object from tradition" (221). For us, the irony that the term "aura" has recently been applied to brand marketing is both suggestive and provocative. In an age when, as Twitchell (159) observes, "the label has moved from inside the collar to outside on the shirt," the brand may be the closest thing to "tradition" that is available to members of consumer culture; in an epoch when "all that is solid melts into air," brands are invested with an "aura" of permanency. As is apparent in the irrational reverence with which teenagers accord the pre-worn and ragged merchandise of Abercrombie and Fitch, brands have become the graven images of the contemporary religion of overconsumptionism. As class definers, brands currently function as the primary currency of a system of distinctions that marks off "insiders" from "outsiders" by conjuring up delusions of individuality while, in reality, promoting rather strict conformity to the carefully-constructed codes of commercial exploitation. In other words, brands are not simply harmless ways of positioning products. Instead, they are, quite literally, ways of "labeling" the self and others. Or to use Hawthorne's lexicon, the collective/individual investment in the "aura" of the brand has become incorporated into the "face" one wears for the benefit of the "multitude" – a face in which the truth of the self may indeed become the source of "bewilderment." Brands brand people. And, like it or not, AOL/Time-Warner, HBO, and *The Sopranos* are all implicated in this branding of human experience. Such is the art of commerce in the age of digital reproduction.

MEN AND WOMEN

SEVEN

"I DREAD YOU"?: MARRIED TO THE MOB IN
THE GODFATHER, *GOODFELLAS*, AND *THE SOPRANOS*

Cindy Donatelli & Sharon Alward

"Kick-ass girls, right?"

Tony Soprano ("Boca"/1008)

In Francis Ford Coppola's *The Godfather Part III* (1990), Kay sums up the vulnerability and imminent danger of being married to a Corleone by declaring coolly: "I don't hate you Michael. I dread you." She, of course, has good reason for her "dread" because by the end of the movie, their daughter Mary will take a bullet for dad, adding to the body count of abused and dead women in the *Godfather* trilogy. By the time Martin Scorsese's *GoodFellas* was released in 1990, Karen Hill, after she gets knocked around a bit *à la* Corleone, survives but only by losing her life when she is forced to enter a witness protection program with her husband Henry, doomed to the suburban domestic ideal in the middle of nowhere. Since divorce for a mob wife is, to quote Michael, "unacceptable," Karen's total makeover is a deal she can't refuse. Fast forward to the end of the millennium and to *The Sopranos*, the HBO mega-hit which has completed three seasons. Carmela Soprano, Livia, Janice, or even Meadow dreading Tony – please! No one is ever again going to slam the door in the face of these powerful, angry women, or he will regret it, as Livia proves when she goads Junior to attempt a hit on her own son. Janice does Livia one better and takes matters into her own hands by blowing away Richie Aprile when the little cocksucker punches her.

Welcome to the HBO 1990s world of "bad girls" who have morphed into a Mafia don's worse nightmare. They are constructed from bits and pieces of Madonna's material girl, Jennifer Lopez's in-your-face attitude, and Andrea Dworkin's post-male feminism. In a "move" that the careful Michael would never contemplate, Tony is sent spinning into the office of Dr. Jennifer Melfi as he looks for a "nice" Italian girl who will nurture him. She is coolly professional and totally in control, as Tony, in his gross, pathetic, male stupidity, is reduced to watching the hemline of her dress-for-success skirts inch up and down and is lost in dreams about Melfi giving him a blow job as he sleeps next to his wife ("Pax Soprana"/1006).

While much has been written about the ways in which *The Sopranos* reflects the circumstances of a post-Gotti fallen world of "real" goodfellas, in this essay we wish to argue that the distance from Michael to Henry Hill to Tony can be plotted in terms of their relation to women. By the late 1990s, books like Susan Faludi's *Stiffed: The Betrayal of the American Man* had declared that masculinity sleeps with the fishes. Tony suffers impotence as a side effect of the Prozac, and Dr. Freid, a self-described "prick doctor," advertises on TV ("Amour Fou" /3012). Tony's best friend is named "Big Pussy," and just in case anyone thinks this is not what David Chase has on his mind, Tony seeks further clarification from Dr. Melfi: "Are you talking about Pussy . . . or about pussy?" ("Funhouse" /2013). While the "graphic" language has almost always been mentioned in reviews of the show, we want to call attention to the fact that, in a doubly transgressive move, women get to use a really juiced Hillary-speak, without bleeps, on prime time. Breaking at once the double bind of ladylike behavior and network censorship, a white, educated, middle-class woman like Janice Soprano can declare in front of a viewing audience in the millions: "this cunt is going to be sorry she ever fucked with me" ("Fortunate Son"/3003). We can just hear Oprah saying, "These ladies actually said the c-word on TV! Did you feel empowered?"

Media have irrevocably spliced Diane Keaton, Lorraine Bracco, and now Edie Falco into a Mafia world. The first question, which prior masculinist discussions have missed, is why would women even show up for this "Sicilian thing"? The double play on "family," which is crucial to the Mafia trope, ensures that women will be prominently cast in violent movies and TV shows which otherwise might see all the lead roles played by men. One has only to compare related genres, like war, westerns, and action films, to observe that while the gun counts are comparable, the female demographics are completely different, except for the occasional sympathetic nurse or love-action interest. Steven Spielberg's *Saving Private Ryan* (1998) is typical – the famous opening D-Day invasion sequence created a screen ecology which completely blocked women's access to any part of the screen, even the smallest corner. Yet in Mafia films, women have always enjoyed relatively high profiles since a Mafia boss, no matter how nefarious and violent his nine-to-five, returns to hearth and home at the end of the day, expecting to find the pasta on the table.

Even though women do make it onto the screen in Mafia movies, they are likely to be found with the children or in the kitchen. Even in the year 2001, women, while having entered the work force in greater numbers than ever before, are still largely identified with domestic space and work, with a combo of child-rearing, food preparation, and maintenance of a neat and attractive home. This identification of women with domestic space delimits their range of movement, activity, and sphere of power, and goodfellas seek out these home-girls – all Italian, except for the Jewish Karen Hill, who might as well be – like heat-seeking missiles drawn to their targets. They must marry immediately, set up house, and live in the double helix sign of family, thereby ensuring that they have a female escort at Jack-and-Jill Mafia events, and of course, have the means to reproduce little wiseguys.

It is possible to distinguish the responses of the wives as they succumb to the Mafia's gilded cage. *The Godfather* (1972) begins as Connie enters into this world at the moment of marriage, though later flashbacks show that she has been preparing for this role throughout her Mafia teen-princess career. While girls learn from their mothers, Connie has seen that Don Corleone's wife, generically stereotyped as Mama, does nothing other than serve pasta to men who eat alone (from behind a partition), hold babies in her arms, and make cameo appearances at family functions where she performs the good-hearted Italian mother on the Lake Tahoe stage. At the wedding, the deliberate camera shots back and forth establish that as the women are outside performing one "family," Don Corleone remains closeted in his study, receiving another family made up exclusively of men. As Ann Haskell has noted in "The World of *The Godfather*: No Place for Women," the play between the brilliant Nevada sunlight and the darkness of the Don's study helps to construct this gendered contrast. This use of chiaroscuro lighting throughout the movie imparts the dignity of Rembrandt-like shadows to men, while women, whose prerogative is lighting in the fashion world, must deal with the relentless sun outside, and you can see perspiration droplets as Mama sings her Italian song. Despite this light, women are rendered invisible in *The Godfather*.

When Connie forces the issue of her visibility after Michael has murdered Carlo, she is reduced to a slut and cut off from her children. Forgiveness is only possible when her sexuality and independence collapse and she becomes an unsexed surrogate wife to Michael. In a declaration which flies in the face of all the rhetoric and images of the women's movement when *The Godfather Part II* was released in 1974, Connie declares: "Michael, I'd like to stay close to home now, if it's alright. . . . You need me, Michael. I want to take care of you." Her fate is to turn into a Lady Macbeth armed with cannoli in *The Godfather Part III* (1990), a black widow whose age and hardness are written all over her tight face. She has become far too much of a bitch to take care of anybody: Connie represents an aging woman who, when her body gives out, gets to read from a power script. We're with Elizabeth Wurtzel, whose book *Bitch: In Praise of Difficult Women* provides a fresh and dynamic reading of women who have serious problems with *everything*, and let everyone know it.

While Karen Hill at first seems to be reading from the adult female domestic script, *GoodFellas* differs from *The Godfather* in giving Karen a narrating voice, and this opens up possibilities for a woman's take on Mafia life. The women in *GoodFellas* won't keep their mouths shut. One of the results of hearing Karen's voice-over is that she can show that she *really* enjoys being wined and dined by Henry. Unlike a lot of media goodfellas, Henry knows how to show a girl a good time. While Kay never really gets over being a WASP "good girl," Karen is freed of that burden by being Jewish, so that dating Henry is already a no-no, and she must lie to her mother from the very beginning, tucking Henry's cross in on his hairy chest. A lot of girls would never even think about going on a second date with Michael since his idea of showing a girl a good time is bringing her to a family wedding, introducing her to Fredo, and pointing out Luca Brasi. We see Kay as a kind of Stepford wife from the very beginning as she vacantly and stupidly listens to these stories of brutality and murder, all the time looking at Michael romantically. Throughout *The Godfather* trilogy, Diane Keaton plays out the role of bored suburban housewife – she pretends that her husband's "business" is beneath her, that she has no knowledge of any of it, that the business is going to go "legit" – but I don't see her walking away from the mansion on Lake Tahoe. Already in *The Godfather*, she wears great Jackie O. clothes and is carrying armfuls of Christmas gifts through the Christmas streets which she surely couldn't afford on her schoolteacher's salary. For all her "good girl" posing, she is enjoying herself, though a nose-stuck-up-in-the-air WASP bitch is not going to admit it.

Karen revels in it. When she first appears as Henry's blind date, she wears red (compared to Kay's pastels), signaling her availability and sensuality. In the shot at the table she is allowed full frame and central position. She is swept off her feet in a whirlwind of fabulous dates, with plenty of hot and steamy scenes. She becomes a celebrity and loves ever minute of it. And Karen makes it clear from the beginning that she is no pushover. After Henry stands her up, she goes looking for him in yet another red dress. She is almost immediately transformed from the "nice" girl that he was able to treat like shit on their first date, screaming in his face: "You've got some nerve standing me up. . . . It's going to cost you. It's going to cost you a lot." Karen speaks the language of money, and it gives her power over a wiseguy, but not quite enough.

While Karen realizes that she's not married to a "nine-to-five" guy, she nevertheless spends a good part of the movie in the domestic realm, barefoot and pregnant. But even in the suburbs with two kids, she manages to fit in being a bad girl who enjoys danger, sex, and drugs. As she says when Henry asks her to hide the gun early in the movie, "I know there are women, like my best friends, who would have gone running. . . . It turned me on." By the end of the movie, Karen is a mess – her hair is all frizzy, she's turned into a cokehead, and she's developed that aged, hard look first modeled by Connie in the *Godfather* movies. One of the most compelling images of her contradictions is to watch her on her knees at the toilet, ground zero of a woman's cleaning rituals, as she desperately flushes the cocaine. It is not a pretty picture, but give us Karen Hill on her knees any day to Kay's sanctimonious and schoolmarmish "my shit doesn't stink" attitude. Karen may look like a mess, but she knows about both Henry's "families" and she finds a source of power in that knowledge. Packing a gun in her panties, Karen becomes what Carol Clover has termed (in *Men, Women and Chainsaws* [35–41]) "a final girl" who survives the male meltdown at the end.

And now with David Chase's *The Sopranos*, the two families have collapsed, and private domestic space has interpenetrated with Satriale's, Pizzaland, and the Bada Bing! in a way that the Genco Olive Oil Company or the Lufthansa heists never did. Tony's nightmarish vision of his father cutting off the butcher's finger at Satriale's ("Fortunate Son"/3003) is juxtaposed with serving dinner at the family table. Living in an upper-middle-class suburban New Jersey no longer provides safe haven for the Mafia boss. Without Don Corleone's study or Las Vegas hotels, Tony cannot distance himself from a very 1990s domestic exurbia in which he hangs around the house for a good part of the day, picks up the newspaper in his bathrobe, watches TV, and eats cold cuts out of the fridge as Carmela watches him with alternating tenderness and disgust. Tony even conducts his other "family" business in a concrete unfinished basement, with the fans turned on – can you imagine Don Corleone giving Tom Hagen an order while the washing machine goes through its rinse cycle?

At one level, this shift can be explained almost entirely in terms of a shift in media: it is well established that television intensifies emotions and makes action seem more private and intimate. Historically, this emotional intensity has been explored most fully in soap operas, and there is no question that *The Sopranos* takes its place in a tradition of prime-time soaps, most notably *Dallas*. But *The Sopranos* is very much like the "real" soaps which rule daytime with a Mafia-like grip and longevity which prime-time capos would die for. While David Chase now promises us fourth and fifth seasons, soaps like *Guiding Light* have been running for almost fifty years on TV, while "newer" soap operas like *Days of Our Lives* and *The Young and the Restless* have been running continuously since 1965 and 1973 respectively. With its references to the domestic, the Mafia genre has always had a soap-opera feel to it, but *The Sopranos* succeeds precisely because it is a serialized soap, with a little violence thrown in for prime-time. Chase goes one step further, however, in *The Sopranos*: his genius is to make violence as domestic as going for a tennis lesson or taking Meadow for a tour of colleges. To some extent this is accomplished by deciding to set the action in the everyday suburban life of northern New Jersey, but violence is also almost always bracketed with homely domestic scenes. Killings are handled economically, and by far the greatest part of any episode is spent in domestic space and dialogue, staples of daytime soaps. Article after article identifies *The Sopranos* as a soap opera, *Soap Opera Digest* routinely covers the show, and in one of those little self-referential moments which *The Sopranos* has borrowed from such shows as *Twin Peaks*, *Soap*, and *Mary Hartman, Mary Hartman*, Tony and Carmela watch a talk show on which Jeffrey Wernick is interviewed about his new book *Mafia: America's Longest Running Soap Opera* ("The Legend of Tennessee Moltisanti"/1008).

As in soaps, there are a very limited number of sets, most of which are domestic: the Soprano home, more specifically the kitchen, functions very much as the main set where various generations of characters come together. Other regularly appearing sets, such as the backroom at Satriale's and the Bing, Artie's restaurant, the tables in front of Pizzaland, and Dr. Melfi's office seem very small-scale, familiar and close, like "The Tuscany" restaurant in *Days of Our Lives*. When the Sopranos venture out to Italy or to New England college campuses, it is, as in soaps, a very temporary excursion away from "home."

By splicing the story of a Mafia boss who sees a female psychiatrist onto a soap opera genre that is still overwhelmingly identified with women (the audience is close to 80 per cent female according to Robert C. Allen's *Speaking of Soaps* and other recent studies), you just know that women are going to rule. In a kind of feminist metatext, Tony and his mob friends are "framed" by rules of domestic television and all their actions are constantly subject to forms of irony and comedy that by now have become inevitably identified with serialized programming. While Tony and his friends may think they're tough, everything that they do is undercut because they are cast in soap-opera episodes that deny them the dignity of a full-length Mafia movie, let alone a trilogy. In the *Godfather* movies, there are stretches of as long as almost forty minutes when the screen is completely controlled by men – for example, the prelude to Michael's climactic shooting of Sollozzo and McCluskey in the restaurant. The sole woman in the restaurant is reduced to a mere speck under the restaurant sign in this scene – this is a man's world. (While we usually expect to see men and women when we eat out, Tony, Henry and Michael find a lot of places that seat guys only.) At the beginning of *GoodFellas*, it takes thirty-one minutes before the first woman even shows up in the opening bar scene. (You wonder, what about cocktail waitresses?)

Tony, who has only one hour at a time in the HBO universe, never enjoys such a run. As lumbering as he is, he is not quick enough to dodge the episodic format of soaps, which is notorious for intercutting brief scenes, intertwining subplots, and emphasizing moments of emotional intensity by holding the camera shot for an extra beat. Without the careful make-up, lighting, and cut pecs that give soaps' leading men their dignity, he is also too large for the screen because of the soap propensity for extreme close-up shots. Tony (played perfectly by James Gandolfini) comes across as bearlike and sweet but physically gross with his large gut. (Indeed, many of the leading characters on the *Sopranos* are losers and would never be cast on a daytime soap that takes place in Genoa City or Salem because of their very ethnicity, but at least they are usually spared the indignity of the close-up shots to which Tony/Gandolfini must subject himself week after week.) But it's kinda cute seeing men as the target of an unforgiving camera for a change, especially compared to the false dignity which lighting gives them in the *Godfather* trilogy. In the tradition of Karen Hill's empowering point-of-view in *GoodFellas*, point-of-view shots through the eyes of Carmela and Melfi reveal Tony as the vulnerable object of their gaze as he squirms in his chair or lumbers around the kitchen.

The Soprano women may not be "made men," but Tony answers to them. Carmela Soprano, Livia, and Janice exercise power over Tony, and while he tries his best to play a Michael Corleone or a Henry Hill to these women, they have him by the balls, and he knows it. In "Pax Soprana" (1006), Tony sums it up for Dr. Melfi: "what my mother, wife, and daughter have in common is that they all break my balls," invoking a phrase that Joe Pesci made obligatory in earlier Mafia movies. (We ask, in an aside, what exactly does it physically mean "to break balls," but we'll leave that for another time since our concern here is with women.) As a television production with much more cutting away between scenes, *The Sopranos* interrupts non-stop flows of testosterone by throwing oestrogen in men's faces before they build up the head of steam that Michael and Henry enjoy during their careers. Tony always has women in his face, both at work and at home.

Though one could hardly call her happy, Carmela enjoys relative independence from Tony as she pursues her tennis lessons, almost has sex with Father Phil ("College"/1005) and Vic Musto ("Bust-Out"/2010), chillingly refuses to talk to family members who have crossed her, and visits Meadow at Columbia while telling her husband to stay at home and watch TV. Her simmering sexual desire on the screen in the episode in which she and Father Phil (who, just like a guy, is confused about whether he wants ziti or sex) spend the night together ("College"/1005) has no equivalent in earlier Mafia movies. Her absolute control over that moment – she brilliantly dismisses him and he goes limp – contrasts with Tony's pathetic string of affairs. While Carmela is a woman who knows her way around passion, she is able to assess her husband's infidelities professionally, from the viewpoint of a suburban housewife. She knows that Tony's whores are "just a form of masturbation to lighten her workload" ("Pax Soprana"/1006). The girls at lunch decide that Hillary Clinton is "a role model for all of us" because "she took all that negative shit that he gave her and spun it into gold" ("Amour Fou"/3012).

Tony is totally defeated by his mother, who is one bitch from hell as played by a melancholic, scowling Nancy Marchand. It is instructive to put Livia and Mama Corleone side-by-side. Livia has internalized the Mafia life of her husband and does not play the usual elderly Italian woman with curled hair, sagging bosom, corsages, and lots of sympathy and pasta for all. Livia is as plain as her hair, and David Chase's casting of anything but an Italian as the mama is brilliant. No stupidity here, as she plots and schemes by manipulating men who are looking, mistakenly, for the stereotypical Italian mama of Mafia movies, a role derived from ethnic stereotyping and reinforced by years of Hollywood typecasting. When men bring her food, she is especially dangerous as when she insinuates to Artie, who has sweetly brought her some cavatelli in the hospital, that Tony set fire to his restaurant. The fact that Tony is driven to murder his mother shows how out of control maternity, the social role that ultimately keeps women subject to men, is in *The Sopranos*.[1] As a woman of advanced age in our society, Livia is thought to be almost completely powerless, invisible, and grotesque, yet she is capable of using her very illnesses and ailments strategically against her son, and he is the one left powerless as she is wheeled down the hall in a hospital bed, with her malicious half-smile visible beneath her oxygen mask.

Janice (played by Aida Turturro) first enters the series during the second season as a seemingly harmless, overweight spaced-out hippie chick who doesn't realize that she is far too old for her clothes and lifestyle. When she first appears, Tony, who has had little success pushing around his wife and mother, zeroes in on Janice as a target to prove his masculinity. In Tony's eyes, she is pitiful, a greedy bitch who is just after a few dollars, and he disdainfully doles out cash to get her car fixed. So far, Tony is reading from the responsible brother script of *The Godfather*, but it becomes clear that Janice, her mother's daughter, has arrived "to bust some balls." The fact of course that she is doing it leads to the inevitable demonization of Janice's character, but she doesn't give a shit.

Her ability to identify her self-interests and pursue them relentlessly, especially when coupled with her weight and tight outfits, enables her to transgress in ways that Carmela wouldn't even dream of because of her continuing commitment to both her shapely and wifely roles.

Like any suburban woman subject to body regimes, Carmela almost always looks put together (like the early Karen Hill), while Janice looks like a slob. She takes up almost immediately with Richie Aprile, one of the most revolting men on the show, and they create a kind of anti-domestic space together ("Oh, look at this" – Tony comments sarcastically when he first discovers their co-habitation – "Ozzie and fuckin' Harriet here. That's beautiful" ["Big Girls Don't Cry"/2005]) in which they have sex with guns (again, Carmela would never go there). An uninhibited woman, Janice can let Richie do her doggie-style and call him "the boss" while he holds a gun to her head. But Janice shows just how dangerous she is to masculinity when she blows Richie away for punching her in the jaw just once. Janice does what Connie could not do to Carlo and makes a very different telephone call to her brother.

Compared to the sustained level of violence against women in the *Godfather* trilogy and *GoodFellas*, Richie Aprile's blow is just a love tap. But women like Janice have their fingers on the trigger in *The Sopranos*, and the stylized gun that forms the "r" of "*Sopranos*" on the title screen is clearly unisex in that women and men, by virtue of their last names, know how to handle themselves in both "families." However, in a patriarchal society which subjects women, whether mobsters' wives or not, to abusive relations, especially domestic ones, the *Godfather* trilogy represents a revolting wet-dream of female degradation. In Francis Ford Coppola's saga, women are inevitably road kill, sometimes literally – Michael's first bride perhaps gets the best deal when she is blown up in a car before she has a chance to suffer through being a mobster's wife. Connie is horribly beaten by Carlo when she is pregnant. Michael terrorizes Kay psychologically with his shouting, pounding, and slamming of doors in her face.

Since there are so many female victims (including the baker's daughter who has been raped and disfigured before *The Godfather* even begins), it is hard to get an accurate body count, but to appear on the screen of the *Godfather* films is to experience the danger of trespassing in a dangerously male world, a space that women continue to live with as the annual "Take Back the Night" marches show. The death of Mary, Michael and Kay's daughter, on the steps of the Palermo opera house in *Godfather III* is particularly disquieting from a feminist perspective – the movie engages in the stereotypical sacrificing of a young woman as "innocent." Kay's expression of stricken grief in the last shot sprays the fixative of female powerlessness as a final sign in the *Godfather* trilogy. Mary's last word is "Dad?" – yet another old story of a daddy's girl who has no respect for mom – and the movie ends with Michael's tortured screams, a conclusion which invites men to experience closure and to contemplate the terrible judgment on his head. But it makes women want to puke. He gets off easy. What is hard to take, as Wurtzel has suggested (discussing Nicole Simpson Brown) is that women may be implicated, and that they somehow set themselves up for this dramatic, once-in-a-lifetime role as victims of brutal violence. Tony can feel this inevitability creeping up on Meadow and, in a touching and personal moment in the kitchen towards the end of the third season, he expresses concern about a girl like Tracee, who suffers a brutal and senseless death at Ralphie's hands ("University"/3006).

GoodFellas doesn't even wait for Karen to get married to slap her around. When a former boyfriend tries to paw her and then throws her out of the car (notice that the film never asks what little Miss Innocent was doing in the car to begin with), Henry avenges her by brutally clubbing him in the face with his gun. Karen peers through a window, watching Henry with admiration, possibly aroused by the idea that such violence and rage may some day be turned against her. Mafia films imitate the circumstances of real-life domestic violence as marriage seems to provide a kind of threshold which, once crossed, empowers husbands to beat their wives. On *The Sopranos*, Richie Aprile says to Christopher, who has been slapping his niece Adriana around: "You want to raise your hand, you give her your last name. Then it's none of my fucking business" ("Toodle-Fucking-oo"/2003). Pregnant women like Tracee and Connie seem to make particularly inviting victims.

In *GoodFellas*, while Karen seems to have a better idea of how to negotiate with male power by holding a gun to Henry's head, she, unlike Janice, allows him to sweet-talk her out of pulling the trigger. While she ends up packing a pistol in her panties, the ending of *GoodFellas* is nevertheless a defeat for Karen. She has no choice but to follow Henry into the witness protection program, yet it represents a victory of sorts for gender equity that the FBI agent doesn't buy her "I'm-so-worried-about-my-parents" story: "C'mon Karen, you're not a babe in the woods." Lorraine Bracco's powerful acting in this film sets the stage for the sexualized, complex, and aggressive women who would be cast in *The Sopranos*, and it seems fitting that she plays a central role on this sequel.

When Tony hulks up, raises his voice, and shouts at Carmela, she either stands there impassively or gives as good as she gets. On TV, Tony stands in a sitcom tradition of stupid fathers who are married to sharp, shrewd, resourceful women – Roseanne, Samantha Stevens, Louise Jefferson. And it doesn't take much to set these women off: Carmela is a bitch when she is ignored at her tennis lesson, and there is a hint of her capacity for Mafia-like revenge in a female register as she drives off in anger. When Carmela marches into Joan O'Connell's office, armed with a ricotta pie, Joan realizes that writing a recommendation letter for Meadow to Georgetown is an offer that she can't refuse ("Full Leather Jacket"/2008). When Svetlana won't hand over Livia's record collection, Janice steals her prosthetic limb and hides it in a storage locker ("Fortunate Son"/3003). She remains impassive, if not sadistic, as she watches Svetlana hop around on one leg. No sisterly feminism here – the personal is not political; it's only business. When the Russians come over and beat the shit out of Janice in return, the episode doesn't represent the scene as if it were the usual victimization of women. It's just payback time, and Tony, rather than avenging his sister (a knee-jerk reaction in *The Godfather*), explains calmly, as if to one of his wiseguys, "I told you not to mess with these people" ("Employee of the Month"/3004). Even a highly professionalized woman like Dr. Melfi, after her rape in the parking garage in the same episode, knows that she "could have had that asshole squashed like a bug" since she has Tony dangling from a string. At the end of that episode, bruised and beaten, she is one breath away from ordering the hit.

In *The Sopranos*, the women *know*, and if they try coyly to forget from one episode to another, David Chase makes sure that they are inevitably reminded. We can turn Dr. Krakower's line ("Second Opinion"/3007) into a metastatement for the whole series – *one thing these women can't say is that they haven't been told*.[2] Carmela candidly confesses, early in the first season with Father Phil: "I have forsaken what is right for what is easy." Easy turns out to be the dreams of a material girl. When Dr. Krakower tells her directly that she is an "accomplice" (a word with a legal ring to it), Carmela tries to hide behind stupid domesticity: "All I do is to make sure he's got clean clothes in his closet and dinner on his table" ("Second Opinion"/3007). When he tells her point blank that she spends "blood money," she goes back home, curls up on the couch for awhile, and finds her solution: to ask her husband to put up $50,000 (as a donation to Columbia University) or else . . .

Meadow is also constantly running into evidence that contradicts her father's "waste management" business: she offers to print out her father's page for AJ from a website entitled *M.O.B. Website: Megabytes of Bad Guy* ("Meadowlands"/1004), and she comes in with her friends, filled with the joy of graduating seniors, only to find him being led away in handcuffs ("Funhouse" /2013). But early in the first season ("College"/1005), she asks him directly if he is a mobster, a huge victory for Mafia-princess consciousness-raising, given Mary's saccharine illusions in *The Godfather Part III*. Unlike Michael's impenetrable "I love you" routine, Tony's half-hearted attempts to lie fall apart under the scrutiny of his bright, sophisticated daughter. She immediately shifts from the realm of generalities, where Mary is forever stuck, to a more effective cross-examination than any FBI prosecutor could muster: "Did the Cusamano kids ever find 50,000 dollars in Kruggerrands and a 45-automatic when they were hunting for Easter eggs?" ("College"/1005). In the final episode of the third season ("Army of One"/3013), Meadow cannot face the fact that her father may have been responsible for Jackie's death. To Mary's "I love you, Dad," Meadow smartly spits out, "this is all bullshit." While Meadow is well aware of her mother's hypocrisy ("Least you don't keep denying it, like Mom" ["College"/ 1005]), her clarity of vision ultimately succumbs to the vacuousness which patriarchy – not just Mafia bosses – forces upon women. At Livia's wake, Tony recognizes her daughter's sad initiation: "She's already becoming a robot like the rest of us" ("Proshai, Livushka"/3002). Yet becoming a robot by no means turns Meadow into a Kay; indeed, as she takes her adult place in the "family," she becomes increasingly more complicated, sexualized and darker throughout the third season. Always close to her "grandma," she is skillfully manipulative and makes the system work for her; perhaps, she will toughen up even more to replace the departed Livia.

"Made men" escape from these shrewd and sharp women by spending time in the exclusively male "families" of social clubs, pizza joints, and the Bada Bing!

While their public heteronormativity is assured by marriage, a social structure without women raises questions about homoerotic desire in organized crime. As in the classic sequence from *The Godfather*, men "go to the mattresses" and spend months living with each other, cooking for each other, expressing concern for each other, and touching each other in very physical ways. Someone like Paulie Walnuts, with his dapper suits and fastidiousness, invites these kinds of readings, especially in light of fetishes like smelling Adriana's panties. This reconstituted "family," idealized in *The Sopranos* as well as in the earlier films, represents an organized retreat from the stink of women. While they may marry them, Mafia guys are definitely not comfortable with women's bodies. Junior, who "is a great artist" at kissing his mistress "down there," asks her not to broadcast it: "Because they think that if you suck pussy, you'll suck anything. It's a sign of weakness. You're a fanuck" ("Boca"/1009). When Junior later goes to play golf with Tony (who has heard the rumor about his uncle's talent), he is greeted by comments such as "What's that smell?" and "Did you guys go to a sushi bar?" ("Boca"/1009) – moronic sexual humor that is given even more of a spin when we think through the metaphor of "sleeping with the fishes." Junior's public embarrassment over giving a woman sexual pleasure, rather than almost invariably being caught in the missionary position like his nephew is, precipitates his dismissal of Bobbi Sanfillipo as "a blabbermouth cunt" who has ratted him out to the guys. But what makes us go ballistic about this episode – *someone on that writing staff really knows women* – is that Carmela, who complains that she only gets it once a year, hardly a laughing matter, is the one who passes along the gossip from the nail parlor and can't stop tittering about Junior at the dinner table.

In *The Sopranos*, the Mafia flow charts which the FBI so love are missing pictures of Livia, Carmela, Janice, and Meadow. At the outset, David Chase said in an interview that he wanted to put these Mafia women under surveillance in his series: "We never see the women in these stories. They're always just like stirring the pot, or pasta, or crying at funerals and weddings. I began to think what it would be like to flesh out these characters" (interview with David Chase, Museum of Television and Radio). Yet for all their empowerment, *Sopranos* women seem no happier or more fulfilled than 1950s versions of mobster wives in *The Godfather* or the 1970s versions in *GoodFellas*. Their lives seem hollow, their power lost on lame men, mindless suburban routines and "spending money like the Sopranos of Park Avenue" ("Pax Soprana"/1006). Carmela buys furniture from Roche Bubois, redoes her wallpaper, and still doesn't get what she wants. So if the Mafia dons no longer rule either "family" and if the princesses have fallen victim to suburban Jersey life, who wins? We would recommend that in a postmodern Mafia world a smart girl would get a job at the Bada Bing! Cunts that are publicly on display and are moneymakers are the only cunts who are granted a degree of autonomy that breaks free of the multiple burdens of "family." These women enjoy a range of camera angles which are closed off to the Soprano women, who are regularly shot in over-the-shoulder sequences. With their heads cut off, the camera focuses on their perfect boobs and asses and shoots them from below, thereby ensuring their anonymity. In other episodes, they remain out of focus in a rack-focus throw shot. Since this is still television, nude shots below the waist, which might show their "shaved twats" (to use Ralphie's term) are out of the question – God forbid that we should actually see a cunt. Long hair in front of the face helps too. And the guys, sitting right under their legs, rarely bother to look up.

Yet, even working girls do occasionally end up dead. Remember Tom Hagen's line in *The Godfather Part II*: "This girl has no family, nobody knows that she worked here. It'll be as though she never existed." But they are treated with "respect" because they are viewed exclusively as commodities. In *The Godfather*, the Las Vegas girls are constantly being herded out of the room, a fate which keeps them free of Mafia "family" entanglements. For these girls, "it's not personal, just business," and they don't have to worry about falling into the trap of Mafia princesses. They are something less than human, and their body parts, whether silicon boobs or braces, are investments. As Tony puts it, "thoroughbreds," and they are granted immunity because they enjoy "an employee/employer relationship," and even made guys are not allowed "to disrespect the Bing!" Perhaps Tracee ends up dead because she makes the mistake of trying to create "family" relations with Tony (the date-nut bread) and Ralphie (the baby). The other girls know their business: "Do yourself a favor," one Bing girl advises. "Keep what you hear to yourself" ("University"/ 3006). Just dance and suck cock.

But the Bada Bing! girls also take aim at Carmela, Nancy, Janice, and Meadow in the historically all-consuming competitiveness among women about their bodies, a subject which has been raised in many feminist studies, including Naomi Wolf's *The Beauty Myth* and Susan Bordo's *Unbearable Weight*. Despite their power, these Soprano women would never be able to compete on the stage of the Bada Bing!: Carmela's late middle-age life-support systems of immaculate hair, makeup, and clothes would crumble if she were on the runway in a g-string (much like Edie Falco's did when she showed up in the wrong dress at the Emmy's and was skewered by those self-appointed doyennes of trash taste, Joan and Melissa Rivers – we're with you, Edie!). Livia is completely overwritten with all the biases, circulated by *both* women and men, against aging which makes even the idea of her wearing less than her hospital gown impossible. And Janice is fat, and though she has a pretty face. . . . So while men may be clueless in the *Sopranos*, it's still not easy being a woman. In a way the wholesale collapse of masculinity on *The Sopranos* has merely served to clear the air for women who were confused, like Kay and Karen, about their life-scripts. As we've suggested throughout, the Soprano women are vulnerable to many kinds of hits (like our bitchiness about their bodies!), but they seem to have a pretty good idea that the men in their lives are tangential rather than central. When Carmela's mother (played by the same actress, Suzanne Sheperd, who played Karen Hill's mother) challenges her about her privileges, she responds with the fierce directness of a mob boss: "I earn it" ("Second Opinion"/3007).

This essay carries a message from kick-ass girls for Michael Corleone, but we must whisper it in his ear: "screw dread."

EIGHT

"FAT FUCK! WHY DON'T YOU TAKE A LOOK IN THE MIRROR?": WEIGHT, BODY IMAGE, AND MASCULINITY IN *THE SOPRANOS*

Avi Santo

BODY COUNTS

Without question, HBO's *The Sopranos* is the series with the largest body count on television today. I am, of course, referring to the show's habitual use of overweight and obese bodies,[1] particularly among its male characters.[2] In addition to the character of Tony Soprano, the show's anti-hero lead, the male body has been represented in its non-idealized form by such characters as Salvatore "Big Pussy" Bonpensiero, Bobby "Bacala" Baccalieri, FBI agent Skip Lipari, rat boy Jimmy Altieri, and Vito Spatofore. And these are merely examples of the extreme. With few exceptions, the male body on *The Sopranos* is regularly shown to be soft and unfit. Male fatness on *The Sopranos* is very rarely an overt signifier of failure, at least not in the traditional sense. Tony Soprano has no difficulties in attracting women, has not been denied work, and is too feared to have his weight openly mocked by his peers, even those few who are fit. In fact, on *The Sopranos*, it is precisely those characters whose bodies are fit or muscled who either wind up dead (Jackie Aprile Jr. being a fine example of this trend) or, at the very least, repeatedly mutilated (Christopher Moltisanti being the most consistent of those assailed). This inversion is noteworthy when compared with what Peter N. Stearns otherwise labels "intense [Western] cultural beliefs in the inferiority of fat . . . [where] failure to live up to the new, standardized body image entails at least an appalling ugliness, at most a fundamentally flawed character" (xii).

How does the male body on *The Sopranos* lend itself to a range of cultural meanings concerning weight and masculinity at the beginning of the twenty-first century? What can be made of this apparent favoring of fatness over fitness in the series? Is the show truly engaged in a redefinition of masculinity through its corporeal representation, or is the fat body a critique of the current definitions of manhood? This essay seeks to answer these questions. Initially, I will trace some of the contradictory discourse on fatness that emerged over the past one hundred years and reveal how these multiple understandings lend themselves to a complex reading of the series and, in particular, the character of Tony Soprano, which both supports and subverts the show's narrative. Moreover, since fitness and appearance have become paramount to an idealized definition of middle-class masculinity, I will also explore how *The Sopranos* has repeatedly engaged in a denunciation of the fit body and the means by which it may be attained, namely sport and diet. On *The Sopranos*, fitness seems intricately connected to dandyism and male bodily display, labeled by Martin Pumphrey in his study of westerns as transgressions of traditional codes of masculinity (54). This inevitably sets up a complicated struggle between fatness and fitness on the show, since both are imbricated in the desire to be looked at and thus, invariably equated with deviant forms of masculinity.

The male body in *The Sopranos* not only exists as a site of struggle over the construction of masculinity – a battlefield on which, inversely, fatness repeatedly wins – but is also an irresolvable manifestation of the inability to resurrect an earlier male ideal, namely that of the self-made man, the entrepreneurial producer. Michael Kimmel has defined this previous designation of manhood as rooted in "economic autonomy – control over one's labor . . . ownership of the products of one's labor" and has further claimed that "when these avenues of demonstrating manhood were suddenly closed, it touched off a widespread identity crisis" (19). In place of this notion of manhood directly related to production, an alternative, consumed version of masculinity emerged, which not only attempted to define itself in relation to material possessions, but also placed considerable emphasis on the fit body as a displayable re-invention of the lost power to produce.

The Sopranos depicts a world run rampant with consumption, where middle-class masculinity has come to define itself not by what it produces but by what it consumes and where even the attempt to reassert control over production outside of the body cannot be achieved. Try as they might, Tony and his crew can only reproduce consumption itself. In the end, the series suggests that a world overwrought by consumption and without the ability to produce anything beyond more consumption will inevitably lead to the consumption of the body itself, in which the corporeal form becomes the ultimate consumer fetish. This, *The Sopranos* repeatedly suggests, is akin to cannibalism, and Tony's awareness of it, I argue, is the ultimate source of his anxiety attacks.

FATNESS, EVIL, AND SYMPATHY FOR THE DEVIL

> "You really are in love with yourself. . . . You deprive yourself of nothing."
> Gloria Trillo to Tony Soprano,
> just prior to lovemaking

"Fat fuck! Why don't you take a look in the mirror, you insensitive cocksucker!"

Bobby "Bacala" Baccalieri reacting to Tony Soprano's insult, after Tony has already left the scene

Fatness, like any other aesthetic definition of beauty or body type, is neither a neutral nor an inherent term. Its meanings are contextually bound and, even then, hopelessly multiple. In short, fatness is a signifier with many overlapping and even contradictory signifieds.

In his illuminating *Fat History: Bodies and Beauty in the Modern West*, Peter N. Stearns frankly states, "awareness and concern about fat forms one of the leading cultural symbols of the late twentieth century" (xii). Stearns' work traces the shift in Western attitudes towards the body away from nineteenth-century associations of corpulence with wealth and power towards current cultural definitions of fatness as analogous with greed, over-indulgence, and a distinct lack of control. Stearns attributes this shifting concern over body shape to a loosening of the moral reins throughout the nineteenth century of Victorian-era notions of sexuality, emotion, and pleasure, coupled with the advent of wide-spread consumerism. These new-found freedoms, in turn, created a moral crisis among the emerging middle-class over the apparent erosion of values related to discipline, moderation, and temperance. "Constraint, including the new constraints urged on eating and body shape, was reinvented to match – indeed, to compensate for – new areas of greater freedom . . . a growing commitment to acquisitiveness generated an even more widespread and durable zeal for attacking fat as a symbol of moral probity" (Stearns 54–5).

Stearns articulates the process by which domination of the body through self-sacrifice became the new compensatory moral outlet for a society that could otherwise consume without constraint. The attack on fat became a means of reasserting control without sacrificing one's appetite for consumer goods. "People could indulge their taste for fashion and other products with a realization that, if they disciplined their bodies through an attack on fat, they could preserve or even enhance their health and also establish their moral credentials" (59).

As an inevitable consequence of this new-found moderation of the body, fatness became separated from its previous class-based connotations of success and wealth and began to take on exceedingly negative attributes. Fatness was now equated with laziness, a lack of discipline, over-indulgence, and even failure. According to Susan Bordo, "the obese elicit blinding rage and disgust in our culture and are often viewed in terms that suggest an infant sucking hungrily, unconsciously at its mother's breast: greedy, self absorbed, lazy, without self-control or willpower" (202).

Bordo defines the ideal body in consumer society as essentially bulimic. Like those afflicted with the disease itself, ideal consumers engage in wild binges followed by violent purges. They desire to consume and in fact do so with great regularity. But they also steadfastly impose restrictions, often oppressive dietary and exercise regimens on their bodies as penance for their indulgences

(201). Bordo does, however, acknowledge that other, more extreme body types must exist alongside the bulimic ideal, in order to legitimate its otherwise contradictory, and somewhat sadomasochistic, tendencies. Obesity and anorexia represent these extreme and polar dysfunctions in consumer society. While the anorexic restrains his/herself to the point of emaciation, the obese person is suggestive of consumption gone unchecked, the feared and loathed outcome of not imposing constraints. Not surprisingly, the obese person's lack of control when it comes to food is often equated with a lack of morality and a willingness to break the social contract. According to Sarah Grogan, "prejudice against the overweight is culturally bound and depends on attribution of blame. Within Western ideology, being overweight is perceived to violate the cultural ideal of self-denial and self-control" (8). Stearns not only concurs but raises the stakes: "The image of fat as essentially evil, the result of personal failure but the cause of additional failures in the outside world, reinforced . . . the need for a moral counterweight in a society of consumer indulgence. Fat people had to wrestle with some inner devils and with the temptations of the outside world" (Stearns 122).

The equation of fatness with evil has certainly not been lost on the film and television industries, which have regularly cast overweight figures in villainous roles, particularly in the gangster genre. Since, as Robert Warshow suggested so many years ago, the gangster is a tragic hero whose very success spells his ultimate self-destruction (133), what better image to use than the criminally obese? Fatness in the gangster genre successfully embodies the self-destructiveness of power as played out on the body. Since in Western culture, fatness is equated with a form of suicidal intention (hence the expression "eating yourself to death"), the obese gangster successfully manifests the eventual price he will have to pay for his gluttony. It is perhaps not surprising that media like film and television, which rely so heavily upon visual imagery, would use the body in order to produce a surplus of meanings that are not otherwise articulated in the narrative. After all, corpulence is so visible. The body is often the first thing that is noticed and only afterwards, the locations it inhabits, the clothing it wears, the liaisons it has, the props it uses. Each of these, in turn, are measured and understood in relation to the body. For his role in *The Godfather,* Marlon Brando gained a significant amount of weight prior to portraying the powerful Don Corleone. Corleone's weight was meant to embody the greed and moral ambiguity that had accompanied his rise to power. This complies with Bordo's assertion that, "Increasingly, the size and shape of the body have come to operate as a market of personal, internal order (or disorder) – as a symbol for the emotional, moral, or spiritual state of the individual" (193).

Significantly, *The Godfather* is often used as an intertextual source of meaning on *The Sopranos.* Similar to Don Corleone, Tony Soprano is also a rich and powerful member of organized crime, whose criminality and ethical haziness are likewise embodied by his corporeal girth. Tony can be characterized as a man of tremendous over-indulgence and lack of control. Aside from food (and Tony is constantly eating), Tony also smokes, drinks, and indulges in multiple women (his wife, Carmela, his goomah, Irina, his "mid-life crisis mobile" girl, Gloria Trillo, strippers at Bada-Bing!, Connie, the born-again secretary at Barone Sanitation, not to mention his recurring fantasies over his therapist, Dr. Melfi. He also regularly loses control of his emotions, often with violent consequences. Upon hearing Dr. Melfi's assertion that his mother might be involved in a plot to kill him, Tony flies into a rage, smashing her coffee table and leaning into her menacingly ("I Dream of Jeannie Cusamano"/1013). Likewise, Tony has exhibited intense and violent emotional bursts of anger over his sister Janice's repeated monetary schemes, Ralphie's killing of the stripper Tracee ("University"/3006), Gloria's threat to tell Carmela about their affair ("Amour Fou"/3012), Christopher's repeated questioning of his authority . . . Tony's temper is likely to flare up at any conceivable moment.

Tony's weight, while rarely mentioned (and even then, never in relation to his criminality), nevertheless plays an important role in signifying that he is, in fact, a corrupt embodiment of the American Dream. His body size sets off a series of cultural associations with greed and moral bankruptcy that lend validity to the show's narrative depiction of Tony's illegal activities and provides a subtext that links Tony's success and wealth in an otherwise decaying set of values. Both the larger cultural criminalization of fatness and the show's intertextual referencing of films such as *The Godfather* contribute to a reading of Tony's body as befitting that of the greedy criminal that he is.

It would, however, be shortsighted to assert that Tony's body type merely lends cultural credence to an understanding of him as a villain. While possessing many bad habits, Tony Soprano is, after all, still the protagonist of the series. Like Don Corleone, he is not utterly despised. In fact, a large amount of empathy is extended towards him in keeping with the mystique of the gangster genre. While an awareness of the gangster's greed and violence persists, the audience roots for him nonetheless. In *The Sopranos*, this is in part due to a recurring narrative thread that repeatedly labels Tony an overgrown child. Dr. Melfi refers to him as a little boy in her therapy sessions with Dr. Kupferberg ("Big Girls Don't Cry"/2005). Carmela regularly chastises Tony to grow up. When Tony expresses anger over Anthony Jr. not wanting to spend time with him, Carmela quips, "What are you? Six years old?" ("Bust Out"/2010). At times, Tony even refers to himself as a child. When he discovers that Janice has removed the "for sale" sign from their mother's lawn, Tony goes into a tirade, angrily asserting that his sister still thinks he is some "little fat kid" ("Guy Walks into a Psychiatrist's Office"/2001). Of course, Tony's behavior suggests that he is precisely that.

Tony's body also plays into this image of him as a child whose tantrums can be forgiven. After all, children are not expected to regulate their bodies, nor are they responsible for their actions. Children are often podgy and show no concern for limitations. They are often depicted as innocent, despite their repeated bad behavior. Stearns' work on why fatness remains so prevalent in America despite the cultural constraints imposed against it confirms this analogy. He contends that children are not subject to the same bodily self-discipline that adults enforce on themselves: "As innocents, children were exempt from any need to compensate for consumer indulgences in which adults must participate" (139).

In the end, Tony's soft, plump exterior inevitably contributes to a reading of his character as childlike and, bizarrely, well-intentioned despite his horrific behavior. Tony, after all, can torch his friend Artie Bucco's restaurant in order to prevent a mob hit from occurring there and still come off seeming heroic. This image of the overweight adult manifesting childish behavior is not new to the genre. In Howard Hawks' *Scarface* (1932), Paul Muni plays the murderous character of Tony Camonte as a child let loose in a candy store. Moreover, from Fatty Arbuckle to Fred Flinstone, fat men have repeatedly been forgiven for their transgressions because of their supposedly ingenuous nature.[3] On *The Sopranos*, however, the line that separates illegal from innocent is repeatedly crossed, making Tony's fatness a disturbingly hybrid signifier of both greed and guiltlessness, which implies that in a world where there are so many things to consume, Tony cannot be held responsible for giving in to temptation. In other words, Tony's body, in this instance, reveals the hypocrisy of consumer culture, which simultaneously encourages limitless self-gratification and vilifies those who take it up on its offer.

In part, however, Tony's transgressions are also lessened due to his own awareness of his corruption. Much the same way that Don Corleone tells his son Michael that he never wants him to get involved in gangster life, Tony continually expresses his own fears that his son AJ will turn out to be like him. A tension clearly exists between Tony's greedy efforts to provide comfort and luxury for himself and his family and his attempts to shield them from the moral degradation he has endured as a result. Once again, Tony's weight plays a subtle but crucial part in negotiating this fuzzy line between villainy and valor. Bordo explains that in order for society to tolerate the obese, they must never be seen as happy with their lives. There must be an acknowledgement of their ultimate failure to achieve normalcy, to fit in, despite whatever material successes they may have realized. "This construction allows people to give their sympathy to the obese, assuming as it does the obese person's acknowledgement that to be 'normal' is the most desired goal, elusive only because of personal inadequacy" (204). Hence, Tony's success, like his body, is presented as deviant. His expressed desire to keep AJ away from the family business is an acknowledgement of that deviance – an awareness that allows Tony to come across as sympathetic, despite his proclivity towards violence and unfaithfulness.

Right from the outset of the series, Tony's psychiatry sessions have been framed as an attempt by him to gain control over his body. While this control is not centered on his weight but on his anxiety attacks, the corporeal connection is still crucial. Reluctant to label fatness a disease that could not be cured without external remedies, the medical profession instead has proclaimed it to be a psychological response to inner demons that need to be brought under control. "Rational people could lose weight or not gain it in the first place. By implication, overweight people were emotional cripples, eating to mask other problems" (Stearns 118). In "The Army of One" (3013), the third season finale, Tony responds to Christopher's lack of respect (brought about by Christopher's belief that Tony has shown preferential treatment to Jackie Aprile, Jr. and has not tried to protect him with the same rigor) by heading straight for the mini-fridge. When he cannot find the leftover romaine he had been "dreaming about all the way the fuck over here" (in other words, when he cannot take solace from his inability to get through to Christopher in food), his reaction is to break the fridge. Tony's lack of control as it relates to his body thus becomes a physical manifestation of deep-rooted psychological and spiritual scars, which, with the help of Dr. Melfi, he must confront.[4] Once again, Tony's effort to gain control through psychiatric treatment – a process which often forces him to confront his deviant and self-indulgent behavior – is one of the narrative tropes employed by the series to elicit sympathy towards his character. According to Bordo, obesity is only tolerated as long as the "perpetrator" acknowledges his/her guilt. Similarly, Tony's base criminality is rendered more acceptable by his own desire to gain control over his body.

All this would make perfect sense if the show was merely concerned with making Tony repentant for his crimes (both corporeal and otherwise). *The Sopranos* succeeds, however, in blurring the line between Tony's excessive indiscretions and his desire for normalcy by continuously playing with the contradictory equation of his fatness with a lack of control, which he exhibits in both bursts of violence and greediness as well as in his anxiety attacks. His fatness is thus both a signifier of his power – labeled evil because of its lack of constraint – and of his powerlessness – evident in his inability to control his own body, and his acknowledgement that his unrestrained consumption (pay offs and kick backs are repeatedly referred to on the show as a form of eating) must be hidden away from AJ.

Adding yet another layer to this complex reading of Tony's body as both a signifier of power and a lack thereof is what Susan Bordo refers to as the relationship of fatness to social mobility (195). As previously asserted, until the end of the nineteenth century, corpulence was often associated with wealth. "The body indicated social identity and 'place'" (191). In particular, it was the bourgeois class that embraced fatness as an outward manifestation of success, while the graceful, slender body was a signifier of aristocratic status. Bordo contends that the emerging middle-class embraced the svelte aristocratic body ideal over its vulgar bourgeois counterpart, partly as a status seeking measure and partly as a response to the shifting definition of power, which came to be identified less with display than with control, and more importantly self-control (191). Soon after, fatness became a distinct sign of the failure to live up to middle-class standards. It no longer demonstrated class location, but rather indicated an inability to grasp the class-based cultural and aesthetic values that accompanied the middle-class economic position. In short, fatness prevented mobility and restricted cultural acceptance regardless of the size of one's bank account.[5]

Seen through the lens of social mobility, Tony's girth thus becomes even more complicated. While on the one hand, it situates him among the capitalist class and embodies his power; on the other hand, it ostracizes him from middle-class standards of acceptability and renders him an outsider. Tony's inability to fit in with middle-class aesthetic and moral values is repeatedly played out on his body. In the pilot episode of the series, Tony is shown ambling down his posh driveway to collect the newspaper. The camera, situated behind Tony and slightly above him captures the incredible wealth that surrounds him. Yet Tony, clad in his bathrobe and boxer shorts, his hairy chest and round belly visibly protruding and his back slouched, seems distinctly out of place. Tony's voice-over commentary confirms his displacement.

> "The morning of the day I got sick, I'd been thinking . . . it's good to be in something from the ground floor. I came too late for that, I know. But lately, I'm getting the feeling that I came in at the end. The best is over. . . . I think about my father. He never reached the heights like me, but in a lot of ways he had it better. He had his people. They had their standards. They had pride. Today, what do we got?"

Tony's monologue suggests a yearning for a time gone by. His body, and in particular the clothing that adorns it, emphasize his reluctant relationship to his class position and indicate his diminished status within it. Quite simply, Tony is a slob, and his appearance is at odds with the visual grandeur of his surroundings. The metaphor is carried to the extreme in this opening sequence when Tony climbs into his pool, bathrobe and all, to play with the ducks that have made a home there. It is the first moment of happiness we have seen him experience; all the while his family stares on in befuddled embarrassment through the kitchen window. Tony is literally a duck out of water in relation to the upper-middle-class lifestyle he leads. Even when Tony is adorned in designer clothing, it often accentuates his girth. His shirts are either too tight or their patterning calls attention to his flabby chest or his expanding stomach. Despite his economic success, Tony seems unable to pass for a middle-class aesthetic ideal.

This inability to pass is the focus of an episode from the first season entitled, "A Hit is a Hit" (1010), in which Tony is invited by his neighbor, the slim and fashionable Dr. Cusamano, for a game of golf. The game, played at an exclusive country club, is an excuse for Cusamano and his friends to pry into Tony's underworld lifestyle. Tony's "otherness" is accentuated by their insensitive snooping, much the same way that his lumbering body seems oddly out of place on the golf course. In the end, however, it is Tony who turns the tables on Cusamano and his cohorts and in a manner that once again calls into question social taboos concerning the body. When asked if he ever knew John Gotti, Tony responds with a story about the Bungalow Bar ice cream trucks. The immediate reaction from Cusamano et al. reaffirms the stereotypical connection between criminality and over-consumption. They ask, rather ridiculously, if Gotti was a silent partner in Bungalow Bar, which essentially sold fattening (and therefore corrupting) sweets to children. Undaunted, Tony dismisses their questioning and informs them that Gotti simply outbid him for the final Bungalow Bar roof that was auctioned off at a bankruptcy sale. Tony then adds that Gotti gave him a lift home, ringing the bell the whole way back.

The story is clearly meant to stump Cusamano's friends, who are expecting a tale of extortion and gangland violence and are instead greeted with an account of utter mundaneness, but the bizarre connections that are drawn between organized crime and ice cream are still disturbing. On the one hand, they again call the hypocrisy of middle-class values into question, suggesting that, despite appearances, Tony and Cusamano are more alike than either man might wish to admit. After all, ice cream trucks are staples of suburbia, and ice cream is one of the many consumer luxuries that the middle-class has simultaneously embraced as sweet and innocent and condemned as fattening. On the other hand, the image of the ice cream truck being driven by a gangster is a powerful symbol of sinful over-indulgence if there ever was one and manages to re-establish the key difference between Tony and Cusamano. Cusamano, the embodiment of middle-class restraint, fits perfectly into the world he inhabits. Ice cream is a temptation he can resist. Tony, like the disturbing image he conjures up of Gotti ceaselessly ringing the ice cream bell, does not. Furthermore, ice cream trucks tend to only pass through middle-class neighborhoods. They do not belong.

Tony's recounting of the Bungalow Bar tale is more than just a reaffirmation of his inability to adhere to middle-class ideals. It is also a tale of power, which implicates Cusamano and his friends as the ultimate consumers of not only ice cream but also Tony's stories, while Tony himself profits from their fascination with the darker side of success. Tony's over-consumptive body might deny him social mobility according to middle-class standards, but as the Bungalow Bar story suggests, Tony is the most mobile of them all. The image of Gotti, childlike and exuberant as he rings the ice cream bell, is ultimately one of freedom from constraint. As has been previously asserted, obesity is despised primarily because it breaks the social contract of self-restraint. Fatness is tolerated in Western society only when it is separated from power (either by associating fat people with children or by forcing them to admit their deviance and seek help).

As the character of Tony Soprano clearly reveals, fatness also carries with it a great deal of force precisely because it is free to challenge the hegemonic demands for self-control in the face of consumable pleasure. Tony can do what Cusamano and his friends cannot. He can break the law. He can consume without constraint. And, despite their efforts to make Tony the object of their amusement, Cusamano and his pals are inevitably shown to be envious of Tony. Their knowledge of gangster trivia and curiosity about Tony's world far exceeds their smug air of superiority and shows them for what they truly are, jealous. While this jealousy might translate into revulsion against the fat body, it is nonetheless a crucial component in deciphering the complex criminalization of obesity in Western culture. While Tony's body might carry a range of negative and emasculating qualities, underneath it all his fatness is envied, precisely because it embodies his freedom and disregard for the social constraints that other middle-class Americans unhappily impose on themselves. In the end, there is a return to the gangster genre and the formula laid out by Robert Warshow. Tony's body is the site of envy, but also of a compensatory disdain intended to reassert dominant middle-class definitions of normalcy – moral, corporeal, and other. Similarly, Warshow has suggested that the audience's response to the gangster film is essentially doubly sadistic. The audience gains pleasure in watching as the gangster violently subverts the codes of society and then in watching him suffer for his indiscretions. "We gain the double satisfaction in participating vicariously in the gangster's sadism and then seeing it turned against the gangster himself" (Warshow, "Tragic" 131–2). *The Sopranos* calls attention to this hypocrisy, which envies Tony's freedom to consume but rejects him on the same grounds.

As a result of this contradictory definition of fatness and its relationship to power, Tony's body becomes emblematic of the hypocrisy that exists in assessing what is normal and what is deviant. In "The Happy Wanderer" (2006), Tony confesses to Dr. Melfi that he has given his daughter a car that belonged to her friend Eric, acquired as partial repayment of a gambling debt incurred by Eric's father, Davey Scatino. When probed as to his reasoning, Tony responds, "this man is a degenerate gambler, but he's also a respected businessman and member of the community and everything that comes with that." Thus, Tony's weight, in addition to criminalizing and infantilizing him, denying him class mobility and providing a physical manifestation of the guilt and mental deficiencies he must work through in order to achieve normalcy, also serves, quite contrarily, as a sign of his rejection of the pretence of normalcy, which merely conceals its excesses under the guise of fitness (it is not accidental that Davey Scatino runs a sporting goods store). Tony is condemned for essentially manifesting corporeally the gluttony that others conceal within. This, in some bizarre way, actually succeeds in rendering the character more genuine and honest than those around him whose bodies do conform to middle-class ideals. The association of fatness with honesty fits well with other popular "positive" stereotypes of fat people as generally kinder and friendlier than thin people (Grogan 7).

Before declaring *The Sopranos* a show that champions the physically ostracized and Tony the leader of the fatties, however, it must be asserted that the fat body as it is represented on the series is not entirely free of stigmatization and disempowerment. It is true enough that Tony's body successfully subverts many of the stereotypically enfeebling caricaturizations of fat people, but to what extent is this the result of Tony's relationship to other obese characters on the program? Though stout, Tony is less fat than all of the other corpulent men on the series. In comparison with Bobby "Bacala" Baccalieri, Tony might even be considered slim. All this might only seem to be a matter of degrees, but for the fact that Tony treats Bacala with the same disgust and contempt that the middle-class has normally reserved for people Tony's size. Simply put, Bacala's presence on the series not only manages to make Tony's body seem more "normal," but it also allows Tony to adapt more seamlessly to middle-class values. As a result, Tony's scenes with Bacala also make him seem more overtly cruel. Perhaps this is the result of Tony's refusal to offer the same sympathy to a fellow fat person that the viewer regularly offers him.

Whatever the case, Bacala's humiliation is not only by Tony's hands. The show has regularly gone out of its way to place Bacala in situations that not only accentuate his humongous girth, but call attention to his embodiment of many of the emasculating qualities associated with corpulence as well. Even though he is a made guy, Bacala is primarily Junior's nursemaid, a role that clearly feminizes him. (In the hierarchy of *The Sopranos*, it also makes him the supporting cast of a supporting cast member.) Aside from the first episode in which he appears, "Do Not Resuscitate" (2002), he is never shown engaging in violent, or even criminal, activity. (Even in that episode, his involvement in the construction site riot was marked by his shortness of breath and Tony's repeated assertion that he is a "lazy fuck.") Moreover, Bacala's body is constantly being placed on display for the amusement of others. In "Pine Barrens" (3011), he shows up to help Tony find Paulie and Christopher, who are lost in the woods, adorned in a gigantic, attention-grabbing, orange florescent hazard jacket. The episode even emphasizes that Bacala is meant to be laughed at by having Tony do just that. When Bacala tries to defend himself, Junior orders him to go with Tony. He is on display and powerless to do anything about it. In "To Save Us All From Satan's Power" (3010), Bacala is once again forced by Tony to be on display when he orders him to be the Satriale Santa Claus. Significantly, Tony chooses to put Bacala on display rather than himself, even though he could easily have worn the Santa suit. As the episode unfolds, we learn that Tony's good friend Pussy, who turns out to be a rat for the Feds, had previously played Santa. The episode focuses on Tony's pain as he reminisces about Christmases past and Pussy's betrayal. In contrast to Pussy, whose body twice criminalizes him (he was a made guy and an FBI informant, and was often shown to be playing both sides against the middle), Bacala embodies all of the jolliness and innocence normally endowed upon Santa and is the perfect remedy for Tony's disillusionment. Bacala, however, is reluctant to be Santa because of his shyness, an attribute normally flung upon fat people who do not want to tolerate the ridicule of others.

In the end, Bacala's body manages to house many of the disempowering features of fatness – from his domesticated, feminized, peripheral, and servile role in the Soprano family to his laziness and his repeated objectification and ridicule – but also the more endearing ones. Bacala is soft spoken and shy; Tony is aggressive and rude. He is trusting and kind to Junior; Tony is suspicious and impatient. Finally, Bacala is Santa Claus, while Tony is not. Suffice it to say that since Bacala's arrival on the scene, Tony has become a much darker character. This is an interesting reworking of the usual criminalization of fatness stereotype. Bacala's obesity makes Tony's body appear more "normal," which in turn, makes Tony more reprehensible.

Crucially, Tony's repeated taunting of Bacala also stresses the power imbalance between them, which imbricates issues of class in any reading of the body. Tony is the boss and Bacala is his underling. Tony's fatness is not ridiculed because he has the class status necessary to prevent this. Bacala, whose caretaker role not only feminizes him but also places him among the working class, simply does not have the leverage to fight back. This argument must, of course, be read into all aspects of the series that implicate the body in power differentials, whether the result of class, gender, or racial divisions. How does an understanding of Tony's body work in relation to his sister Janice's or his wife Carmela's, or any of the naked strippers at the Bada Bing!, or Officer Wilmore's, the African American police officer who pays the price for giving Tony a speeding ticket? ("Another Toothpick"/3005). Moreover, how have audiences responded to James Gandolfini's body in comparison with female actresses on the show? When Jamie Lynn Sigler (Meadow) gained weight in season two, a huge outcry could be heard across Internet chat rooms, but Gandolfini has been labeled a sex symbol, despite his bulk. Clearly different standards prevail. While beyond the scope of this essay, these remain crucial areas of exploration in filtering out the complex meanings that corpulence embodies on *The Sopranos*.

THE FIT BODY AND THE DANDY

> "You wanna know what I'm interested in? Men's fashion. Not the faggy part of it, but, like, to be Hugo Boss."
>
> Jackie Aprile Jr. explaining his goals in life to Meadow Soprano

> "You finished? Cuz that sugarless motherfucker is the last fucking drink you're ever gonna have."
>
> Tony Soprano to Matthew "Drink Water" Bevilaqua
> just before he and Pussy kill him

While Tony's body lends itself to multiple and contradictory readings of his character, at least one thing remains fairly consistent. On *The Sopranos*, fatness wins and fitness regularly leads to an early grave. In the previous section, I traced the connection between differing cultural associations made with corpulence and their complex reworking upon Tony Soprano's body. I suggested that the series regularly calls attention to the conflicting need for and vilification of consumption in Western society through its exploration of the body and its relationship to power. By making the body itself a symbol of constraint and moral virtue, I also argued that the middle-class has successfully elided its own deviance by concealing its over-indulgence under the façade of fitness. In this section, I will explore how the show has regularly attacked the fit body and the means by which it is achieved, namely sport and diet. I will show, too, how the fit body has repeatedly been equated on the show with a distinct lack of discipline, the very thing that it was expected to instill. Instead, I will argue that *The Sopranos* has implicated physical fitness in a consumer-oriented conception of masculinity, which emphasizes external superficialities over internal codes of honor and loyalty.

Peter Stearns has suggested that the emphasis placed on disciplining the body at the beginning of the twentieth century was meant to counterbalance the expanding realm of consumer society and the purchasing freedoms encountered by middle-class Americans. While consumption ran wild, the body remained a site onto which constraint could be levied and control re-established. The primary means for ensuring the maintenance of the fit body became sport and diet, which were heavily endorsed by the medical profession as well as an array of businessmen eager to capitalize on America's need for restraint (38–43). While being fit quickly became an aesthetic ideal, looking fit was often stressed as a sign of good character and inner resolve. "The need to fight fat remained a matter of demonstrating character and self-control in an age of excess" (117).

Michael Kimmel has similarly argued that sport and diet provide a means for middle-class manhood, stripped of its productive power, to reinvent itself according to a new consumable aesthetic, namely the muscular physique. Kimmel asserts that masculinity entered into a crisis period following the demise of the self-made man, or, "Marketplace Manhood," which had previously characterized masculine ideals at the turn of the twentieth century. "'Marketplace Manhood' describes this 'new man' who derived his identity entirely from success in the capitalist marketplace, from his accumulation of wealth, power, and capital" (13). Stearns suggests that the erosion of the relationship between manhood and production accompanied the emergence of the middle-class, which neither owned the means of production nor physically labored to create it, but profited greatly from the labor of others. "Greater abundance and intense but not clearly meaningful work in corporate management and service jobs created a real crisis in values" (118).

It also created a need, particularly for white, heterosexual manhood, to raid the proverbial cupboard for symbols that could be used to convince itself that it still had a firm grasp on the reins of power. "If manhood could no longer be produced, then it could be consumed, by the appropriation of symbols and props that signified earlier forms of stability." This transition from producible to consumable manhood engendered a shift from a notion of masculinity that was essentially inward-focused and defined itself according to principles of integrity and honor to one that was outwardly visible and concerned mainly with its appearance (Kimmel 20). The body became the primary focus of this external masculinity. If the fit body was a sign of self-constraint in the era of mass consumption, then it was equally a sign that masculinity had survived the move to the suburbs. "If the body revealed the virtues of the man, then working on the body could demonstrate the possession of virtues that one was no longer certain one possessed" (Kimmel 22).

Kimmel suggests that this aesthetically defined notion of manhood eventually became separated from its representational purpose of revealing the man within and became the principle means of assessing "real" masculinity.

> This preoccupation with the physical body facilitated the transition from inner directed men, who expressed their inner selves in the workplace and at home – that is, in their "real" lives – to other directed men, concerned with acquiring the culturally defined trappings that denoted manhood. The increasing importance of the body, of physicality, meant that men's bodies carried a different sort of weight than expressing the man within. The body did not contain the man; it was the man. (26)

Contrastingly, on *The Sopranos*, sport and diet have both been exposed as essentially sadomasochistic performances of violence upon the body, and furthermore, following Kimmel, the show has suggested that the connection between corporeal constraint and moral piety is an illusion. The inhabitant of the fit male body on the show is often less disciplined than his obese counterpart. In fact, on *The Sopranos*, it is corpulence that embodies the qualities of inner manhood, not vice versa.

With all the talk about obesity in this essay, it would be easy to assume that sport plays a minor role on *The Sopranos*. Quite the opposite. Tony's kids are both active in sports; Meadow in soccer and volleyball, AJ in football and swimming. Tony regularly attends his kids' sporting events and even frequents little league baseball games with Uncle Junior. On occasion, Tony has even been seen working out in his basement. Without fail, sports have been marked as either corrupt or potentially crippling. In the previous section, I suggested that it was not incidental that Davey Scatino, the "degenerate gambler," owns a sporting goods store. His public face in the world of fitness functions as a means of concealing his inner lack of constraint. Likewise, Meadow's soccer coach turns out to be a child molester, AJ vandalizes the very same swimming pool that he competes in, and Tony uses little league baseball games to conduct underworld meetings with Junior. In the third season, the relationship between sport, corruption, and a lack of restraint becomes even more explicit as Tony's sports betting operation becomes a prime focus of his criminality. Quite simply, Tony thrives off of "degenerate gamblers" who bet their money on sporting events. They represent his "busy season."

Sport on *The Sopranos* often functions, as well, as a site of violence against the body. This violence comes in many forms and is alternately sadistic, sadomasochistic, and voyeuristic. For instance, in "Big Girls Don't Cry" (2008), *The Sopranos* reveals the real function of a baseball bat, when Tony sends Furio into Bahama Skies Tanning Salon to collect an outstanding debt. Likewise, the psychological violence of Tony's golf game with Cusamano is dwarfed by the head bashing that Mustang Sally gives Bryan Spatafore with a golf club in "Another Toothpick" (3005). Even Mikey Palmice meets his demise while jogging in "I Dream of Jeannie Cusamano" (1013). The mere assertion that sports are violent, however, would be essentially redundant if not for the fact that on *The Sopranos* that violence is both self-inflicted and joyously consumed. In "A Hit is a Hit" (1010), Dr. Melfi is having dinner at the Cusamano's home when she hears what sound like violent shrieks of pain coming from Tony's house next door. Later in therapy she confronts him, asking if he heard anyone screaming in *agony* that night. Tony is mystified. At the culmination of the episode, however, it is revealed that it is, in fact, Tony who is torturously howling as he struggles to lift the weights on his Nautilus machine. The episode does not end, however, with Tony working out, but instead, we cut back to the Cusamano residence, where "Cooz" and his wife, Jeannie, are staring worriedly at the box that Tony has asked them to conceal – a box that the audience knows is filled with nothing but sand. In this sequence, the box, like Tony's body, becomes a vessel into which meaning is inserted. The Cusamanos assume that it contains heroin or a weapon, much as they assume that Tony is deviant partly because of his corporeal lack of restraint. As they fret, Tony's screams come bellowing through their kitchen window, and they look up alarmed at each other. They remain oblivious to Tony's self-inflicted pain and assume, like Melfi, that the screams are related to Tony's criminal behavior. The scene effectively communicates how little they know and, moreover, that the true sources of deviance in society remain unseen: namely the damage inflicted on the body through efforts to get it under control and the social inequities that place judgment on people (and boxes) according to external features, perpetuating this corporeal violence.

Tony, of course, is not innocent of these same hypocrisies. Not only does he participate (sparingly) in the infliction of pain on his own body through sport, but he actively gains pleasure in watching others suffer as well, including his own son. In "Fortunate Son" (3003), Tony attends AJ's high school football game. After a fumble and an attempted recovery, the camera dollies forward, capturing a pile of players toppled on top of one another. As the players pile off of one another, it becomes evident that AJ is at the bottom of the pile. The shot is filmed in slow motion, and even the soundtrack is slowed down so that it sounds warped. Overall, the sequence is both chilling and ominous. It adheres to oft-seen generic conventions that usually foreshadow some impending sport-related injury (think about any sports movie and this becomes immediately clear). A cut to Tony, standing and bellowing on the sidelines, adds to our distress. By slowing down the motion and the sound, it almost appears as if he is rising from his seat out of concern. As the camera cuts back to AJ, however, it quickly becomes evident that he has recovered the fumble. A final shot of Tony is accompanied by speeding up the image and the soundtrack to their normal speed. What appeared as frantic concern is instantaneously redefined as ecstatic cheering. The speeding up of the camera midway through the shot melds these supposedly opposing scenarios into one. Thus sports are revealed to be not only instruments of violence, often self-inflicted in the hope of gaining control over our bodies, but also sources of pleasure to be consumed precisely because of the imminent possibility of bodily harm. Rather than a source of discipline, on *The Sopranos* sports unleash our wildest indulgences in brutality and call attention to the sadomasochistic pleasure we gain in inflicting bodily pain on ourselves as well as wishing it upon others. Susan Bordo confirms the link between sport and the secret desire for aggression it unleashes when she claims that "as spectators, we find these 'displays of masculine aggression' exciting . . . precisely *because* they break with the taboos of civilization, and act out the (forbidden) aggression in us all" (*Male* 236). Or, as Dr. Melfi astutely responds to Tony's gloating about having sent Furio into the massage parlor with the baseball bat and his musing that he only wished it had been him instead, "giving the beating or taking it?" ("Big Girls Don't Cry"/2008).

Dieting, while rarely mentioned on the series, also occasionally figures into the fatness/fitness debate. The irony cannot be lost, for example, when Matthew Bevilaqua requests a diet soda as his last meal in life (though, in his defense, he is not smart enough to realize this, nor, as Pussy informs Tony, are there any non-diet drinks available even if he had a change of heart), especially when his execution scene is followed by one in which his executioners (Tony and Pussy) gorge themselves on steak and beers. Even in death, Bevilaqua denies himself anything fattening, which might lead to corporeal excess on his otherwise fit body. Tony and Pussy, on the other hand, reward themselves for their efforts with a full course meal. Instead of food, fit-bodied characters on *The Sopranos* consume drugs. Without passing judgment on drug usage, it is fair to say that fitness and drugs are not often understood as belonging in the same camp, and, at least on *The Sopranos*, drug usage is associated with irresponsibility, poor judgment, and a lack of discipline. Ralphie blames his violent outbursts at the Bada Bing! on his cocaine habit ("He is Risen"/3008). Likewise, Brendan Fallone blames his heroin addiction for his repeated, and finally, bungled, attempts to hijack trucks that belong to Junior, despite Tony's warnings to the contrary. He later pays the ultimate price for his lack of discipline ("Denial, Anger, Acceptance"/1003). Jackie Aprile Jr. also continues to pedal Ecstasy and engage in petty crime despite Tony's warnings against his getting involved in Mob life. Furthermore, when Jackie goes on the ill-fated hold-up that eventually costs him his life ("Amour Fou"/3012), the show makes sure to include a scene in which he and his friends comment on their being high. Impatient and eager to prove their manhood through reckless actions rather than careful planning and inner resolve, Jackie and his friends bungle the hold-up, and Jackie is later whacked by Vito Spatafore ("The Army of One"/3013). Similarly, Matthew Bevilaqua and his partner, Sean Gismonte, are seen lounging about their house, practically naked, smoking a bong just prior to their rash and ill-advised decision to shoot Christopher in order to score points with Richie ("Full Leather Jacket"/2008). They both later wind up dead because of their impetuousness (and arguably, because of their bodily display; more on this below). In each of these cases, the fit body is shown to engage in vices that simply are not corporeally visible. Moreover, as the narrative continuously emphasizes, these hidden vices prove a lot more costly than Tony's bodily excesses.

While dieting may not figure prominently on the series, the medical profession that endorses fitness does. This is significant because *The Sopranos* has repeatedly inverted the medical establishment's denouncement of fat bodies. Contrarily, illness on the series is often equated with weight loss and, more importantly, with a direct attack on the area of the body that has received the most attention from physicians and ordinary citizens alike when it comes to fat, namely the stomach. When Junior develops cancer it is in his stomach. Janice refers to Junior as "another toothpick" ("Another Toothpick"/3005), stressing the relationship between illness and thinness. When he goes in for surgery to have the tumor, along with a part of his stomach, removed, he experiences an hallucination in which the FBI cuts a deal with him, promising to cure his illness in exchange for his testimony. The medical invasion of Junior's stomach is analogous to the law seeking to bribe him into betraying his friends.

In "Funhouse" (2013), Tony contracts food poisoning. In that episode, his infirm dreams reveal to him what he had been denying all season long: that his close friend and corpulent conspirator, Pussy, has been working with the Feds. Tony's illness can thus be understood as a metaphor for Pussy's betrayal. In his dream, Tony envisions Pussy as a talking fish set upon a market display table. His first comment to Pussy is that he has lost weight. In the episode just prior to this one, "Knight in White Satin Armor" (2012), Pussy admits to FBI agent Skip Lipari that he realizes he has led a life of evil and corruption and wishes to repent. In other words, Pussy confesses that he, like his body, is deviant. (As previously asserted, obesity is tolerable only when the culprit admits his/her guilt.) This signals a complicity with the social order and a desire to achieve normalcy through slimming down. When Pussy doubly confesses to Tony in the dream that he is both working with the Feds *and* that he only weighs eight pounds, the two must be seen as inextricably linked. Pussy's betrayal of Tony is a betrayal of his own body and acquiescence to the society that criminalized him in the first place. Through the show's equation of Pussy's disloyalty with weight loss (the result of exercise, since he claims to have lost the weight swimming), a reworking of the fit body's supposed reflection of inner virtue occurs. Pussy's betrayal of his friends is a direct affront against the values that Tony repeatedly stresses to Dr. Melfi, which separate him and his men from more despicable criminals who enjoy inflicting pain on others – Tony and his crew act out of a sense of loyalty, honor, and a desire to preserve their heritage. In order to drive this point home, Pussy is depicted as a double rat, who lies to both sides and has no loyalty or honor other than to himself. As he tells Agent Lipari, "President Franklin is my best friend, and right now he's sitting in your pocket." The fit body thus carries none of the allegiances that Tony's corpulence seems to engender. Pussy's betrayal of this code is not only a betrayal of his body but also a disclosure of the essential moral hollowness of the fit male body.

As previously asserted, the fit male body has come to take the place of inner-directed manhood in Western culture. According to Michael Kimmel, however, it is merely an aesthetic, consumable image of masculinity that relocates a lost sense of productive power, and the resolute values that supposedly accompanied this position, onto the muscled physique. On *The Sopranos*, this body has been both stripped of its virtues and revealed to be complicit in the betrayal of the values of inner-directed manhood. Moreover, the fit male body has repeatedly been feminized on the show by placing it on display and calling attention to its concern for appearances. The problem, according to Susan Bordo, is that masculinity, in addition to redefining itself on the basis of the fit and muscled body, has also continued to be defined according to its blatant disregard for appearances. "Men are not supposed to enjoy being surveyed *period*. It's feminine to be on display" (Bordo, *Male* 173). To be looked at and admired has been repeatedly dismissed by white, heterosexual men as something desired by the "other," namely women, racial minorities and gay men. The latter two have often been feminized due to their supposed desire to call attention to themselves and their bodies. "The man who cares about his looks the way a woman does . . . is unmanly, sexually suspect" (Ibid. 200). Accordingly, masculinity, understood as the hegemony of straight, Caucasian men, has defined its power base as the ability to look without being looked at in return.

In "Why Do Cowboys Wear Hats in the Bath," Martin Pumphrey asserts that the visual display of the male body in cinema is highly problematic, denoting both effeminacy and weakness. Pumphrey's analysis centers less on the fit body than on the display of male nakedness and, alternatively, male concern for appearance that goes beyond mere functionality, which Pumphrey labels Dandyism. Both nakedness and Dandyism, Pumphrey argues, are cinematic signifiers of unmanliness precisely because they indicate a desire on the part of the perpetrator to call attention to the body, to be looked at.

> Not surprisingly, male display causes problems. For a man to betray a desire to be looked at (to make himself a willing object of the gaze) is to transgress the natural order of the genre. Though the hero may be distinguished by style, cleanliness and appearance, he cannot be seen to invite the pleasure-seeking gaze of other characters. Equally, although he is the focus of narrative attention, he cannot be explicitly transformed into an object for the spectator's (potentially erotic) contemplation. (54–5)

Not surprisingly, the fit male body on *The Sopranos* bears the brunt of these moments of nakedness and dandyism. In "Full Leather Jacket" (2008), when Furio goes to collect Tony's money from Matthew Bevilaqua and Sean Gismonte, they are both caught in their underwear. Their bodies are tightly muscled, but still, their nakedness adds to their vulnerability in the scene, which Furio capitalizes on by demanding an additional one thousand dollars. Their bodies, placed on display, also trigger a homophobic remark from Furio, who asserts (in Italian) that they must suck each other's cocks. (This insult is thrown back in Furio's face in "Amour Fou" [3012], when, after having been shot in the leg by Jackie Aprile Jr. and grimacing in pain on the doctor's table with his pants down, Tony comments about his girlish underwear.) Male nakedness on *The Sopranos* is often presented as a potentially dangerous and/or humiliating situation. Brendan Fallone is shot while taking a bath by Mikey Palmice. Paulie orders Christopher to strip as part of the policy of checking for wires on newly made guys. Once Christopher's pants are down, Paulie quickly berates his manhood: "I guess you could call that a dick" ("Employee of the Month"/3004).

Gismonte and Bevilaqua's emasculation is also accentuated in an earlier scene from "Full Leather Jacket" (2008) when they spot Tony going into the washroom at the Bada-Bing! Deciding to go into the washroom after Tony (thus placing Tony on display), they fastidiously adjust each other's hair and squirt breath spray down each other's throats. The concern for appearance is paramount. This over-emphasis on display is further ridiculed when they bungle their bathroom introduction to Tony and incur his ire by openly discussing their recent string of robberies. Real men, the show appears to suggest, are less concerned with looking the right way than with doing the right thing. In the end, Gismonte and Bevilaqua's nakedness and dandyism spell incompetence, as they not only screw up the bathroom encounter with Tony, but the attempted hit on Christopher as well. (Gismonte is killed by Christopher when he cannot get his seat belt unbuckled.)

Additionally, Gismonte and Bevilaqua are depicted as both desiring to be looked at and desiring to look, a particularly dangerous position to be in on *The Sopranos*, where bodily display already exists as a bit of a paradox. While there can be no doubt that the fit male body is the one regularly displayed unclothed (Tony even wears an undershirt during sex) as well as overly concerned with its appearance, fatness remains the more visible of the two body types. It is hard not to notice body types like Tony's, Pussy's, Skip's, Bacala's, Vito's. They stand out despite the rarity with which the show's narrative calls attention to them. There is simply so much more of them to be seen. Thus, the *desire* to be seen (or not to be seen) becomes of equal importance with the actual display of the body. In "Nobody Knows Anything" (1011), Paulie tries to ascertain if Pussy is a rat by inviting him to take a schvitz with him. Pussy declines on the grounds that his doctor has told him to stay away from steam. The scene, however, is accentuated by Paulie's increasing irritation over Pussy's refusal to take his clothes off. Despite Paulie's aggression and threatening pose, Pussy refuses to place his body on display. In "Full Leather Jacket," however, Gismonte and Bevilaqua, by following Tony into the washroom, potentially expose Tony's penis to their, as well as our, gaze. They force Tony to place his body on display. Similarly, in "Do Not Resuscitate" (2002) they spot Tony and Pussy parked at the top of a hill surveying the riot scene. As they approach, they turn the tables on Tony, who becomes the object to be looked at instead of the one doing the looking. As Tony speeds off, he angrily admonishes them, "I'm not supposed to be seen here." Thus, by the time Gismonte and Bevilaqua meet their demise, there is a growing list of reasons for them to be gotten rid of, which far exceed their botched attempt on Christopher's life. In addition to displaying their bodies and expressing excessive concern over their appearance, they have implicated Tony in the process as well.

As in the previous section, it must once again be pointed out that inconsistencies exist in the series. Clearly, Bacala is repeatedly placed on display by Tony, complicating the "fit body on display" pattern I have thus far established (though it should be noted that Bacala protests his exhibition, while the fit bodied examples I have provided, for the most part, do not). Bacala's objectification might serve to offset Tony's, but contrarily, it also manages to further vilify Tony by implicating him in the middle-class hypocrisy his own body otherwise rejects. A further inconsistency, particularly when it comes to the apparent rejection of the fit body that occurs on the show, can be found in Tony's encouragement of AJ's football career. Though Tony's body has been established as a bizarre mix of villainy and empathy, power and powerlessness, it nonetheless remains deviant to the extent that it breaks with the middle-class veneration of self-restraint. It has also been asserted that Tony is aware of this deviance and wants to prevent AJ from following in his footsteps. To this extent, Tony's support of his son's participation in sport makes perfect sense. Tony desires that AJ learn the values of discipline and good judgment, characteristics which consumer-based manhood has inscribed onto athletic competition.[6] Yet, as the show has continuously emphasized, these avenues for learning moral values are often self-destructive and counter-productive to their initial intent. AJ's violent displays of "manliness" are cheered on the football field but admonished when carried over to the real world, as in his destruction of school property when he vandalizes the swimming pool. Tony's inability to instill the values of "inner-directed" manhood in AJ without resorting to the very means that he, himself, has rejected as duplicitous and corrupt, namely fitness and sport, actually calls attention to one of the key paradoxes addressed by the series: the impossibility of reproducing the "self-made man" in a world ruled by consumption; the very consumption that was bread and butter of the "self-made man." This paradox is the focus of the concluding section of this essay.

The Self-Made Man as Cannibal

"Take me to the river."

Song sung by Big Mouth Billy Bass,
Pussy's reincarnation as a consumer fetish

"What was I supposed to do? That's my livelihood. It's how I put food on the table."

Johnny Soprano explaining to Tony, age 11,
why he had to cut off Mr. Satriale's pinkie finger

Until now, this essay has explored some of the ways the fat and fit body have been implicated in constructing meaning on *The Sopranos*. I have suggested that Tony's corpulence is vilified precisely because it is the object of envy within a culture that desires consumption but punishes itself for its indulgences. I have intimated that the fat body is merely an outward manifestation of the gluttony and corruption concealed by ideals of fitness. Thus Tony Soprano might be understood as a representation of what the middleclass does not want to admit about itself: that it loves to consume and that even its attempts at constraint only produce more sites of consumption, whether sporting events, drugs, or cosmetic touch ups. Finally, I have asserted that definitions of masculinity have been greatly affected by the decline of the "self-made man" and its replacement with a more aesthetic and consumable version of manhood, which reinvented itself according to superficial displays of fitness and muscle rather than internal systems of value. Consumable manhood developed out of a loss of direct contact with the means of production that accompanied the rise of the middleclass.

I have argued that on *The Sopranos* consumable manhood has been regularly attacked for its over-emphasis on appearance over codes of conduct.

Initially, Tony and his crew might seem to be the last remaining vestiges of "self-made manhood." For the most part, they exhibit indifference to their appearance and adhere to a code of conduct that values mental fortitude over a muscular physique. At this level of analysis, it might even be plausible to assert that *The Sopranos* as a series is concerned with trying to reassert self-made manhood in place of its more consumable version and that the distinctions between self-made and consumable masculinity are written onto the bodies of the show's characters. After all, in the *Sopranos* universe, fat people kill fit people. Fit people are often shown to be incompetent copycats of the lifestyle led by fat people. When fat people die, it is because they have betrayed their corpulent brethren and sided with the same law that criminalized them in the first place.

While generally accurate, this reading of the show misses out on much of the complexity that is involved in the corporeal relations depicted. In the end, it cannot be forgotten that Tony and his crew profit from the over-indulgence of the corporeally fit but spiritually weak. They run the sports betting racket; they run the drug trade. They produce the consumption by which middle-class masculinity has come to define itself. In fact, it might be argued that Tony's entire existence is the product of consumption. His office is in a strip club, where alcohol and naked women are constantly being consumed. His other bases of operation are Satriale's, the butcher shop, and Nuovo Vesuvio, the restaurant run by his friend Artie Bucco – both sites where consumption is produced and sold. Even Tony's "legitimate" business, waste management, profits from discarded consumer products.

If, on the one hand, Tony were truly interested in destroying consumer-based notions of masculinity, then it would seem paradoxical that he and his corpulent cohorts were doing so through over-consumption. After all, if consumable manhood is defined according to the fit body, then fatness would definitely be the antithesis, but fatness, of course, also requires a greater degree of consumption. If, on the other hand, Tony were simply attacking the constraints placed on the body as hypocritical in a world where consumption is not only rampant but also encouraged, then the fact that he violently imposes his own bodily constraints on those who defy him might seem to be a real contradiction.

In the end, Tony's body must be understood as the expression of self-made manhood's subsistence, which is consumption itself. In order for Tony to embody the values of self-made manhood, which asserts its identity through battle in the free market and the accumulation of capitol, then his girth can only be read as resulting from the profits he has reaped. Those profits are the result of producing the very consumption that causes overindulgence and its repressive counterpart constraint, and which lead, inevitably, one way or the other, to the destruction of the body. In other words, the self-made man that Tony embodies is, essentially, a cannibal, since he feeds off the destructive consequences of consumption. Is it mere chance that Matthew Bevilaqua, the fit-bodied dandy who merely wanted to emulate the type of masculinity that Tony and his crew project but which he could not produce himself, is killed by Tony and Pussy in a snack bar? At the very least, the location of his death begs the question, who is the snack? The answer, of course, is Matthew Bevilaqua. Alternately, is it a coincidence that in Tony's fevered dreams, Pussy confesses his betrayal in the body of a fish that is for sale at the market? Not only is Pussy's treachery equated with weight loss; he also literally becomes food that can be consumed. By submitting to the guilt and penance imposed by consumer society on those who over-indulge, Pussy becomes a mere object of consumption, defining himself in relation to the aesthetic symbols of manhood that are bought and sold on the open market. He becomes yet another image of deviant masculinity trying to reinvent itself. Furthermore, Pussy's transformation into an object of consumption is not complete until he shows up on Tony's desk as a singing, plastic mounted fish, Big Mouth Billy Bass, the ultimate consumer fetish with zero use value. When Tony sees the plastic mounted fish that has been placed on his desk as a gag, he is initially amused but is soon reminded of his dream and, in particular, of Pussy informing him that he now costs four dollars per pound. The human body has become a site of transaction, and what is being sold serves no tangible function. At least as food, Pussy's sacrifice to the realm of consumption might have provided nourishment, but as a plastic fish, he is merely an object of amusement. He has become the ultimate reminder that fatness is not only a symbol of scorn and ridicule in Western culture but, more importantly, as marketable a symbol as fitness is. Finally, Pussy's conversion into a commodity is a reminder to Tony of the role that he plays in the process. As a self-made man and a gangster, Tony is responsible for buying and selling the human body all the time, whether through bribes, extortion, intimidation, or murder.

It is this awareness of his essentially cannibalistic nature that is ultimately the greatest source of Tony's anxiety. Though he might loathe the lack of values, the hypocritical restraints, and the over-emphasis on appearance that dominate consumed-masculinity, Tony cannot abolish it without destroying himself. He also cannot live without the violence inflicted on the body or the restraints imposed to control it. These are his chief methods of ensuring his power. Tony is implicated in the creation of the very corporeal contradictions his own body seems to unravel.

In "Fortunate Son" (3003) Tony has a flashback to the first time he ever experienced an anxiety attack and lost control over his body. He was eleven-years old and witnessed his father, Johnny Boy Soprano, chop off the pinkie finger of Mr. Satriale, the butcher, who had owed Tony's father a gambling debt and had not paid up. As penance, Johnny Soprano took a pound of flesh. Tony, however, does not collapse until after he witnesses his father carving up the roast that Satriale has delivered as partial payment of his debt. It is the very connection between the infliction of violence on the body and the meat that he consumes that sets off Tony's attack. In this flashback, the cannibalistic metaphor is rendered nearly literal as the butcher shop that feeds the Soprano family becomes the spot where Satriale's own flesh is carved up by Tony's father, who later explains to his son, "this is my livelihood. It's how I put food on the table."[77] Tony's anxiety attacks are not only brought about by meat, as

Dr. Melfi suggests, but by the knowledge of where that meat came from – the body itself.

Tony Soprano's body arouses both revulsion and empathy precisely because it is caught up in a cycle of consumption from which it cannot escape. Tony is both in a state of revolt against middle-class validations of consumed masculinity, with their sanctimonious norms and self-imposed constraints, and the beneficiary of the successful commodification of the male body that has accompanied its rise. Self-made manhood is thus doomed to destroy itself. Its very reliance upon success in the capitalist marketplace in order to define its identity requires that it constantly exploit new areas of consumption. In *The Sopranos*, the search for consumable markets eventually leads back to the body and the various acts of violence and constraint that can be imposed upon it. Tony's body is the self-destructive body, not because fatness is unhealthy or aesthetically devalued, but because it represents the barbarous failures of self-made manhood to sustain itself without resorting to cannibalistic consumption, and hence destruction, of the very ideals of inner-directed masculinity it adheres to.

NINE

ONE FOR THE BOYS? *THE SOPRANOS* AND ITS MALE, BRITISH AUDIENCE

Joanne Lacey

If you really want to understand what the media means to people then you have to ask them.

Rodger Silverstone, *Why Study the Media?* (64)

Contextualizing *The Sopranos* for a British Audience

This essay sets out to explore what makes *The Sopranos* appealing to a male audience. In order to explore this question I undertook individual and group interviews with ten British men ranging in age from sixteen to fifty-five. (Short biographical profiles of the interviewees can be found at the end of this essay.) The respondents were gathered together through word of mouth contact and, in the case of the younger interviewees, through contact with a local college. Eight of the men are English, one Welsh, one Polish/Irish. They are white, non-Italian, and with the exception of one, are either from middle-class backgrounds and/or doing middle-class professional jobs. Two of the men are Catholics. In focusing on a male audience, I am not assuming either that all men like this show, because clearly they do not, or that it doesn't also attract a loyal female audience, because clearly it does (myself included), but that's another study.

The empirical, qualitative approach taken in this essay has a long history in media studies, where various kinds of audience study, using a range of different methods, have been undertaken. My commitment to qualitative research in relation to the media rests very strongly on the assertion put forward by Rodger Silverstone in the epigraph above. A qualitative approach to media audiences, however, is not without its limitations. Important markers of caution need to be placed around the selection, recording, and analysis of interview data. I would nevertheless argue that, as an approach, it gives us better access to the place of media texts in people's everyday lives. Men's relationships to popular media are under-represented in academic audience research. As Fred J. Fejes argues, "the paucity of empirical media research on masculinity at this point represents a challenge and an opportunity to media researchers, but also to the examination and redefinition of one of the fundamental ways we define and act out our reality" (22).

This essay seeks to explore the ways in which a particular group of British men make use of *The Sopranos* to understand their masculinity. In doing so it seeks to answer several important questions. How do men's investments in media texts negotiate the boundaries between men's psychological/emotional states and social existence? How might men make use of media texts in order to figure out what it means to be a man and to fantasize about possessing a different kind of masculinity? How, in short, does the media mediate between fantasies of masculinity and everyday life?

There are a number of avenues of investigation open to researchers who want to examine the cultural reception of a TV program – in this case *The Sopranos* in Britain. Thomas Austin, a British film researcher, argues for an integrated approach that looks at (1) an analysis of industry audience figures; (2) the reception and reviews around the media text in the press and on TV; and (3) empirical audience research. A combination of these three approaches may give researchers access to a fuller picture of how a media product is received culturally at a particular place and time. If we use such an approach to map *The Sopranos* in Britain what we begin to see is its status as a cult TV show, rather than one with mass appeal.

The pilot ("The Sopranos"/1001) was first shown on Channel 4 on 15 July, 1999. *The Sopranos* has never, despite its favorable reviews in the British press, made either the top ten in the viewing poll figures for digital and cable television (thus always drawing less than 1.2 million viewers) or the top 30 viewing poll figures for terrestrial television (thus always drawing less than 1.8 million viewers). On the digital channel E4 the third season of *The Sopranos* drew significantly fewer viewers than repeats the same weeks of *Ally McBeal* and *Sex and the City*. It is important to understand that the audience of *The Sopranos* in Britain may well be considered a cult one. It is followed avidly not by a mass audience such as exists for *Friends*, *Big Brother*, or *Ally McBeal* but rather by a significant number of people within a particular sector of the public (older, professional, educated) whose relationship to the show has been carefully represented and reviewed in particular newspapers, specifically *The Observer*, *The Independent*, *The Guardian*, and *The Telegraph*. Since it helps to pinpoint who actually watches it, the relationship between viewing figures and the coverage and review of the show in the British press is significant. The tabloid press have scantily covered it, focusing mainly on the humor of a balding Mafioso with a mid-life crisis. The broadsheets, however, whose target audience is a middle-class educated one, have given the show extensive coverage in their review sections, thus indicating that the British audience for *The Sopranos* has also been drawn from this section of society. The cultural reception of *The Sopranos* in the broadsheet press has framed it as a quality, unmissable drama: "A modern masterpiece" (*The Guardian* 6 June 1999); "The best show on television" (*The Observer* 15 October 2000); "The best television drama to have come out of the US in decades, and currently the best drama showing anywhere on British television" (*The Financial Times* 1 September 1999). I would not want to characterize the British audience for *The Sopranos* in absolute terms; there are, of course, crossovers in the social classifications of its viewers. However, the cultural reception of the show in the British press may well indicate viewing trends, which may well, in turn, be reflected in the responses of my interviewees.

When I have spoken to people about my *Sopranos* research, the response has often been: isn't it obvious why men would like it – gangsters, guns, and violence? What else is there to say? This kind of comment reduces the narrative complexity of the show and of the male viewer's experience to caricatured levels of engagement. However, a number of key themes emerge out of the analysis of the interviews. The interviewees' responses raise extremely interesting questions about (1) the male audience's relationship to drama on television, particularly to American drama; (2) the structure of men's lives today and their negotiation of codes of work, family, leisure, and the relationship between masculinity and responsibility; and (3) the enduring (and perhaps problematic) potent appeal of the Italian-American gangster as a signifier of masculine power, control, and protection.

THE SOPRANOS AS TV DRAMA

For all of the interviewees, the main stated reason for enjoying *The Sopranos* was its status as well written, well crafted, well acted television. This was not, the interviewees insisted, "trash" TV:[1]

"I picked up on stuff that was written here in the media. . . . I read a review by Simon Hoggart who I've got some time for, who said that *The Sopranos* was the best thing on TV. I'm usually fishing around for something worth watching, and it set me up to watch it. I'm interested that you're doing this because I've been thinking myself about why I found it attractive. I think there's something about the *vérité* appearance of it isn't there? Although it clearly isn't that. . . . I have to say that I was extremely impressed by the way that it was structured, by the characters, by the very peculiar idea of a Mafioso going into psychoanalysis." (John)

"It's a quality American drama, it's got a bite of reality to it. At its bottom line it's just a well crafted, a well-written piece of drama that has different story lines. It's a more hard hitting drama than you would typically get on British TV." (Alex)

"Great writing, great acting. Intriguing premise – all-powerful crime overlord when at work, neurotic family man with parent problems when at home." (Dereck)

"This was a good show, something more serious, not in a lad's mag kind of way." (Rodger)

"If it was a cowboy film or a cowboy series, it almost has to follow a logic where one character is introduced into it, and there's problem, conflict, resolution, there's a problem, there's a solution, one of them gets shot. In gangster films, if you like, the characters are introduced ten years before, and you watch the way that people respond to the character over time. You don't perceive the problem there and then, so I think with *The Sopranos* it didn't really matter that I didn't see it in sequence." (Nathan)

"Most of the stuff that comes out of America is rubbish, it's sanitized and simplistic, but this isn't, it's terrific, it has this richness of character . . . it's great entertainment, and it's quite Shakespearean. . . . *The Sopranos* are like little self-contained dramas every week." (Chris)

For the interviewees the Americaness of the show is significant. This Americaness is, of course, a particular version of Italian-Americaness that may represent as much of a fantasy, mythology, and stereotype to American audiences as it does to British. From my research it is apparent that America operates in *The Sopranos* as a landscape of both the foreign and the familiar. The filmic urban signifiers of mob life are familiar to this audience, particularly New York, Vegas, and the eerie serenity of the Corleones' Lake Tahoe. All of my interviewees have built up a fairly detailed mob "cultural capital."[2] They are fans in general of mobster movies. *The Sopranos* is, of course, TV not film, but its visual iconography and its intertextual references to other representations of the Mafia on film align it quite closely to a filmic heritage. If *Public Enemy* (1931), *The Godfather* trilogy (1972, 1974, 1990), *Married to the Mob* (1988), *GoodFellas* (1990), and *Analyze This!* (1999) didn't exist, then neither would *The Sopranos*. If Don Corleone, Paul Cicero, and Tony Russo didn't exist on film, then Tony Soprano wouldn't exist on TV. David Chase has said that "my biggest challenge was to change the way that the Mafia are represented, and to show that those films are out of date" (*The Guardian* 6 June 1999). If all of these film texts did not exist, then a British audience would not be able to "get" *The Sopranos*. My interviewees could articulate quite clearly how *The Sopranos* was similar to and different from *The Godfather*, for example:

"Just because it's about gangsters doesn't mean that it's the same as *The Godfather*. That's like saying that all war movies are the same or all sci-fi is the same." (Dave)

"The godfather is the Italian-American immigrant, which is where the roots of *The Godfather* lie. Tony is a second/third generation American with American roots. *The Godfather* was that much more . . . operatic, sort of like grand scale cast of thousands . . . it's very different, it's got a different kind of feel to it. You get the sense in *The Sopranos* that these guys are much more in the trenches." (Alex)

"Vito and Michael are nowhere near this street level. *The Sopranos* is much more *Donnie Brasco*, that level. Al Pacino trying to knock open a parking meter, you know what's all that about? The big end deal is *The Godfather* series, this is street level crime." (Nathan)

For this audience *The Sopranos* works because it can be generically differentiated. They know their American mobsters, and they know where and how Tony fits. This audience also knows its British gangsters, and has followed the British cinema's resurgence of interest in the genre lately in recent films such as Guy Ritchie's *Lock, Stock and Two Smoking Barrels* (1998) and *Snatch* (2000), yet when the interviewees were asked if they could imagine a dramatic serial based on the life of a British gangster being as compelling to them, they all said no. Clearly part of the appeal of this show for the interviewees is that it continues to represent the iconography of a particular Italian-American culture and mob masculinity in which they are already invested. For the younger interviewees, there is a more blatant articulation of the Italian-American mobster as a powerful, stylish renegade, whose ethnicity and geographical location lend heavily to his appeal as Other. The British gangster is too close to home. "The Mafia mobster is cool, the way that they speak, the cars, the clothes, I could quite fancy being there" (Tom). "There" is not specified as a geographical location; "there" is more of a fantasy landscape of cool. When I asked them about the "coolness" of recent British gangsters in film, Matt said, "It's not the same, they speak with cockney accents, and we can get on the train and be in London in an hour, and if you went to find them in Soho or whatever then you could." Whether or not Matt actually could isn't significant here; what is significant is the geographical and otherworldly distance between a non-Italian British audience and the Italian-American mobster. The cultural codes and rules of belonging to "the family" – codes and rules that they have acquired watching film and television – manufacture a world, an already dramatic world that they can never really see on the street. This idea emerged even in some of the interviews with the older men. Unanimously, the Americanness of the show constitutes a huge part of its appeal, but that Americanness is a specifically coded Italian-Americanness equated to mob existence; it's a surface, a set of stylistic signifiers (suits, cars, and jewelry), dialects (learning mob speak),[3] and geographical markers (the pizza parlor, the coffee shop, the restaurant, the basement, the butcher's). These ingredients are needed in order to map out the coordinates of their knowledge of mob culture and to mobilize their engagement in an escapist narrative.

Because it stretches the co-ordinates of a landscape of fantasy the men already know to encompass precisely the same kinds of domestic, emotional, and work-related dramas they are negotiating in their own lives, *The Sopranos* becomes particularly potent as a representation of the "known" codes of mob life for the older men, who have to negotiate a different set of responsibilities in relation to work, finances, and home. Tony not only embodies the powerful and seductive signifiers of Mafia masculinity (power, belonging, protection) but also negotiates the drudgeries, normalcies, and tensions of domestic life. He's getting older, he has a belly, he's balding, and he's a bit lost. As a compelling and beautifully crafted dramatic character, Tony Soprano functions as a cipher for the lived contradictions of the British middle-aged, or middle-aging, middle-management lifestyle but with the escapist fantasies attached to Mafia masculinity. As a point of identification for male audiences, he has the fantasy components integral to the Italian mobster's dark, ethnic charisma: "Mafia gangsters are just gangsters who happen to be Italian," *The Sopranos'* fictional mob expert Jeffrey Wernick states, anxious to correct a wrong impression. "Not for me. If they weren't Italian through and through, from the cut of their suits to the cut of their pasta, I wouldn't be interested" (Rucker). And David Chase argues, "we love mobsters because they look like they have strong identities and the rest of us don't" (Rucker interview). Chase's position is echoed in my interviews. Chris explains, "the *idea* of [gangsters] is just so fantastic, they are the antidote to bland existence" (my emphasis). As Chris goes on to say:

> "Modern life is about suburban life, it's quite prosaic really, modern life is about that and nothing else, you know going to the supermarket, getting your trolley, parking your car, how dull. So you've got that world, but then it's embedded in this mediaeval, you know war lords and robber barons, that sort of thing, and you almost long for the soup to be stirred a bit, so that life isn't just about parking the car, weeding the garden, although that's nice enough, so it's seductive in that way, but of course the reality is that you wouldn't want to go anywhere near it, it would be absolutely horrendous, but you are attracted by it."

The Sopranos also moves the action out of New York and into the suburbs of New Jersey, thus contextualizing the action of Tony's world in an (at times) suffocating local space. Somehow, the local vernacular brings Tony closer to the audience. "It's a good thing, you don't get this stereotypical kind of Italian-American little Italy kind of thing. It's refreshing to see a different set of shots about and around New York" (Dave). "It's New 'Joisey' but that's also a product, that's his operating environment, his particular patch. They have it all sewn up, stitched up between them" (Alex). Tony's world is as circumscribed by the demands of home and work as most of the interviewees. His office may be in a strip club, but it's still an office, and his wife still calls him there to get home early for dinner.

THE SOPRANOS AS A SOAP OPERA

The emphasis on the uninspiring suburban vernacular of New Jersey and the limited spaces within which we actually see Tony and other characters operate invites the interviewee's identification of *The Sopranos* as functioning like "soap opera for men." The generic characteristics of soap are multifaceted, and the distinction between a soap and a dramatic serial is complex. Traditionally, soaps place narrative emphasis on the domestic and emotional lives of characters. A narrative openness, a rejection of anticipated endings or closure characterizes the action, which takes place in a very localized setting. One of the defining characteristics of soaps, of course, has been the assumption that they are made for a female audience – that they follow stories and characters that will engage women, are scheduled at times that they can watch, and provide a community of gossip for female viewers. These audience demographics have been changing for some time in Britain and in America as soaps have found new audiences, including millions of college students and non-college age men (shift workers, the unemployed).

Among those I interviewed *The Sopranos* was viewed like a soap in the way that the men became intensely involved on a weekly basis with the characters (particularly Tony) and their stories, feeling as if they had got to know them and, also significantly, discussing the show with other men at work, or in the pub. When *The Sopranos* was positioned by them as a kind of soap opera, it wasn't done in a derogatory sense, as though this somehow softened/feminized its status, but rather as a means of generic re-possession that at once recognized the importance of the dramatic structure and the characterization of soap opera for women as a means of extra-textually providing them with a community of discourse and gossip at work or at leisure. They had been missing out on something, and *The Sopranos* gave them a way into owning a drama and at the same time marking it as masculine TV territory. Dave and Chris both said that they talked about the show with other men at work or in the pub. As Dave remarked, "it's unusual because I don't ever have conversations about telly." Some of the other comments about *The Sopranos* and soap are equally as interesting.

> "Sometimes it has a touch of *Dallas* about it when you think, oh that dream sequence is a little over-worked, but there's a definite element of escapism about it, Adorno and Horkheimer aside (laughs). The pleasure is of course not realized pleasure; you are always hanging on for the next bit of the story. Interest and pleasure is carefully sustained." (John)

> "Its important to me, and to the people around me who are talking about it. We care what happens to these people, more than any soap opera. It's not just for men though, a lot of men watch soap operas. It's a soap opera for men who are different from the normal culture, from *Sun* and *Mail* reader culture. There's so much more to it than a soap, and things last a lot longer, but yes basically it's soap opera." (Nathan)

THIS THING OF OURS

Tony Soprano's difficult juggling of the responsibilities of home, work and family resonates strongly with those I studied. A poignant and deeply felt identification with Tony Soprano as a man struggling to do his best in a difficult world was apparent. Undoubtedly one of the great dramatic achievements of the script is the phenomenal way in which Tony Soprano is at once Capo and suburban husband and father, doing a job and living a life. This sentimental/empathetic identification is especially apparent in the following dialogue with Dave.

> Dave: Tony Soprano is a gangster and a husband and a father. In lots of ways he's just a bloke, any bloke, earning and living under stress.
> *JL: Is that how you see Tony, as someone who's just earning a living?*
> Dave: What comes across to me quite strongly is that he's trapped in it.
> *JL: What would you say it's about? What's the main theme?*
> Dave: I'd say the main theme is, like I said, it's about life, earning a living, dealing with your wife, dealing with your family.

And it is echoed many times in the interviews.

> "These boys don't lead a nine to five life do they? They don't have to get up and do the commute to work everyday; they are all wealthy . . . they have their stresses! They have strains on them. Tony has to juggle his work and his personal life; he has issues and stresses the same as any other business man." (Alex)

> "He's in many ways an ordinary 'Joe Schmoe' – has problems with his kids, his mother/uncle, and doesn't always win. . . . In *The Sopranos* there is at least as much about domestic matters as about racketeering. The Sopranos have as much of the Simpsons about them as the Corleones, and Tony is often as much like Homer as he is Vito." (Dereck)

> "He's very protective of his family and business. Hard, but also vulnerable – probably a bit too thoughtful for his own piece of mind." (Nathan)

> "I can identify with Tony because the fact that he does a stressful job, he's a man in the workplace, just like anybody else, he's a gangster, he kills and he lives with the threat of being killed . . . but really there's not that much violence, and this fellah, if he was a doctor or a lawyer or a dentist or a high powered business exec, would still have pressures, would still have stress. He has to deal with his job, with his wife, with his fucking mother, with his fucking kids . . . I mean this guy has needs, blokes have needs too. . . . You feel for the guy, you can identify with him, at the same time there's the fantasy, looking at him and thinking wouldn't it be good to be able to dot, dot, dot." (Rodger)

Rodger goes on to say later in the interview, "the old social roles for men don't hold up anymore, and the main theme I suppose is that men are trying to find their way. It's very unclear, very unclear, how men should react." Rodger's position prises open a contemporary and far-reaching cultural and political debate relating to the status of masculinity in crisis. The discourse of masculinity in crisis has been played out in TV, film, newspapers, magazines, novels, education, social and welfare policy, psychology, sociology. Men are in trouble. Barbara Ehrenreich traces the historical decline of patriarchy in America. She defines patriarchy as "the intimate power of men over women, a power which is historically exercised within the family by the male as breadwinner, property owner, or armed defender of women and children" (284). Ehrenreich's detailed historical analysis is important and scholarly. Other academics and social commentators have pursued a similar quest in seeking to trace the decline of men's certainties in their role and identity. Because of the intersection of a number of social and historical factors, men are lost. The image of a mobster on Prozac and in therapy has been read by the British press as not only a humorous generic development in representation of the mob boss, but also as a comment on the state of men's lives in general. "He is carrying the weight of his generation on his shoulders," we read, "a generation that's failed the promise its parents gave it. 'I feel like I've come in at the end,' he says to his shrink, 'like I missed the best bits'" (*The Guardian* 6 June 1999). James Watson, writing in *The Telegraph* in July 1999, links the representation of the Mafia's mid-life crisis to the mid-life crisis of the middle-aged audience for *The Sopranos* in Britain.

Among my interviewees, Rodger articulated identification with Tony on this level most strongly:

"I'd like to see [Tony] find a way out, away from the expectations of his family, of everyone. I'd like to see him figure out who the fuck he wants to be, to do what he wants to do so that he can say 'fuck you.' I'd like the same for myself."

Rodger was certainly not the only man to feel his own social estrangement in relation to the characterization of Tony. Nathan, the youngest interviewee, identified what he saw as his own loss of men's spaces for socializing and communicating and described how he felt envious that Tony and his friends could be in the back room at the Bada Bing! where there were no women, and they could talk and be together. Nathan also articulates the specific loss of a heterosexual "lads" culture in Brighton – a Southern English town that has a significantly larger gay community than most others and a significant number of social spaces in which gay men can come together. He expresses a resentment drawing on his own experiences and sense of loss as a young heterosexual male:

"I do think there's something that is lost. Maybe it's this town. I'd have to go back home. There blokes and women go out, they do this pub tour, but they are always one behind each other, and then meet up at the end, and so you've got the lads space. In Brighton that doesn't happen. In this town, for me, if there's any one culture that's been eroded, it's the lad's culture. That's what's missing, and then I look at that [*The Sopranos*] and I think, what a great life, they get to hang out with their mates and talk rubbish. . . . I remember in [Season 2] when they've got all that stuff from the war ["House Arrest"/2011], and they're just playing, you know it's wonderful."

The young men (aged sixteen to eighteen) that I talked to dipped in and out of *The Sopranos* on a week to week basis; neither loyal nor dedicated viewers, they often watched the show with their parents. These young men were critical of imagined older viewers' heavy investment in the show, both in terms of time and identity. Their sporadic viewing of the show was the result of the fullness of their social lives; they watched "depending on what else was going on" (Tom). Jon argued that "we can't watch every week or think that much about it because we're not saddo's sitting at home – we have a life." Interestingly, however, these young men did follow soaps on a regular basis, particularly *EastEnders* and *Neighbours*; unlike some of the older men, they did not need to find substitute soaps. *The Sopranos'* schedule on British Television has clearly influenced viewing practices. First runs of the first two seasons of *The Sopranos* were shown on a Thursday night – an important night in the young men's social calendar, marking the end of the week and "getting ready for Friday" (Liam). *Neighbours*, on the other hand, is shown nightly at 5.35pm, and *EastEnders* is broadcast three times a week at 7.30 or 8.00pm. The scheduling of these shows does not intrude into a night out; *The Sopranos* would. For the young men that I talked to, a dedication to any show screened after the 9.00pm watershed was seen as a bit "sad." In a group setting only one young man, Liam, was open about his loyalty to the show.

The young men, however, did not articulate the same sense of end-of-the-week-fatigue the working men expressed. For them the most common reason for missing episodes was exhaustion. "I made a special effort to watch it. I'm normally knackered by then" (Dave). "I simply can't guarantee to watch it. If I'm awake enough and haven't got anything else to do then yes I will watch it" (John). "It was on quite late, so it depended on whether I was awake or not, but I watched it regularly" (Chris).

Within the structures of everyday life of the older men interviewed *The Sopranos* occupied a significant location. Older men connected to the representation of generation and work and family responsibilities shown in *The Sopranos*. At 24, Nathan – who straddles the lack of responsibility for work and family of the 16–18 year-olds, all of whom still lived at home, and the family and work responsibilities of the 33–55 year-olds – was especially interesting. With no children or mortgage but a responsible high-pressured job and a career to build, Nathan's use of *The Sopranos* to imagine a space in which men had power and autonomy, a space in which they could figure out who they were as men, opens up interesting possibilities for understanding a cross-generational reception of the show. In many ways Nathan's investment in *The Sopranos* was the most passionate, in as much as he used the embodiment of social spaces by the characters in the show to reflect on the different spaces he inhabited in his own life. The 16–18 year-olds did not make the same kinds of links between the show and the circumstances of their everyday lives. In many ways the narrative exploration of Tony's contradictory relationships between home, work, and family passed them by as something that "my parents are probably interested in more" (Jon). They identified more strongly with Meadow Soprano (struggling with her identity as the child of a mobster), Livia Soprano (who was perceived as funny), and Christopher (whom they thought cool). They did not regard the show's focus on an aging mobster and his world as excluding them as viewers and judged the show as "appealing to all ages" because of the depth of characterization of different generations within familial framework of *The Sopranos*.

The fantasy of being a mobster and a "made" guy provided an interesting generational cross over point in the interviews. All of the 16–18 year-olds, apart from Liam (who acutely observed the characterization of the mob life in *The Sopranos* as mixing in equal measure "cool autonomy with terrifying violence and social responsibility"), saw the appeal of the mob life as offering a chance for men to "live beyond the expected rules of society" (Tom). "They don't have to obey the rules and they belong to something" (Jon). "I'd love to live with that sense of being protected, of having another family to call on" (Matt). The older interviewees were also invested in the escapist potential of the figure of the mobster as a point of mediation between social existence as a man and fantasies of masculinity, as is apparent in the following exchange:

JL: *This genre has a particular history, an appeal as being somehow glamorous. Why do you think that is?*

Alex: It's the same as being a rock star or a football star, or anything like that, it has the potential to be a very glamorous lifestyle. Look at Tony's rise through the ranks, going to smart restaurants, drinks bought for him, all the rest of it, yeah it's that sort of stuff really, but every so often you get the price being paid for it by at least one character, and that's the violence that goes with it because they live outside the law, you don't have recourse to lawyers to sort out your contractual obligations. But that's the other side to it – obviously that has a certain glamor as well as long as it's happening to somebody else.

JL: *Do ever dream of being a made guy?*

Dereck: Only when I'm treated with disrespect.

JL: *What is it about the gangster that's so compelling for you?*

Nathan: I think about this, and my dad's literature and films are cowboy films, and I think it's the modern-day cowboy film. As blokes we can't walk into bars and punch people out straight away, but we can sit back and look sultry and powerful, and I think that element there it's always the dream, not entirely, but sometimes you think, yeah that would be OK.

Chris further situates the idea of the gangster as a compelling "antidote to bland existence." He goes on to say,

> "Modern life is so prescribed, you know you do your nine to five, structures in society are very clear, but here you have a world that's outside of that, that works with a totally different code of ethics, power structures that have no relation to the law, democracy might just as well not exist . . . it's about deep loyalties and betrayals and that's why it's quite mediaeval."

Rodger talks a lot about the imagined fantasies and fears of living Tony's life. What appeals most to him about the gangster as a fantasy figure here is his ability to live a life beyond accepted social structures and expectations. Interestingly, he sees Tony as the embodiment of the millennium gangster as a good role model for a man who knows his place in the world. He finds Tony's vulnerability to be symptomatic of his willingness to take responsibility for his actions: "These guys know that they are doing wrong morally, but in a lot of ways they can't act any differently, they were born into it, it's an accident of birth. In some ways that's what everyone else might think, what else could I have done if I were born someone else."

The space between fantasy identification and the distancing of male viewers is one that is mediated by the materiality of everyday life. The figure of the gangster in general (in terms of the male interviewees' filmic/media mob education) and its performance in *The Sopranos* in particular offers an escapist fantasy, a surface, a heavily styled body upon which to play out fantasies of power, protection, belonging – living outside the law. This is grounded by the knowledge that being a gangster means being violent, or living under the very real threat of violence. In *The Sopranos* the violence is seen to be realistically portrayed as an integral part of the gangster's everyday life:

> "It's all ruthless and nasty. I suppose, it's just business, part of the job."
> (Dave)

> "It does push at the edge of screen violence versus grizzly real-life violence. In *The Sopranos* one has to keep reminding oneself that one is dealing with art violence, rather than true-life violence . . . the mediocrity of everyday violence they seem to have got over rather well, with an artistic kick and a moral question mark." (John)

> "The violence is shown as being necessary. Richie Aprile is shown as being unnecessarily violent, and that's why we see him as being bad. For Tony violence is for a reason and is seen to be completely justified. Chris is seen to have gone off the rails because he was violent against a civilian. It is a violent world that they live in, but everything is necessary." (Nathan)

Chris also sees the violence shown as representing an integral part in their world: "It's unsanitized, it's not voyeuristic, not violence for its own sake." Apart from Dave, none of the men interviewed said that they had ever lived with violence or knew gangsters in real life. Nevertheless, Tom, Jon, Liam and Matt all said that they would quite fancy living the life of a made guy, describing it as being "a laugh," admiring its surface or style – great clothes, great mates, freedom, protection. This surface was also tempered by their knowledge of the other side of it. As Matt says, "in some Mafia stuff that you see, like *Analyze This!* or *My Cousin Vinnie* or *Married to the Mob*, the comedy takes away from the violence. In *The Sopranos* it's just so brutal. It makes you see it how it probably is. I couldn't live like that." Liam says, "I would quite fancy looking the part and having the respect and all that, but I know that there's no way that I could ever hurt anybody, let alone kill anybody. If you can't do that then you can't really be a gangster can you?"

Given the very clearly articulated critical examination of the show that John offered at most points in the interview, he still had anxieties about his own pleasure and enjoyment of "gangsterdom as a kind of deprivation of culture that has become a force and one could say the major crime force in the twenty-first century." His anxiety was rooted in a concern that "it might just be about the producers, creators and purveyors. It's about them. One could draw out the example of a nice macho boy's movie. In which case that's nasty." I asked him why he though this was nasty.

> "Oh you know boy's toys, boy's guns, the idea that you can be swaggering and nasty and also humane. It's an idea that we were all brought up with. It's an old fashioned form of thought. It doesn't offer the possibility of a new kind of non-macho, non-violent. New forms of thinking. It's a form of masculinity that's reprehensible, but I think that it's a form of the constructed male that's very difficult to avoid. You try to be self-conscious and you try to avoid it, and yet when you go into automatics, and find that you are playing it out, so yes it's very dangerous and insidious. If the film is good, or the series is good, it's offered up for you to reflect on, to think about what you can do with it, but if it merely reinforces it . . ."

In focusing on men and the media, this essay has stepped into a gap in the audience research market. It is important to look at the ways in which men make use of the media, and at the ways in which the media mediates their everyday lives. I am not trying to prescribe the ways in which all men watch *The Sopranos*. I have offered extracts from particular readings of the show. I have identified a number of key areas of interest that emerged across the interviews. These relate to men's relationships to dramatic structures on television, questions of fantasy and identification and the negotiation in daily life of the structures of work, family, and leisure. A supposed crisis in masculinity has been extensively debated across the pages of the popular press and in academic writing. If we use the media in order to make a certain kind of sense of who we are, then an exploration of men's uses of particular media might enable a greater understanding of how men see themselves, and how men would like to be seen. An exploration of the particular cultural uptake of specific media texts might allow deeper insights into, not only the media text itself, but also the communities in which it circulates and produces meanings and identities at specific times.

Biographical profiles:

Alex, 33, Welsh – finance director
Rodger, 35, English – chartered accountant
Dereck, 43, English – solicitor
Chris, 43, English – web developer
John, 55, Irish/Polish – lecturer
Nathan, 24, English – bar/restaurant manager
Liam, 17, English – student
Jon, 17, English – student
Matt, 16, English – student
Tom, 18, English – student

"CUNNILINGUS AND PSYCHIATRY HAVE BROUGHT US TO THIS": LIVIA AND THE LOGIC OF FALSE HOODS IN THE FIRST SEASON OF *THE SOPRANOS*

Joseph S. Walker

"I don't have to admit anything."
Livia Soprano

"I'm a man. And you're a woman. End of story."
Tony Soprano to Dr. Jennifer Melfi

Actually, the story *begins* with a man and a "woman": in the first shot from the first episode of *The Sopranos*, as Tony Soprano sits on a small couch in Dr. Jennifer Melfi's waiting room, his body is framed for the viewer by the green metal legs of the small statue of a female nude across the room. Hands folded passively in his lap, his eyes initially closed and his head tilted downward, Tony blinks, then appears to look up into the offscreen nether regions of the figure; a reverse shot gives us the serene face of the sculpture, her own arms raised gracefully above and behind her head, her nipples prominent. The third shot, from a different angle, returns to and brings us nearer to Tony, and the camera begins a slow tracking movement to come still closer to him; his facial expression at this point registers confused apprehension as he continues to look at the sculpture. Again, an answering reverse shot tracks in on the face of the statue, reinforcing the impression of a connection or even an exchange between the two; the brief, completely silent sequence is then disrupted by the entrance of Dr. Melfi and her call for "Mr. Soprano." These subsequent shots only enhance the effect of extreme restriction and excessive anxiety immediately conveyed by the initial image, in which Tony is contained, pinned in, not only by the legs of the statue (which are barely far enough apart to permit a view of him), but also by the blinds dropped across the window behind him (unavoidably calling to mind prison bars), by the cluttered furniture, and perhaps most of all by the small size of the room, particularly in relation to his already obvious physical bulk. It is a visual composition which is easily read, which indeed demands to be read, as a symbolic foreshadowing of the program's central drama of Tony's conflict with his mother, Livia – a shorthand reference to the complex relations of birth, subservience, sex, fear, desire, and guilt which connect them, and which have essentially incapacitated Tony.

Such a reading, of course, depends upon the viewer having an existing knowledge of the remainder of *The Sopranos* text. It depends no less upon a careful positioning of the camera, the purely hypothetical eye; Tony himself, clearly, cannot share our perception of his appearance in this frame. For that matter, despite the shot/reverse-shot structure which links them, we get no sense here of Tony's distance from the statue, or even its actual size. Our understanding of the relationship between the two figures and its meaning, then, is necessarily dependent upon knowledge and perspectives utterly external to the actual content of the scene, and, vitally, utterly external to Tony's own experience. The treatment of Tony here creates a sense of distance rather than sympathy or identification; he is made the object of our televisual gaze, but equally the object of our narratively and visually informed judgment. His silence and immobility throughout the sequence speak to his powerlessness, his almost total lack of agency, as the focus of such objectification.

This becomes particularly clear if the waiting room scene is contrasted with the opening scene of the *second* episode of *The Sopranos*, "46 Long." This episode begins with a tight close-up of a television screen on which a talk show host is saying, "John Gotti – life in prison, no chance of parole." Between "prison" and "no chance," a cut reveals that the television is in the back room of the Bada Bing!, where Tony, Silvio Dante, and Paulie Walnuts are sitting around a table counting a large pile of money. Christopher is at another table, smoking and lifting weights; a few seconds into the scene Big Pussy enters the frame, dumps more money onto the pile, and then crosses to a desk where he begins reading a newspaper. For the remainder of the scene – which lasts a little over three minutes – the television host and his guests (including Vincent Rizzo, a former Mafia soldier turned "government witness and best-selling author") discuss the decline of the Mob in America, while Tony and his four associates chat idly and continue to count their money.

It is immediately obvious, even from this minimal description, that the opening moments of these two episodes differ in at least one important respect: the oppressive silence of the waiting room is displaced by the multiple voices of conversation, both from the TV and in the counting room itself. The visual contrast is equally striking. Where Melfi's waiting room is clean, sterile, well-lit, and filled with soft colors, the counting room is cluttered with cheap furniture and waste, broken up by bright lights (including several neon advertisements) and deep shadows, and filled with garish images. Put most simply, an array of cultural codes tells us we have moved from a feminized to a masculine space. Where Melfi's waiting room is dominated (at least in the views given the audience) by the figure of an empowered and austere woman, the back room of the Bada Bing! – a strip club, let it be remembered – is not only occupied by five aggressively masculine characters (themselves further echoed by the three men chatting around a table on the talk show), but ringed with posters of boxers (including Robert De Niro in *Raging Bull*, one of the show's obsessive nods to the Coppola/Scorsese film cycle in particular and Italian-American culture in general) and of scantily clad women in films such as *Leather Bound Dykes From Hell*. This marginalization and dismissal of the feminine extends into the scene's spoken discourse; when Christopher challenges Paulie's assertion that he has been to Paris, the older mobster replies that he "went over for a blow job. Your mother was working the bonbon concession at the Eiffel Tower." Where the visually overbearing statue in the first scene can be taken as representing the considerable power which Livia exerts over Tony, the maternal presence has here been dismissed, recontextualized as nothing more than a crude joke. Paulie then turns to Silvio and repeats the comment in full, an unusual repetition which effectively highlights the nonchalant misogyny of the entire scene.

The most significant shift, however, is in Tony's casual domination of the counting room space and scene, which is at least as total as the statue's influence over Melfi's waiting room. While he does not talk as much as the other men, it is Tony – frequently positioned in the center of the frame – who clearly serves as the focal point of their social structure; he has moved from extreme restriction to a place of considerable authority in a rigidly hierarchical system, even if that authority is expressed here in essentially trivial ways. When Paulie changes the TV channel away from the Mob discussion, it is Tony who demands that the original station be restored. It is Tony who passes judgment on the television experts, mournfully acknowledging that "the shoe fits" when the decline in the Mafia is attributed to a disregard for the old rules, then firing a rubber band at the screen when the traitorous Rizzo appears. It is Tony who calls for Silvio to "cheer me up, babe" with his imitation of Al Pacino in *The Godfather Part III* – "Just when I thought I was out, they pull me back in" – and then praises the performance – "That Pacino or is that Pacino?" Tony has now become the possessor, rather than the target, of the controlling gaze that manifests fundamental narrative knowledge and power.

He enjoys this authority within the context of a range of cultural codes and narrative frames that are woven through the scene. Such contexts are necessary for any textual moment to bear meaning; even in its silence and brevity, the waiting room scene itself evokes the audience's knowledge of the rituals of medical care, gender roles, sexual anxiety, and so on. In the case of the second scene, the multiple frameworks invoked are primarily hierarchical networks structured around rigid assumptions about truth and power – and Tony's understanding and employment of them reveal both the depth of his investment in these systems, and his assumption that such power is identified with the masculine. In a later episode ("Nobody Knows Anything"/1011), Tony will assert his absolute control over his children's discourse by telling them that "in this house, it's 1954." In the opening moments of "46 Long"

(1002) it is already clear that this also applies at the Bada Bing! When Tony responds to a discussion of cloning by saying, "I tell my kids, only God can make a life," for example, he is not only asserting his own authority as The Father (and, not incidentally, again eliding the mother, another giver of life), but also aligning that authority with a highly traditional understanding of divine power. These hierarchical structures of family and religion are further arranged in a sort of metahierarchy as superior to the relatively new power/knowledge claims of science.

The dominant narrative frame at work in this scene, however, is clearly that of the Mob; like *The Sopranos* as a whole, the counting room scene depends upon the audience's knowledge, or at least awareness, of a long tradition of stories about organized crime in America. In Tony's world, this Mob narrative is so powerful and so elemental as to insistently insert itself into any other framework, any discussion. Cloning, when it is first mentioned, is assumed to refer not to the replication of life but to the theft of cell phone codes. The hypothetical cloning of Princess Diana in turn prompts Silvio to muse about the possibility that the Royal Family had the Princess "whacked," while Tony, presumably angry over "business" concerns, declares that "the fucking mayor of New York" should never be cloned. Politics, fame, economy, science – from Tony's perspective in the Bing, all are connected to the fundamental logic of crime, and all are thus subject to his knowledge and assessment. That said, Tony here is also aware, as he is throughout *The Sopranos*, that the power of the Mob narrative is widely perceived to be on the wane; recall his lament to Melfi, in their very first meeting, that he "came in at the end – the best is over." Despite Melfi's immediate assurance that "many Americans" share this feeling (a first expression of the show's treatment of the Mob as an analogy for the American endeavor in its entirety), it is clear that Tony is specifically referring to the decline of the Mafia at the end of the twentieth century. While the Mob genre has throughout its history demanded the eventual downfall and destruction of its central figure – demanded that, in David Remnick's words, "the brutal man who believes himself invulnerable . . . ends up dead in the gutter" – such a painful fate seems particularly unavoidable in a period when the Mob has almost completely vanished from our consciousness of the real world, when even stories of what Rizzo calls "the golden age, or whatever" of the Mafia have reached a point of tired familiarity. The grim diagnosis of the Mafia given by the TV speakers in the counting room scene, glumly endorsed by Tony, is itself an echo of the widespread conviction that the Mob has lost both its real and its fictional power; even David Chase, the creator of *The Sopranos*, has spoken repeatedly of his initial reluctance to engage the dying form, and the mobster has long seemed ready to join the cowboy as a figure revived out of nostalgia or parody rather than immediate interest.

The net effect of the counting room scene, however, is to subvert precisely that conviction that the mob story as such is "over." At the exact moment that a government prosecutor on television describes the Mob's situation as "confusion, instability, vacuum at the top," we see a close-up of the pile of money in front of Tony as Pussy pours still more bills out of a paper bag.

In a time when financial transactions have increasingly become an abstract matter of electronic signals, the pile of money is a transgressive throwback, an immediately present and visible sign of power; it is neither confusing nor instable. Nor is there a vacuum at the top; we have already seen how unmistakably Tony wields his power. By the end of the scene, Rizzo is asserting that "you're always going to have organized crime" as long as humans have "certain appetites" which cannot be legally fulfilled. Even the *Godfather* dialogue, twice repeated during the scene, is at its base a statement of the continuity, the undiminished influence, of the Mob. For all Tony's *agita* over the pressures of his "job," it is here made clear that the Mob of *The Sopranos* has not truly reached its end; it remains at least vibrant enough to offer Tony the agency, the identity, he is denied in Melfi's waiting room.

The very placement and form of the counting room scene is no less significant than its content. It is not simply the opening scene of "46 Long" (1002); it is the only scene in all of *The Sopranos* to be shown *before* the opening theme and credits, and none of its events relate directly to any others in the episode. Thus isolated, the scene works primarily to establish characters and relationships (although we have already met these characters, we have already seen these relationships), but also exists as a mini-narrative in its own right; it would function perfectly well as an independent short. Seen in this way, the scene is appropriately representative of the complexity marking the entire structure of the *Sopranos* narrative – or rather, narratives. It is, after all, virtually impossible to identify the boundaries of any definitive *Sopranos* text; that the series is uncompleted at this writing effectively denies us the certainty of closure, while such non-televisual works as Allen Rucker's *The Sopranos: A Family History*, which greatly flesh out the story, might well demand to be included.[1] Traditionally, narrative unity demands, at the very least, a sense of completion; on this basis, it is surely legitimate to treat any single episode of the series – or any season – as a distinct narrative text. This is particularly true of the first season, which is structured and internally unified by the central plot idea David Chase originally had for a Mafia film: a Mob boss's psychiatrist helps him to realize that his own mother is trying to have him killed.[2] For that matter, the pilot episode was written and shot with no knowledge of whether a series would actually be made and was designed to stand on its own if necessary.

The counting room scene thus serves as a bridge, a transition which redefines a potentially closed narrative as part of a larger whole. Its establishment of Tony as a dominant figure whose power is guaranteed by a network of patriarchal frames is a vital part of this function, a corrective to the passive, anxiety-ridden Tony of the waiting room scene and, in fact, of much of the first episode. It is in the first episode, after all, that we twice see Tony pass out, once while cooking and once while touring Green Grove Retirement Home with a female guide; it is in the first episode that we see him inert in a hospital gown, hectored by a wife who tells him he is going to hell; it is in the first episode that both Uncle Junior and Artie refuse Tony's requests, forcing him to the subterfuge of burning down his friend's restaurant; it is in the first episode that he cries over the loss of the ducks and his dream of castration. While he certainly has moments of self-assertion and authority in the pilot ("The Sopranos"/1001), he exhibits nothing like the confidence and certainty in himself, or the control over the narrative space, visible in the counting room scene and in many later points in the series. Even his encounter with the deadbeat he runs over and assaults is disrupted (however comically) by Melfi's insistence that she cannot be told of any crime. In countering this troubled representation, the counting room scene makes possible the central conflict, the tension which structures not just the contrast between the two opening scenes but the entire first season: is Tony to be a coherent subject, or a hysterical object?

If this essential dynamic for *The Sopranos* can be conceived of as an internal struggle for Tony, it nonetheless operates externally as well, in a series of clashes between two opposed logics of narrative operation – clashes between visible and invisible power, between presence and absence as fundamental signs of power. Tony's desire to be a coherent, integrated self, visibly operating under control within well-defined systems of meaning and authority, is continually subverted and disrupted by the operations of secrecy, uncertainty, fragmentation, evasion – by, that is to say, an entirely different style of power/knowledge. While there is nothing necessarily gendered about either style, it is undeniable that *The Sopranos* continually associates Tony's methods and preferences with the conventionally masculine and the subversion of that style with the feminine and with female characters – most notably, of course, Livia. These associations may well be among the more troubling aspects of the series, but, given its use of many long-established tropes and types, they may also be inevitable.

Near the beginning of Rucker's *The Sopranos: A Family History*, an FBI agent rather improbably states in an email message that "I like Tony Soprano. I genuinely like him. If he wasn't a professional thug, I think we could be friends." This unlikely, and oddly insistent, endorsement speaks directly to the self Tony would like to create, like to take for granted – Tony as the hero of his own story, recognized and respected for exactly what he is. Nearly all of Tony's "business" relationships – whether with competitors, victims, underlings, informants, or even law enforcement authorities – are characterized by a phallocentric, linear representation of self, a strictly hierarchal organization of power, and aggressive, straightforward communication. Even when Tony is confronted by government agents seeking evidence against him, both parties clearly understand the identity and purpose of the other; the relationships are always grounded in visible power and shared knowledge. For all his occasional concerns about the morality of his actions, Tony is, more often than not, fundamentally happy with his identity – and anxious that that identity be clearly recognized by those around him.

One consequence of this is that Tony's most visceral moments of violence and anger are frequently associated precisely with some misrecognition, some challenge to this sense of his own identity. Fabian Petrullo, the rat Tony is strangling in "College" (1005), makes a desperate final attempt to bargain for his life – "Teddy, there must be something we can do" – and Tony, for no reason at all, angrily corrects him: "Tony, it's Tony, you fuck." Actually, of course, there is a reason, the same reason that Tony believes Fabian must die: "You took an oath, and you broke it." Tony's sense of honor demands that he keep his own oath, and thus his own identity; Fabian, after all, voluntarily surrendered his identity, his very name, in talking to the government. To Tony, the betrayal and the loss of identity are synonymous. In "Denial, Anger, Acceptance" (1003), Tony reacts with similar anger to Shlomo's assertion that he is "a living golem": "what the fuck is a golem?" Perhaps most tellingly, in his encounter with the deadbeat in the pilot ("The Sopranos"/1001), Tony seems enraged less by the man's failure to pay than by his vocal lack of respect: "You tell people I'm nothing, compared to the people that used to run things." One of those people, of course, was Tony's father, and it is easy to see Tony's desire for a stable identity as an aspect of his desire to be everything his father was, to live up to his role in the continuation of the patriarchy. It is the meaning he derives from this sense of his place in a larger system that makes him, as he tells Melfi in "Denial, Anger, Acceptance" (1003) unafraid even to die, if the death is "for something." This sense of a meaningful context for his selfhood extends back far beyond the Mob itself; as he makes clear on several occasions, Tony sees himself and his crew as the modern continuation of the Romans.

Other threats to Tony's identity, however, are less easily dealt with than the protests of frightened victims. In "A Hit is a Hit" (1010) Tony's flirtation with the legitimate society of upper class, integrated Italian-Americans – "mayonnaisers" – is disrupted by his anger and hurt over their amused questions about John Gotti and *The Godfather,* their treatment of him "like a fucking dancing bear." Of course, Cusamano and the others have only recognized in Tony exactly what he wishes to be recognized – but they have done so in a reductive, insulting way, precisely by removing him from those contexts in which his identity is truly meaningful (moreover, in imposing this identity upon him they have robbed him of the agency which is basic to it). Shlomo's labeling Tony "a monster, a Frankenstein" is similarly reductive. When Melfi asks him if he feels "like Frankenstein, a thing lacking humanity," we do not hear Tony's answer – but we see him smile as the music from his daughter's recital begins to play, and a few minutes later we see him at the concert, seeking to make contact with his wife, and then crying. Tony is no monster and no cartoon gangster. His revenge on the mayonnaisers – asking Cusamano to conceal a mysterious box, insisting upon the crude nickname "Cooz" – works because it operates in reverse, imposing *his* world – his contexts – upon the safe and clean one in which Cusamano's own comfortable identity is based.

Melfi herself, at various points, embodies many of the complications that come between Tony and his desire for a coherent identity. When Tony believes he is in love with her, in "Pax Soprana" (1006), he is baffled and angered by her insistence that his feelings are illusory, a byproduct of successful therapy, and that she cannot respond to them: "I'm a man. And you're a woman. End of story." For Tony, this should indeed be the end of the story: their identities established, his desire stated, what other outcome is possible? In part, Tony's frustration here is caused by the failure of the external world to meet his expectations, to act as directly and predictably as he believes himself to act, to shape itself to his desire. Figuratively speaking, Melfi, like Fabian, is not living up to her "oath," not fulfilling the role provided for her within the narrative framework that gives Tony's life meaning. Such frustrations are recurrent in *The Sopranos*, providing much of the conflict in Tony's life. He expects the insurance company to pay promptly when he destroys Artie's restaurant, and its failure to do so greatly increases his sense of guilt. He expects his mole, Detective Makazian, to act like a responsible cop in following Melfi for him; when he instead assaults her date, Tony is again disappointed and enraged. He expects his mother to be a sweet little old lady. He expects his associates to be unquestionably loyal. If the exterior world would play its part as well as Tony plays his, he would undoubtedly have a simpler life.

But not, perhaps, a simple one. What truly disturbs Tony about Melfi's denial of his "love" is her insistence that it is not love, that he does not truly know himself any more than he can know the external world: "You've made me all of the things you feel are missing in your wife – and in your mother." Essentially, Melfi is telling Tony that the coherent self is an impossibility, that he, like everyone else in the world, is fragmented, complicated, confused; an object, not a subject. She is reasserting his powerlessness before certain forces, and that these forces are a hidden part of himself is no matter. To a great extent, this dilemma is already fundamentally fixed and represented for Tony in the particular identity he attempts to take such pride in, that of a "made guy." Though he is threatened by any failure of recognition, he must at the same time, as a purely practical matter, cultivate and encourage such misrecognition in order to avoid prosecution or even death. Tony's dilemma is dimly mirrored in Father Phil, the priest who openly accuses himself of being a *schnorer* in order to, consciously or unconsciously, divert attention from the deeper pathologies Carmela accuses him of in the closing moments of the first season ("I Dream of Jeannie Cusamano"/1013): "I get exactly the same 'who, me?' shit with Tony . . . I think you need to look at yourself." Like the priest, Tony is caught in a network of false appearances and real selves in which a stable identity becomes increasingly difficult to locate and sustain; looking at himself, given this realization, becomes increasingly painful. Near the end of "College" (1005) Tony, waiting for his daughter in a Bowdoin College hallway, is troubled by a quote from Hawthorne on the wall: "No man can wear one face to himself and another to the multitude without finally getting bewildered as to which may be true." Given the masquerade he has played for Meadow throughout the episode, it is easy to see this, as it is clearly intended, as a statement of Tony's essential problem: he cannot be at once a criminal and a respectable member of society. In reality, however, his crisis is deeper: beneath the face he wishes to wear is not another, but something which stubbornly remains unseen and unknown.

Given the logic of the insistently masculine world from which Tony derives meaning and identity, it is perhaps necessary that the subversion of such meaning and the disruption of that identity should be so obsessively identified with the feminine which is regularly marginalized within that context. However sincere his love for his family, Tony's primary reality is clearly his business world (asked how he is by Melfi, Tony invariably replies with comments about "work"), and that world is centered on and embodied by the Bada Bing! club, where nude female dancers are almost always visible – but rarely included in the discourse. Indeed, they are so far out of the loop that one of them must be told, in the pilot episode, that Tony is not charged for his drinks; on the rare occasions when they ask questions (as in "46 Long" [1002] when they overhear Tony's concern over the fire at his mother's house), they are routinely ignored. This is, of course, only the most visible manifestation of a pattern that recurs throughout the series, a repression of the feminine in the name of the power of the masculine. What the pattern reveals, in its most excessive forms, is the hysteria and fragmentation underlying not merely Tony's apparently secure identity, but the entire Mob – and, by extension, any pattern of narrative logic structured on a stereotype of the hypermasculine self.

Consider, for example, the panic which erupts around the topic of cunnilingus in the episode "Boca" (1009) and which ultimately contributes to the violent showdown between Tony and his Uncle Junior. Asked by Roberta why his talent for oral sex must remain secret, Junior can say only that "they think if you'll suck pussy, you'll suck anything." Despite clearly being a heterosexual act, cunnilingus threatens the sexual identity – and thus, the complete identity – of the man who performs it. It is not difficult to speculate on the psychological underpinnings of this reasoning; to perform the act is to surrender the self, giving up even the ability of speech, of self-assertion, in the name of female pleasure. It is a privileging of the feminine, a muffling of the male. This is, of course, only one example of the hysteria continually suffered by the masculine characters at the possibility of any form of emasculation, a possibility continually raised and continually denied by their own discourse. In "Denial, Anger, Acceptance" (1003), Tony, stymied by Ariel's apparent invulnerability to torture, must call Hesh, who suggests threatening castration ("Make like a mohel. Finish his bris" ["Denial, Anger, Acceptance"/1003]) – but it is surely curious that Tony, a man well versed in giving pain and who himself dreads castration (recall the dream of the ducks), could not arrive at such an idea himself. Clearly, the thought is both ever-present and eternally repressed, another aspect of the mysterious, hidden Tony the straightforward surface man cannot control or comprehend. Nor does it seem coincidental, given the symbolic logic of the entire program, that it is the mobster named Big Pussy whose ambiguous loyalty becomes the cause of Tony's most acute crisis and uncertainty, eventually disappearing (only, of course, to return and be unmasked and killed in the second season). When *Entertainment Weekly* ran the cover line "Where's Pussy?" as part of their preview of the second season of *The Sopranos*, it might well have been expressing the thoughts of every male character mystified and terrified by the very concept of feminine sexuality or power – of absence rather than presence.

Feminine subversion is thus a recurrent threat within the discourse of *The Sopranos*, but it finds its most disruptive embodiment, of course, in Livia. Her own discourse, in marked contrast to Tony's characteristic bluntness, is marked by evasion ("I don't know what you're talking about"), self-denigration ("I'm a babbling idiot"), and misdirection (her continual fascination with mothers who kill their children). Where Tony seeks certainty, Livia revels in revisionism and ambiguity; consider her repeated insistence that the husband she hounded and nagged "was a saint," or her condemnation of Brendan: "The other one? Filone? I don't know." Livia's every utterance, however casual, has the potential to disrupt Tony's precarious sense of his selfhood. Her barbed "look who calls his mother," or "oh, he knows everything," addressing Tony in the third rather than the second person, objectify him as effectively as the scene in Melfi's waiting room, symbolically fragmenting him into observer and observed. Perhaps the truest statement Livia utters in the course of the first season is her defensive "I know how to talk to people" after she has driven away her caretaker in "46 Long" (1002). Still more powerfully, however, she knows how – and when – to *not* talk to people. Although Livia has become infamous as the mother who put out a hit on her own son, it is surely worth noting that she never once utters such a command, or even such a suggestion; her agency is expressed through silence, analogy, innuendo. When FBI agents play Tony the damning tapes of his mother and uncle, it is Junior who says "I have to"; Livia does not answer. If her manipulation of Junior is clear – to the audience, to Tony, to the FBI, even to Junior himself – it is nonetheless silent and invisible.

Given the fact that Livia is clearly perceived as pathological – Melfi suggests that she has borderline personality disorder – it is rather troubling that the other significant female characters are themselves so frequently represented as sharing in her patterns and methods, or even identified with her. While Junior is easily influenced and Tony remains blind to the depth of her animosity, both Melfi and Carmela understand what Livia is doing and how she does it: "I want you to cut the drama," Carmela warns her mother-in-law, "it's killing Tony." Presumably, they understand her for the same reason Makazian and Christopher understand Tony: because they speak the same language, they comprehend the same codes. Tellingly, Tony refuses to believe the warnings both of them give him; it is only the FBI tapes, played for him in the context of his preferred criminal narrative, that convince him of his mother's malevolence, bringing her into the open. Moreover, the dreams Tony has in which Carmela becomes Melfi, in which Melfi becomes Livia, like his casual promiscuity, only echo the program's unspoken treatment of women as endlessly interchangeable. This is perhaps least visible in Carmela; for all her badgering of Tony, she is ultimately willing to accept the identity he wants for himself and to stand by him. For that matter, she can at moments – as when she seizes an assault rifle to defend her home – seem like little more than an extension of her husband. Carmela's disruptions, when they come, are minor; her eagerness to study Buddhism, for example, stands in marked contrast to Tony's purely traditional understanding of religion. It is also worth noting her fast and effective deconstruction, in the first season's final episode, of the carefully constructed and maintained public character of Father Phil – a particularly brutal version of what Melfi has been trying to do for Tony all along.

The association between Livia and Melfi, however, only becomes more pronounced as the first season progresses, just as the statue so clearly associated with Livia in the waiting room scene will in later episodes frequently reappear on a shelf behind the doctor's chair. Both Livia and Melfi, after all, are attempting to do essentially the same thing: disrupt the coherent identity and meaning which sustain Tony, and sustain his power. That Melfi's motives are constructive while Livia's are destructive does not change the essential fact that both deal in the realm of the invisible, the silent, the repressed. It is possible to see Melfi's office as the place where the opposing systems of logic which structure *The Sopranos* most immediately meet in conflict and, occasionally, dialogue. Indeed, for part of the first season it appears that Tony will successfully integrate the two styles; for a time he averts war with Junior by allowing the older man to believe he is in charge, while in fact Tony runs things behind the scenes. It is a piece of manipulation – giving "the illusion of control" – which Melfi suggests, although she wishes him to employ it against Livia; he is never able to do so, perhaps because his mother would understand the attempt all too well.

Ultimately, however, the two styles of power at work in *The Sopranos* cannot truly coexist, let alone merge; ultimately there must be conflict. As the season progresses, Tony's rising anxiety and Livia's rising influence over Junior both testify to the fundamental disjunction between the assertive style the Mafia framework demands and the quiet subversion the feminine represents. The turning point, when compromise becomes impossible, comes in the season's ninth episode, "Boca." The episode's two main plots each concern the revelation of a sexuality deemed deviant within Tony's world, though they are, no doubt, wildly different for most audiences: Uncle Junior's suddenly public talent for cunnilingus, and the soccer coach's molestation of one of Meadow's friends. What is vital is Tony's reaction to these events. Initially, he intends to kill Coach Hauser – but in response to the pleas of Melfi and Artie, and his recognition that he would only be serving himself, he finally decides to hold back, allowing the man to be taken into custody instead. Similarly, his first reaction on learning of Junior's oral skills is to laugh at the man in the privacy of his own bedroom, but to leave him alone in public – to allow him, in other words, to retain the kind of masculine identity Tony himself values so highly. Needled by Junior on the golf course, however, Tony cannot resist retaliating with his own subtle jokes, flaunting his knowledge.

In both cases, Tony essentially follows the logic not of his own masculine style but of feminine subversion and misdirection. In allowing the police to handle Hauser, Tony abrogates his own sense of ultimate responsibility and authority, turning aside from his own desire in a denial of the privilege he usually feels free to exercise. In expressing his disdain for Junior, he chooses to forego direct confrontation and honesty in favor of the sorts of hints and associative thought more typical of Livia. At the end of the episode, Tony, high on booze and pills after the strain of acting in such unnatural ways, comes home in the middle of the night and proudly tells Carmela "I didn't hurt nobody." While this may be true of Coach Hauser – and while Tony might be justly proud of that – he must, or should, recognize that he *has* hurt someone: Junior (and, indirectly, Roberta, who will be left sobbing and alone in the wake of Junior's rage). It is in the locker room after the golf game that Junior first seriously considers the idea of killing Tony, setting in motion a chain of events that will ultimately demand Tony's reassertion of his authority and identity within its original, masculine context.

For there can be little doubt, finally, about which style emerges as dominant in the resolution of *The Sopranos'* first season. Having been reduced to extreme depression – an immobility almost echoing his passivity in the waiting room scene – by Pussy's disappearance, by his alienation from his family, by the impending indictments, Tony is reinvigorated and newly empowered by the attempt on his life in the penultimate episode, "Isabella." Indeed, the direct conflict of the battle, the most primal expression of the masculine logic that characterizes his world, seems to do more for his mental stability than Melfi ever could. Moreover, whatever of the feminine style he has previously taken from her office is amply balanced by the moment in which, finally understanding what Melfi is saying about his mother, he throws aside furniture and charges across the room to breathe disgust and threats into her face ("I Dream of Jeannie Cusamano"/1013). It is one of the most frightening and immediately felt moments in the entire series, and it represents nothing less than Tony's rejection of Melfi's rules and his violent imposition of his world into hers – indeed, almost onto her very body. Even when he returns to her office after hearing the FBI tapes which vindicate her interpretation, it is less to apologize than to reassert that she is now part of his world and therefore endangered; his insistence that she must leave town is, at least in part, an insistence that the authority within her office now belongs to him.

The victory cannot be complete, however. In part, of course, this is demanded by the necessity of denying complete closure in order to facilitate continuation of the series; Junior's arrest and Livia's "stroke" allow them to remain viable characters, as an assassination and a smothering pillow would not. Aside from this, however, there is something entirely appropriate in the ending of the first season, and particularly in Tony's final confrontation with his mother. His anger and violence, now brought fully into the presence of her silence and ambiguity, encapsulate perfectly the conflict that has structured the entire narrative. For all Tony's violent insistence, we cannot even be sure at the last whether she is smiling, whether the stroke is feigned; she remains an enigma, an absence, a disruption to Tony's certainty and authority (that her silence is matched, in the subsequent scene, by Melfi's absence only reinforces the connection between them and the subversive potential of the feminine as a whole). Still, if she escapes her son's revenge, Livia is, in the end, moved offscreen, moved into the realm of a purely potential disruption, and what we are left with, as the first season draws to a close, is Tony Soprano, the patriarch, toasting his family, his lieutenants nearby, his authority unchallenged; as Silvio tells Paulie, "he'll be the new boss now – in name, in everything" (and, of course, the montage which opens the second season will confirm the happiness and success Tony has found in this renewed assertion of and belief in himself). For all its radical elements, for all its revisionary moves, in the end *The Sopranos* cannot help but celebrate that most powerful of mythic figures: the male as coherent subject, the male as the self-validated hero of his own story.

GENRE AND NARRATIVE TECHNIQUE

ELEVEN

"TV RUINED THE MOVIES": TELEVISION, TARANTINO, AND THE INTIMATE WORLD OF *THE SOPRANOS*

Glen Creeber

"It won't be cinematic."

> Patsy Parisi to Gloria Trillo as he points a gun
> to her chest and describes how she will be killed if she
> continues to stalk Tony Soprano ("Amour Fou"/3012)

INTRODUCTION

Surprisingly perhaps for the creator of *The Sopranos* (what one American critic has referred to as "the best television drama ever made" [Holden ix]), David Chase seems to hold a less than favorable view of the medium in which he works. "All my life I wanted to do movies," he explained to Bill Carter in the *New York Times*. "I just resented every moment I spent in television . . . for me it was always cinema, cinema, cinema" (90). Despite previous credits to his name such as *The Rockford Files*, *Northern Exposure* and *I'll Fly Away*, Chase seems to regard television as cinema's poor cousin, unable to ever capture its magnitude and visual spectacle. "There's so much more to the movie experience," he told the British journalist Alex Blimes, "music and pictures and rhythm. I miss that" (169). Chase clearly feels that cinema has inevitably suffered for allowing itself to be increasingly influenced by its small screen rival. "I saw television take over cinema," he told Allen Rucker. "I saw TV executives moving into movies. I saw the pandering, cheerleading, family entertainment shit dominate everything. Low attention span stuff. It all came from TV. TV ruined the movies . . ."

As this suggests, Chase seems to resent the increasing influence of television on a new generation of filmmakers and cinemagoers. Quentin Tarantino's own much-hyped employment in a video store perhaps most famously suggests such a trend, revealing a writer, director, and actor as openly influenced as much by the small screen as the big. As Roger Avary, Tarantino's friend, co-worker, and (frequently over-looked) co-writer *of Pulp Fiction* (1994), points out: "We were the video store generation, right after the film school generation, the first generation of people who wanted to be filmmakers who had grown up alongside computers, videos, the information highway" (cited by Botting & Wilson 7). Indeed, the phenomenal success of Tarantino's *Reservoir Dogs* (1992) on video is sometimes cited as evidence that the aesthetics of cinema and television are perhaps gradually beginning to merge.[1] According to *New York Times* film critic Vincent Canby:

> Since the videocassette recorder has become, in effect, the second run of the theatrical film, there has been a televisionization in the look of movies. An interesting number of today's theatrical movies give the impression of being photographed almost entirely in the close-ups and medium shots that register best on the small screen. (Cited by Wasko 166)

Few genres perhaps illustrate this trend towards "televisionization" as perfectly as the gangster genre. While movie critics like Peter Cowie have praised *The Godfather* (1972) for epitomizing the "classical style" of modern film-making (209–23), newer gangster movies such as *Reservoir Dogs, Pulp Fiction,* or more recently *Lock, Stock and Two Smoking Barrels* (1998) have often been associated with the type of "cartoon imagery" and "MTV aesthetics" more generally associated with TV. Indeed, *Lock, Stock* was recently made into a British television series, quickly cashing in on its big screen success.[2] For many critics, then, cinema's apparent movement towards adopting televisual aesthetics has produced a new breed of gangster film, one that is inherently different in style, form, and content from its big screen predecessor.

In this essay, I will argue that *The Sopranos* implicitly critiques the "televisionization" of the gangster genre – parodying its gradual development (Chase might say decline) from cinematic epic to standard video or television fare. In particular, I will illustrate how its constant self-reflexive referencing to its own generic history reveals a television narrative desperately trying to re-invent and re-examine itself; searching for the means by which it can both deconstruct and possibly reconstruct its own narrative dynamics. By critiquing the very medium it both utilizes and exploits, the drama ironically produces a complex and sophisticated narrative structure that simultaneously denigrates and celebrates its own inherent potential and artistic possibilities. Above all, then, *The Sopranos* can be seen as an investigation of genre, not only an attempt to "modernize" the portrayal of the Mob, but also an attempt to look back longingly to a genre that was once perhaps more morally stable and secure than it can ever be today.

It is clear, even to the most casual of viewers, that *The Sopranos* self-consciously positions itself (however ironically) as part of a long and illustrious cinematic tradition. As Caryn James points out, "One man has a car horn that blares out the first bars of *The Godfather* theme; another routinely impersonates Al Pacino as Michael Corleone" (29). As other essays in this volume demonstrate the drama seems intent, even in areas such as casting, on offering reminders of an earlier generic tradition. This implicit referencing to an earlier generic tradition seems to be paralleled by Tony Soprano's own longing to return to a now forgotten era. "Out there it's the 1990s," the Prozac munching Mobster tells his children, "in here, it's 1954" ("Nobody Knows Anything"/1011). In particular, this depressed Mafia boss seems obsessed with the standards and the values epitomized by an earlier generation of gangsters. "He never reached the heights like me," he says of his father, "but in a lot of ways he had it better. He had his people. They had their standards. They had pride. Today, what have we got?" As this suggests, Tony appears to believe that the world of organized crime is clearly less noble and respected than it once was in its Golden Age.

This notion of a "Golden Age" could refer as much to the *dramatic universe* Tony inhabits as it does to the reality of the Mob itself. For it has been argued that, like the Mob, the contemporary gangster movie has also rejected the traditional conventions of *its* past. Interestingly, a TV mob expert suggests ("46 Long"/1002) that the Mafia itself is partly to blame for its own decline, particularly for turning its back on the "rules which once served the old Dons so well." Indeed, such a statement could equally refer to a *genre* that has perhaps similarly rejected its own (cinematic) heritage, disregarding a set of moral "standards" and aesthetic "rules" that once governed it in the past. Seen in this light, Tony's depression is symptomatic of a character who unconsciously feels he exists at the wrong end of a long and illustrious tradition (literally, in the form of the Mob and metaphorically, in the form the gangster genre). "Lately I've been getting the feeling that I came in at the end," he tells his psychiatrist. "The best is over."

As such, Tony Soprano is clearly meant to represent an earlier *generic* tradition, a world that still remembers the "rules" and the "standards" that once "served the old Dons so well." In cinematic terms, this perhaps most famously refers to Coppola's classic portrayal of the Mafia, particularly Marlon Brando's modern (yet inherently old-school) Don Vito Corleone.[3] According to his wife Carmela, her husband "watches *The Godfather* all the time." On his new laser disk, she adds, "he says the camera work looks as good as in the movie theater." Consequently, Tony's choice of film and his specific appreciation of the genre appears to reflect a particular cinematic tradition, a time when the gangster movie had not yet succumbed to the increasing influence of television. In contrast to more recent examples of the genre, critics have argued that Coppola's original movie was made primarily for cinema and therefore can never be fully appreciated on the small screen. As film critic Anton Wilson puts it:

Coppola created the magnificent "underworld" texture by extensively exploiting the shadow detail capability of film. Most of the action in many of the interior scenes existed in the lowest regions of the exposure curve. In my opinion this subtle feel of the texture was lost when the film appeared on television as the medium could not cope with the range of exposure, especially the shadow details. (cited by Wasko 167)[4]

As this suggests, Tony Soprano epitomizes the "classical" gangster genre, one that was inherently at home on the big screen.[5] As such, it is no wonder that he finds it difficult to adjust to the smaller dimensions of television. In what is now regarded as one of the founding texts of Television Studies, Horace Newcomb argued that television could never emulate the sheer "expansiveness" of the cinema. Instead, the small screen (particularly through its use of close-up and medium shots) achieves a more *personal* and *intimate* view of the world (243–64).[6] Tony's tragic predicament can be viewed as an essentially cinematic creation, desperately trying to conform to the apparently *intimate* dynamics of the small screen. Looking like extras from *The Godfather,* his crew are deposited uncomfortably into a world of soap operas, docu-soaps, and confessional talk shows – forced to take their personalities beyond their traditional generic boundaries. "Nowadays," Tony complains, "everybody's gotta go to shrinks, and counselors and go on *Sally Jessy Raphael* and talk about their problems" ("The Sopranos"/1001). As such, Tony's long-running battle with therapy implicitly parallels the narrative's own struggle with the personal requirements of television. Frustrated by the constant need to express his feelings, this Mafia boss is not simply resisting the contemporary preoccupation with self-analysis but also struggling to adapt to television's obsession with the *private* and *personal* dynamics of human experience.

It comes as no surprise, then, that he frequently longs to escape from this "intimate" world and return to the traditional conventions of classical Hollywood. "Whatever happened to Gary Cooper, the strong silent type?" he asks his psychiatrist. "He wasn't in touch with his feelings. He just did what he had to do." In this context, it is clear that Tony's fear of *intimacy* is not just a symptom of his *psychological* condition but is also perhaps an inevitable reaction against his own *generic* confinement.

In contrast, Tony's impetuous nephew, Christopher Moltisanti, is clearly meant to represent a new breed of both gangster and genre. Brought up on a steady diet of television, videos and computer games, he is, as the *New York Times* puts it, "a soldier of the MTV generation." Tony clearly feels his nephew has been spoiled, citing his $60,000 Lexus automobile as an example of a generation that has been over-indulged ("The Sopranos"/1001). However, both men do seem to share a love of the movies, although for Christopher it is a passion that threatens to almost overcome his allegiance to the Mob. Indeed, he secretly enrolls in an acting class and begins (with the help of *How to Write a Movie in 21 Days*) to write a screenplay. "You Bite, I Bark" is based on his experiences in the Mob, although as Holden points out, "his stolen laptop seems to come without a spell checker" (129). Later Christopher even visits a movie set with his cousin's girlfriend who just happens to have worked for Tarantino.[7] As this might suggest, Christopher's perspective on the cinema perhaps reflects the cultural attitude of a new generation of filmmakers and movie buffs. Although clearly obsessed with film, his local video store is as near as he actually gets to the cinematic experience. "I love movies," he tells his girlfriend Adriana. "That smell at Blockbuster, that candy and carpet smell, I get high off" ("The Legend of Tennessee Moltisanti"/1008).

As a symbol of the new "video store" generation, Christopher clearly seems to reflect the contemporary genre's more violent and perhaps increasingly "amoral" sensibilities. He certainly seems unable to disconnect movies from his real life, frequently reacting self-reflexively to volatile situations. "This is the *Scarface* final scene," he shouts at Tony and the crew, "Fucking bazookas under each arm. Say hello to my little friend" ("Pax Soprano"/1006). However, his older colleagues seem unimpressed by his uncontrolled outbursts of anger. "Always with the scenarios," Pussy comments sarcastically. As this implies, this new "video store" generation simply fails to appreciate many of the more subtle ingredients of the classic gangster movie. Even when Christopher travels to Naples with Tony and the crew, he spends most of his time in his hotel room doing drugs, missing a rare chance to see and experience his ancestral homeland. Not surprisingly, then, he also seems unable to fully grasp the details of his own cinematic heritage, even managing to misquote from Coppola's original masterpiece. This contrast between Tony and Christopher's viewing habits clearly reveal characters at different ends of the same generic spectrum – perhaps representative of the old "film school" and new "video store" generations respectively. While both characters are clearly corrupt, dangerous, and violent individuals, they appear to represent a fundamentally different set of moral and ethical values.

"They Just Don't Give a Damn"

Some critics argue that the new gangster movie is representative of a "new brutalism" in modern cinema. Julia Hallam and Margaret Marshment argue that rather than constructing "narratively adequate motivations . . . for violent acts," these films tend to portray *natural* born killers who are not apparently motivated by any "narrative causality" (225). Similarly, in his discussion of *Reservoir Dogs*, the film critic Geoff Andrew argues that "Tarantino does not appear to be concerned with the moral implications of the film; rather, it is primarily a stylish variation on traditional genre conventions, designed to thrill, shock, amuse and surprise" (323). This apparent "amorality" has certainly helped to characterize this new breed of gangster film, distinguishing it from the kind of realism that critics have associated with the genre in the past. As Hallam and Marshment put it:

> By the 1980s and the 1990s, the gangster film's roots in any antecedent discourse of social reality is largely obscured by "high concept" aesthetics

that foreground stylistic excess, its entertainment value articulated through accrued layers of generic self-reflexivity and intertextuality. (92)

Consequently, it has been argued that these new films are inevitably more concerned with creating intricate aesthetic worlds, rather than with exploring the wider *moral* and *ethical* considerations of the genre. For some critics it is a cinematic tendency seen in the contemporary depiction of crime and violence as a whole. According to Philip L. Simpson, "the popular 1990s films that mythologize serial murderers' exploits are unremittingly conservative in many aspects and generally dispense with social critique in favor of apocalyptic (as opposed to cathartic) levels of violence" (120). As a TV psychiatrist says of Mickey and Mallory (the postmodern Bonnie and Clyde of *Natural Born Killers* [1992]): "They know the difference between right and wrong. They just don't give a damn." According to Phil Hardy's introduction to the *BFI Companion to Crime*, "These [new] films are deeply pessimistic and very violent." Comparing Scorsese's *Mean Streets* (1973) with *Pulp Fiction*, Hardy argues that "for all his freneticism" Harvey Keitel's character (perhaps like Tony) "has a secure sense of society." This is in stark contrast to John Travolta's who (perhaps like Christopher) "can only innocently wonder about the odd thread that connects the events of his life . . ." (23)

Put crudely, then, it could be argued that there has been a tendency in the contemporary gangster genre – embodied in the contrast between Tony and Christopher – to swap its classical sense of realism with "cartoon style" violence and "high concept aesthetics." In this sense, the new gangster movie may have taken on many of the most excessive characteristics of the television action series, replacing ethics with exhibition and personality with spectacle. As Toby Miller has recently put it, "Several genres within US and UK [television] drama focus on action rather than character [such as] police programs that feature violence rather than detection . . . war shows that stress fighting over politics . . . and action packed historical . . . and science fiction epics" (17–18). As such, films like *Reservoir Dogs* have been criticized for glamorizing a similar televisual tradition, carefully tuning into and articulating the stereotyped themes and repressed motifs of the classic 1970s television action and crime series. As Taubin puts it:

What makes *Reservoir Dogs* such a 90s film is that it's about the return of what was repressed in the television version of 70s masculinity – a paranoid, homophobic fear of the other that explodes in hate speech, in kicks and blows, in bullets and blades. *Reservoir Dogs* is an extremely insular film – women get no more than thirty seconds of screen time, people of color get zero – yet not a minute goes by without some reference to coons and jungle bunnies, to jailhouse rape (black semen shooting up white asses), to the castration threat of "phallic" women like Madonna or that 70s icon Pam Grier. (124)

Seen in this light, *The Sopranos* ultimately offers the viewer a critique of the "classic" TV action series, particularly in the way this TV genre has now infiltrated and "contaminated" the narrative dynamics of the "classical" gangster movie. The repressed sexism, racism, and homophobia present in such programs become the subject of a television serial that seeks to re-invent and re-position its own narrative point of view and generic construction. However, rather than blatantly renew and reinvigorate the stereotypes of the past, it could be argued that *The Sopranos* re-employs these very tropes so that both Tony and the genre itself become the subjects of analysis. In this way, the viewer may be forced to reconsider the hidden and repressed desires that have produced and manufactured them both.

In "D-Girl" (2007), for instance, Christopher meets up with film development girl Amy Safir and actor Jon Favreau. Clearly sophisticated and middle-class, this Hollywood pair simply engineer to use Christopher (and his script) to help them with their next project, *Crazy Joe* – based on the life of the real gangster, Crazy Joe Gallo. "Mob theme stories," as Amy tells Christopher, "are always hot." Visibly turned on by his Mob connections, she begins an affair with him that she clearly has no intention of continuing beyond her hotel room. Later, both she and Favreau become excited when Christopher tells them real stories from the Mob, secretly hoping to appropriate them for their own screenplay. One tale revolves around a gangster who unknowingly has sex with a transsexual and is horrified when he discovers she still has male genitalia. In retaliation he buys a can of acid and seeks her out. He "burns everything" Christopher explains, "pours it on her arms, on her face . . . on her prick." Favreau is clearly shocked; forced to confront the reality of a type of violence he prefers to think of only in cinematic terms. However, the hard-nosed Amy is simply concerned that the story lacks originality and mentions *The Crying Game* (1992). "This is a true story," Favreau has to quickly remind her. In this way, the exploitative tendencies of the new gangster genre are clearly satirized, contrasting the comfortable lives of these two affluent filmmakers with the people they depict, stereotype, and inherently use.

COMPLICATED SHADOWS

An implicit critique of the contemporary gangster genre is discernible in the style of *The Sopranos* as a whole, particularly in the way that it appears to deliberately echo the mise en scene of the "classical" gangster movie. The narrative, for example, frequently employs the technique most famously used in *The Godfather* of cross-cutting (as Holden puts it) "between scenes of extreme violence and domestic warmth" (xiii). At the end of Coppola's movie the innocence of a family christening and a number of brutal murders are carefully edited together. As Michael Corleone renounces the devil in his role as Godfather to his sister's child, so his role as a Mafia Godfather is graphically foregrounded by the cold-blooded murders that we see carried out in his name. The end of episode three of the first season ("Denial, Anger, Acceptance"/1003) clearly borrows this technique, mixing the killing of Brendan and the mock execution of Christopher with a choral recital from Meadow's school concert. This kind of montage gives an important moral and ethical context to the story, graphically revealing the hypocrisy that lies beneath the Mafia's respectable veneer.

A similar technique is loosely applied in "College" (1005). When Tony visits Maine with his daughter Meadow for a college tour, he accidentally comes across a notorious "rat" now living under the pseudonym Fred Peters. As a result, the normality of this everyday trip is suddenly juxtaposed with a bloody tale of Mafia revenge. As with Brendan's death, Tony's brutal strangling of "Fred" from behind is also reminiscent of a scene from *The Godfather*, the infamous murder of Luca Brasi. Such a treatment of violence is clearly meant to unsettle viewers, forcing them to contemplate the different facets of Tony's life and personality. As if to reinforce such a reading, Tony himself spies a plaque on a wall while waiting for Meadow to be interviewed at Bowdoin. "No man can wear one face to himself and another to the multitude," it reads, "without finally getting bewildered as to which may be true" (Hawthorne in *The Scarlet Letter*). In this way, rather than allowing Tony's Mafia persona to dominate the narrative point of view, the viewer is given a number of contrasting perspectives (father/parent/ husband/mobster) from which to view the action. This offers a complexity of characterization seldom witnessed in movies such as *Reservoir Dogs*, where colors replace even the names of its principal characters. As Stephen Prince puts it: "Tarantino is drawn to violence because he knows it as a movie style, and it is one that he finds compelling. The style itself is the subject and form of his work. Accordingly, he has not moved to explore the psychological and emotional dynamics of violence in terms that might reference life apart from the movies" (241).

A similar approach can be detected in *The Sopranos'* use of music. Although the series frequently employs popular songs, they generally lack the catchy intensity of the music that so often punctuates more recent examples of the genre. Indeed, the low-key beat of Nick Lowe's "The Beast in Me" or Elvis Costello's "Complicated Shadows" is in direct contrast with the frenetic dance beat of *Pulp Fiction's* "Jungle Boogie" (Kool & The Gang) or the infectious pop of *Reservoir Dogs'* "Stuck in the Middle with You" (Stealer's Wheel). Consequently, the choice of music tends to avoid constructing the sort of rapidly edited sequences that have become associated with the new sub-genre. Instead, the series' use of music frequently helps to create a mood and an atmosphere that is reminiscent of Coppola's famously languid pace, perhaps echoing the classical eloquence of Nino Rota's memorable theme tune.

The second season of *The Sopranos*, for instance, begins with the lazy and melancholic tones of Frank Sinatra performing Ervin Drake's "It Was a Very Good Year." As the song plays, so we are given a long and leisurely paced selection of apparently unconnected scenes. Sequences such as Livia lying motionless and depressed in her hospital bed, Carmela baking at home, Silvio trying on a new pair of shoes, AJ self-consciously combing his hair, and Tony and Paulie making love with their girlfriends/prostitutes provide an essentially "domestic" montage. However, the music fails to extenuate or exaggerate the pace of the action (as, for example, George Baker's "Little Green Bag" famously does at the opening of *Reservoir Dogs*). Instead, Sinatra's unhurried and mournful ballad (played in its full four and a half minutes) explicitly heightens the scene's leisurely construction, deliberately slowing down the story's narrative pace and transforming the generic spectacle of the modern gangster genre into an essentially domestic and intimate display.[8]

This leisurely pace and implicit sense of intimacy is further heightened by the drama's deliberate excursions away from the traditional world of the gangster genre. If, as I have argued, Tony finds himself implicitly trapped in the relatively restricting dynamics of television, it is not surprising that televisual aesthetics are frequently employed to break up and fragment the narrative's more traditionally "cinematic" images and techniques. As in the domestic (sitcom-like) story lines surrounding Tony's family, the psychiatry sessions seem to deliberately utilize some of the essential elements of the small screen. Relatively static (at least, compared to the "high concept" techniques favored in newer examples of the genre), the emphasis here is on dialogue, close-ups, and human interaction, employing what many critics regard as some of the most basic ingredients of television drama (see, for example, Jacobs 7–8).

Indeed, these scenes are perhaps more reminiscent of the conventional TV chat show or the "head-to-head" political interview than they are of the contemporary gangster or action movie. In this way, the therapy sequences appear to deliberately fragment the series narrative dynamic, perhaps forcing the viewer to stand back for a moment from Tony's exotic (and perhaps essentially "cinematic") life-style so that they can briefly distance themselves from the genre's historically seductive appeal.[9] Like Tony, then, the aesthetic intimacy of the small screen is unexpectedly thrust upon the viewer and the narrative expectations of the genre suddenly denied.

The first episode, for instance, opens with Tony sitting alone and in silence for a full twenty seconds in Melfi's waiting room. Once in her office, it is another thirty seconds before she finally breaks the silence, a bravely austere opening for a pilot episode of a gangster series.[10] Compare this, for example, with the hectic opening sequence of *Lock, Stock and Two Smoking Barrels*, or the famously seductive credit sequence of *Reservoir Dogs*.[11] Later in the episode, Dr. Melfi interrupts one of Tony's recollections to get, as she puts it, "some ethical ground-rules out of the way." This interruption similarly breaks up the narrative pace of the action, while the rock soundtrack that accompanies Tony's violent memory is suddenly replaced by the abrupt silence of Mefli's office. In this way the therapy sessions unexpectedly forces the viewer to take time out from the traditional attractions of the gangster genre, giving a possibly "ethical" and spatially contrasting perspective from which to view the events taking place. As a result, the typically high powered conventions of the genre are temporarily suspended and the audience given a brief moment away from its visual and audio excitement.

In this way, *The Sopranos* implicitly reflects the use of the psychiatry narrative as employed in a television series like *The Singing Detective* (Potter/ Amiel, BBC 1986).[12] In a manner seldom matched by cinema (hence perhaps the more comedic inflection of a film like *Analyze This!*), the sheer breadth of the television series (what Newcomb refers to as its tendency towards "continuity") enables the inherently slow and *gradual* process of psychotherapy to be more realistically represented and explored. Like Dennis Potter's equally reluctant patient in *The Singing Detective*, Tony's therapy appears to progress slowly, operating in a time-frame clearly not affordable in the relatively limited time-span of the cinema. It is not until "Down Neck" (1007), for example, that we are given our first direct glimpse (in the form of a flashback) of his childhood. As a young boy in 1967 we see him discover (for the first time) his father's involvement in the Mob, accidentally witnessing him and his Uncle Junior "beat the crap" out of a man from the neighborhood.

Interestingly, the way this scene is shot is strikingly reminiscent of the childhood trauma at the heart of *The Singing Detective*, when Marlow (as a young boy) accidentally comes across his mother having sex in the woods. Like Marlow, Tony stands at the foot of a tree, voyeuristically witnessing the action from a concealed spot, both repulsed and excited by what he secretly witnesses.[13] The echo of this famous scene perhaps implicitly pays homage to the depth of characterization that the cumulative narrative of a television series like *The Singing Detective* can achieve. Tony is ultimately struggling with the claustrophobic dynamics of television but (despite its apparently limiting restrictions) may ironically gain a greater understanding of himself – and perhaps the genre in which he unknowingly exists – through serialized drama's gradual excavation of character, desire, and perhaps even unconscious motivation.[14]

By reluctantly allowing the "intimate" world of television into the more "masculine" world of the gangster genre, both Tony and the drama itself are gradually forced to recognize the limitations of their own restricting worlds. This employment of televisual techniques may seem contradictory (especially for a drama that implicitly critiques the impact of television on an essentially cinematic genre), but the critique of a certain type of television remains intact. Indeed, Tony's therapy sessions are a world away from of the classic action series, of "cartoon violence" and "MTV aesthetics." In this way, the drama critiques not the medium itself (of which it is clearly now an important exponent) but the refusal of the medium to utilize its basic strengths and inherent possibilities.

CONCLUSION

Tony Soprano is clearly sexist, homophobic, and unashamedly racist, but in his journey through psychoanalysis we learn some of the reasons for his complex condition (a psychological journey that, as we have seen, is seldom equaled in the new gangster genre). As such, we are given the means by which we can start to unravel the historical and personal dynamics by which this character has arrived at such a complex and neurotic state. *The Sopranos* does not pretend to resolve these problems for Tony – indeed, in the process of therapy little real change seems to have been made either to his mental health, life-style or personal views. However, the series does attempt to examine its own narrative desires, asking difficult and uncomfortable questions that simultaneously harness and investigate the genre that Tony both inhabits and ultimately subverts.

As such, Tony's continual nostalgia for his father's long forgotten "moral" standards can be partly regarded as a yearning to return to the age of the "classical" gangster genre – certainly before the rise of the "new brutalism" and the increasing influence of television on this apparently "most cinematic" of all genres. The clash between these two opposing worlds is most clearly played out in the conflict that exists between Tony and his impetuous young protégé, Christopher. While Tony's "traditional" sensibilities appear to represent Coppola's old "film school" generation (represented by the series' own homage to "classical" film aesthetics), Christopher clearly encapsulates the new priorities of Tarantino's "video store" generation, particularly its apparent obsession with the forms and moral aesthetics of the television action series. However, this "televisionization" of the genre is clearly both critiqued and celebrated by the series that both deliberately employs and subverts the intimate dimensions of the small screen, forcing its cinematic heroes into strangely intimate and uncomfortably private situations. In the way, the drama simultaneously modernizes and parodies a genre that has seemingly lost touch with a heritage that was perhaps more morally stable and secure than it can ever appear today.

It is clearly ironic that *The Sopranos* attempts to do all this on the very medium that it implicitly set out to examine and critique. However, by incorporating both elements of television and cinematic practice into its essentially hybrid form, the drama implicitly forces the viewer to confront the very means by which the narrative is produced, contained and finally received. In this way, Chase and his team of writers and directors have created a form of drama that transcends traditional generic boundaries, but still retains the moral framework upon which the gangster genre was originally (if not ambiguously) based. In doing so, the narrative self-consciously satirizes and subverts the changes and developments that have recently taken place in the gangster genre as whole. Perhaps the overriding message of *The Sopranos* is that we are all capable of overcoming and transcending our inherent prejudices and "generic" limitations; that heroism and tragedy resides not just in the epic and the spectacular but also in the personal and the everyday. A view of the world, it could be argued, that is more successfully examined and explored within the inherently "intimate" dynamics of television.

TWELVE

MOBBED UP: *THE SOPRANOS* AND THE MODERN GANGSTER FILM

David Pattie

The characters in *The Sopranos* are obsessed by *The Godfather,* but their maker is obsessed with Martin Scorsese and his street-level view of things. David Chase thought the Mafia movie had finally exhausted itself in 1990 with *GoodFellas.* Scorsese's gangster films, beginning with *Mean Streets* in 1973, are about guys who sit around all day eating, gabbing, and collecting money in bags, guys who intimidate truck drivers and mailmen, guys for whom no petty scam is an indignity . . .
> David Remnick, "Is This the End of Rico?" (43)

At this point in our cultural history, mob movies are classic American cinema, like westerns.
> Jason La Penna, "The Legend of Tennessee Moltisanti" (1008)

During the 1990s American media were saturated with the postmodern. *The Simpsons, Beavis and Butthead* (and MTV in general), *South Park, Buffy the Vampire Slayer* – these and many other programs operated on the assumption that their media-literate audiences were sufficiently skeptical of broadcasting norms to find self-referentiality and intertextuality inherently amusing and worthwhile. When, in 1998, the cable network HBO started to broadcast *The Sopranos,* it seemed as though another program had joined the swelling ranks of TV postmodernity. As David Lavery notes, *The Sopranos* "comes heavy"; it is supersaturated with intertextual references to literature, culture, television, and, of course, the modern gangster film (modern, in this context, denoting a period that begins with the first *Godfather* movie in 1972). These references are neither deeply embedded nor diffuse; they are obsessively foregrounded.

If one thinks of *The Sopranos*, Silvio's Pacino impersonations and Christopher Moltisanti's reprise of De Palma's *Scarface* – "This is *Scarface*, final scene, fuckin' bazookas under each arm. Say hello to my little friends" ("Pax Soprana"/1006) – immediately come to mind. As Ellen Willis observes in this volume,

> Tony and his men love *GoodFellas* and the first two *Godfathers* (by general agreement *III* sucks) and at the same time are objects of fantasy for civilians steeped in the same movies. Tony accepts an invitation to play golf with his neighbor Dr. Cusamano, who referred him to Melfi, and finds that his function is to titillate the doctor's friends; during a falling out with Jennifer he tries to connect with another therapist, who demurs, explaining that he has seen *Analyze This!* ("It's a fucking comedy," Tony protests). Tony's fractious nephew Christopher, pissed because press coverage of impending mob indictments doesn't mention him, reprises *GoodFellas* by shooting an insufficiently servile clerk in the foot. He aspires to write screenplays about mob life, and in pursuit of this dream is used for material and kicks by a Hollywood film director and his classy female assistant. Meanwhile Jennifer's family debates whether wiseguy movies defame Italians or rather should be embraced as American mythology, like westerns . . .

The point can be extended. For one thing, a glance at the cast list reveals that actors in *The Sopranos* have a long history of involvement in the gangster genre: Lorraine Bracco, most famously, starred as Henry Hill's wife in *GoodFellas*; James Gandolfini had parts in *Bullets Over Broadway* and *True Romance*; Dominic Chianese appeared (as Johnny Ola) in *The Godfather Part II*; David Proval (Richie Aprile in the second season) took a leading role in *Mean Streets*, and so on, and so on. For another, the TV series occasionally replays moments from other gangster texts. In "The Legend of Tennessee Moltisanti" (1008), Christopher Moltisanti reprises a scene from *GoodFellas*. In "Denial, Anger, Acceptance" (1003), Don Corleone's castigation of Sonny for revealing his private thoughts in their initial meeting with Sollozzo finds an odd echo in Shlomo Teittleman's rebuke of his complaining son during their sitdown with Tony and crew. Near the beginning of *The Godfather*, a gangster leaving home on his way to commit a murder is reminded by his wife to pick up some cannoli along the way; at the beginning of the second season of *The Sopranos* ("Guy Walks into a Psychiatrist's Office"/2001) a gangster (Philly Parisi) on his way to his own death (he is whacked by Gigi Cestone) hears his wife shouting after him, "Don't forget the pastries." In both sequences, a mobster is killed by someone he trusts; both sequences conclude with a dead body in a car. At the funeral of Jackie Aprile ("Meadowlands"/1004), the mise en scene echoes the burial of Don Corleone: a large headstone prominently displays the dead man's family name, a group of Mafiosi stands apart from the seated head of the family, and a member of that group receives tributes from those at the funeral – a sure sign of a potential shift in the family's power structure. (In *The Godfather* Barzini receives the tributes; in *The Sopranos* Tony occupies Barzini's position.)

The Sopranos, then, patterns itself on previously existing Mafia texts; it relies on our knowledge of those texts for much of its effect. However, simply to say that a text contains moments of self-referentiality is not necessarily to say that it is postmodern, self-consciously or otherwise. To pick a genre example, when the minor Mafiosi in Martin Scorsese's *Mean Streets* receive an unexpected windfall, or find themselves at a moment of crisis, they go to the movies – to see John Ford's *The Searchers* (1955) or Roger Corman's cheap and cheerful Poe adaptation, *The Tomb of Ligeia* (1964). These references, though, cannot be said to be self-referential in the same way as, say, a reference to *Cape Fear* (1991) or *Dr. Strangelove* (1963) in *The Simpsons*. In *Mean Streets*, references to, and quotations from, films have a meaning contained within the text. *The Searchers* is an ironic comment on the failed loners and uncooperative communities in Scorsese's film; the clip from *The Tomb of Ligeia* (the typical ending to a Roger Corman horror film; a visually impressive – and above all, cheap – conflagration) mirrors the impending chaos and destruction that will engulf the central characters.[1] In *The Simpsons*, however, a movie reference (or a joke about the Fox network) stands separate from the development of the main text, commenting both upon the series and on the audience's own cultural knowledge.[2] In *The Simpsons*, if you don't get the reference as a reference – as a moment that stands outside the development of the plot – you don't get the joke.

We have, therefore, two ways of looking at self-referential programs: one in which readings of other media texts can be contained first of all within the film or program in which they occur; and a more overt type of referential work, which relies almost exclusively on the audience's detailed, constantly-updated, cultural intelligence. *The Sopranos*, as the above comments might suggest, has been read as an example of the second kind of text; and certainly it contains moments – Christopher shooting the shop assistant, for example – whose impact is immeasurably heightened for a viewer who has seen *GoodFellas*. I will argue, however, that most of the references to Mafia movies are best understood, not as examples of postmodern self-referentiality *per se*, but as a symbolic framework within which Tony, Paulie, Christopher, Silvio and most of the other Mafia characters in *The Sopranos* attempt to find a meaning and justification for their lives.

THE SOPRANOS AND MOB FILMS

"Let's go to the movies."
Charlie, *Mean Streets*

The characters in *The Sopranos* live in a media-saturated world. References to films, to television series, and to the news pepper their conversation; the viewer is left with the distinct impression that, whatever failings the characters might have, they are at least adept at reading and commenting on the various codes each medium uses. Tony is addicted to the History Channel; Meadow and her friends are similarly addicted to MTV. Christopher provides a skeptical assessment of a televised arrest (on Fox's "Cops": "Like the cop would be calling this asshole 'sir' if the fucking cameras weren't around"); in the same episode, Junior counsels against killing Christopher with the admonishment "We're not making a Western here" ("Denial, Anger, Acceptance"/1003). Movies and television provide raw material for humor: Tony to Junior: "you want my DVD player . . . you can watch *Grumpy Old Men*" ("46 Long"/1002); Junior to FBI Officer: "I wanna fuck Angie Dickinson. We'll see who gets lucky first" ("I Dream of Jeannie Cusamano"/1013); quick descriptions: "Those were feds, right? Just like in *Godfather I*? ("Down Neck"/1007); and name-tags: "Hey, Donnie Brasco!" ("A Hit's a Hit"/1010); "George Clooney. Don't get in the middle of this" ("I Dream of Jeannie Cusamano"/1013). They even feature strongly in more romantic moments; Father Phil and Carmela have a bizarre pseudo-relationship that revolves around food and films; when Carmela eventually rejects him, he responds "I thought you liked movies. *Mea culpa*" ("I Dream of Jeannie Cusamano"/1013). Some characters can provide culturally literate glosses on media images (Meadow, watching a horror film – *The Howling 3* – in which a woman's face splits apart, comments admiringly "Whoo, Georgia O'Keefe! ["I Dream of Jeannie Cusamano"/1013]); hospital workers are understandably amused to find that a US marshal is named McLuhan ("House Arrest"/2011). It is no surprise, then, to find Christopher attempting to write his own movie, even though his script is filled with mis-spelled clichés ("I thought I was daed but I managed to get the drip on him . . . I must be loyle to my capo" ("The Legend of Tennessee Moltisanti"/1008).

In *The Sopranos*, however, mob films are themselves arranged in an ascending order – at least, if judged by the number and relative importance of the references made to each film. At the bottom of this hierarchy-within-a-hierarchy are comedies like *Mickey Blue Eyes* and *Analyze This!*; slightly higher are epics like the De Palma/Stone remake of *Scarface* (an operatic, coke-fuelled and spectacularly gory take on the genre, guaranteed to attract Christopher's approval); and at the top, obsessively referenced (especially in the first season), and watched over and over again, *The Godfather* and *The Godfather II*. There is, though, something profoundly revealing about this obsessiveness, and the desperation it betrays; there is something instructive also in the absence of another set of films whose place in the hierarchy should be assured: Martin Scorsese's *Mean Streets*, *GoodFellas*, and *Casino*. After all, if *The Sopranos* is a postmodern Mafia tale, one might expect that these texts, prominent examples of the genre, would be featured alongside Coppola's films. They do not, however, and the reasons for their absence, as with the reasons behind the *Godfather* films' omnipresence, bring us close to the center of Tony's troubled life.

FRANCIS FORD COPPOLA AND *THE GODFATHER*

When Francis Coppola's original *Godfather* was in production, it attracted some rather unwelcome attention from the very organization whose history it attempted to present. The Italian-American Friendship Association, a pressure group with strong links to the Mafia, moved to deny the film crew access to suitable locations in New York.[3] Over a quarter of a century later, the Mafia had become far more comfortable with the idea of a fictional representation of their activities. An FBI phonetap at the time of the first season found Mafia members enthusiastically discussing *The Sopranos*.[4] It is not that the Italian-American community has entirely accepted the idea of mob movies and TV programs; *The Sopranos* itself has come in for criticism, and the series itself includes discussion of the stereotyping of Italian-Americans as proto-hoods. Something has shifted, however; not only have the activities of a small percentage of a particular prominent American ethnic group become part of the media culture of the US; they also seem to have found an answering echo among the very people who were so wary of Coppola and Evans in the 1970s.

In part, this could be explained by the nature of Coppola's original film. The young director (in his own nervous estimation) took Mario Puzo's graphic, explicit source novel and "turned it into a bunch'a guys sitting around in dark rooms talking" (Biskind 159). He took a project that the studio intended to be a cheap crime thriller and turned it into a monumental study of the importance of the family in Italian-American life (albeit that he chose a family whose members were involved in organised crime). In doing so, he elevated the status of the gangster from small-time hood to tragic American anti-hero. This change was sanctioned by Puzo's novel (in a documentary made for the film's twenty-fifth anniversary, Puzo even noted that, in portraying the Corleones, "I made them out to be good guys"); the film elevates the Mafia further:

> Coppola concedes that the film projects a certain idealized image of the Mafia in the public consciousness. "People love to read about an organization that's really going to take care of us," he has said. "When the courts fail you and the whole American system fails you, you can go to Don Corleone and get justice." (Cowie 66)

The *Godfather* films portrayed the Mafia as a rogue police force for the poor; whatever else they were involved in (and however many bodies littered their path), they fulfilled a necessary function in a country whose justice system was biased in favor of the Anglo-Saxon rich. As Biskind has noted, there is something profoundly reactionary in the film's attitude about the Mafia:

> *The Godfather* looked forward to the conservative family values of the Reagan era. . . . In its emphasis on generational reconciliation, on ethnicity, and on the Mafia as, in effect, a privatized government of organized vigilantes that performs functions that the government can't or won't, it foreshadows the Reagan Right's attack on the Washington establishment in the next decade. "In the seventies, we felt families were disintegrating, and our national family in the White House was full of backstabbing," said [Robert] Towne [a screenwriter who worked on *The Godfather* script]. . . "Here was this role model of a family who stuck together, who'd die for one another. . . . It was really kind of reactionary

in that sense – a perverse expression of a desirable and lost cultural tradition." (164)

Not surprisingly, David Chase regards *The Godfather* as a crucial text in the lives of *The Sopranos'* characters. It is not simply a film; it is an original myth, both for the series and for the community it reflects:

> *The Godfather* is everything to these people. . . . It's their Bible, their Koran. Their Mona Lisa, their Eiffel Tower. It's their thing. . . . Many Italian-Americans simply love it as entertainment . . . or on some level, either overt of covert, revel in the fact that you have these tough guineas. The movie came at a time of race awareness and civil rights progress in America, and the Godfathers can be seen as something like a manifesto of strength and pride for Italian-Americans. The people who made them had to have felt strong about themselves and assimilated . . . (cited in Curtis)

As noted above, *The Sopranos* is littered with references to, and quotes from, the *Godfather* films. We hear about Tony's favorite scene from *The Godfather Part II* – he loves the sequence in Sicily near the film's end when the young Vito Corleone avenges his family's deaths at the hands of Don Ciccio ("Commendatori"/2004). Silvio impersonates, *ad nauseam*, Pacino from *The Godfather Part III*. Another line from *The Godfather Part III* – "Our true enemy is yet to reveal himself" – first heard at the beginning of the second season ("A Guy Walks in to a Psychiatrist's Office"/2001), is ominously repeated in a dream sequence at the season's end ("Funhouse"/2013). Junior makes a Coppola-themed racist joke ("You hear about the Chinese Godfather? He made them an offer they couldn't understand" ["Meadowlands"/1004]). AJ notices that the FBI are taking advantage of a funeral (for Jackie Aprile) to indulge in *Godfather*-style anti-mob surveillance ("Down Neck"/1007). The mobsters prepare for a trip to Italy by watching (or attempting to watch) *The Godfather Part vII* on DVD ("Commendatori"/2004). A dialogue exchange from the first season ("Meadowlands"/1004) gives a good indication of the reverence in which the *Godfather* films are held:

> Christopher: Brendan's dead . . . Brendan's brains are floating in the bathtub. Message job through the eye. Moe Greene special.
> Paulie: What you talking about, Moe Greene?
> Big Pussy: In "One." Moe Greene's eyes got too big for his stomach so they put a small caliber in his eye.
> Christopher: Fucking Mikey Palmice does all their hits.
> Paulie: In his glasses, you mean.
> Big Pussy: Glasses, eyes, why you quibbling with me?
> Paulie: The eye is just how Francis framed the shot. For shock value.

Coppola's films are scrutinized with the kind of attention that only a devoted *cineaste* (a Martin Scorsese, for example) would bring to the study of film. Other gangster films are referenced occasionally (Christopher's direct quotation from the De Palma/Stone remake of *Scarface*, for example), but there is no doubt that the *Godfather* films (or rather, the first two films in the trilogy – only Massive Genius ["A Hit's a Hit"/1010] has a kind word for *The Godfather Part III*) occupy a central place in the characters' affections. They do so, because they enshrine the crucial central myth about the Mafia's place in American society that Chase, Towne, and Biskind outline above. The *Godfather* films provide an image of the Mafia that is romantic, heroic, and above all stable; even though the times might change, the organization's need for a strong central male figure and the desirability of adhering to the old standards (*omerta*, the love of the traditional family) is never seriously questioned. In one of his early sessions with Dr. Melfi, Tony bemoans the absence of traditional male role models in American life: "Whatever happened to Gary Cooper? Now that was an American" ("The Sopranos"/1001). He might also cite Don Vito Corleone; a strong man whose love of family and tradition is ingrained and unassailable; a man who is monumentally certain, implicitly sure of his own judgment, and able to keep his own counsel even in the most adverse circumstances.

However, the elevation of *The Godfather* is not without its problems. It provides Tony and his crew with a secure reference point; but it also establishes a code of behavior that is well-nigh impossible to follow. The Mafia in *The Sopranos* might look up to Coppola's characters, but they also look back on them; the world has changed, and the kind of honorable and free-wheeling behavior set in the 1940s and 1950s and celebrated in the 1970s is not available to the 1990s mobster. Drugs, the RICO statutes, and something less easy to define – a decline in deference, the splitting up of the old communities, the loosening of an implicitly hierarchical social structure – has weakened the modern-day Mafia. Furthermore, the relation between the generations celebrated in *The Godfather* emerges in *The Sopranos* as one of the central points of conflict in the characters' lives. It is not simply that there is no respect any more; it is that the older generation – the Juniors, the Livias – are not worth respecting. The old in *The Godfather* are the repositories of the mob's collective wisdom; in *The Sopranos*, the old are vengeful, fearful children. No wonder that, when the possibility of conflict between Tony and Junior is mooted, the gangsters signal their unwillingness with a phrase taken directly from *The Godfather* ("No-one's going to the mattresses this day and age" ("Pax Soprana"/1006).[5] The *Godfather* films, then, represent an unattainable (if not downright dangerous) myth for Tony and his associates; they offer the illusion of ultimate power, a universe with the Mafia squarely at the center of American life – an image which contrasts painfully with the mob's present status.

Martin Scorsese's Gangster Films

Ellen Willis is wrong. Tony and his crew don't love *GoodFellas*; in fact, they rarely mention it. (In "Big Girls Don't Cry" [2005], Christopher is asked what he'd like to write. He replies "*GoodFellas* and shit" – the only reference.) In the pilot episode, Carmela and Father Phil discuss Tony's taste in films; when the priest asks "What does Tony think of *GoodFellas*?" the conversation is cut short before she gets a chance to reply ("The Sopranos"/1001). Other characters do: at a dinner party, Dr Melfi's extended family discusses the role of gangster films in Italian-American culture, and *GoodFellas* is mentioned. And other Scorsese films are also evoked by non-mobsters. Dr Cusamano gleefully recalls the moment in *Casino* where "Joe Pesci puts the guy's head in a vice . . . " ("A Hit is a Hit" /1010). When Tony takes Meadow to New England to look at colleges, they begin to broach the awkward subject of his work:

> Meadow: Kids in school think it's actually kind of neat.
> Tony: Seen *The Godfather*, right?
> Meadow: Not really, *Casino* they like. Sharon Stone, 70s clothes, pills . . .
> Tony: I'm not asking about those bums. ("College"/1005)

Scorsese himself (or, at least, an actor who looks like him) even puts in an appearance: in "46 Long" (1002): he breezes into a nightclub while Christopher, Brendan, and Adriana are forced to wait outside. (Christopher, ever the movie buff, shouts after him "Marty! *Kundun*! I liked it!")

And yet, if *The Sopranos* is indebted to any gangster movie, it is to the Mafia as depicted in *Mean Streets*, *GoodFellas*, and *Casino*. Tony and his crew are "blue-collar guys" (as Henry Hill's wife puts it in *GoodFellas*); affluence has not significantly changed their tastes or their manners. (In comparison, the Corleones – and especially Vito – have acquired something of the graciousness of royalty.) The world that Scorsese's gangsters inhabit is unpredictably violent, as is the New Jersey of *The Sopranos*; and in both worlds there is no clear separation between the business of crime and the characters' personal lives. There are other, more direct echoes: as noted above, Christopher gets to replay a scene from *GoodFellas* (and to exact a little revenge for the indignities his character suffers in Scorsese's movie). Also, Scorsese's films make use of music as an ironic counterpoint to the onscreen action: in *GoodFellas*, for example, Henry's coke-fuelled mania is scored against a soundtrack that includes the Stones' "Monkey Man." *The Sopranos* uses music in similar fashion. In "The Knight in White Satin Armor" (2012), for example, Tony's sister Janice shoots Richie Aprile, thus removing the man Tony sees as the main threat to his position. After ordering Furio and Christopher to dispose of the body, Tony goes back home, only to find his wife contemplating a trip to Rome without him (she tells him that if she has to perform one more thankless task for Tony and the kids, she "might just commit suicide" – just like Tony's goomah, Irina). Tony is left alone and deflated on the family sofa, while on the soundtrack we hear The Eurythmics comment ironically on the image in front of us: "Hey hey, I saved the world today."

In the world of *The Sopranos*, then, Scorsese's films are the dogs that don't bark. They are part of the series' fictional universe, and yet they are never mentioned by the very people who should by rights have the greatest interest in them. This apparent distaste is surprising; Tony is otherwise keen to stress the achievements of other Italian-Americans, and Paulie (in particular) is comically sensitive to any perceived cultural slights (he even goes so far as to steal a coffee pot from The Great Seattle & Tacoma Roastery Company that looks suspiciously like Starbucks; "We invented this shit," he says in partial justification ["46 Long"/1002]). Why, then are the films of perhaps the most famous Italian-American director not given the same kind of veneration accorded to Coppola's movies?

A partial answer is given by David Remnick in an epigraph to this essay. Scorsese's mob films are despairing, blackly humorous tales of a mob in decline. Even in *Mean Streets*, the first (and least ironic) of the series, the small-time hoods are always at the mercy of each other and of their own stupidity and short-sightedness (one of the characters buys a consignment of camera lenses, only to discover on closer examination that he had paid for camera lens covers). In *GoodFellas*, Henry (Ray Liotta) promises his boss that he won't get involved in the drug trade – and then promptly gets involved in the drug trade. In *Casino*, Nicky Santoro (Joe Pesci) operates betting scams that are chronically inept and makes up in violence for what his schemes lack in intelligence. In each film, the characters have no long-term strategy, no detachment, and no sense of community; their activities, and even their lives, are as contingent as the lives of the mobsters in *The Sopranos*. To be a mobster in these movies is to live in a disintegrating world, as Robert Kolker has observed:

> In all three films, centers come apart. The gangs in *Mean Streets* and *GoodFellas* disintegrate when they turn on each other. This happens with the suddenness of an angry word and a trip out of the safe neighborhood in *Mean Streets*. It happens with a glance at the camera in *GoodFellas*, a glance that has itself been prepared for by other glances: The troubling, Hitchcockian sequence where Karen visits Jimmy at his own warehouse in Queens, for example. Henry's act of betrayal is his own act of salvation. He redeems himself into the banality of a suburban life in the witness protection program, and betrays the audience with a wink and a nod. Irony bites. The thing that bites in *Casino* is a baseball bat, with which two characters are beaten, before the viewer's eyes, into a bloody pulp at the end of the film. (202–3)

At the end of the films, the central characters are left with nothing. Charlie in *Mean Streets* loses all hope of redemption; Henry in *GoodFellas* turns informer and ends the film as nothing more than a completely miserable civilian (and with the ever present threat of discovery by the hoods he has betrayed); Sam Rothstein (Robert De Niro) loses his wife and his casino, watches the old Las Vegas turn into a corporate operation, and has nothing more to say than "And that's that."

This sense – that life is meaningless and that the activities that fill one's days will never amount to anything – haunts Tony Soprano. When AJ discovers existentialism ("D-Girl"/2007), Dr. Melfi identifies his new philosophy as an understandable reaction to a teenager's growing awareness that death robs life of meaning; Tony ruefully concedes that his son has a point. He complains to his therapist that he can't go through life as 'the Happy Wanderer' – that is, in that state of unreflecting joy available to those people who don't examine the basis of their lives too closely ("The Happy Wanderer"/2006). Feverish after a bout of food poisoning, he cries out in his sleep that his life has been for nothing ("Funhouse"/2013). Indeed, the word *nothing* haunts Tony; contemplating his friend Jackie Aprile's imminent death, he says: "I'm not afraid of death, not if it's for something. . . . If all this shit's for nothing, then why do I got to think about it?" ("Denial, Anger, Acceptance"/1003). Later, he tells Dr Melfi that "I'm not a husband to my wife, I'm not a father to my kids, I'm not a friend to my friends, I'm nothing" ("Isabella"/1012).

Scorsese's films, then, dramatize one of Tony Soprano's deepest fears: that the organization to which he has devoted his life does not give that life a meaning. They also play to another fear: that the organization itself has seen better days, and that the Mafia's time has passed. In *GoodFellas*, Mafiosi get involved in the drug trade with disastrous results; *Casino* documents the failure of the Mafia to maintain its share of the gambling business in Las Vegas. Both films dramatize the end of an era in the Mafia's history; simply put, they show the end of the good times. In *The Sopranos*, this process is further advanced. Tony's attitude to the Mafia is neatly summed up in the pilot episode. "Lately I got the feeling I came in at the end," he tells his therapist; for his generation, the "the best is over" and "things are trending downward." His attitude is generally shared; as noted above, the mob in *The Sopranos* no longer practices the old codes celebrated in *The Godfather.* Old notions of honor, of *omerta*, and of the separation of emotion and business no longer apply; the organization of the mob is shambolic; as Christopher says to Brendan, "Nobody knows who runs things any more" ("46 Long"/1002); and betrayal is a fact of life (we learn, for example, that Big Pussy's involvement with the FBI predates the series' beginning; even when he seemed to be a loyal member of Tony's crew, he was already working with its enemies). The idea of the Mafia's inevitable decline has made its way beyond the Mafia itself; the mob has become the property of media pundits and ex-Mafiosi ready to debate on television the long-term future of organized crime in America ("It's not like it was," former member of the Genovese crime family Vincent Rossi tells an interviewer. "Organized crime – the heyday, the Golden Age. . . . That's gone and it's never coming back, and they've only themselves to blame" ("46 Long" /1002). The game is over; in *The Sopranos*, as in Scorsese's films, the Mafia is at a very low ebb indeed.

Conclusion

Gangster movies feature heavily in *The Sopranos* not because they provide the audience with the kind of pleasures more normally associated with an episode of *The Simpsons*, or the sudden arrival of Dracula in Sunnydale at the beginning of the fifth series of *Buffy the Vampire Slayer*; but because Tony and his crew are men adrift, and sorely in need of the kind of comfort only a total immersion in Coppola and Puzo's universe can bring. Tony, Paulie and Silvio's love for a particular type of mob movie is as revealing as, say, Don Quixote's passion for heroic epics, or Catherine Morland's marked partiality for the Gothic novel (it might be worthwhile to note in passing that any definition of postmodernity that can stretch to include both *Don Quixote* and *Northanger Abbey* has, perhaps, lost a certain intellectual suppleness). They are not so much comments on the status of the genre, or on the current state of Postmodern America, as signposts to the emotional health of both of Tony's families.

And the clear lesson is that, emotionally, the outlook is bleak. The Mafia in *The Sopranos* has given itself over to a defining myth that it cannot sustain. Tony is caught between an idealized version of the Mafia's past (which reflects – can't but reflect – badly on the organization's present state) and the unwelcome truth that things were always pretty much as they are now: that his father suffered from the same symptoms as he does; that his mother was always a destructive force in his life; that his marriage is an uneasy compromise between respectability and expediency; that his friendships are distorted and destroyed by his work; and that he himself is driven to violence not because it is good business but because the logic of his world demands that he periodically give way to overwhelming anger. The contradiction at the heart of the character – and the contradiction at the heart of the world he inhabits – is neatly expressed in his attitude toward Coppola's and Scorsese's work. *The Godfather* and its sequels provide a distorting mirror in which Tony and his friends can see an idealized version of their lives; but this vision is doubly displaced – into fiction and into the past – and is unattainable. On the other hand, Scorsese's work is ignored (even though *GoodFellas* and *Casino* are key points of reference for those characters not directly involved in the Mafia) because the fictional mirror Scorsese creates is perhaps too close to Tony's grubby, meaningless, and contingent reality.

THIRTEEN

BEYOND THE BADA BING!:
NEGOTIATING FEMALE NARRATIVE AUTHORITY
IN *THE SOPRANOS*

Kim Akass & Janet Macabe

> Unlike Francis Coppola's *Godfather* epics or Martin Scorsese's *GoodFellas*
> and *Casino*, David Chase's *The Sopranos* deals brutally and honestly with
> the relationship between men and women. And it paints the female
> characters just as vividly as the male ones.
>
> Karen Croft, "Made Women" on Salon.com

Mobsters doing it "doggy-style" to their half-smothered mistresses, bare-breasted pole-dancers ignored by whiskey-swilling gangsters, kept women modeling a Donatella Versace dress with a $2,400 price tag, the long-suffering housewife cooking lasagne alone in her pristine kitchen, the battering to death of Ralphie's pregnant girl, and the brutal rape of Tony's female psychiatrist. These representations of women seem to offer little room for negotiating female narrative authority in *The Sopranos*. Reviewing "the thoroughly regressive portrayals of women" at the beginning of the third season, Martha Lauzen claims that "the show's writers give these psychologically and physically brutalized women no means of escape and . . . no power" (Lauzen, http://www.sicilianculture.com/news/sopranos women.htm). She contends that while the male gangsters are represented as psychologically complex individuals, the females are "one-dimensional characters . . . deserving of their less-than-desirable fate." On the surface at least, the series appears to confirm Lauzen's damning critique by showing Tony Soprano, the Mafia boss from New Jersey, moving freely, unimpeded and unintimidated, between different narrative spaces that he believes he commands, while the females, limited to particular interiors, are denied similar mobility. If reactionary representation and circumscribed marginality define women in *The Sopranos*, then it begs the question: what possible opportunity do the female characters have in asserting their voice within this predominantly male narrative context?

In a series where the mobster finds himself in an unfamiliar generic territory characterized by mundane chores and domestic worries, women play an important role in referencing the new narrative spaces through which the Mafia don progresses. Each week, as he drives from the fringes of New York City up to his front door in the leafy New Jersey suburbs, home to his wife Carmela, or attends his therapy session with Dr Jennifer Melfi, the narrative structure demands that Tony relinquish mob violence in order to function within feminine – and feminizing – spaces. Women, long denied an authoritative voice within the self-contained cinematic world of male violence and defined action (Sacks 9), subtly shape the serial arc, a television narrational structure defined by ambiguity and contradiction. Using strategies associated with soap opera and family drama – listening and confession, gossip and silence, talking-heads and inter-personal skills – women constantly negotiate Tony while consolidating an assured narrative position for themselves. Furthermore, as the series progresses, a meta-narrative emerges that reinvents the gangster type for a media literate television audience. In uncovering how the complex female narrative authority operates, we offer a feminist perspective on why one female fan felt compelled to write in response to the Lauzen article, "I wonder if Lauzen is watching the same show [that] I am?" (Letters to the Editor).

STRUCTURING FEMALE NARRATIVE AUTHORITY

"Lately, I get the feeling that I came in at the end"
Tony to Dr Jennifer Melfi ("The Sopranos"/1001)

Orthodox studies on the gangster genre note a narrative hostility toward women (Sacks, Schatz). As representational types, they tend to fall into two broad categories of virgin (mothers, sisters) and *femme fatale* (sophisticated molls, "broads" who "put out." The mobster shows little regard for the narrative position of these women, focusing instead on the generic need "to assert himself as an individual, to draw himself out of the crowd" (Warshow, "Tragic" 130). Even in more recent film examples, James Wolcott notes how "women in mob movies tend to be either nightclub bimbos decked out in acrylic hair and Christmas-tree-ornament jewelry-Rat Pack chicklets – or troubled spouses minding the fort" (Wolcott 26). So much so that he concludes, "women are seldom the [narrative] activators." Establishing the woman as inferior "other" emerges as a generic necessity, for it is against her that the film gangster can define himself and strengthen his own narrative authority. The ambivalence created by, and embodied within, the Madonna/whore dichotomy serves to construct women as narratively subservient and subject to sexist practices, male humiliation and violence, and patriarchal control.

Outwardly Tony's paradoxical attitude toward women seems to confirm the misogynist generic paradigm related to the position of women. Despite telling long-suffering wife Carmela "you're not in my life; you *are* my life" ("Pax Soprano"/1006), he repeatedly cheats on her with a string of prostitutes, dancers and mistresses, including a Russian whore named Irina, and Mercedes-Benz saleswoman Gloria Trillo. He thinks nothing of instructing a Bada Bing! dancer to give a casual acquaintance a blow job but reproaches his teenage daughter Meadow for talking about fornication at the breakfast table: "Out there it's the 1990s; in this house, it's 1954" ("Nobody Knows Anything"/ 1011). Herein lies Tony's dilemma, as his creator, David Chase notes: "He wishes he'd been born when organized crime was in its heyday, when they had more, controlled more" (Flaherty & Schilling 25). Tony recognizes that the old-world values are fast becoming outdated as he struggles with the new. He feels his life is slowly spinning out of control, that "there is some knowledge that things are out of whack" (Flaherty & Schilling 24). His confusion triggers panic attacks and blackouts, the catalyst being not a violent gangland hit but a family of migrating ducks that have chosen his backyard pool as a temporary resting place.

It is our contention, however, that underpinning this most patriarchal of cinematic forms, complex women come to guide, reshape, and reorder, for better or worse, the complicated narrative world of Tony Soprano brought to television. In particular, we concentrate on two of the most intriguing women in his life: Carmela Soprano, his long-suffering wife and most trusted confidante, and Dr Jennifer Melfi, his analyst and the other woman to whom he unburdens himself.

Similar to other "quality dramas," *The Sopranos* alludes to existing generic texts both as starting point and as cultural reference for its imagined, media-savvy viewer. The presence of Lorraine Bracco as Dr Jennifer Melfi, for example, recalls the 1990 Martin Scorsese film *GoodFellas*, in which she plays Karen Hill, wife of mobster and FBI informant Henry Hill (Ray Liotta). In a male-orientated genre where female characters outside the Mafioso crime circle rarely get the chance to speak, her enunciation of the hitherto untold feminine perspective rechannels the gangster first-person narration through an intimate voice defined by melodramatic conventions. In many ways, *GoodFellas* can be read as a breakthrough gangster film for the female narrator. Bracco indeed recognizes the continuation of the project in *The Sopranos*: "The whole thing about *GoodFellas* was that in showing Karen and the kids . . . it was much more than the stereotypical mama-in-the-kitchen kind of Mafia film. Part of *The Sopranos*, too, is that it shows the . . . humanization" (Bracco 108).

Carmela Soprano in so many ways reminds us of Karen Hill. Both enjoy the good life with beautiful homes and expensive designer clothes while tolerating their husband's philandering ways. Living with the knowledge about the source of the family fortune makes Karen and Carmela uneasy, a tension that places constant strain on both marriages. Yet, despite telling a different story, Karen's voice has little impact upon the narrative arc beyond describing an alternative perspective. As if to learn the lessons from the failure of this cinematic prototype, it would seem that Karen has evolved into two complex television characters to complete this generic transformation. Jennifer and Carmela thus emerge as key to "the slow consolidation of a complex fictional world" (Johnston 10) defined by drama conventions associated with television.

Research into television family dramas has revealed how its formal and generic conventions give nuance to the feminine voice. Jane Feuer, for example, analyzing the ideological consensus in prime-time soap opera serials like *Dallas* and *Dynasty*, determines that such dramas emerge as a "potentially progressive form," precisely because the serial formula and multiple plot structure do away with obvious ideological standpoints and delay narrative resolution. "Since no action is irreversible, every ideological position may be countered by its opposite" (Feuer 15). Ellen Seiter has developed these arguments further in the context of gender. "The importance of small discontinuous narrative units which are never organized by a single patriarchal discourse or main narrative line, which do not build towards an ending or closure of meaning, which in their very complexity cannot give a final ideological word on anything, makes soap opera uniquely 'open' to feminist readings" (Seiter 4).

It is through Carmela and Jennifer appropriating these "open" narrative strategies that we learn just how complicated Tony Soprano really is. Stephen Holden suggests that, "in forcing us to empathize with a thug whom we watch committing heinous acts, *The Sopranos* evokes a profound moral ambiguity" (xviii). Rather than suggest that contradiction originates through seeing two sides of Tony, we contend that this "profound moral ambiguity" is connected intimately to the narrative position of women. For it is from their perspective that we get to know (as he tells his most intimate secrets to both women), someone we morally judge (as Carmela confesses his crimes to her priest and later a psychiatrist), and someone we psychologically study and analyze (as Jennifer dispenses advice while talking about him to her own therapist as well as her ex-husband). The point is that Tony's character emerges as ambiguous precisely because he is being represented within ambiguous narrative spaces defined by women whose attitudes towards him are profoundly morally confused and paradoxical.[1]

The central structuring issue for the female narrative authority is how to integrate the brutal "man of the city, with the city's language and knowledge" (Warshow, "Tragic" 131) into the language and knowledge of respectable middle-class America. In part, this is achieved by a shift between narrative action (personal crisis or cathartic violence) and narrative reflection (the therapy session that allows Tony to talk and be listened to). Consultation with Jennifer emerges as a privileged space for narrative assessment and control, functioning not only to shed light on what has happened, but also to affect the outcome of future events through offering a series of coping strategies. The episode "Boca" (1009) clarifies this pattern when Tony communicates to Jennifer his confusion over why Meadow's school-friend Ally Vandermeed should want to commit suicide, saying "Life is putting Prozac to the test." Later Meadow confesses to her parents that the reason why Ally slit her wrists was because she had slept with Coach Don Hauser, the high school soccer coach. Tony goes ballistic. Jennifer is called upon to give her verdict. In spite of her reluctance ("I don't know why I tell you anything") and his plan for vigilante justice ("Why do you have to set things right?" Jennifer retorts), she advises him to hand the man over to the authorities. The next time we hear about Coach Hauser is from a television news report, in which the police are leading him away in cuffs. The shot/reverse shot between mobster and shrink mirrors this formal pattern, oscillating from narrative conflict to narrative commentary and temporary resolution. This back and forth movement between commentary and action emerges as a central structuring device within *The Sopranos*, allowing the male to speak about his problems and the female to listen and make sense of this information. "The doctor and her patient battle and flirt, and the closer she gets to help him unearth the true cause of his problems, the more explosive their relationship becomes" (Rudolph 63) – a structural pattern repeated within individual episodes and extended across the series arc, a struggle between different formal styles, generic models, and alternate types of gendered action.

Another narrative dynamic operates through the textual construction of gendered authority. The challenge is integrating the violent mobster into the safe respectable American middle-class home, a movement that replaces his usual spheres of action with new ones. Within this re-configuration, the inappropriateness of Tony's brutal cause-and-effect action must be relinquished and substituted for different modes of behavior. It is a problem with civilizing the male that taps into the American mythology of the action hero, an archetype that stretches from the frontiersman, through the westerner, to the urban gangster, and on to Tony Soprano. Repeated across American cinema history, and worked through in each single text, the narrative cycle creates an arc that takes the male hero from being un-socialized to the point of becoming civilized – with the formation of the couple and the promise of domestic stability and home which the union brings. This latest manifestation finds the male in the domestic generic phase shaped by the tranquility of the Soprano family estate efficiently run by Carmela. Indeed, it is *only* through Carmela's understated but dominant position within the home that Tony's masculinity is determined as problematic; she defines the appropriate gendered behaviors, making his unacceptable in the process. Her economical use of words goes right to the heart of Tony's problems: "You know what Tony, maybe you should explore your own behavior, maybe you pass out because you're guilty over something, maybe the fact that you stick your dick into anything with a pulse. You ever thought of exploring that as the root cause?" ("Another Toothpick"/3005). He must, therefore, be temporarily expelled, to discharge his violence before being reintegrated at the end of the evening as he slips into bed with Carmela. This civilizing textual pattern is repeated each week, a cycle from which Tony cannot break free. No wonder he needs therapy. But, as Tony soon discovers, his options are circumscribed by a morality defined by civilizing women, including his female therapist. For example, after informing on Coach Hauser, he stumbles through the door, high on a mix of Vicodin and alcohol. The episode concludes with his garbled confession: "Carm, I didn't hurt anyone." She, in turn, stands impassively over his body while looking up at her daughter sitting on the stairs ("Boca"/1009).

Another textual tension that emerges in the "Boca" episode is how women (in this case, Meadow) often set a chain of narrative events in motion through indiscretion and revelation. Meadow, for example, uses precisely the same words as her grandmother ("Now what have I done?") after she has told her parents the truth behind Ally's attempted suicide. Despite her protestation, she knows exactly what effect her words will have on her morally righteous father whose day job just happens to be a mob boss. "I'm losing my fuckin' mind," Tony rants, making it clear how, once again, the women in his life contribute to his perception that the world is somehow out of whack. Women are instrumental in controlling the distribution of hidden knowledge, able to keep secrets but knowing when to reveal them. Some women, however, are better at this narrative task than others. Carmela, for example, knows exactly what to say and when to say it. Her no-nonsense straight-talking manner belies a complex yet authoritative narrative position. In the same episode, Carmela tells Tony, as they prepare for bed, that his Uncle Junior performed oral sex on his mistress Bobbi Sanfillipo ("Let's just say he has acquired a taste for her"). The information about Junior's unmanly sexual etiquette will be used later by Tony against his older relative, further precipitating the breach between uncle and nephew. In her subtle and not so unconscious way, Carmela has shaped a complex narrative arc for the two men as personal animosities and deep-rooted family bonds intermingle with a bitter leadership struggle that underpins the series' epic sensibility.

Finally, women in *The Sopranos* know how media representation of the gangster works, a knowledge that is played out between women as receivers of media texts and gangsters as products of them. Warshow contends that the gangster is a "creature of the imagination," the invention of an "imaginary city" related to the modern urban world ("Tragic" 133). Whether on television, the Internet, or in newspapers, media representation of FBI attempts to crack down on New Jersey's most infamous Mafia figures proliferates throughout the series, once again replaying the inexorable appeal that the mass media and mobster have for one another. While women may be absent from the equation, they are positioned as spectators, either as eyewitnesses interviewed by the press, television viewers or readers of the press accounts. It is Carmela who watches the news coverage as the high school soccer coach is taken into police custody, for example. Earlier, Meadow shows AJ a web-site entirely devoted to the Mafia family and their exploits, including police profiles of their male relatives ("Meadowlands"/1004). Denied direct access to the sites of male action, women come to hear the mobster stories from the thrilling and dramatic accounts that appear in different media. Yet, in listening to these tales of daring criminal-do, women point to the gap that exists between fictional gangsters and their real-life selves living normal lives in the suburbs. In so doing, they use that knowledge to their advantage.

> "Cunnilingus and psychiatry have brought us to this."
>
> Tony tells Carmela, in "Boca" [1009]

Gender discord and dysfunctional familial relations soon emerge as the root cause of Tony's panic attacks and repeated blackouts. As Charles Strum writes, "the audience sees Tony in all his many guises, including the inner Tony, a man not fully understood by his wife, his girlfriend, his passive-aggressive mother" (104). Our first impression of Tony sitting outside Jennifer's office seems to confirm what Strum is saying about gendered miscommunication ("The Sopranos"/1001). Tony is framed between the legs of a female bronze statue ("The Matriarchy," Chases calls it on the commentary on the first season DVD). A shot/reverse shot pattern moves back and forth between the nude torso and a bemused Tony who is unable to take his eyes off the enigmatic feminine form. Here is the articulation of the gangster's (narrative) breakdown. For rather than suggest as Strum does that women misinterpret him, it is clear that Tony is depressed precisely because they know him *only too well*.

Despite Tony's privileged narrative position, *The Sopranos* opens with the upwardly mobile gangster visiting a female psychiatrist who proscribes Prozac to help him cope with depression. He tells his new therapist about Gary Cooper, his idea of a real American man: "The strong, silent type. He wasn't in touch with his feelings, he just did what he had to do." Referencing a cinematic world where heroes had defined goals allows him to voice his anxiety that the field of male action is not what it was. Nothing has prepared the Mafia don for his aging mother's incessant griping, the guilt she burdens him with, the disrespect he gets from his wife and daughter, and crew members breaking old world codes of loyalty. "I feel exhausted just talking about it," he laments. "Talking about it," however, is precisely what he must do.

The "potentially progressive [television dramatic] form" of uncertainty and ideological contradiction allows women like Carmela and Jennifer to take control. Reworking generic conventions of the gangster film through strategies associated with open-ended television discourses, female narrative authority comes from its knowing-ness, for while knowing the forms are not perfect, they know how to work them to their advantage all the same. For example, the Mafia capo does what no screen gangster has done before him – he visits a female psychiatrist. Urban corruption exposing the underbelly of respectable society becomes reconfigured as dark family secrets and an emotionally starved self buried beneath Tony's pathologically brutal exterior. Encouraging Tony to talk allows Jennifer to gradually reveal a distracted mother figure with borderline personality disorder rather than a case study of pure criminality. But, as is the nature of therapy, nothing happens straightaway and Tony's journey toward self-knowledge is a long, drawn-out and often confusing process. It is little wonder, then, that Tony feels unable to affect control over his narrative arc. Trying to convince Carmela that there is nothing going on between him and his therapist, just after he has confessed his love to Jennifer, he says: "What you feel is not real; and what you're not feeling is the real agenda" ("Pax Soprana" /1006).

Direct action is rendered problematic and resolutions unclear for Tony as women prevent him from revealing the true horror of his lifestyle. Answering Jennifer's question about the day he had the first panic attack, he begins to elucidate his experience of anxiety during a recent business deal – "We saw this guy, and there was this issue of an outstanding loan." Jennifer interrupts. She warns him that anything said in her office is strictly confidential; however if he were to divulge something, "say, a murder," she is bound by the law to report it. Her action effectively blocks the gangster from telling his story. Tony is momentarily silenced. Just as Jennifer instructs him to be careful in what he tells her in the consulting room, Carmela also censors the information that flows from Tony. Both women know who he is; but for different reasons they do not want to hear his version. In so doing they close down his cause-and-effect gangster narrative to replace it with a more open-ended ambiguous one. Limiting what he can say compromises Tony's therapy and his authority in the home but, by censoring him, Carmela and Jennifer come to re-order and rewrite his violent and socially unacceptable behavior.

This subtle ordering of Tony's narrative world is a feature from the start. It begins in understated ways, with Tony simply adopting what his therapist has said to him. For example, he stands around the barbecue with his cronies, telling them that "hope comes in many forms," a phrase used only moments earlier by Jennifer ("The Sopranos"/1001). Time and again he repeats her word-for-word – for example when he tries to persuade his mother to move into Green Grove Retirement Home: "I know seniors who are inspired," he rants to Livia as he prowls around her living room ("46 Long"/1002). He may not be convinced about what he is saying but he knows that it is the right thing to say: the next sequence finds the Soprano family looking around Green Grove with Livia. Jennifer's words are also bounced around between him and Gloria as they begin a short but torrid affair in Season Three. The assimilation of Jennifer's psychoanalytical vernacular by Tony thus allows a feminine voice to penetrate into a generic text that has traditionally excluded it.

Hers is a voice to which Tony will come to listen as he attempts to regain precarious control both of his New Jersey businesses as well as the series narrative. Soon Jennifer is providing strategies that will help him deal with his mid-life crisis. For example, Tony faces a power struggle with his Uncle Junior while having to deal with a recalcitrant mother who wants him dead for putting her in Green Grove. Jennifer offers practical advice on managing elderly relatives, advising that the best way to handle them is "to let them have the illusion of being in control." A narrative shift between the therapy session to the Bada Bing! finds Tony reading *Eldercare: Coping with Late Life Crisis* when news of mob boss Jackie Aprile's death comes on the television. Later at the funeral it becomes clear that Tony has taken all the advice to heart, and made his uncle the nominal head of the family while taking over behind the scenes. Season Three finds Tony counseling Patsy Parisi ("Fortunate Son"/

3003) whose twin brother, Philly, was killed execution-style on the orders of Tony ("Guy Walks into a Psychiatrist's Office"/2001). He adopts Jennifer's professional manner as, facing him in a chair, he tells him: "Tell me you've put this grief behind you." When Patsy merely agrees with him, Tony, in the most professional therapist's manner, tells him: "Now let me hear you say it." Only when Patsy has actually repeated his words does Tony appear finally satisfied ("Mr. Ruggerio's Neighborhood"/3001). Tony is being equipped with the new interpersonal skills needed for dealing with the human resource problems facing the mob at the beginning of the twenty-first century.

Jennifer uses psychoanalysis as a tool to unlock the narrative for Tony, explaining the real meaning behind unexpected events. In "Nobody Knows Anything" (1011), Tony asks Jennifer why his friend Salvatore "Pussy" Bonpensiero should be experiencing severe back pain when nothing physical seems to be wrong. Reluctant to put forward a theory at first ("Every time I offer my opinion about any of your friends, you go crazy"), she finally speculates that he may have secrets that are proving a heavy burden. In so doing, she plants the seed of suspicion that will be played out in Season Two culminating in Tony's dream when Pussy, appearing to him as an Abalone, confesses his guilt ("Funhouse"/2013). Analyzing the significance of his Lithium-induced hallucination involving the beautiful Isabella; she proffers the theory that the mystery woman is his Madonna fantasy, a substitute for his cold, dyspeptic mother. Without prompting, she furthers the theory that Livia could have been behind the recent attempt on his life, inadvertently revealing the truth ("Isabella"/1012). Jennifer says what Tony can only suspect and reveals what is unthinkable within the gangster genre: betrayal at the hands of both the gangster's most trusted friend and his mother. This powerful narrative position – to say what should not be said – is, however, a precarious one. Jennifer finds this out to her cost when she identifies Livia's nihilism and borderline personality disorder. It takes her several weeks and numerous bottles of vodka to recover from her patient's violent reaction.

Carmela is much better at narrative negotiation than Jennifer, more used to having to deal with feminine exclusion from two patriarchal worlds: Catholicism and the Mafia. Her handling of Tony emerges as much subtler than Jennifer's direct psychoanalytical approach. When AJ's science teacher has his car stolen, she casually mentions it to Tony as she serves up breakfast ("46 Long"/1002). (AJ is only getting Ds in science so Carmela knows Tony will want to help.) Mr. Miller's car (or a reasonable facsimile) mysteriously reappears in the school playground as Carmela requested. Tony and Uncle Pussy get the final credit as AJ boast to his chums: but this is a mere detail. Carmela has got her own way; she is the real power behind Tony Soprano. Far from being trapped by the all-embracing patriarchal structures, she has found solutions that work to her advantage. Outwardly beleaguered, and frustrated by his atheism and constant womanizing, Carmela repeatedly uses this knowledge as an "emotional leverage" (Croft). On one level, she is able to get Tony to do what she asks, from offering money to friends ("Denial, Anger, Acceptance"/1003), to letting Parvati/Janice, his estranged sister, stay in the house ("Toodle-Fucking-oo"/2003), and her change of heart over the vasectomy ("From Where to Eternity"/2009).

On another level, Carmela's response to Tony's sexual indiscretions takes the form of silent reproachfulness. In "Employee of the Month" (3004), after giving Tony Jennifer's telephone message about her "car accident," she sits and looks while Tony talks about the long-term scarring effects of a knee injury. Her silence becomes pregnant with indignation and reproof. The more he speaks, the guiltier he seems to be for caring *too much* about Jennifer's welfare. Carmela forces a confession as he finally blurts out that she has been invited to join his therapy session. In so doing, Carmela's silence, accompanied by a harsh reproving look, forces Tony to act to ameliorate his unease and sense of guilt.

The clash of these two different female narrative approaches precipitates a crisis for Tony. Jennifer may have told Tony that he accords his mother "an almost mystical power to wreak havoc" but these two "good" mother-substitutes, pulling him in conflicting narrative directions, cause the real havoc in Tony's mind. "Is this a woman thing?" he asks Jennifer. "You ask me how I'm feeling. I tell you how I'm feeling and now you're going to torch me with it." In contrast with Carmela's reaction to the recovery of Mr. Miller's car, Jennifer's response to the replacement of the starting motor on her vehicle is of quite a different order. She watches through the window as Paulie Walnuts steals her car to get it repaired and berates Tony for his trouble as a violation of her privacy on its return. He brings Jennifer coffee ("Pax Soprana"/1006), but she refuses his "gift," telling him that it is not appropriate. Carmela, on the other hand, rejoices in the sable coat that he gives her and, although she knows it is a payoff for his guilty conscience, accepts it gratefully ("Funhouse"/2013). Tony is confused by the different reactions: he *did* for Jennifer what Carmela *expects* him to do. What Tony yet has to learn is that the two narrative authorities are struggling for supremacy through, and for, him.

Surviving in a shaky marriage is the price Carmela must pay for her narrative position. Her dilemma is constantly being articulated, such as when she counsels Angie against divorcing Pussy despite suspecting her own husband of infidelities while on business in Naples ("Commendatori"/2004). In Season Three, Carmela is referred by Jennifer to a psychiatrist (Dr. Krakower), who tells her that she is living on blood money and should take her children and leave Tony and all her belongings ("Second Opinion"/3007). Instead she tells Tony to donate $50,000 to Columbia University, thereby resolving her crisis, and resorting to the narrative strategy that works for her. She returns to the confessional to talk over her dilemma as she did with Father Phil in Season One. Outside of the confessional Father Obosi reassures her that divorce from Tony is out of the question. He counsels her to "live on the good part, and forgo those things that lie without it" ("Amour Fou"/3012), Carmela chooses the advice that suits her narrative arc and continues to subtly handle Tony, ignoring his misdeeds with a conscience cleared by her Catholicism. At a lunch attended by the Mafia wives, Carmela agrees with Rosalie Aprile's summation of Hillary Clinton's decision to stand by her man: "She's a role model for us all." Rosalie asserts that Hillary stayed with Bill because she was obviously planning her own thing and was rewarded for putting up with her husband's infidelities ("Amour Fou"/3012). According to the mob wives, serial infidelity is a small price to pay for the more beneficial task of being in control of their husbands' narrative arcs.

Long-suffering she may be, but Carmela is no archetypal Mafia wife. Unlike her predecessors, she makes full use of the social advantages of being married to the mob. Nowhere is this display of quiet power more apparent than in "Full Leather Jacket" (2008). Realizing that Meadow will need more than good grades to get into a prestigious school like Georgetown, and not wanting her to go to school in California, she secures a letter of recommendation for her daughter. It is a narrative moment where she shows the "vein of steel" that she usually keeps hidden under her "manicure, plucked and dyed eyebrows, fur coats [and] piety" (White 13). At first she asks her neighbor Jeannie Cusamano to intercede on her behalf, and inquire if her sister Joan O'Connell, a successful lawyer and a graduate of Georgetown, will write the letter. Joan is adamant that she will not do it. Armed with home-baked goods, Carmela decides to visit Joan in person. Ricotta pie with pineapple may be all that Carmela can offer Joan in return for Meadow's reference, but it is enough for Joan to understand the meaning of the gift and its gesture accordingly. While denying Joan's accusation that she is threatening her, she brooks no arguments. Joan *will* write the letter for Meadow: it is an offer she cannot refuse. No threats have been uttered, no explicit warnings issued, but her silent intimidation is clearly understood by Joan. It may be dressed up as another kind of neighborly gesture but it is powerful as when Fabian "Febby" Petrullo sees Tony driving around Maine with his daughter ("College"/1005). Carmela thus makes the stereotype work for her.

The price Jennifer pays is more problematic. Living outside the Soprano clan, she is not automatically protected by the family name. Although she initially reaps the benefits of being associated with Tony Soprano, getting a table in an exclusive Manhattan restaurant and having her car fixed after a string of excuses from her mechanic, Jennifer soon discovers her life may be in danger as a consequence of her privileged access to Tony's story. Season Two finds her operating out of a motel room and her practice seriously compromised because of her sudden flight. This uncomfortable narrative position is fully realized with her savage rape ("Employee of the Month"/3004). With her attacker released on a technicality, she confesses to Dr. Kupferberg that she only has to tell Tony to get the vigilante justice she wants. At their first meeting after this revelation, Jennifer struggles with her dilemma within a shot/reverse shot pattern involving her and Tony. Covering her mouth to ensure her silence, she bursts into tears. It is a moment of narrative crisis, for not only does she change her mind about terminating Tony's therapy so that the narrative can continue, but she also resists the temptation to tell him about her rape and knowingly unleash mobster retribution. By keeping both therapeutic and narrative barriers intact, as the credits roll, Jennifer has regained control of herself and her narrative authority.

If these women are powerful alone, imagine the confusion that they can wreak together. If Tony was bouncing between narrative strategies before, his confusion becomes more intense when, in couple therapy, he has to accommodate both narrative authorities within the same fifty-minute slot. At their first meeting Carmela is antagonistic towards Jennifer ("Another Toothpick"/3005), reminiscent of their first conversation when Jennifer called the family home to change an appointment. Carmela, assuming Tony is sleeping with his therapist, refuses to take down the number, acidly saying that she "lost [her] pencil up his ass" ("College"/1005). So it is not too surprising that Carmela gives vent to her frustration when, in response to her question about how Tony's panic attacks make her feel, she cuttingly remarks that she is concerned by Melfi's "inability" to cure Tony's panic attacks. He in turn jumps to Jennifer's defense. Silence and tears mark the journey home. Carmela is upset not because her marriage is in trouble but because Jennifer took his side. Next time Carmela goes alone. At this meeting both women realize how difficult it is to be married to Tony. Their looks acknowledge the other as being an important narrative voice for Tony. From this encounter, Jennifer takes away the knowledge that Tony's wife may leave him but he will never leave her. So, when Tony ruminates to her that the reason he is attracted to dangerous women is because he is subconsciously looking for a way out of his marriage, she swiftly discounts his theory ("Amour Fou"/3012). Such a moment of narrative revelation once again exposes the power that these two women have over Tony Soprano.

Revealing the Narcissism of the Gangster

"I thought we'd made some progress on your narcissism."
Jennifer Melfi to Tony, in "Meadowlands" (1004)

"It's like watching a train wreck – I'm repulsed by what he might tell me but somehow I can't stop myself from wanting to hear it."
Jennifer Melfi to her therapist, in "House Arrest" (2011)

Media self-reflexivity operates throughout, as well as being embedded right into the very form of, *The Sopranos* text. Women play an important role in foregrounding these intertextual references, for it is through her agency that the gangster's fascination – and ours – with his own generic story is exposed. In the episode "The Legend of Tennessee Moltisanti" (1008), Christopher Moltisanti bemoans the fact that his friend Brendan's death ("Denial, Anger, Acceptance"/1003) has been reported in the media while there is no mention of him. He does not have long to wait. His moment of glory comes with a phone call from his tearful mother telling him that his name is in the paper "with other lowlife wise-guys." Whereas Tony moans that "every piss I take is a fuckin' news story" ("Big Girls Don't Cry"/2005), Christopher is jubilant and runs out to obtain (that is steal) as many newspapers as possible. As if we did not get the message, this scene is inter-cut with Jennifer's family therapy session. While her ex-husband Richard is moaning about her involvement with Tony Soprano, Dr. Reis, the therapist, interjects to say that his uncle was a driver for Louis "Murder Inc" Buchulter Lepke. There are different levels at work in revealing the glamor of being a mobster, the gangster's narcissism, the irresistible attraction we have for the mob, and the role that women play in animating and exposing this fascination.

Warshow has identified narcissism as a key character trait of the American gangster: an individualist whose self-centered pursuit of fame, fortune, and media headlines excludes all else ("Tragic" 133). The gangster has always been in love with his own mythic image; and his latest incarnation proves no exception. Just as Silvio Dante, admiring himself in his new stolen Italian suit, reprises his Michael Corleone "When I thought I was out, they pulled me back in" impression, his fellow crew members "model themselves after their screen idols" (Strum 108). With few appropriate role models left alive, it would seem right for Pat Sierchio to conclude that the "gangster uses his fictional anti-heroes as a kind of instructional manual on how to act like a mobster" (Sierchio 39). "Where's my arc?" Christopher passionately pleads to Paulie. "I got no identity" ("The Legend of Tennessee Moltisanti"/1008). If Christopher cannot get his name in the press for his violent exploits, he will ensure his own cinematic immortality by writing his own Hollywood script ("D-Girl"/2007). What is clear is that our gangster has begun to believe his own press and fallen in love with his media representation.

Women use this knowledge about the media-obsessed gangster narcissist to their advantage. An example can be found in the use of music. As if to invert its conventional use in melodrama, music, both diegetically-motivated and non-diegetic, operates as a soundtrack for the mobster's imagined life in the (media) spotlight. Carmela may love listening to opera, but gangsters *live* the poignancy of Frank Sinatra singing "It Was a Very Good Year." The beginning of Season Three sees Tony driving away from home singing, "I'm a fool to do your dirty work, I don't want to do your dirty work, no more . . ." Tony imagines he is back in control to the words of Steely Dan.

Non-diegetic music is further used to indicate male emotional excess that cannot be accommodated into the feminine text. Since Carmela has no need to displace her emotions onto the mise en scene as her melodramatic predecessors have done, she is perfectly able to articulate her dissatisfaction. Tony, in contrast, makes full use of the soundtrack to articulate his bewilderment as he struggles to find a language to adequately express his emotions. Melodramatic inversion is demonstrated in the penultimate episode of Season Two ("The Knight in White Satin Armor"/2012). Although Tony has spent the last days cleaning up after his unruly women (his sister has just shot her fiancé dead, and his mistress has her stomach pumped for twenty Halcyon washed down with vodka), and exchanged insults with the most unruly of them all, Livia, Carmela has had enough. Her caustic retort – "You want me to feel sorry for a whore that fucks you?" – makes clear her position. She and Rosalie Aprile are off to Rome, because, as she says, if she does not get away she "just might commit suicide." To the strains of "I Saved the World Today," Tony sits alone. The non-diegetic music does not speak of Carmela's anger but resounds with his desperation. He surely feels that he did the right thing. Annie Lennox singing "Everybody's happy now/the bad things gone away" might ironically celebrate the engagement of Janice and Richie but its non-diegetic use here carries an emotional charge when laid over Carmela's rejection of Tony. His narcissism suffers yet another puncture wound from Carmela. There being nothing more for him to say, Tony leaves the expression of his emotional state to The Eurythmics as the credits roll.

Carmela is the one who brings the narcissistic Tony and the fascinated audience back down to earth. The first episode from Season Three finds the FBI laying a bug in the Soprano family home. Accompanied by the savvy remix of The Police's "Every Breath You Take" and "Theme from *Peter Gunn*," the agents miss vital details as they are so absorbed in being hip, cool detectives from classic television shows. All they have on tape is an exchange between Tony and Carmela about his diet and teeth. Carmela gives him instructions: "You need more roughage in general"; "You should use floss." The excitement of the mission ends with the reality of domesticity behind this narcissistic world. The FBI may have infiltrated the Soprano household but the basement is Carmela's domain, and she knows how the fiction works. They may be watching Tony, but they will learn little from listening to a woman who knows the first rule of a Mafia wife: keep your mouth shut. *Capisce*?

While Carmela has no delusions, Jennifer's response to the gangster's narcissism is more complex. As Carmela functions to point out Tony's uncivilized flaws as the urban gangster rubs elbows with his respectable "mayonnaiser" neighbors over the barbecue, Jennifer is positioned to analyze and dismantle the ego-ideal of an American frontiersman so that he can function without violence. As soon as Carmela exposes his vulnerabilities with her insightful and no-nonsense critique, Jennifer is there to ask him: "How are you doing with this?" Her interest in the psychology of the Mafia don functions to probe deep into the reasons for his "Machiavellian calculation and brutal violence" (Flaherty & Schilling 25). But despite purporting to demystify his tormented soul and pathological dysfunctionalism, she is, in fact, responsible for keeping his narcissistic self – and our fascination with it – in place. With her motives for wanting to treat him remaining paradoxical, as she becomes irresistibly drawn to him "even as she is disturbed by his lifestyle and tendency to erupt – in anger" (Flaherty & Schilling 26), her ambivalent fascination with Tony Soprano functions as a surrogate for ours.

While the viewer *is* able to see the unpleasant and bloody reality of his criminal life, the series consistently denies Jennifer that privilege. It allows for a space to open up in which the adrenaline rush of the latest hit can be interrogated. In the standard pattern for the series, violent cathartic action is followed by therapy with Jennifer. In "Big Girls Don't Cry" (2005), her final decision to take him back over a glass of Chardonnay is structured next to Tony's visit to the Bahama Skies Tanning Salon with his new crew member from Naples. Furio collects the protection money with ruthless efficiency, and just at that moment, Jennifer rings Tony on his mobile phone: "Ah, fuck it. No cure for life," he replies. The movement back into therapy offers a space to possibly analyze why Tony responds in a sexually charged way. Not so: instead Tony begins to tell us a story about his father. Jennifer's reaction is predictably oblique, responding with a question rather than an answer: "Giving the beating or taking it?" The id is the body armor of Tony Soprano but it is constantly deconstructed and interrogated by an ambiguous feminine narrative mediator, revealing a complicated ego to television viewers complicit with Jennifer's repulsed yet captivated position.

Warshow argues that to a certain extent the gangster "is what we want to be and what we are afraid we may become" ("Tragic" 131). Despite knowing all the risks she takes in treating Tony Soprano, the reasons behind her decision to keep seeing him contribute to a narrative tension. Each season Jennifer considers breaking off the therapy but at the last minute decides to keep seeing him. After recounting her *Wizard of Oz* dream/fantasy involving Tony to her therapist, he dares to voice the real reason for her fascination: "I'm concerned that treating a mobster provides you some vicarious thrill" ("Big Girls Don't Cry"/2005). Her response is surprisingly fierce. Cursing in a profane manner reminiscent of her mobster client, she storms out. But the truth has been revealed.

Throughout the series, she expresses unexpected interest in, and uninhibited moments with, the Mafia boss. After being invited to dinner at the Cusamanos, the Sopranos' neighbors, she seizes the opportunity to glimpse his home ("A Hit is a Hit"/1010). Balanced precariously on the toilet seat, she strains to see out of the window. Sometimes it appears difficult for her to conceal her fascination with his stories. As Tony recalls the sound of Jefferson Airplane when he first found out his father was a gangster, he ends his 1967 musical tour by making Jennifer laugh out loud ("Down Neck"/1007). Later, after recounting his mother's response to his boyhood request for an electric organ ("I could stick this fork in your eye"), the young Livia, with fork in hand, staring straight into the camera, is cut with a close-up of Jennifer who is leaning slightly forward, both intrigued and appalled by what she has just heard. The therapy sessions are peppered with these moments when Jennifer, in her silence, cannot quite hide her complicated attraction to Tony; as he asks her after confessing to having a 24-year-old mistress: "How are you doing with it?" ("Down Neck"/1007).

That Tony is the center of the narrative is not in question, but why he should seem so uneasy about this position has been the purpose of this essay. If Tony's favorite expression, is "those who don't understand history are doomed to repeat it," then Carmela and Jennifer's could be "those who do not understand how complex media narrative strategies work are condemned to an anachronistic cinematic past." These women have read the books and seen the films on television. They know how the patriarchal script reads but are still able to shape Tony's narrative arc, precisely because they know how to make it work for them in the familiar generic world of television where rules are not constant. The end of the episode "Guy Walks into a Psychiatrist's Office" (2001) clarifies how this nuanced narrative position allows women to gain control. Tony returns home to find Carmela in the ergonomic kitchen. Suspicious of his early return, she sets the table and prepares pasta. "Cheese. Something to drink?" she tartly asks. Tony sits down to eat and she gently straightens his collar. She sits down next to him and starts to go through the mail. No words are spoken. So far so submissive. Yet it is the very sparseness of the scene that unsettles the viewer so used to the relentless dramatic pace of television drama. It strikes one as strange, even unsettling. The stillness articulates Carmela's formal authority over a savvy, media-saturated series that is punctuated with film references, pop songs, and media-hip gangsters. But the silence also represents her authority as Tony accepts her disapproving looks and her orders to sit down. It is his tacit acceptance of her authority that the silence acknowledges. At the moment we recognize the significance of the silence and the unspoken nature of their relationship, the song "Time's On Your Side" filters in and across the final credits. Tony may still want to problem-solve in fifty-minutes but Carmela and Jennifer are in it for the longer duration and already making plans for Season Four.

FOURTEEN

WISEGUY OPERA: MUSIC FOR *SOPRANOS*

Kevin Fellezs

Christopher: Our thing once ruled the music business. Did ya know that? We bankrolled acts . . . blacks, everybody. Paid the deejays or busted heads to get 'em played on the air.

Adriana: There were some great Italian singers.

Christopher: Fuckin' A. Franki Valli, Dion, The Rascals, that whole Philly thing. My dad used to talk about those guys. Now? Fuckin' drum machines, some ignorant poetry and any fourth grade dropout *ditsoon* is "chairman of the board."

("A Hit is a Hit"/1010)

VERISMO AND CONTEMPORANEITY

"Music," William Congreve once said (in *The Mourning Bride*), "hath charms to soothe the savage breast." The savage breasts that gather at the Bada Bing!, contrary to Congreve, are more often moved to confrontational, if not violent, outbursts while the soundtrack underscores their antagonisms. David Chase, in his decision to forgo music scoring and rely exclusively on source music,[1] heightens the role music performs in *The Sopranos*.[2] In an interview on the HBO website devoted to *The Sopranos*, Chase reveals the strong link music provides for the series.

HBO: Music's a very important part of the show as well. Can you tell us a bit about the music?

Chase: I don't know why that is. Music has always been intrinsic to me with movies. It's television but I consider it movies but . . . as a writer

> I've always been inspired by music. I listen to music while I'm trying to think of ideas and I just like it. So even from the beginning I said [that] we really need to have a good music budget. And originally people said "Why, I don't get it, what do you mean music budget?" And, now I think they see it. It creates a tremendous mood and it also creates a sense of contemporaneity. I think that's the word, whatever the word is, contemporaneousness.

The HBO series, while often described as soap opera, can also be compared to "real" opera. To cite an example, when Frank Sinatra sings "It Was a Very Good Year" over scenes tracing the activities of various characters in the opening episode to the second season ("Guy Walks into a Psychiatrist's Office"/2001), the correlation between opera – soap or otherwise – becomes apparent. Montage and music relate to each other in complicated and expository ways. Ellen Willis, in her article in this volume, writes:

> While the sheer entertainment and suspense of the plot twists are reminiscent of Dickens and his early serials, the underlying themes evoke George Eliot: the world of Tony Soprano is a kind of postmodern *Middlemarch*, whose inhabitants' moral and spiritual development (or devolution) unfolds within and against the norms of a parochial social milieu.

While Willis sees correlations between *The Sopranos* and Dickens and Eliot, I maintain that Rossini, Verdi, and Puccini can also be seen as precursors to the series in the interrelation of music, plot, and character development.

The *verismo* (realist) style with which Puccini was loosely associated closely resembles the form *Sopranos* creator David Chase envisioned for the series. Verismo opera, influenced by movements outside of music such as the naturalist writings of Emile Zola, developed libretti concerned with peasants, petty criminals, and their everyday lives. This stood in stark contrast to the operas of, say, Wagner, which dealt with gods and goddesses or historical and mythical figures – certainly not the starving artists of Puccini's *La Bohème*. As one commentator notes, "The aim of the Italian verismo composers at the turn of the twentieth century was to write emotionally raw operas with realistic depictions of everyday people" (Tommasini 1). These "everyday people" were invariably drawn from the underworld or the artistic communities. The parallel between verismo opera and *The Sopranos* is more than just thematic, however.

The comic savagery of Gioacchino Rossini's *Il Barbiere di Siviglia*, Giuseppe Verdi's *Rigoletto*, and Giacomo Puccini's *Tosca* are readily recognizable in the dark comedy of *The Sopranos* (particularly if one recalls Jonathan Miller's famous production of *Rigoletto* [English National Opera, 1982] recast as a 1950s New York mob story). Where Rossini wielded his comic ear in grand *buffo* (comic) style (particularly in *Il Barbiere di Siviglia* and *La Cenerentola*), Verdi drew on what Italian censors of the time derided as obscene and repellant scenes of debauchery and vice. Puccini's popular audiences, meanwhile, recognized in the melodies and lyrics a dramatized reflection of their emotional and social lives, no matter the often melodramatic libretti. The writers of *The Sopranos* depict similarly drawn characters and situations that point up both the characters' exaggerations as well as their realism and have drawn similar complaints.

While Puccini relied on a supposedly true story for *Madama Butterfly*, many verismo operas naturally relied on figures familiar to their audiences – some pulled from vernacular cultural practices such as *commedia dell'arte*. Similarly, in scenes that have been commented on elsewhere, the many references to popular culture – including those that point directly to Mafia movies such as Paulie "Walnuts" Gualtieri's Cadillac horn that plays the love theme from the first *Godfather* movie (1972) or Michael Imperioli's (as Christopher Moltisanti) reprise of the foot-shooting scene from Martin Scorsese's *GoodFellas* (1990), in which he reverses the victimized role he once played – help carry a self-conscious and humorous element throughout the series. There are also the many malapropisms sprinkled throughout the dialogue such as Tony's announcement that his girlfriend, Gloria, looks like "one of those Spanish princesses in a painting by Goyim" ("Amour Fou"/3011). The juxtaposition of black humor and violence, comic play and serious themes, while not the focus of this essay, do link *The Sopranos* and verismo opera such as *Rigoletto* and *La Bohème*.

Ironically, as Chris Heath reveals in his *Rolling Stone* cover story on *The Sopranos*, the one significant conflict with HBO was about the show's title: they thought that *The Sopranos* would confuse people, that people would expect it to be about opera singers (46). Music, in fact, is self-consciously utilized throughout *The Sopranos* both as commentary and material for character and plot development similar to the way they complement each other in opera. In "A Hit is a Hit" (1010) from the first season, the business world of Tony Soprano merges somewhat uncomfortably with the social climbing Carmela is advocating. The urging that Christopher, a nephew of Tony and Carmela as well as an up-and-coming lieutenant in Tony's crew, receives from his girlfriend, Adriana, to widen their social contacts parallels this development. These two women stand on opposite ends of a continuum: Carmela looks for respectability and financial stability, while Adriana searches for a life other than Carmela's "stretch marks and houseful of kids." Music plays a big part in Adriana's hopes for a more fulfilling life. While Adriana's hopes are not realized in this episode they are later re-visited in the third season when she opens her club, The Crazy Horse, with alt-rock band, The Miami Relatives ("The Telltale Moozadell" /3009).

The plot of "Hit" also involves the negotiations between Herman "Hesh" Rabkin, a Jewish associate of the Soprano organization, and Massive Genius, a rap entrepreneur, in an episode that addresses the racial dynamics in rhythm 'n' blues recording history. While Tony and his crew face down challenges to Hesh's music empire from Massive Genius (a storyline that later evaporates), Meadow Soprano's involvement with her school chorus group as well as her vocal performance in the first two seasons are seen, by Carmela as well as Meadow, as a strategy for academic advancement and upward social mobility. Janice (aka Parvati) Soprano, in the third season, engages in a life-long search for spiritual and material enrichment, finds a sense of fulfillment in Christianity and composing Christian music, using her "born again" faith as an avenue to explore her growing interest in more orthodox spiritual teachings. It doesn't hurt that, as she remarks to Tony, "In the larger sense, Christianity's more about a business with the CCM . . . Christian Contemporary Market. It's the fastest growing sector in the music business today" ("Amour Fou"/3012).

The "contemporaneity" that Chase creates is due, in large part, to the music soundtrack of *The Sopranos*. Music functions in the series, as Chase's remarks indicate, as a means of relaying information about a character or a situation that is otherwise "silent" or unspoken. Dialogue and imagery convey information that the soundtrack either supports or emphasizes. For instance, in "Amour Fou" (3012), Bob Dylan's version of "Return to Me" plays in the background as Ralph Cifaretto attempts to comfort Rosalie Aprile about the disappearance of her son, Jackie Jr., following his attempt at "stepping up to the A leagues." Dylan's request to "return to me" echoes Rosalie's hope for Jackie Jr.'s return home. Significantly, Dylan's opening line introduces the scene and predominates the soundtrack as Rosalie greets Ralph home. Their dialogue enters as Dylan ends this first line, his song sinking into the background of the soundtrack. Just as significantly, the song returns to predominate the sound mix whenever the dialogue pauses, emphasizing its role as a third "voice" in the scene.

The domestic scene at the Aprile household cuts to the kitchen of the Soprano house where Carmela Soprano is seen in the foreground while Tony enters the house in the background. Dylan continues to sing, the song tying the two scenes together. In the scene with Tony and Carmela, however, the song underscores the "return" of Tony to the family hearth – as he has just ended an extramarital affair with Gloria Trillo, a woman he met in Dr. Melfi's waiting room. (Gloria, an exciting but unstable personality, stands in contrast to Carmela, a woman who, in Tony's words, "doesn't have those loony tune moods.") It is obvious, as Tony watches Carmela bake ginger snaps for a church benefit, that he *has* returned home (if only briefly, given the nature of television entertainment narrative), re-assessing his marriage and marriage partner. The lyrics which play over the ending of the scene (where no dialogue is spoken) – "My darling, if I hurt you, I'm sorry" – underline Tony's renewed appreciation for the relative stability marriage to Carmela provides for his otherwise tension-filled life.

In an earlier scene in the same episode, Jackie Jr. and Dino Zerilli meet with Ralph in order to pay him a part of their "earnings." As they discuss their business relationship, Dean Martin's version of "Return to Me" plays in the background. This earlier version of the song – from an era that Tony has referred to as "the good days" of the mob – reinforces the way in which the old rules, and the context in which they were formed, have changed. Martin's version, evoking the "GoodFellas" era of mob lore, also indicates the ways in which Jackie Jr.'s view of criminal activity is permeated with Hollywood imagery and popular cultural constructions of the Mafia.

Utilizing different versions of this song also illustrates the way in which contemporary concerns impact the lives of these mobsters. The fact that Dylan and Dean represent an antagonistic generational difference nearly forty years ago reveals the way in which the music of the series draws on an audience's familiarity with popular culture. It is also pertinent that the song both men sing is drawn from the repertoire of Italian Dean Martin (née Dino Crocetti), a "return" to older popular music that reflects the hopes, if not the realities, of Tony's agonistic relationship with his two "families" as well as Ralph's mentorship of a soon-to-be executed Jackie Jr. Importantly, Martin's version does not play as a "third voice" to the meeting but is almost subliminally inserted into the background of the soundtrack, reflecting the failure of the "old ways of doing things" in the present moment.

In another interview, Chase unveils another aspect of his musical aesthetic:

> When I was like 17 or 18 back in [New] Jersey, my friend Donny and I, we used to get high in his basement and we'd put a single on the stereo, like "Peppermint Twist," and play that single against whatever was playing on the TV, and turn the TV sound off. You would notice strange synchronicities like the rhythm of the cutting of the TV show would miraculously fall in with the rhythm of the song. And the chance juxtaposition of, say, Joey Dee and wheat harvesters rolling across the plains was very funny. *It blew out the idea of "score."* (Rucker interview, my emphasis

Chase is clearly aware of the way soundtracks can increase the interaction between the music and the action onscreen – the music not only cues the audience to any number of interior processes a character may be going through but is also used by the character her/himself to engage the process. The character and the viewer are thus often hearing the music in a similar, if not identical, way. In a larger sense, because there is no scoring, the music that is selected to accompany the series contributes significantly to the visual images.

"Core 'Ngrato"

As one readily sees, Chase's construction of "contemporaneity" is set in opposition to non-contemporaneous social life – an opposition between an imagined past of honor and tradition-bound social interaction and a contemporary world that has forsaken those social binds, letting loose a relativism that undermines, for example, the fraternal codes of the Italian mob. For the moment, I would like to focus on a song whose performance occurs in the ultimate episode of the third season ("Army of One"/3013), when Corrado "Junior" Soprano sings the classic Neapolitan song, "Core 'Ngrato."[5] Here, the role of source music is accentuated, since it is one of the few times that a character performs the music and allows both the audience and the *dramatis personae* to come together as one listening group. As we learn through Adriana's questioning of *consigliere* Silvio Dante's wife, Gabriella, "core 'ngrato" means "ungrateful heart," a subject with which Tony is only too comfortable. Themes of infidelity, familial tensions, and

166

betrayal by family and childhood friends bear witness to the questions that "Core 'Ngrato" enunciates. This song underscores many of the themes that have been explored throughout the series: infidelity, ingratitude, insolence, and indifference, particularly in the ways that they undermine or emphasize the rhetoric of fidelity to familial and fraternal obligations. As Chase, in an interview published on HBO's *Sopranos* website, remarks:

> Certainly I think [*The Sopranos*] describes American materialism. American . . . psychobabble. The victim society that we have, that we're developing. *The society of non-accountability.* You know, the rugged Yankee American guy, who doesn't really seem to exist anymore. So in that sense it's an American phenomenon. But then I go to Europe and I hear the same things. That it's a welfare state and half the people are on the dole and nobody takes responsibility, you hear the same thing all over. (my emphasis)

In the case of the Soprano *familia*, Naples and "Core 'Ngrato" link the old-world sensibilities that Tony attempts to maintain in the face of contemporary American "materialism and pyschobabble." The song also underlines the sentimentality "Core 'Ngrato" serves for the Italian-American gangsters.[4] The placement of the song in a funereal situation also contributes to its poignancy. Contrasted with the first two season finales where the audience is a witness to the Soprano family and close associates in scenes of seemingly normative domestic bliss, the funeral dinner underlines the tensions that threaten the cohesion of both of Tony's "families," his crew as well as his genetic family.[5]

In the episode "Army of One" (3013), Paulie Walnuts expresses his growing disaffection with Tony in a scene prior to Uncle Junior's singing in the restaurant (the scene also becomes an opportunity for Paulie and Johnny "Sack" Sacramoni to further the cross-generational conflict that is yet another site of tension and express the strain between "traditional (mob) family values" and "American materialism and psychobabble"); Christopher, who has always voiced impatience with the slow pace of his "career," is in an increasingly tense relationship with Tony over the handling of Jackie Jr.'s part in a card game heist; and Artie Bucco, owner of Nuovo Vesuvio, who has always maintained an ambivalent friendship with Tony Soprano, has been recently questioning the role Tony plays in his life – a question which has been aggravated by his impending divorce due, in part, to his friendship with Tony as well as his unrequited love for Adriana.

Additionally, Meadow exits Jackie Jr.'s funeral dinner after throwing pieces of bread at Uncle Junior – indicating both her suspicion concerning Jackie Jr.'s actual murderer (despite her argument with Kelli Aprile) and her growing antipathy toward her father's business and business associates. It is also significant that she leaves halfway through Uncle Junior's rendition of "Core 'Ngrato." Her gesture, not only the throwing of bread but her invocation of Britney Spears ("Oops, I did it again . . ."), in opposition to Uncle Junior's Neapolitan song, accentuates the tensions between "traditional" Italian mob codes of familial fidelity and patriarchal obedience with Meadow's growing independence and antipathy towards the "family business." Her articulation of her growing autonomy – at least, as she perceives it – is shaped through her defiance of Tony's authority in her mocking of her granduncle's singing as well as her physical escape from the dinner. As she announces to Tony, before running away from the funeral dinner, "This is such bullshit!" ("Army of One" /3013).

If those problems weren't enough, Tony and Carmela are bickering over the educational direction of AJ. The knowledge that AJ also suffers from the "family curse" (anxiety attacks) causes Tony added pressure; he cannot make his son realize that "the world [doesn't] run on his feelings" ("Army of One"/3013) by sending him to a military academy. Tony also realizes that the same code of behavior that he hoped a military academy would have instilled in AJ was once provided by Mafia "rules" such as *omerta* (code of silence). But this, too, has changed. As Christopher remarks to his running mate, Brendan Filone, "Maybe one reason things are so fucked up in the organization these days is guys runnin' off, not listenin' to middle management. . . . We have to stick together. Why be in a crew? Why be a gangster?" ("46 Long"/1002). Why, indeed, be someone who "lives outside the rules" if all the old rules are being thrown out?

The balancing Tony must accomplish between "tradition" and "contemporaneity" is exemplified by the plaintive tone of "Core 'Ngrato." The anxiety Tony feels between the pull of old-fashioned values and the resourcefulness that he must employ in order to maintain control over his crew and his home puts an enormous strain on his own coping abilities. When Uncle Junior sings of once having given his heart to a now-rejecting lover, it reflects how Tony's own conflicts center on the two things dearest to his heart – his crew and his family. The crew with their infighting are partly fueled by the wider problem of wiseguys who, rejecting the old rules of mob conduct because they no longer have the stomach for "the penal experience" (Tony to Dr. Melfi in "The Sopranos"/1001), can no longer be counted on to act on a stable set of guidelines – guidelines that provided formerly unassailable parameters for discipline and punishment. Meanwhile, his family provides no refuge from the pressures of mob life. Rather, his son and daughter resist his authority at every opportunity, while Carmela reveals herself to be a stronger adversary than the stereotypical "Mafia wife," all adding to his already dangerous levels of *agita* (anxiety).

Contrast "Core 'Ngrato" to the song played at Livia Soprano's funeral dinner ("Proshai, Livushka"/3002), when Janice attempts to coerce everyone to reminisce about Livia. The song, "If I Loved You," sung by Shirley Jones in her screen debut role as Julie Jordan in Rodgers & Hammerstein's *Carousel*, highlights the contrast between Janice's desire to enact a remembrance of a recently-departed maternal figure and Carmela's voiced recognition that Livia was not only unloved by most of the people gathered at the remembrance but also "a dysfunctional" woman.[6] In the song's denial of an obvious and apparent affection, "If I Love You" confronts "Core 'Ngrato" as the opposing poles of familial and communal cohesion and disintegration. While "If I Love You" speaks of a "non-existent" relationship, "Core 'Ngrato" speaks of unrequited love.

It is also significant that of all the many deaths in the series, these are the only two that are given "musical accompaniment" – their own death arias, so to speak. While *Carousel* uses "If I Loved You" in a playfully facetious manner, *The Sopranos* uses the song to delineate the very real antagonism between Livia and her "mourners," notably her son Tony, who was almost killed because of her. There is no playfulness here but a darkly rendered dysfunctional mother/son relationship that underlines the fragmented, and fractious, nature of Tony's professional and familial bonds. Equally significant is the relationship between verismo opera and David Chase's recognition of the similarities between Livia and his own mother (he has been quick to point out, however, that his mother never wanted him murdered) as well as his apparent focus on the musical element of the series.

These themes – family and business tensions, conflicts between "traditional" values and what Tony registers as a form of utilitarianism or instrumental relativism – unfold through the metaphor of unrequited love. Searching for meaning, Tony only finds more questions and unresolved dilemmas. As in the second season's ending, when the Rolling Stones' Keith Richards sings of unrequited love ("Thru and Thru"), Uncle Junior also sings of instability and inconstancy. The failure to count on traditional forms of behavioral norms and regulations puts Tony's control over his two families in jeopardy. This is especially important in a world where no one is bound to any rules in an "age of non-accountability."[7]

As "Core 'Ngrato" makes clear, Catari is inaccessible. In similar ways, the insular world of the mob precludes any possibility of finding relief from these tensions on the "outside." Tony sees himself as "the sad clown; laughing on the outside, crying on the inside" ("46 Long"/1002). This sad clown, tormented by unresolved conflicts, finds only attenuated resolution in the psychiatric sessions with Dr. Melfi. When "White Rabbit" plays over scenes of Tony's growing depression ("Down Neck"/1007), the "little pills" that Tony takes "don't do anything at all." The profound dissonance between his responsibilities as mob boss, father, and husband with his valorization of "traditional" values are reflected in the lines of "Core 'Ngrato": "Core, core 'ngrato/t'aie pigliato 'a vita mia/tutt'è passato e nun'nce pienze chiù!" (Ungrateful heart, you wrenched my life from me!) For Tony, the "ungrateful hearts" – beyond his would-be killers (Uncle Junior and his mother, Livia) – include Salvatore "Big Pussy" Bonpensiero who "ratted out"; Meadow, who fights against Tony's authority at every turn while accepts his financial and material sustenance; Paulie, who is dissatisfied with Tony's ruling "against" him in a sit-down with Ralph Cifaretto ("Army of One"/3013); Jackie Aprile Jr., whose continual refusal to listen to Tony's advice to "smarten up" ("The Telltale Moozadell"/3009) eventually leads to his demise; and Janice, who chafes at having to bow to his will in order to secure his favors but accepts the protection her brother's reputation and position give her. This partial list elides the very real tensions his in-laws, Hugo and Mary DeAngelis, provide as they condemn Tony's business activities while enjoying his largesse. Finally, and most importantly, Carmela is also an "ungrateful heart" who, instead of easing Tony's tensions, "never thinks of [his] pain."

Carmela, though, has very similar anxieties. Her conflicts between Roman Catholicism and the knowledge regarding Tony's mob activities engage the same psychological and moral compass as those provided by the tensions between "traditional" values and "non-accountability" for Tony. Her platonic affair with Father Phil also addresses how the secular and the sacred co-exist in the world of the Sopranos.[8] Their mingling of sexuality and spirituality registers the same mixture of ambivalence and ambiguity that Tony experiences in his inability to integrate his vision of the "right" way to act and the ways he is compelled to act in order to maintain his professional world. As she states to Father Phil regarding various Biblical concepts, "Well, let's face it, Father. We've got some major contradictions here" ("College"/1005). Father Phil's response is to cite love as a method of seeing through these contradictions.

Carmela's relationship with Father Phil also allows her to articulate her perspective, in the time-honored tradition of Christian dogma, on the world of human activity in opposition to a higher plane of existence. Carmela faces her own dilemma in a highly sexualized confession and communion with Father Phil. Her confession reveals how her dreams of material well-being conspire to assist in her denial of Tony's actual business "practices." The platonic – though highly sexualized – nature of her relationship with Father Phil underscores as well as undermines her urge to reconcile her moral quandary. While Father Phil willingly participates in the sexually charged atmosphere of his female parishioners' spiritual quests (a situation for which Carmela eventually reprimands him ("I Dream of Jeannie Cusamano"/1013) – although it is her petty jealousy about his relationship with Rosalie Aprile that initiates her censure), it is Carmela's dialectic between the earthly and the heavenly that situate her own moral dilemma.[9]

Still, while seeking counsel from Dr. Sig Krakower, who tells her bluntly to leave Tony, Carmela argues feebly against this advice by enlisting to her aid parental responsibilities, the greater material comforts a man of Tony's income provides, and the sanctity of holy matrimony ("Second Opinion"/ 3007). Dr. Krakower points out, however, that she is only misleading herself. Her unwillingness to divorce Tony will need other sources of validation. Later, when Carmela confesses to another priest, Father Obosi, about the ways her life with Tony seem to compromise her creed, she finds the validation she needs in order to remain married to Tony ("Amour Fou"/3012).

Carmela: The psychiatrist said that I should leave my husband. May God forgive me, when he said that, it seemed so right.

Fr. Obosi: You made a sacred vow. Divorce is out of the question, unless . . . Is he abusive, your husband?

Carmela: Not to me but he is unfaithful. He's a good man, basically. But I talked to Father Intintola about all this years ago and here I still am.

Fr. Obosi: And you love your husband?

Carmela: I do. I love my husband and I love God. But my life is financed by crime. His crime. $50,000 to my daughter's college. . . . The psychiatrist says it's all blood money. And now to maybe bring another child into this?

Fr. Obosi: God understands that we all live in the middle of tensions. You say your husband has good in him. What you have to do is learn to live on what the good part earns.

Carmela: The . . . the what?

Fr. Obosi: There's a point inside yourself – an inner boundary beyond which you feel culpable. You've got to come to an awareness of where that line is and forego those things which lay without it.

Carmela: The church has changed so much.

Fr. Obosi: It's a complex world.

Carmela: Learn to live on the good part. Forego those things which lay without it. I think I can do that, Father. I'll try.

It is apparent in this exchange that Carmela has found a process for working out the contradictions between what she believes as spiritual truth and how her belief system is attenuated by Tony's activities. It is also obvious that in her view, Tony's criminal activities are solely his own and that, legal practice or no, she is no accomplice to his mob life. She is merely being financed by crime but feels no moral entanglement beyond accepting its spoils. When she gives up her sapphire ring, she is practicing Father Obosi's advice – advice that is clearly meant to keep her satisfied with her marital choice. In a rudderless world, Carmela has managed to find a means to hold on to the fiction that her husband's working world and his domestic one can remain separate.

"CON TE PARTIRO"

In a similar fashion to the way "Core 'Ngrato" functions for Tony, Andrea Bocelli's rendition of "Con Te Partiro" ("I'll Go With You")[10] operates for Carmela. Her scenes are not often underscored by music. In this sense, "Con Te Partiro" holds greater significance – it almost functions as Carmela's *leitmotif* in "Commendatori" (2004). In one scene, Carmela, Angie Bonpensiero, and Rosalie Aprile are having lunch when Bocelli's singing inspires Rosalie and Carmela to express their admiration for his singing as well as leading Carmela to confess that, "God, he is so handsome . . . " ("Commendatori"/2004). The luncheon conversation, centering around the two themes of death and divorce – indeed, both embodying distinct forms of separation – is reflected in the lyrics to "Con Te Partiro." In the song's promise to share in new experiences, to visit "countries I never saw and shared with you," each of these Mafia wives hears a distinct meaning. Angie contemplates divorce from Big Pussy; Rosalie has lost her husband, Jackie, to cancer; and Carmela is physically separated from Tony while he conducts a business trip to Naples, Italy. More poignantly, Carmela has been separated from Tony in ways that have nothing to do with physical proximity. Her anxiety over Angie's decision more accurately reflects her unarticulated concerns about her own marital situation than her desire to be a true friend. Consoling Angie, Carmela is talking to herself when she remarks, "In the end, I know you're not going to leave him. I know you won't do that" ("Commendatori"/2004).

The romance that "Con Te Partiro" represents for Carmela points to the lack of it in her life. (The allure that Italy holds for her also operates on Paulie as he attempts, unsuccessfully, to connect with "real" Italian people in Naples.) In her imagination, Italy represents an Old World order of romance, family, and Catholicism – a world of stable relationships between honorable people. Her connection to Tony – especially in light of his life outside of the marital home: his *goomahs* (girlfriends), his criminal activities, and, meaningfully, his trip to Italy *without* her – appears more tenuous the deeper she questions her position as wife and mother. In fact, the lack of romance in her marriage has spelled near-disaster for her sense of moral equilibrium as she has flirted with the idea of extra-marital affairs.

In another scene, "Con Te Partiro" plays in the background as Carmela and Janice discuss the "medieval fucking outlook" of Tony and his business associates. Janice elucidates the madonna/whore complex that rules these men's view of male/female relationships. Again, Carmela's "leitmotif" underscores the lack of feminist perspectives in the world of these underworld families. While articles on *The Sopranos* have argued for the strong women in the series, this episode undermines such easy announcements.[11] Carmela is unfulfilled despite her material wealth. The promises that "Con Te Partiro" enunciate are empty for Carmela, and the distinctions that some commentators delineate between Carmela and "old-style mob wives" are superficial and do not challenge the power relations between mob husbands and their wives. Her outbursts, for instance, fail to change Tony's extra-marital habits or his criminal decisions. While he certainly respects her in ways that seem to attenuate older stereotypes of husband/wife relations in popular imaginings, the idea that Tony and Carmela are equals is not entirely supportable.

In addition to these scenes, the song enters in the final scene as Carmela, putting away some freshly laundered clothes, hears Tony announce his return from Italy. Carmela, shown in her domestic role as housekeeper, is situated in opposition to Tony's other women. In Italy, Tony conducted business with Annalisa Zucca, the beautiful acting boss. Though there was no physical affair, the sexual attraction between them was palpable. The dichotomy between Carmela as wife and mother and the *goomah*s and women such as Annalisa posed in Tony's mindset undermines Carmela's seeming self-awareness of her position in her world. She cannot "compete" with these women and even if Dr. Melfi is correct in assuming that Tony will never leave Carmela (though Dr. Melfi doesn't preclude the possibility that Carmela may leave Tony), Carmela's position in Tony's world will be fraught forever within a madonna/whore binarism. "Con Te Partiro" announces itself to Carmela as a promise, forever broken.

It is in this way that the two songs, "Core 'Ngrato" and "Con Te Partiro," both explicate and illustrate the spiritual and psychological dilemmas that Tony and Carmela find themselves in at the end of three seasons of fighting, loving, accommodation, and negotiation. *The Sopranos* opera, however, does not look to remain static in this tense and dramatic situation; the libretto is leading to a dénouement. Whether that ending is tragic, comic, or some combination of the two, remains to be seen.

In any event, it is only a matter of time before the fat man begins to sing.

"CORE 'NGRATO" (music: Salvatore Cardillo; written for Enrico Caruso, 1911. Translation by Anne Lawson.)

Catari, Catari, pecché me dici
sti parole amare;
pecché me parle e 'o core me turmiente,
Catari?
Nun te scurdà ca t'aggio date 'o core,
Catari, nun te scurdà!
Catari, Catari, ché vene a dicere stu parlà
ca me dà spaseme?
Tu nun'nce pienze a stu dulore mio,
tu nun'nce pienze, tu nun te ne cure.
Core, core 'ngrato,
t'aie pigliato 'a vita mia,
tutt'è passato e
nun'nce pienze chiù!

"UNGRATEFUL HEART"

Catari, Catari, why do you tell me
only words of bitterness,
why only things that torment me
Catari?
Don't forget that once I gave you my heart,
Catari, don't forget!
Catari, Catari, why do you say
these things that make me suffer?
You never think of my pain,
you never think if it, you don't care.
Ungrateful heart,
you wrenched my life from me!

"CON TE PARTIRO" (Italian lyrics and English translation courtesy of bocellionline.com. Music and lyrics by L. Quarantotto and F. Sartori)

Quando sono solo
sogno all'orizzonte

e mancan le parole,
si lo so che non c'e luce
in una stanza quando manca il sole,
se non ci sei tu con me,
Su le finestre
mostra a tutti il mio cuore
che hai acceso,
chiudi dentro me
la lace che
hai incontrato per strada

Con te partrio'
Paesi che non ho mai
veduto e vissuto con te,
adesso si li vivro'
Con te partiro'
su navi per mari
che, io lo so,
no, no, non esistono piu'
con te io li vivro'

Quando sei lontana
sogno all'orizzonte
e mancan le parole,
e io si lo so
che sie con me,
tu mia luna tu sei qui con me,
mio sole tu sei qui con me.
Con te partiro'
Paesi che non ho mai
veduto e vissuto con te,
adesso si li vivro.
Con te partiro,
su navi per mari
che, io lo so,
no, no, non esistono piu',
con te io li rivivro.
Con te partiro'
su navi per mari
che, io lo so,
no, no, non esistono piu'.
con te io li rivivro.
Con te partiro'
Io con te.

"I'LL GO WITH YOU"

When I'm alone
I dream on the horizon and words fail;
yes, I know there is no light
in a room where the sun is absent,
if you are not with me, with me.
At the windows show everyone my heart
which you set alight; enclose within me
the light you encountered on the street.

I'll go with you,
to countries I never saw and shared with you,
now, yes, I shall experience them.
I'll go with you on ships across seas
which, I know, no, no, exist no longer;
with you I shall experience them.
When you are far away
I dream on the horizon And words fail,
and, Yes, I know that you are with me;
you, my moon, are here with me,
my sun, you are here with me,
with me, with me, with me.

I'll go with you,
To countries I never saw and shared with you,
now, yes, I shall experience them.
I'll go with you on ships across seas
which, I know, no, no, exist no longer,
with you I shall experience them again.
I'll go with you
On ships across seas which, I know,
No, no, exist no longer;
with you I shall experience them again.
I'll go with you,
I with you.

CULTURAL CONTEXTS

FIFTEEN

NO(RTH JERSEY) SENSE OF PLACE:
THE CULTURAL GEOGRAPHY
(AND MEDIA ECOLOGY) OF *THE SOPRANOS*

Lance Strate

SOPRANOLAND

I live in Sopranoland. I didn't fully realize this fact until I was driving south on New Jersey's Route 17 one day, and I passed Satin Dolls, a gentlemen's club located in Lodi. Below the "Satin Dolls" sign the management had added another display that said, "AKA Bada Bing!" As viewers of *The Sopranos* television series know, the Bada Bing! is the strip joint owned by Silvio Dante, Tony Soprano's consigliere.[1] In many of the episodes, we see Tony and his crew hanging out at this club, and these scenes are filmed at the real-life Satin Dolls establishment. No doubt, the management of Satin Dolls intended to capitalize on its association with the HBO hit by taking "Bada Bing!" as its alias. But this blurring of the line between fictional setting and actual location also reflects a shift in New Jersey's *cultural geography* (Burgess & Gold; Duncan & Ley; Fry), a redrawing of our shared mental map of the North Jersey region.

Ramsey Outdoor is a sporting goods store that was featured in a story arc during *The Sopranos'* second season. Unlike the Bada Bing!, Ramsey Outdoor is not an assumed name. It is a real store, also on Route 17, but on the North-bound side, in Paramus. On television, Ramsey Outdoor was owned by the fictional character Davey Scatino (Robert Patrick), a childhood friend of Tony's. Davey's gambling addiction leaves him heavily in debt to Tony, who bleeds Davey's business dry, "busting it out," sending it into bankruptcy. In reality, the store was doing fine. At least, it was until the end of this story arc, when customers stopped coming because they thought it had really gone out of business; the management had to run advertisements insisting that they were still open. I related this story, noting that I myself have shopped at Ramsey

Outdoor both before and after the second season, in a conversation I had with some out-of-town colleagues during the 2001 meeting of the Media Ecology Association. Kidding around, I also said that I don't shop there anymore, and when asked why, I deadpanned, "because it's owned by the mob!" I thought this line would get a laugh. They thought I was serious.

And then there was the time that they were filming a scene at the Garden State Plaza in Paramus, New Jersey's largest mall. It was for the second season episode "Toodle Fucking-oo," where Tony has a talk with Richie Aprile, recently released after a ten-year prison sentence (in the background they pass the Brooks Brothers store I've bought suits in). While the scene was filmed on the lower level, crowds had gathered on the upper level to look down at the filming. Everyone was excited – after all this was *The Sopranos*! This was New Jersey's own, the home team! And they had even chosen a few Eddie Bauer employees to appear in the background as extras. They would be on TV. But we all were in the mall that would be on TV. Either way, television was our environment, and we were living, and shopping, in Sopranoland.

The funny thing about this process of cultural landscaping is that no flags are planted, no borders established or defended or violated, no governments set up or overthrown. All it took, in this instance, were cameras and cable. And no one had any idea of what was going on when *Sopranos* producer David Chase started filming the first season. I drove by them a few times in Montclair and I noticed the bright lights, but there didn't seem to be all that much of a crew, certainly not like one of those big productions you see over in New York City. I even asked my friend Thom Gencarelli, who teaches broadcasting at nearby Montclair State University, whether it might be some of his students. But he had no idea who it was. Of course, by the second season just about everyone knew who they were. And by the third season, they were no longer shooting in Montclair, due to the protests over their portrayal of Italian-Americans. Not everyone here is happy to find themselves living in Sopranoland.

Those who do favor North Jersey's new cultural geography are most likely experiencing the many pleasures of recognition. For one, there is the simple pleasure of seeing your local environment depicted on TV. For example, I'm watching the second season episode "Commendatori" and there's a scene where Sal "Big Pussy" Bonpensiero, a member of Tony's crew who has turned informant, meets with FBI agent Skip Lipari, and they accidentally bump into Jimmy, an Elvis impersonator with mob connections. Suddenly, I realize that they are inside Party Box, a store I've gone to many times for birthday decorations, balloons, and New Year's paraphernalia. "That's *my* Party Box," I say to myself, as I reflect on the convenience of the setting for the production crew – it's only a store or two down the road from Satin Dolls.

Then there's the third season episode "Another Toothpick," during which Tony gets even with a traffic officer who gave him a ticket. Tony's crony, Assemblyman Zellman, has the officer taken off of traffic duty, which also means that he is no longer eligible for overtime, and has to moonlight as a salesman to make ends meet. When Tony accidentally runs into the officer in his new role, he experiences a touch of guilt and offers an enormous tip, which the officer refuses. But what stands out is the background: "Fountains of Wayne!" my wife shouts, as we're watching the episode. "That's where I bought our snowman!" (She was referring to one of those electric snowmen that light up lawns during the winter.) My wife is a native New Jerseyan (I've only lived here for the past decade) and has many more of these moments of recognition than I do. For example, she easily identified the cemetery used by the Sopranos and Apriles in several episodes as the Jersey City Cemetery (my wife's family is from Jersey City, but her parents moved to the suburbs of Bergen County after she was born).

The Jersey milieu has been very much a part of the series-creator's vision. David Chase grew up in Clifton and North Caldwell (the latter being the site of the private residence that serves as the Soprano family's home in the series). And Chase's locations manager, Mark Kamine, has lived in Jersey City, Wayne, and Montclair. In an interview with Peter Bogdonovich that is included on *The Sopranos: The Complete First Season* DVD set, Chase explains that when the series was originally in development for the Fox network, his insistence on shooting in New Jersey did not go over well with the executives. HBO, in contrast, very much wanted that authenticity, and at least three quarters of the exteriors are filmed on location in Jersey. The remainder come from New York City, Long Island, and Connecticut, and much of the interior shooting takes place in the New York City Borough of Queens, at Silvercup Studios. Chase looked for East Coast actors in the casting for *The Sopranos* and certainly struck paydirt with James Gandolfini, born in Westwood and educated at Rutgers University. Also inspired was the selection of Steven Van Zandt, alias Little Steven, appearing in his first dramatic role. As a musician, Van Zandt played a major role in the development of New Jersey's Asbury Park sound as a member of Bruce Springsteen's E Street Band, working with South Side Johnny and the Asbury Jukes, and with his own band.[2] Both the crew and the cast have been mostly drawn from the New York-New Jersey region, a decision driven in part by aesthetics, but also by the practicalities of producing the program in this region. The East Coast working environment has influenced cast selection, and the North Jersey settings have influenced the very process of acting, according to Chase (as quoted by Matt Zoller Seitz of Newark's *Star-Ledger*):

> There's no question that shooting on location lends believability to everything we do. It helps the actors, too. It might sound funny, but the mere fact that you, the actor, are actually in the place you say you're in means a lot when you're shooting a movie or a TV show. As an actor or a writer or a director, you can learn a lot just from being in an area, having a chance to live and work there and get to know the people.

While there is a certain pleasure to be found in knowing that people are filming in your hometown or region (even more if you can actually observe them), the greater gratification comes from viewing the finished product, knowing that millions of other people are watching it along with you. Consider, for example, the following introductory message written by Sue Sadik, also known as SopranoSue, a contributor to the Sopranoland.com website (www.sopranoland.com/sightings/index.html):

> Welcome to SopranoSue's Sightings. I'm just a fan, but I happen to be lucky enough to work in Soprano territory. In fact, the majority of my day is spent driving all around New Jersey. This is great, I get paid and I also get to see a lot of the filming and hear great little tidbits about the filming and the locations. I saw a lot of the filming from the first season, but I didn't pay too much attention because I see working film crews all the time. Some major pictures were filmed at some of my accounts. When I got hooked on *Sopranos*, mainly because of the opening credits, (hey I know where that is, I was there today, etc.) I suddenly became more interested.

The opening from *The Sopranos*, with its dozens of shots of different North Jersey locales, is most definitely a hook for the local audience. Everyone recognizes some of the images, at the very least the shots of the New Jersey Turnpike and Newark Airport. The quick succession of scenes warns us to pay close attention, to be on guard for the next spot to be shown, for it may be a place that we know. It is an invitation to a game that only we, the hometown crowd, can play. And it is a promise that our attention will be rewarded, sooner or later, by a familiar site.

Clearly, this mode of viewing is unique to New Jerseyans. We pay more attention to the settings and backgrounds of *The Sopranos* than other viewers would. We watch the show on alert, prepared to ascertain the identity of the show's locations. New Jersey fans enjoy the narrative and aesthetic elements of the program along with the rest of the television audience, but there is this added pleasure of recognition. More than pleasure, it is an added level of meaning, derived from the links between the video images and the familiar locales. The specific meanings are local, often personal, but the general meaning that is being conveyed is that we are insiders, that we are (dare I say it?) *family*.

The local media jump onto the bandwagon, discussing the Jersey references in newspaper columns and through radio chat, reinforcing the effect. This also serves to widen the scope, as more local residents are clued into the game. For example, during the third season, Bergen county's newspaper, *The Record*, ran a column by Raymond A. Edel and Virginia Rohan entitled "Hits and Misses: A Weekly Guide to 'The Sopranos'" (which I read religiously). One line from 18 March 2001 reads, *"Recognizable locations:* Applebees, Harmon Discount on Route 46 West in Totowa" (YT-2). Another section from 22 April 2001 includes, *"Did you catch?* How Ralphie pronounces [with a New Jersey dialect] the word "whore" (who-er)? . . . That this is the first Thanksgiving we've celebrated with "The Sopranos"? (That stolen-turkey sequence behind the Bada Bing! really was filmed in November.) . . . That Jackie Jr. has a big New Jersey Devils poster over his bed?" (YT-2) *The Record* had also been running a regular column about the TV program

Ed, which employed frequent North Jersey location shoots. But for *Ed*, New Jersey was just a backdrop representing the program's fictional small town setting, Stuckeyville. *Ed* was not representing New Jersey to New Jersey (and the rest of the world), it was not feeding back into everyday life in the region. It therefore could not have the kind of impact on geographic identity that *The Sopranos* has had.

The pleasures of recognition flow backwards as well as forwards. Places like Ramsey Outdoor and Party Box may be physically unchanged, but they seem different after being televised. They have gained the kind of *aura* that Walter Benjamin wrote about, in this case an aura gained through electronic reproduction. The act of driving on the New Jersey highways is no longer simply a matter of transportation. It has become a ritual reenactment of the program's opening. Put *The Sopranos: Music from the HBO Original Series* CD on the car stereo, turn the volume up as A3 comes on with "Woke Up This Morning (Chosen One Mix)," and the experience is complete.[3]

While driving down the Garden State Parkway through David Chase's hometown of Clifton one day, I took note of an elevated sign advertising an Italian supermarket, Corrado's Family Affair. I must have passed by this sign dozens of times in the past, but on this particular ride it dawns on me that this store might be connected – not to the mob, but to David Chase's muse. After all, Tony's Uncle Junior, who Tony makes titular boss of the North Jersey mob, is actually named *Corrado* Soprano Jr. And "family" constantly figures into the advertising and promotion for *The Sopranos*. (Even the song "Family Affair" by Sly and the Family Stone finds its way into the program's soundtrack, as a sample on "Blood is Thicker Than Water" performed by Wyclef Jean, and included on the soundtrack recording.) And consider the following text taken from the website for Corrado's (www.cfamarket.com/about.html):

> Another reason for Corrado's success is the quality, caring and personal touch that people have come to expect from us. That "Family" atmosphere is prevalent throughout the store. You can always find a family member to help with any requests. Jerry, Joey, Peter, Cousin Sal, Carmela, Joanne, Uncle Tony are available if you need help.

Even if Carmela (the name of Tony Soprano's wife) and Uncle Tony of Corrado's Family Affair represent nothing more than a coincidence, they have taken on new meaning now that they are living in Sopranoland. Everything is seen in a new light as *The Sopranos* aura extends to the North Jersey region as a whole. It is not only a matter of a limited number of landmarks reproduced on the program. All of us North Jerseyans are part of a new cultural landscape, one that has suddenly become sharply defined and highly visible. As geographer Yi-Fu Tuan explains:

> We may say that deeply-loved places are not necessarily visible, either to ourselves or to others. Places can be made visible by a number of means: rivalry or conflict with other places, visual prominence, and

the evocative power of art, architecture, ceremonials and rites. Human places become vividly real through dramatization. Identity of place is achieved by dramatizing the aspirations, needs, and functional rhythms of personal and group life. (178)

By dramatizing North Jersey, *The Sopranos* has put the region on the map, bestowing upon it a visibility and reality for North Jerseyans and others alike. And as Daniel Boorstin makes clear in *The Image*, the geographic counterpart to the media event is tourism. It should come as no surprise, then, that North Jersey has now become tour-worthy. On Location Tours, Inc., offers a thirty dollar *Sopranos* bus tour that leaves from midtown Manhattan. The advertising copy on their website (www.sceneontv.com/sopranostour.html) reads:

Get a "shakedown" on a tour of sites used on *The Sopranos*, including Satriale's Pork Store, the cemetary [sic] where Livia Soprano is buried, the Bada Bing! night club, the diner where Chris was shot, and much more! This three hour bus tour . . . takes you through New Jersey's Sopranoland. . . . You'll learn *Sopranos* trivia, origins of the show, and production information on the way. . . . Not to "fugged aboud" Mafia speak and a stop for cannolis!

This same company offers a *Sex and the City* Tour (clearly cornering the market on HBO programming), and a Manhattan TV Tour that takes you to sites familiar from programs such as *Friends, Mad About You, Cosby, The Nanny, NYPD Blue,* and *Seinfeld. Seinfeld* was in fact the focus of the first such television tour, pioneered by Kenny Kramer (on whom the *Seinfeld* character Kramer was modeled).[4] Although the *Sopranos* tour leaves from New York, they do have a pick up in Secaucus for New Jerseyans who want a guided tour of Sopranoland, or just want the voyeuristic pleasure of watching tourists and tour guides treating their domestic environment as exotic, and even erotic.

The feeding back of televised reality into everyday reality, and the concomitant blurring of the boundaries have long been noted by media scholars. For example, anthropologist Edmund Carpenter, a colleague and collaborator of Marshall McLuhan's, reproduces the following *New York Times* article, dated 8 April 1972, in one of his major studies of communication, consciousness, and culture:

Joseph Gallo, reputed Mafia leader, was scheduled to give the keynote address before the A. J. Liebling Counter-Convention of Publishers. His topic: "The Image of Joe Gallo, in the Press and as I See It." However, he was murdered a few days before the conference opened. Gallo's sister, Mrs. Carmellia Fiorella, sobbing over her brother's body, said, "He tried to change his image – that's why this happened." She was treated for shock. (8)

A related form of reversal occurred on 4 July 2001, when Robert Iler the young actor who plays Anthony Soprano, Jr., was arrested on charges of robbery and possession of marijuana. Just a few short months ago, his character had gotten thrown out of school, after engaging in vandalism and pot-smoking. This is what Baudrillard would refer to as the *hyperreal*, an instance in which media simulation serves as a model for reality, rather than an imitation of what already exists. This event has been treated with humor by journalists, whose only reason for reporting the story in the first place is the irony of life imitating art.

On the other hand, a series of recent New Jersey political scandals have had a major social impact. They have involved, separately: New Jersey Supreme Court Justice Peter G. Verniero (accused of covering up racial profiling policies while State Attorney General), United States Senator Robert Torricelli (accused of accepting personal gifts from a campaign contributor), and Acting Governor Donald DiFrancesco (accused of unethical business dealings and forced to withdraw his gubernatorial candidacy). Incredibly, all three scandals came to light during *The Sopranos'* third season. An editorial published in *The Record* on 22 April 2001 called it the "Curse of 'The Sopranos'" and went on to argue:

> It's very possible we brought this on ourselves. New Jersey is in the national headlines again, for all the wrong reasons. It wasn't long ago that we looked positively respectable in the nation's eyes. Former Gov. Christie Whitman had an upscale, suburban image. She wore pastel suits and tasteful jewelry. No one looked at her and thought of landfills. But apparently we were not satisfied with this new WASP-like identity. Looking back, maybe it all started with "The Sopranos."
>
> The hit show – which depicts the trials and tribulations of a New Jersey family – is set in the present, but it's not about Princeton or Ridgewood or anything to do with a state aspiring to good taste. "The Sopranos" gives New Jersey back its old, familiar image: the mob, the turnpike, the sleaze, the bad taste. Politicians in "The Sopranos" are in the mob's pocket.
>
> And the fans love it. The gritty series has been a hit with viewers and critics alike. It's about sex and violence and crime. But it's also art.
>
> "The Sopranos" gives New Jersey status, buzz, cachet. The show glamorizes everything we'd felt inferior about for decades. And we don't have to pretend anymore that we have moved on. Now we can revel in our corruption.
>
> Maybe that's why the state's karma has begun to turn bad, at least in politics. . . . It might make a colorful backdrop for a TV series, but in reality, it's pretty depressing. (RO2)

Sopranoland may have generated a kind of Jersey chic, but at a price. As noted above, not everyone enjoys living in Sopranoland, and the pleasures of recognition come at the cost of stereotypical depiction, particularly of New Jersey's Italian-American population (an implicit but obvious point in the above editorial). That is why Essex County Executive James Treffinger and

Sheriff Armando Fontoura denied Chase and his crew permission to film on county-owned property last year. And on 23 May 2001, Representative Marge Roukema from Ridgewood proposed a Congressional Resolution chastising the producers of *The Sopranos* for their depiction of Italian-Americans. There have been protests from the National Italian-American Foundation, the Sons of Italy Foundation and the Italian-American Democratic Leadership Council. My friend Camille Paglia, a professor of communication at Philadelphia's University of the Arts, has become an outspoken critic of Sopranoland. For example, in one of her columns for the online magazine *Salon*, she writes:

> I have yet to watch a single entire episode of that show, which I find vulgar and boring as well as rife with offensive clichés about Italian-Americans that would never be tolerated were they about Jews or blacks.
>
> What I find especially repugnant about "The Sopranos" is its elitist condescension toward working-class life, which it distorts with formulas that are thirty years out of date. Manners and mores have subtly evolved in the ethnic world that "The Sopranos" purports to depict and that extends from South Philadelphia to central New Jersey and metropolitan New York. ("Energy Mess")

Philadelphia and New York are the two metropolises that are situated across the border from South and North Jersey, respectively. Of all the immigrant groups that came through Ellis Island, just off the Jersey coast, the Italians were the largest, and they settled in great numbers along the corridor between Philly and New York, the corridor otherwise known as New Jersey. (The two cities are now linked by Interstate 95, which for most of that span is also the New Jersey Turnpike.) And while Italian-Americans are prominent in both Pennsylvania and New York State, they have achieved a unique dominance in many of the towns and neighborhoods of Jersey. Sopranoland is in large part a Little Italy, and while some Italian-Americans (such as David Chase) don't mind America's Mafia mythology, others cringe.[5]

Even if Sopranoland is not an ideal place to live in, it does provide us with the pleasure of recognition, in this case the pleasure of being recognized. In interpersonal communication, this form of recognition is referred to as confirmation. According to communication theorists Paul Watzlawick, Janet Helmick Beavin, and Don D. Jackson, phatic communication, our rituals of everyday life (Hello. How are you? Fine, how are you?), allow us to acknowledge each other's existence and importance, satisfying a deep-seated psychological need. But there is also a need for cultural confirmation, in order to insure social cohesion and morale. New Jersey has long suffered from being rejected, and disconfirmed. As Watzlawick, Beavin, and Jackson explain, "while rejection amounts to the message, 'You are wrong,' disconfirmation says in effect 'You do not exist'" (86). In this respect, it is better to have a negative identity than no identity at all. Watzlawick *et al.* suggest that disconfirmation within the family may explain the development of juvenile delinquency and criminal behavior – it's an extension of acting out to get attention. Thus, Sopranoland's love affair with the mob may be connected to the fact that Jersey has for long been ignored and given the message that it does not exist.

JERSEY

Without a doubt, New Jersey has an identity problem, even with its very name. New York is never referred to as just *York*, nor is New Hampshire ever known as *Hampshire*, and New Mexico is certainly not called *Mexico*. But New Jersey is often called *Jersey*. *Jersey* has an informal feel to it, familiar and slangy. Add an exaggerated accent to it, and you have former *Saturday Night Live* comedian Joe Piscopo's famous routine: "Hi! I'm from Joisey! You from Joisey?" However it is pronounced, *Jersey* does not elicit respect.

There are historical reasons for this linguistic eccentricity. New Jersey traces its origins to the colonies of New Netherland (which also included parts of New York State and Connecticut), founded in 1621, and New Sweden (which also included parts of Pennsylvania and Delaware), founded in 1638. In 1655, New Netherland conquered and annexed New Sweden, meaning that the colony that would one day become New York now controlled most of modern-day New Jersey. New Netherland became New York in 1664, when it was taken over by the English. Portions of New Jersey were granted to Lord John Berkeley and Sir George Carteret and became known respectively as West Jersey and East Jersey. The two Jerseys were consolidated into the crown colony of New Jersey in 1702, but the colony was administered by New York, and did not get its own governor until 1738.

The colloquial use of *Jersey*, therefore, is a venerable alternative to the official state name, but most experience it as simply peculiar. It is reflected, however, in the name of the state's second largest municipality, Jersey City, which was incorporated in 1820 (and at that time also called "the City of Jersey").[6] And because *Jersey* is not inextricably bound to *New*, it is free to combine with other modifiers such as *North*, so that it is just as common to speak of *North Jersey* as it is to speak of *Northern New Jersey*. While the names East Jersey and West Jersey are not used anymore, their legacy of the *Jerseys*, of New Jersey as a plural rather than singular location, remains.

The east-west division remains significant, and Sopranoland is definitely in East Jersey. Northwest Jersey, especially past Morristown, is a country environment that the North Jersey mobsters would find alien. On the other hand, they would be perfectly comfortable heading south down the New Jersey coast, which is referred to as *going down the shore*, even as far as Atlantic City. West Jersey has an affinity for Pennsylvania, East Jersey for New York (and while Atlantic City is sometimes considered part of the Philadelphia region, it has much in common with New York as a center for the entertainment industry).

The fusion of East Jersey and West Jersey in the past has contributed to the confusion about New Jersey in the present. But just as East-West oppositions have given way to North-South contrasts on a global scale, today, the most common reference to two different Jerseys is based on the distinction between North and South Jersey. This reflects New Jersey's position between two major metropolises, New York to the Northeast, and Philadelphia to the southwest. The boundary between North and South Jersey is therefore defined, in large part, by which of the two cities is closer, which has the greater magnetic pull on a given locale, and most importantly, whose electromagnetic signals you are receiving. New Jersey has no major television stations of its own, and what can be more disconfirming when we are living in an electronic media environment (McLuhan, Carpenter)? This means that we often do not receive even the most basic affirmation that local television news programming provides. Not that they ignore Jersey altogether, but the geopolitics of information on this local level resembles that of global information networks (Smith), with Jersey in the role of a third world nation.[7]

This also makes it inordinately expensive to reach the New Jersey population through television. Much was made of the fact that Jon Corzine's successful 2000 campaign for the United States Senate was the most expensive to date, but television spots were essential for an unknown like Corzine, and he had to pay for time in two of the nation's top ten markets. And he had to pay for millions of Pennsylvania, New York, and Connecticut audience members who were irrelevant to his campaign in order to reach the minority of the TV audience living in New Jersey.

Of the two Jerseys, North Jersey has it worse. Some parts of South Jersey are considered Philadelphia's suburbs, but they are at a distance from the city, in contrast to the close proximity between the New Jersey's northeast coast and Manhattan and Staten Island. And while Philly's pull may be strong, how could it possibly be as powerful as the Big Apple? South Jersey is also distinguished by the state capital, Trenton, by the Jersey shore resorts and Atlantic City, and by the state's leading institutions of higher learning, Princeton University and Rutgers University (the latter sometime considered Central Jersey).

The northeastern coast of North Jersey, on the other hand, is practically on top of New York City. Admittedly, this makes for spectacular views and easy commutes. After the George Washington Bridge was completed in 1931, Bergen County became know as "the bedroom of New York." Neil Genzlinger, author of *The New York Times'* Jersey Column, complains about the "residents of Brooklyn and Queens who take an hour to get to their jobs in Midtown Manhattan and then ask [how you] can stand the commute from Jersey, when it takes maybe 20 minutes" (1). This underscores the fact that while the geographic distance is miniscule, the psychological gulf is huge. The state line that separates New Jersey makes it an alien world to New Yorkers.

I can attest to it, as I was born in Manhattan and moved to Queens when I was two weeks old (my parents thought the more suburban environment would be a better place to raise a child). I probably would still be living in Queens if I hadn't married a Jersey girl (who convinced me that the more suburban environment of Bergen County would be a better place to raise our kids). When I lived in New York, even though I didn't know very much about

New Jersey, I was always ready to express my disdain for the Garden State. Most New Yorkers do so as a knee-jerk reaction, it's simply expected behavior. Of course, the put down is common in New York culture: in Queens we put down Brooklyn, in Brooklyn they put down Queens, the Bronx puts down both Long Island boroughs and is in turn put down by them, and Manhattan puts down all of the outer boroughs, even Staten Island. But they all put down New Jersey, even in the suburbs of Nassau and Westchester. Clearly, this can't do much for New Jersey's self-image.

One reason for all of the disrespect is the olfactory association that so many New Yorkers have with New Jersey. I myself have very strong memories, going back to early childhood, of the horrendous smell of industrial waste one still encounters on the turnpike, in the vicinity of Elizabeth and elsewhere, of my parents rolling up the windows, myself complaining bitterly, and everyone coughing. In this regard, Tony's official occupation of "waste management" is more than a Mafia cliché; it is a commonplace of North Jersey's heavily industrialized areas. It is hard to miss the irony of claiming to be the *Garden State*, as Robert Duffy explains in his "New Jersey 101" essay:

> Let's face it. To the rest of the world, there's nothing cool about New Jersey. People have called it a huge toxic waste dump, The Garbage State (a witty turn on our state nickname, The Garden State), and yes, New Jersey has even been called the armpit of the United States.

Incredibly, The Garden State did not become New Jersey's official nickname until 1954, and despite the veto of Governor Robert B. Meyner. According to New Jersey State Librarian Robert Lupp:

> Alfred M. Heston, in his two-volume work, *Jersey Waggon Jaunts* (Camden, NJ, Atlantic County Historical Society, 1926), twice credits Abraham Browning of Camden with coining the name at the Centennial Exhibition in Philadelphia on New Jersey Day, August 24, 1876. On page 310 of volume 2 he writes: "In his address Mr. Browning compared New Jersey to an immense barrel, filled with good things to eat and open at both ends, with Pennsylvanians grabbing from one end and the New Yorkers from the other. He called New Jersey the Garden State, and the name has clung to it ever since." The problem with this is that the image of a barrel tapped at both ends dates back at least to Benjamin Franklin, so this statement crediting Browning with naming the Garden State can not be taken at face value.

Apparently, New Jersey's subordination to its neighbors was apparent as far back as the eighteenth century. As for the Garden State nickname, Governor Meyner opposed it on the grounds that New Jersey was distinguished by a great many activities, and agriculture was hardly the foremost. Among them, we have been a leader in the chemical industries, which has also given New Jersey one of the most polluted environments in the nation.

Insults like "you stink!" may sting, but it is the disconfirmation that has the most powerful effect. Unless someone mentions Jersey, eliciting the automatic response of ridicule, New Yorkers simply don't think about the place. It's not on their mental maps – out of state, out of mind. This is reinforced not only by the absence of major television stations and local news programs, but by our exposure to the New York City media. New Yorkers are constantly being confirmed and celebrated by the media. New York is familiar, not only to those who live and work in the metropolitan area, but also nationally and internationally. As the media capital of the world, New York is highly self-reflexive, continually turning to itself for settings and subject matter. Images of Manhattan have long been part of America's mythic landscape. The outer boroughs of Brooklyn and the Bronx made their mark in Hollywood movies, and became a mainstay of early television programs such as *The Honeymooners* and *The Goldbergs*. Queens came into its own in 1971, when it was featured in *All in the Family*. But where was New Jersey before *The Sopranos*? Yes, there is the rock icon, Bruce Springsteen, whom New Yorkers like but New Jerseyans worship (and yes, there is also Hobokon's Frank Sinatra, but unlike Springsteen, Sinatra ignored his roots and preferred to identify himself with New York, New York). But in so often being eclipsed by New York, New Jersey frequently is given the message that it doesn't exist. Moreover, as Duffy puts it:

> New Jersey also has a bit of an identity crisis. When national and international events come to town, such as the Final Four, World Cup Soccer, and even the Net Aid concert, all of these events were billed as being in New York. If that isn't bad enough, the two biggest sports teams that play in the state, the Giants and the Jets, both say they're from New York when in fact they play in East Rutherford, New Jersey. With Manhattan shadowing us in the north, and Philadelphia biting our heels in the south, it's no wonder that Jersey has a bad rap.

In all fairness, sports franchises have relocated to the suburbs before and retained their inner city identification. And the Nets basketball team did adopt a New Jersey identity when it moved west from Long Island. But given the fact that Giants Stadium was built in the New Jersey Meadowlands for that team to play in, their rejection of a New Jersey Giants identity becomes "just another brick in the wall." Similarly, New York has for long owned Ellis Island and Liberty Island, even though they are closer to the coast of New Jersey – Jersey City's Liberty State Park has a magnificent view of the Statue of Liberty, but she has her back turned to us.

Having been overshadowed by New York for so long, it is no wonder that *The Sopranos* are causing such a sensation in North Jersey. And yet, the very same geographical tension is reflected within the program. The program's opening shows Tony coming out of the Lincoln Tunnel, leaving New York City. Across the Hudson is the New York skyline, while looking in his rearview mirror, he sees the twin towers of the World Trade Center (geographically inaccurate, but culturally right on target).[8] From the beginning, then, Jersey is defined in opposition to New York. Also, from the beginning of the series, Tony's North Jersey mob has been portrayed as having ties to New York's Mafia. While the relationship is distant, during the third season there is a suggestion of a threat as Johnny Sack, the leader of one of New York's five families (Rohan), moves out to North Jersey. Although he still "works" in New York, he becomes a subtle influence (and potential interference) in Tony's business.

Meadow's search for a college was also fraught with significance. Tony himself went to Seton Hall University, a Catholic institution in South Orange, not far from his West Orange home (i.e., his mother Livia's house, later occupied by his sister Janice), but he dropped out after a semester and a half. In contrast, the first season episode "College" (1005) has Tony driving Meadow to Maine to look at Bates College, a nonsectarian, and highly liberal, liberal arts school (they also visit Bowdoin and Colby Colleges in Maine, similarly elitist institutions). During the second season, Tony and his wife Carmela make it clear that they want their daughter to go to Georgetown, a Washington, D. C.-area university, or to Holy Cross, a college in Worcester, Massachusetts, an hour south of Boston. Both are Catholic and Jesuit schools, both out of town. But significantly, Boston and D. C. are the northern and southern ends of the northeastern United States' megalopolis, which is linked together by Interstate 95. In other words, were Meadow to attend either of these schools, she would be directly connected to the New Jersey Turnpike, only a matter of five or six hours away by car.

In contrast, Meadow's desire to attend Berkeley, an airplane trip across the country, horrifies her parents. While I wonder why my own institution, Fordham University, which is New York's Jesuit university, never came up, Meadow's ultimate choice of Columbia speaks volumes. Just across the Hudson River, Columbia University looks out at the New Jersey Palisades. The proximity means safety for Meadow, who is very much the Italian-American Princess, but situated in Manhattan, in Harlem, the cultural distance between the Soprano North Caldwell home and Columbia is as great as it would be for Berkeley.

The beginning of Meadow's freshmen year, depicted in the third season, shows her having trouble adjusting to her new environment. Ultimately, she reaches back across the Hudson for the security of the familiar, frequently visiting her parents in part for food and laundry services, in part for her emotional support. Moreover, after being dumped by the exotic Noah, she begins dating longtime friend of the family Jackie Aprile Jr., son of the late North Jersey mob boss who wants to be like his dad, drops out of Rutgers, and ultimately gets himself whacked. While it is not unusual for college freshmen to get homesick, there is a strong sense in which Tony's two families are defined by their turf and have difficulty on unfamiliar ground.

This was shown with great effect in the third season episode "Pine Barrens" (3011) when two members of Tony's crew, Paulie and Christopher, get lost in the South Jersey Pine Barrens following a botched execution. "How can we be lost? We're in New Jersey," moans Paulie. And it is true that you cannot truly get lost in the densely populated and well-developed environment of northeastern New Jersey. But the Pine Barrens are another story. They are part of the largest body of open space on the east coast between Massachusetts and Virginia, a national reserve 1.1 million acres large. The Pine Barrens are also the home of the legendary Jersey Devil, and the episode is reminiscent of *The Blair Witch Project* (Erica Leerhsen from the film's sequel has a minor role as a tennis instructor in an earlier episode from the same season). Thus, David Chase's New Jersey has something in common with *Blair Witch* creators Eduardo Sanchez and Daniel Myrick's Maryland, Stephen King's Maine, and H. P. Lovecraft's Massachusetts. The Pine Barrens are a part of another of the many Jerseys, *Weird New Jersey,* which is the title of a local periodical that covers a Jersey that lies hidden beneath industrial Jersey, a folk Jersey full of devils, ghosts, and unexplained phenomena.[9]

NEW AND OLD JERSEY

North Jersey is defined in opposition to New York in one direction, and in opposition to South Jersey in another. Internally, it is defined by yet another opposition, which I would call *Old* Jersey vs. *Nouveau* Jersey. By *Old* Jersey, I mean the urban areas like Newark, the state's largest city. Even here, there is the linguistic problem that *Newark* sounds like a garbled pronunciation of *New York*. And no doubt Newark's proximity to New York has kept it from achieving any degree of prominence. Also, Newark never quite recovered from the race riots of 1967, although recent efforts to build a performing arts center and a sports arena for the Nets and Devils are hopeful signs. Still, Newark is the old neighborhood, the place where poor immigrants and minorities raised their families, the place where Tony's father ruled the streets. This is where Satriale's Pork Store is situated within the show, although its actual location is Kearny. *Old* Jersey also includes Jersey City, Hobokon, and Paterson, but there are urban neighborhoods distributed throughout North Jersey. In contrast to New York's traditional proxemics of inner city, outer boroughs, and outer suburbs, *Old* Jersey and *Nouveau* Jersey areas are scattered around the North Jersey region, forming a patchwork or postmodern pastiche, an episodic arrangement that reflects the aesthetics of the television series, as New York City's more coherent layout reflects the traditional linear narrative of the cinema.

Old Jersey is much like New York City, in contrast to *Nouveau* Jersey which has more in common with the New York suburbs of Long Island, Westchester and Rockland, and southern Connecticut. Significantly, the ascendancy of Nouveau Jersey is reflected in the fact that New Jersey has replaced Connecticut as the state with the highest median household income, according to the 2000 census. Connecticut lifestyle-icon Martha Stewart secretly reflects the move from Old to Nouveau Jersey, insofar as she is a Polish-American born in Jersey City as Martha Kostyra, and grew up in Nutley (not far from David Chase's Clifton).

Tony Soprano's drive during the opening credits takes him out of New York to *Old* Jersey, and then finally to *Nouveau* Jersey. Geographically, the sequence is incoherent. It is not a route that you can follow on a map. The sequence is a montage of images shot at many different locations in North

Jersey, some south of the Lincoln Tunnel, some north of it, and some to the west. But the drive from *Old* Jersey to *Nouveau* Jersey is a drive through time more than space, from the old to the new. It also reflects the drive needed for upward mobility, for making your way through the American class system. Additionally, the drive simply represents the activity of driving. That's what we do in New Jersey (we have the highest automobile insurance rates in the country to show for it). And if the opening drive doesn't follow a linear route, the fact of the matter is that neither do we much of the time. We don't just drive up and down a given highway. We drive *around* North Jersey. We navigate a dense web of highways, parkways, turnpikes, and roads. There is an almost hyperactive relationship to the highways here in New Jersey, or at least so it seems. Crossing the George Washington Bridge from Manhattan to Fort Lee, the driver suddenly encounters a bewildering array of road signs for the Palisades Interstate Parkway, Routes 1, 9, and 46, Interstate 95 and the New Jersey Turnpike, Routes 4 and 80, and Routes 17 and the Garden State Parkway. Drivers unfamiliar with this busy highway area (e.g., New Yorkers) have been known to stop completely despite the obvious danger, paralyzed by information overload.

After ten years, my experience of North Jersey remains fragmented and discontinuous. For example, I know David Chase's hometown of Clifton, not as a neighborhood that constitutes a geographic whole, but as exits on Route 3, Route 46, and the Garden State Parkway. I know a little of the area surrounding each exit, but not how they fit together to form a coherent place. A more traditional sense of place would require walking around a town, or at least driving around a grid of streets, rather than driving through, and exiting and entering highways. In this respect, then, the opening credits reflect the experience of the North Jersey's driver's "no sense of place."

I am used to it now, but when I first moved out here I was amazed at most people's casual attitude towards driving. In New York City, your first instinct is to stick to your neighborhood. Your second is to travel to another neighborhood, and stay there until you are ready to go home. Traveling is associated with a great deal of overhead, in the time it takes to move through congested areas, in the cost of parking and tolls, and in the risk of accident or theft. And from a New York point of view, New Jersey is a journey, not a destination. It is a place to pass through to get to somewhere else.[10] You might cross the George Washington Bridge to cut through the northeastern corridor of New Jersey, which would take you to New York's Rockland County suburbs, the Catskill Mountains, and upstate New York.[11] Or you might take Route 80 West and cut across Northern New Jersey on your way to Pennsylvania, southwestern New York State, and on into the midwest. Or you might head down the New Jersey Turnpike and follow I-95 to Philadelphia, or to points south, from Delaware, to D. C., to Disneyworld. Of course, your destination might just be Newark International Airport, considered *New York*'s third major airport, an alternative to the older, more congested Kennedy and Laguardia airports in Queens.

Old Jersey is a bit more automobile-friendly than New York City, but it still emphasizes neighborhoods. And while the mass transit options may not be as extensive as they are in New York, they do exist there, unlike *Nouveau* Jersey. Bruce Springsteen often paints poignant pictures of *Old* Jersey, but his most popular works are the songs that romanticize the road, that describe how *Nouveau* Jerseyans were "born to run." In this, his music mirrors *The Sopranos* opening. Joe Piscopo's famous line, "You're from Joisey? What exit?" cemented the image of New Jersey as a state that had been paved over by superhighways. "What exit?" has become a Jersey commonplace. And it suggests that North Jersey/*Nouveau* Jersey has more in common with Los Angeles and Dallas than it does with New York, meaning that there is no *there* there.

The region is characterized by urban sprawl, but it has a certain coherence that may also qualify it as a "regional city" (Calthorpe and Fulton), a region whose parts, *Old* Jersey's traditional urban areas and *Nouveau* Jersey's suburban settlements, add up to the equivalent of a traditional city. The Sopranoland regional city would encompass Essex County, which includes the city of Newark, as well as Montclair and the Oranges; Passaic County which includes the cities of Paterson and Clifton; Bergen County which includes Fort Lee, Hackensack, and Paramus; Hudson County which includes Jersey City and Hoboken; and Union County which includes the town of Elizabeth.

Throughout the series, as in the opening credits, Chase conveys a strong image of New Jersey, one that is culturally confirming, one that reworks our cultural geography. But it is also true that North Jersey comes across as atmosphere, albeit sometimes polluted, rather than an established geography. Jersey is reduced to bits and pieces, which are put together according to dramatic and aesthetic needs, not according to the realities of the actual landscape. This sort of editing has long been a part of film production, as Benjamin has pointed out – an early form of Baudrillard's hyperrealism. And that makes Sopranoland the kind of postmodern scene that Fredric Jameson has detailed. But most of all it suggests a geographic environment that mirrors the electronic media environment. Marshall McLuhan provides one of the best known commentaries on the displacements brought about by the new media ecology, and Joshua Meyrowitz sums it all up with his book title, *No Sense of Place*.

Electronic media defy distance and dissolve boundaries, undermining a stable conception of space. Space becomes decentered, discontinuous, and dynamic. The electronic media encourage a sense of space that is acoustic, circular, encompassing, and involving, rather than visual, linear, and objectively distanced. Chase makes New Jersey cool, both in making it chic, and in McLuhan's sense of placing us in the midst of it, forcing us to participate in the construction of his *new* Jersey geography.[12]

Much more so than New York, which is a city born out of print and mechanical technologies, Jersey is an electronic environment. It is the home of Thomas Edison, the great electrical pioneer. Also, because of Edison, Jersey was America's motion picture capital until 1916 – how ironic, then, that Chase must now travel to Queens for a production studio. And New Jersey's car culture also reflects an electronic sensibility. Anyone who thinks that an automobile is not an electronic medium has never tried to start a car when its battery is dead. More to the point, the highway system is as much a decentered network of nodes and links as electrical wiring, the telephone system, and the Internet.

Sopranoland is an electronic environment, a television map that has altered Jersey's cultural geography. The electronic media ecology retribalizes, according to McLuhan. Similarly, Walter Ong suggests that electronic cultures are characterized by secondary orality, sharing some of the characteristics of nonliterate, oral cultures. Tony Soprano's Old School harkens back to traditional and tribal societies, with their emphasis on kinship, loyalty, and honor (Goode). It should also be noted that tribal societies can be extremely violent (Carpenter). But the main thing is that such societies are group-centered – no one in Tony's crew ever bowls alone (Putnam). Perhaps that is why we have been so fascinated with Mafia mythologies over the past few decades (it also accounts for the fascination with street gangs). In contrast, Dr. Melfi represents print culture, with her emphasis on the individual psyche and depth analysis. McLuhan would conclude that her approach is therefore obsolescent, and doomed to failure, except insofar as she herself trades her modern ethics in for postmodern moral relativism.

But the Sopranos' world is ultimately one of secondary orality, reflected in their electronic gadgetry, surrounded as they are by home theater systems, DVD players, videogame machines, and home computers. The Sopranos are wired, and wiretaps and recording devices also figure into their world. Informants such as Big Pussy carry wires, and in the first episode of the third season, "Mr. Ruggerio's Neighborhood," the FBI bugs the Soprano home. There are no private spaces in the electronic media environment, reflecting the fact that we are all under surveillance. At the same time, there is no sense of public space, for the private and the public are only defined as polar oppositions. The extreme cursing that the *Soprano* mobsters and family members engage in is symptomatic of the electronic media environment's blurring of the public and private, of no sense of place or propriety, and also of secondary orality's retrieval of primary orality's use of vituperation.

The great conflict that the Sopranos face is the conflict between family values, Old School traditions, and the pressures of the tribe on the one hand, and the individualism, desire for freedom, and downright selfishness that motivate them and much of American society on the other. The new North Jersey sense of place does not give them a stable environment within which they might resolve this conflict. Left with no sense of place, they find themselves lost, struggling to achieve a new synthesis between orality and literacy, community and individualism, a synthesis for the electronic age. And they are not alone, as *The Sopranos* presents the media, academia, and even religion as Mafias in their own right. Sopranoland expands outward to encompass New York and Philadelphia, indeed all of the United States, and perhaps even the world. It turns out that Sopranoland has an alias: the global village. Suddenly, we're all from Joisey, we're all living mythically and integrally while driving around Sopranoland. But we don't know how to answer the question, "what exit?"

SIXTEEN

"SOPRANO-SPEAK": LANGUAGE AND SILENCE IN HBO'S *THE SOPRANOS*

Douglas L. Howard

"Network TV is all about people saying *exactly* what's on their minds. . . . This show is about people *not* saying what's on their minds, and then acting in very passive-aggressive ways."

David Chase

Language may be the vehicle of communication, but meaning is not universal and interpretation is never absolute. Given language's inherent ambiguity, in fact, the interpreter is often forced to rely upon nonverbal cues or to consider context and intent in order to make sense of a linguistic statement. In assessing the value of this unspoken element of language, the French critic Pierre Macherey states that "it assigns speech to its exact position, designating its domain. . . . Speech eventually has nothing more to tell us: we investigate the silence, for it is the silence that is doing the speaking" (85).

While poststructuralism and contemporary literary and linguistic criticism have prided themselves upon revealing the complexity of verbal expression, ultimately they have offered analyses that organized crime and its cinematic representations have realized all along. Meaning is perhaps best conveyed beyond or outside of language. As Al Capone once explained, "you get a lot more with a kind word and a gun than you do with a kind word alone" (Thompson 29).[1] (Although "the kind word," in both instances, expresses the speaker's desire and represents an attempt to influence the listener's behavior or gain the listener's favor, the gun is the nonverbal exclamation point that clarifies the meaning of the statement and drives home the speaker's murderous intent.) If ambiguous verbal expression is characteristic of everyday speech, however, it is nearly a way of life within this world of the mob, where candor and direct speech can lead to arrest, imprisonment, and even death. Picking up on this idea, contemporary cinematic representations like *The Godfather, GoodFellas, The Untouchables, Get Shorty, Donnie Brasco,* and *A Bronx Tale* (to name a few) have deftly considered the ways in which language is used and meanings are implied, diverted, or deferred in the Mafia, and HBO's *The Sopranos* certainly continues this tradition. But David Chase's brilliantly scripted, directed, and acted series raises the bar on language play by blending Mafia intrigue with the mundane world of family responsibility and domestic stress, where the harsh realities of violence, theft, and murder must be even further diverted in order to maintain the façade of suburban tranquility.

MOB HISTORY: *OMERTA* IN ACTION

From its rise to power in America in the early twentieth century, the mob has always survived on a code of silence (*omerta*) and linguistic diversion that is not, according to Francis Ianni, so much a condition "of membership . . . but [based upon] ingredients of culture passed on through the socialization process" (58). Within the Italian-American crime syndicate or within organizations that follow their model, the "family" is the primary unit of order through which all moral value is determined, all social relationships are hierarchically defined, and all linguistic expression is processed, confirmed, or denied. Lies, half-truths, and omissions are all justifiable in the name of the family; mobsters consistently attempt to deceive the public by presenting themselves as members or heads of legitimate organizations in order to conceal their criminal activities. Al Capone began his business in Chicago as "Alphonse Capone, second hand furniture dealer" (Kobler 101). Not unlike Tony Soprano himself, Capone even lied to immediate family members about his illegal dealings, perhaps to protect them or to avoid an embarrassing and extensive explanation. During a 1929 jail term for possession of a deadly weapon, he let his son believe that he was away "in Europe" (Kobler 263). Head of the New York syndicate in the late 1960s and 1970s, Joe Colombo Sr. was also the leader and founder of the Italian-American Civil Rights League, a political body ironically dedicated to eliminating criminal stereotypes about Italian-Americans. Colombo successfully managed to have the words "Mafia" and "Cosa Nostra"[2] removed from certain newspapers and films – the term "Mafia," in fact, never appears in Coppola's *The Godfather* – because they constituted a perpetuation of an ethnic slur. Nicholas Gage points out that "no one has ever caught a Mafioso using the word 'Mafia' even in monitored conversation with his fellow members" (27), in part because the term is outdated. And, through this act of omission, family members create a silence that necessitates interpretation and allows for the possibility that, as Colombo disingenuously maintained, the mob itself is a myth. The "Teflon Don" John Gotti also used legitimate business contacts in construction and sanitation to establish an air of propriety around his racketeering enterprises; he simultaneously conducted "La Cosa Nostra" initiation ceremonies (various forms of these rituals have been part of mob memberships since their inception) that required members to commit to a code of loyalty, dedication, and silence, and pledge that they would "serve forever" (Blum 18).[3]

If the distortion or absence of language is a sign of family loyalty, then candor, clarity, and free expression are most certainly the marks of betrayal. Convinced that he was an informer, crime boss Vito Genovese sentenced Joe Valachi to death. Genovese never specifically said that Valachi would be killed, but he did communicate his intentions outside of language by branding him with the notorious "kiss of death," a nonverbal gesture that Michael Corleone also uses to mark his traitorous brother Fredo in *The Godfather Part II* (1974). Although Genovese was mistaken about his soldier, Valachi went on to testify against the mob (perhaps, as Gage suggests, out of "anger and a desire for revenge") and provided authorities with one of the most complete pictures of "how the organization's activities [menaced] American society" (Gage 35). Mob boss "Big Paul" Castellano was gunned down in front of his favorite restaurant in 1985 when other members feared that he would strike a deal with the federal government and "sing." Inasmuch as his killers permanently "silenced" Castellano, the public nature of the hit, like the "kiss of death" had its own meaning that Mafia regulars would clearly interpret. As Joseph O'Brien and Andris Kurins note, "in the language of the Mob, [it] sent a message: the murder was not a rebellion by some splinter faction of the Gambino clan, but a stratagem sanctioned by the five major Cosa Nostra families of New York" (10). While he played an active part in Castellano's death, Gotti himself was done in (he died in prison in 2002) by specific acts of verbal expression, both on his own part and on the part of Sammy "the Bull" Gravano. After negotiating with the FBI and federal attorneys, Gravano testified against Gotti in court, but not before he had been spurred on by surveillance tapes of Gotti verbally discrediting him to other family members, tapes that Gotti apologetically dismissed as "just talk" (Blum 379).[4] Gravano violated the terms of *omerta*; yet, in his own way, Gotti, giving voice to his opinions about the inner workings of the family and the family business in general, had, too. Where he had previously taken pleasure in eluding conviction, he now had become, according to federal officials, "a man trapped by his own words" (Blum 392).

SILENT FILMS: THE MOB GOES TO THE MOVIES

Aware of the complex lines of communication that must accompany life in the mob, contemporary film-makers have developed intriguing character studies that have not only contributed to the growing number of films within the genre, but that have also become classics of modern cinema in their own right. Vito Corleone (Marlon Brando) and his son Michael (Al Pacino), the focal points of Francis Ford Coppola's compelling Mafia drama *The Godfather* (1972), are both successful "dons" precisely because they know how to manipulate language, truth, and meaning toward their own ends. Conducting "business" on the day of his daughter's wedding, Vito is visibly offended by the mortician's demand for bloodshed, not so much because of the nature of his request, but because of the explicit manner in which it is made. Voicing such immoral or obscene acts is crass and dangerous – the don is later gunned down because Sonny makes the mistake of telling "someone outside of the family what [he] is thinking" in their meeting with Sollozzo "the Turk" – whereas "respect" is demonstrated through the linguistic veneer of propriety. When the troubled mortician learns the don's "language lesson" and instead asks for "friendship," the don grants his request for justice, in the same way that he also agrees to solve singer Johnny Fontane's problems with unyielding Hollywood producer Max Woltz by making him an ominously ambiguous "offer that he can't refuse." The Godfather never defines the unspoken, never breaks the terms of *omerta* in order to get his point across, but, like the fish that signals the end of Luca Brasi, the horse's head that Woltz finds in his bed becomes a bloody signifier that contextually (and graphically) drives home the force of the signified. Michael uses this same technique in *The Godfather Part II* when he uses the silent presence of Frank Pantangelo's brother – his brother cannot speak English – to keep Pantangelo from testifying against him at a Senate committee hearing.

Although all of the films in the *Godfather* trilogy end with the swift, violent, and unannounced resolution of family business, the first installment masterfully reveals the linguistic hypocrisy that is the godfather's legacy. As Michael, succeeding his father as don, swears to renounce the works of Satan during his goddaughter's baptism, his soldiers viciously murder the other heads of the five families. Even Michael's traitorous brother-in-law Carlo, the father of his goddaughter whom he promised to spare in exchange for an admission of guilt, is brutally strangled for his part in Sonny's death. And, when his wife Kay apprehensively questions him about Carlo's murder, a stone-faced Michael denies involvement, just as the other family members pledge their loyalty to him. Within the world of *The Godfather*, then, the truth must be determined through the unspoken, through what can be tangibly felt or seen or contextually interpreted beyond the words themselves, since language is consistently used as a means of deception. Looking back through the doorway, Kay glimpses the truth of Michael's family business, but she cannot bring herself to accept the dark reality (at least not until the sequel).

In the same way that Don Corleone sends his message to Max Woltz without speech, Robert De Niro's Al Capone, angered by Eliot Ness's raid on his liquor shipment, concludes his discussion of baseball and the value of teamwork by beating one of his men to death with a baseball bat in Brian DePalma's 1987 *The Untouchables*. Capone could have expressed his displeasure by simply chastising his men for their incompetence, but, from the murderous intensity of his attack to the dark red pool that forms on their white tablecloth, he dramatically imposes the meaning of his metaphoric comparison with a force that the language could never achieve. Henry Hill (Ray Liotta), the protagonist of Martin Scorsese's fact-based *GoodFellas* (1990), learns the "two most important things in life," according to De Niro's Jimmy Conway, at an early age: "never rat on your friends" – as Lefty Ruggiero (Al Pacino) explains in *Donnie Brasco* (1997), "rats" have no name – "and always keep your mouth shut." (Conway later murders most of his partners in the Lufthansa heist because he fears that they will not keep quiet and will implicate him in the crime.) Both "lessons" essentially amount to variations on the Mafioso dedication to silence, a dedication that Henry ultimately abandons by entering the Witness Protection Program and "speaking out" against his accomplices. Like Henry, the young Calogero (Lilio Brancato) is taught the value of silence at a very young age in *A Bronx Tale* (1990). When he refuses to rat on local gangster Sonny (Chazz Palminteri), who rules the neighborhood through a Machiavellian use of fear and violence as opposed to language, he is brought into the mob world of money and glamour. As a mob "shylock" trying to make it in the Hollywood movie business in the 1995 comedy *Get Shorty*, John Travolta's "Chilly" Palmer conceives that his collection techniques largely rely on his ability to communicate, outside of language, through visual contact with his target. Explaining his "role" to actor Martin Weir (Danny DeVito), he notes that he convinces delinquent borrowers that he "owns them without saying it" and that they are just "entries in his book" all through the specific "look" that he gives them. And the varying demands of language and silence also compete in the dark world of FBI agent Joe Pistone in *Donnie Brasco*. While he cannot tell his wife about his undercover activities in the mob and is sometimes unable to speak to her at all for weeks at a time, he must essentially lie to his mob contacts in order to infiltrate their organization. Acquiring an understanding of their unique vocabulary in order to speak to them as one of their own, Donnie not only learns the important difference between being introduced as "our friend" and "my friend," but he also masters the various shades of meaning that accompany the phrase "fuhgeddaboutit," linguistic subtleties that he must later define for his fellow agents.

SOPRANO-SPEAK

HBO's *The Sopranos* clearly owes a debt to this history of *omerta* and to these contemporary cinematic representations of mob life. Tony's problems with Uncle Junior in Season One, in fact, stem largely from linguistic issues that are not unlike Jimmy Conway's tragicomic paranoid concerns about the Lufthansa heist or Don Corleone's demand for respect from the grieving mortician. Although Uncle Junior is suspicious of Tony's growing power in the family – Uncle Junior is only boss because Tony (the irreplaceable James Gandolfini) understands the value of linguistic propriety and has allowed him to assume the title in order to keep the peace – he does not feel compelled to move against him until he learns, from Tony's mother Livia, that Tony is seeing a psychiatrist to help him with his panic attacks. For Junior, the fear that Tony might be mentally unstable and violating the code of silence, even under the confidential terms of Dr. Melfi's care, amidst the threat of FBI indictments is enough to warrant his removal, and, in Episode 9, the cleverly titled "Boca" (a reference to Boca Raton that in its literal translation of "Mouth" also applies to Uncle Junior's interest in oral sex as well as to the various secrets that are revealed), their conflict comes to a head (no pun intended). During a casual game of golf, Tony, stung by Uncle Junior's reference to a baseball error that he made when he was younger, sarcastically notes that Junior's ball has landed "in the muff," and he reprimands him in front of Silvio and Mikey P. for "eating sushi." As Tony well knows, other family members would look down upon his sexual preoccupation;[5] rather than explicitly embarrassing him with his knowledge of Junior's "oral habits," Tony uses humor to obscure the truth, but pointedly conveys his awareness to Junior himself. And Junior, in turn, defends himself by affirming that he, at least, can deal with his own problems, "not like some that [he knows]," an obvious allusion to Tony's therapy visits that he tells him to interpret "however [he wants]." Both Tony and Uncle Junior obey the linguistic rules of respect. Neither one openly humiliates the other, yet, within the ambiguity of their comments and within the silence that envelops them, each one takes the measure of the other by subtly exposing his weakness. In Junior's case, though, Tony's effrontery is the proverbial straw that leads him to plan his nephew's death.

Tony is an effective family leader, however, because his ability to manipulate the language (and others) is not limited to sexual puns or sarcastic innuendo. After Jackie Jr.'s (Jason Cerbone) attempt to rob Gene Pontecorvo's card game goes horribly awry ("Amour Fou"/3012)[6] – the dealer is killed and Furio is wounded – Christopher and some of the other family members cry out for justice. Since Tony promised Jackie's father (and former family boss) that he would look after his son, he feels honor bound to spare him, an obligation that prevents him from verbally giving the order for Jackie's death. Therefore, in a masterfully orchestrated scene from "Amour Fou" (or "Crazy Love") he places the responsibility on Ralphie Cifaretto because Jackie is technically a member of Ralphie's crew. Ralphie admittedly wants to "give the kid a pass on this one," a decision that Tony seemingly endorses. But, as he encourages Ralphie to ignore what people will say behind his back and as he returns Ralphie's gun to him, Tony's true intentions are clearly communicated and, as Ralphie's face drops, are clearly understood. Strategically plotting his way through this moral dilemma, Tony thus skillfully accomplishes both of his objectives, keeping his pledge to Jackie Sr. yet dispensing family justice from the unspoken implication that eventually leads to Jackie Jr.'s demise.

The Sopranos also dares to go where no mob drama has gone before by juxtaposing Mafia intrigue with domestic responsibility. For all of the crime and murder and violence that is part of his life, Tony is still a suburban family man with commonplace concerns. In fact, from this perspective, he is even rather average. But, as his underworld activities continue to impinge upon his bid for normalcy, Tony finds that he must apply the same linguistic discretion that characterizes his business dealings to his daily interactions. While Tony's drive up to Maine with his daughter to look at colleges in "College" (1005) could easily be an event in any father-daughter relationship, their car-ride conversation focuses on Tony's true profession, as he is forced to dance around Meadow's curious inquiries. Blandly confessing to his gambling operations, he denies the true extent of his influence. When Meadow later goes off to tour the Colby campus, Tony excuses himself on the pretense of finding his missing watch, a lie that conceals his murder of FBI informant Fabian Petrullo.[7] And as

Meadow later quizzes him about the incriminating cut on his hand and the mud on his shoes, Tony claims to honor their commitment to the truth, although his deception is perhaps a better metaphor for their relationship.[8] Tony similarly conceals the truth from Dr. Cusamano and his friends in "A Hit is a Hit" (1010) because he realizes that their friendship is really based on a vicarious attempt to experience the thrill of mob life. Not only do they exclude him from their stock discussions around the barbecue, but, during their golf game at the country club, they crassly quiz him about the authenticity of *The Godfather,* mob rituals, and John Gotti. Rather than give in to their line of questioning, Tony instead teases them with a story about how Gotti outbid him for an outdated "Bungalow Bar" ice cream truck, a humorous anecdote that he uses to pacify the other golfers and simultaneously indicate his unwillingness to speak out on family business. Recognizing that he does not belong in such circles, he ultimately plays off Cusamano's preconceived notions by asking him to look after a plainly wrapped package. The package is only filled with sand, yet, in deliberately failing to disclose its mysterious contents, Tony uses the ambiguity of his silence to get back at the doctor for taking advantage of him.

Even within the confines of his psychiatrist's office, Tony must walk the line of language and silence with Dr. Melfi, for her safety as well as for his own,[9] and the linguistic conflict that is at the heart of their relationship forms the basis for one of the show's central and most intriguing storylines. During his first visit, Tony believes that seeing a psychiatrist "is impossible" for him precisely because it demands verbal candor for psychological progress ("The Sopranos" /1001). In order to get to the heart of the panic attacks that plague him, he must discuss the personal and professional responsibilities that cause him so much stress. However, in talking about his problems and opening himself up in this way, he violates the very vow of silence that he has sworn to uphold and demonstrates a weakness that, in the world of the Mafia, could be fatal.[10] Torn by these conflicting value systems, the troubled Tony nostalgically longs for the days when "pinched" family members honored the code and "strong, silent types" like Gary Cooper "just did what [they] had to do" (1001) without talking about their feelings.[11]

Yet Tony does talk to Dr. Melfi about his feelings, although he typically obscures his discussion of the incidents that precipitate them and, in doing so, perhaps psychologically compromises with the demands of his Mafia oath.[12] He claims that he only "has coffee" with the "degenerate gambler" Mahaffey, when, in reality, he runs him down with Christopher's Lexus and beats him senseless for his outstanding debts. While he is clearly impressed by Ariel's courage in the face of their intimidation and death threats ("Denial, Anger, and Acceptance"/1003), a show of faith that later leads him to contemplate the meaning of life during his therapy session, Tony likewise describes their encounter as merely "business" and fails to mention that he had to threaten the Hasidim with castration in order to get him to comply with his father-in-law's wishes. And in Season Three's "University" (3006), he similarly glosses over the tragic story of pregnant Bada Bing! stripper Tracee, beaten to death by her lover Ralphie. Instead, he ambiguously tells Dr. Melfi that he is grieving over the loss of a co-worker. For Tony, Tracee's death clearly triggers important psychological and therapeutic issues. He overtly perceives a parallel between the stripper and his daughter Meadow, yet the incident, a sensitive "family problem," must remain outside of language and outside of his treatment.[13] But, as *The Sopranos* continually demonstrates, Dr. Melfi is also the one who can best interpret Tony's linguistic ambiguities. From his preoccupation with the ducks in his pool to the Oedipal issues involving his mother to his concerns for the future well-being of his family, she is the one that guides him (and us) through the internal, often unspoken conflicts that torment him and gives voice to the silence that most definitely must figure in the show's inevitable resolution.

While the question of "who gets whacked" certainly provides enough material for coffee clutch conversations and talk radio shows, these yearly "hits" alone cannot account for *The Sopranos* entertainment value or explain the public's ravenous appetite for the growing Soprano lore. Clearly, the show's addictive drama is fuelled, season after season, by the compelling interplay of converging lines of linguistic conduct, as domestic, mafioso, and therapeutic guidelines of behavior collide within the world of Tony Soprano and his "families." As viewers, we must also appreciate and navigate the subtle nuances of innuendo, implication, and silence in order to understand the conflicts that the characters themselves face; in these moments of interpretation, the true interactions between them take place and true friendships and oppositions are formed. Like the characters themselves, we are drawn into the puzzle of meaning, where we, too, are led to wonder how expressed intention relates to true intention without the same fear of retaliation or assassination. This is also what makes us believe in the future of television drama and what reminds us that silence can indeed be golden.

SEVENTEEN

THE EIGHTEENTH BRUMAIRE
OF TONY SOPRANO

Steven Hayward & Andrew Biro

Hegel remarks somewhere that all the great events and characters of world history occur, so to speak, twice. He forgot to add: the first time as tragedy, the second as farce.

Karl Marx, "The Eighteenth Brumaire
of Louis-Napoleon Bonaparte"

"Those who do not learn from history are doomed to repeat it."

Home Box Office, advertisement
The Sopranos summer reruns, 2001

It has often been suggested that the works of Karl Marx are more relevant to North Americans than ever in this era of neo-liberal globalization, corporate downsizing, and relentless commodification. From protests against global free trade in the West to revelations of sweatshop exploitation in the "Third World," one is confronted every day with fresh evidence of the existence of exploitation and class struggle. The presence of tens of thousands of protesters at recent meetings of the WTO (Seattle), the IMF (Washington), the FTAA (Quebec), and the G8 (Genoa) suggests the sustained importance of Marx's theorizations of the nature of a capitalist economy. But with formerly socialist regimes reverting to capitalism in the last decade of the twentieth century, Marx's dialectical materialist understanding of history seems obscure, if not irrelevant. If in the nineteenth and early twentieth century Marxists could confidently predict that capitalism would doubtless be succeeded by socialism, the dawn of the twenty-first century has left many (even on the left) unable to imagine an alternative to capitalism. The gravity of the situation, and the felt obligation to adhere to Marx's indispensable eleventh thesis on Feuerbach, leads us – like so many intellectuals – to write an essay on a television show.

We are kidding. Half kidding. We begin by observing *The Sopranos* is partly a parody – however, like this essay, not *all* parody. In what follows we will be suggesting that an understanding of the series as parody is the key to rendering it visible as an instance of the ideological, objectified by the work of aesthetic production – or, if you prefer, a work of art that says something true about real world manipulations. We will be working to situate the show and the problems of its protagonist as exemplary within its historical moment; we ask in other words, what *The Sopranos* has to do with us, its audience.

This is not an original question. It is a question Tony Soprano asks himself. Indeed, in the pages that follow, many of the questions we ask of *The Sopranos* have been asked already, and with more eloquence, by *The Sopranos*. This question with which we begin – how to understand the relation between yourself and what you see on television – is a question Tony asks Dr. Melfi, part way through Season Two ("House Arrest"/2011). Tony is sitting in Melfi's office, complaining about being bored. He is uninterested in his wife and children (who seem entirely uninterested in him), uninterested in his work (his lawyer has told him to "insulate himself" from "shenanigans"), and even Melfi (who, having insulated herself through compulsive drinking, is singularly unresponsive) seems uninterested. An indication of how entire Tony's ambivalence has become is that he finds himself no longer interested in television. He describes for Melfi his beginning to watch the movie *Se7en* (1995) (it is identified, initially, as a movie starring Brad Pitt and Gwyneth Paltrow; the invisibility of Morgan Freeman is a matter to which we will return). It is a good movie, Tony concedes, but he nevertheless loses interest and shuts off the television. "What do I care who the killer is?" Tony asks Melfi. "What difference is that information going to make in my life?" This question bears not a superficial resemblance to the questions we raise in the pages that follow. What does what we watch on television have to do with us? What does *The Sopranos* have to do with our lives? We suggest *The Sopranos* does make a difference and argue the cultural contradictions staged in and by HBO's "family drama" are resonant because they speak to larger cultural anxieties. But what does this have to do with parody? To answer that question we need to go all the way back to Marx's theory of history, and to the French Revolution.

Marx begins "The Eighteenth Brumaire of Louis-Napoleon Bonaparte" with the epigraph that heads this essay. Marx is referring specifically to the coup d'état by Louis-Napoleon Bonaparte in 1851. (The "Eighteenth Brumaire" of the title refers to the date – on the revolutionary calendar – on which Louis-Napoleon's more famous uncle, Napoleon I, seized power.) With respect to the two coups, Marx suggests that the first Napoleon performed a revolutionary function, helping to sweep away the old aristocracy and spread the liberal values of the French Revolution across Europe. However, his nephew's seizure of power a half-century later served a conservative, even reactionary, function. Among other things, it consolidated the power of the

French bourgeoisie against the more radical demands for equality made by the Parisian proletariat. Both were Napoleonic coups, but the two events had political consequences that were diametrically opposed.

For Marx, this developmental arc is not unique to nineteenth-century France: "all history is the history of class struggle," and all political movements are movements that represent the interests of particular classes. In order to be successful, however, a political movement must present itself as representing more than merely a fraction of society. One of the ways this is accomplished is by "conjur[ing] up the spirits of the past" (146). For example, the French Revolutionaries' defeat of the *ancien regime* was accomplished in part by the fact that the former arrived "in Roman costume and with Roman slogans" (147). This need to "resurrect the dead . . . to exalt the new struggles . . . to exaggerate the given task in the imagination" (Marx 148) arises from the fact that these struggles are partial or contradictory struggles – struggles on behalf of a particular class. The French bourgeoisie in the mid-nineteenth century (whose goals no longer corresponded with those of the masses, as they did a half-century earlier) are able to present their particular goals as the goals of the French people as a whole only by finding their own Napoleon. The coup of Louis-Napoleon is "farcical" in that the bourgeois republic is preserved only by assuring the ascent to power of someone who can rule in an arbitrary and despotic fashion. Marx thus concludes that a truly universal political movement must be one that is willing to "let the dead bury their dead." This observation forms the basis for a programmatic assertion: "The social revolution of the nineteenth century [i.e. socialism] can only create its poetry from the future, not from the past. It cannot begin its own work until it has sloughed off all its superstitious regard for the past" (149).

Tony Soprano, we suggest, represents a contemporary Louis-Napoleon, and the "farcical" elements built into his character indicate the specificity of his place in the history of filmic gangsters. For instance, if *The Godfather's* (1972) Don Corleone represented the attempt to assert some control over their lives by a marginalized immigrant group in the face of Anglo control over society and the economy (a point also made with respect to African-American gangsters in the Hughes brothers' *Dead Presidents* [1995]); if, and even more pointedly, Coppola's trilogy charts an attempt to reassert the primacy of loyalty and "family values" against the corroding influence of the market economy, then Tony Soprano's anxieties are indicative of a moment when a recuperation of these values has become unthinkable. A number of times during *The Sopranos'* first season, Silvio cheers up Tony and the others by doing an impression of Michael's (Al Pacino's) line from *The Godfather Part III* (1990): "Just when I thought I was out, they pull me back in!" While the *Godfather* films treat Michael's predicament as tragic, in *The Sopranos*, Silvio (former E Street Band guitarist Steve Van Zandt, who hardly has the intensity or star power of Pacino) plays the line for laughs.

The Sopranos, of course, is self-consciously farcical. The series is constructed out of characters who know they are witnessing a "Family breakdown" *and* who know how bourgeois lifestyle precludes the appropriate *gravitas*: when

Tony objects to Junior's men selling cocaine, Junior says the drugs provide a "nice income stream" and lists his medical expenses; when Pussy is late for a meeting with a federal agent, the agent tells Pussy he's "got a life outside of this"; when Paulie discovers he is followed around by undead specters of those he has murdered, he tells his priest he "should have been covered by [his] donations." The point is made repeatedly: mob life is increasingly difficult under the historical and political conditions represented in the show. As one of the shows' promotional tag lines (on the box of the first season DVD collection) reads: "These days, it's getting tougher and tougher to make a killing in the killing business. Just because you're 'made' . . . doesn't mean you've got it made." *The Sopranos* represents a world in which the logic of the market is everywhere triumphant, and where loyalty (whether corporate or familial or, in the case of the Mafia, both of these at once) is increasingly treated as a commodity to be bought or sold. In the preface to the second edition of the "Eighteenth Brumaire," Marx argues that Louis-Napoleon's rise was neither a result of the individual's sheer force of will, nor the inevitable result of preceding historical developments. Instead, "the class struggle in France created circumstances and conditions which allowed a *mediocre* and grotesque individual to play the hero's role" (144; emphasis added). Similarly, the nature of contemporary capitalism allows a mediocre mob boss like Tony Soprano to capture the popular imagination.

Let us consider a particular example of what we mean by Tony Soprano's mediocrity. In the pilot ("The Sopranos"/1001) Tony is talking to Dr. Melfi about his business problems, and more particularly about the kinds of compromises he is required to negotiate. Tony is able to sum up his problems in a single sentence: "It would have been good," he laments, "to have gotten in on the ground floor." It is an unapologetically nostalgic, self-pitying statement. Tony is imagining how his life, his career, his family, and his Family would have been different had he been born into a different time. However, what Tony means by the "ground floor" is left vague. It could refer to his father (who we see in a later episode ("Fortunate Son"/3003) coming home, like Marlon Brando at the beginning of *A Streetcar Named Desire* (1951), and throwing meat on the table). But the "ground floor" might also allude to a fictional or filmic space such as that which exists in Coppola's *Godfather* chronicle (where both getting in and getting out of the ground floor are a possibility) or William Welman's *Public Enemy* (where mothers, and audiences, cry for their gangster sons). The "ground floor" could also allude to the straightforwardly brutal and relatively uncomplicated life of the Depression-era gangsters (where prohibition created, morally and geopolitically speaking, a relatively uncomplicated nexus of supply and demand). Born into the latter half of the twentieth century, Tony Soprano finds himself an unwilling participant in the postmodern condition, subject to a historical moment where the pressures of globalization of the economy and the information technology revolution have effected a generalized disintegration of community. The wording of Tony's wish – his desire to have "gotten in on the ground floor" – is instructive. He is isolated both temporally and conceptually and is no more able to imagine getting in on the ground floor than he is able to imagine (as does Michael Corleone, a more properly modernist mob-boss) a moment of reconstruction which might involve a return to the ground itself.

Tony's desire is repeated in overtly parodic form in "House Arrest" (2011) during a conversation between Dr. Melfi and her college student son. The two are eating dinner when Melfi asks Jason about his comparative literature course. He reminds his mother he is not taking comparative literature; he is taking a course in Lacan, or as he puts it "deconstructive theory." Melfi shakes her head. "Deconstructivist theory," she says, "and your grandfather a contractor." Her son replies: "My droll mom." It is a predictable gag; like Dr. Melfi, the writers of *The Sopranos* cannot resist it. This is because the joke articulates the desire residing at the center of the series, the desire behind Tony's lament for the ground floor – a desire for an originary moment, for some kind of beginning. Construction, however, is no more a viable alternative for Melfi's son than it is for Tony Soprano. Not only is the ground floor closed, the ground itself has disappeared. Tony Soprano arrives in the world in much the same way as the television viewer arrives at the series itself: late, with a sense of himself as a kind of parodic repetition, of not being the real thing. He arrives *after The Godfather*.

But what does it matter that Tony inhabits the post-*Godfather* condition, if Tony himself has asked the question of why we should care about what happens on television? The idea of looking to popular culture – and, in particular, to fictional figurations of the criminal – as a means of diagnosing and identifying cultural contradictions is not a new one. This line of reasoning is undertaken as early as the late 1970s, by Marxist literary critic Fredric Jameson, in an essay entitled "Reification and Utopia in Mass Culture." Jameson's argument is that the conventions of the Hollywood gangster film change to reflect the ideological needs and utopian longings specific to the period of American capitalism in which a film is made:

> Thus the gangsters of the classical 1930s films (Robinson, Cagney, etc.) were dramatized as psychopaths, sick loners striking out at a society essentially made up of wholesome people (the archetypal democratic "common man" of New Deal populism). The post-war gangsters of the Bogart era remain loners in this sense but have unexpectedly become invested with tragic pathos in such a way as to express the confusion of veterans returning from World War II, struggling with the unsympathetic rigidity of institutions and ultimately crushed by a petty and vindictive social order. (31)

By the 1970s, a period coinciding with the emergence of "late capitalism," a further shift has taken place. By the 1970s the filmic gangster is no longer a "loner" but a member of a criminal organization or "family." The paradigmatic example is, predictably, Francis Ford Coppola's classic *The Godfather*. Rather than alienated individualists ultimately doomed to failure, Coppola's film (released in 1972, in the dying days of the long post-war economic boom) presents us with Don Corleone: a *successful* gangster – the head of a vast and many-tentacled criminal organization – who manages to place himself well beyond the reach of the law. Crucially, the success of the criminal here is not attributable to his ability to "strike out" at society or to resist the social order, but is rather an indication of the strength of the social bonds within the criminal organization: the Mafia's ability to keep disputes "within the family."

This essay is attempting to come to grips with the fact that, a quarter century or so later, at a point when "late capitalism" is all but fully consolidated, we are presented with yet another shift in the figuration of the gangster in popular culture. Tony Soprano, like Don Corleone, is the head of a large and lucrative criminal enterprise. But while *The Godfather* paints a picture of the Mafia as a community in which loyalty to the organization is the overriding value, in Tony Soprano's world, loyalty, like everything else, has its price. Further, anti-racketeering laws make it easier for law enforcement officials to "flip" members of the Mob, and the police have started to act – through wiretapping, extortionist tactics, and a single-mindedly businesslike approach – like criminals. This is emphasized by Tony's lawyer, Neal Mink, who, in attempting to convince Tony that he needs to protect himself from prosecution says: "The Feds are running a business, and sooner or later, they're going to want a return on their investment. Just like you" ("House Arrest"/2011). The series' reduction of the Racketeer Influenced and Corrupt Organizations Act to an acronymical personification who seems always in pursuit of Tony indicates the extent to which the relation between the cops and robbers in *The Sopranos* is represented as a breakdown of social structure. With a name ending in a vowel, with seemingly limitless resources and powers of intimidation, the malignant RICO sounds often like the name of someone in a rival crew who has put a contract out on Tony. This, too, is a point we reiterate – a point made in and by the series itself. Says Dr. Melfi to her own analyst, Dr. Kupferberg, about the absurdity of her trying to treat such recalcitrance: "The RICO Act, Elliot. We sat there and we talked about the fucking RICO Act. . . . Two years ago I thought RICO was a relative of his" ("House Arrest"/2011).

But even more insidious than changes in the tactics law enforcement agencies are allowed to use are the corrosive effects on organizational solidarity unleashed by the Mafia's own success. It has been suggested that for many years the Mafia refused to get into the drug trade because it feared dealing in such strongly addictive substances might erode the bonds of loyalty crucial to the organization's success.[1] But *The Sopranos* makes clear that the substance that is truly corrosive of familial-corporate bonds is not white but green: the scene in which Vincent Rizzo expounds his theory begins with Tony's crew emptying bags of cash in front of him, while the voice-over (from the television in the room) catalogues the Mafia's recent decline. Don Corleone might have inhabited a world in which certain things (honor, community, and so on) had a value in and of themselves, but Tony Soprano is forced to inhabit a world in which dollar values are the only values that matter. While Tony's nephew Christopher wants nothing more than to become a "made" man – to become a fully-fledged member of the Mafia community, bound by the *omerta* (code of silence) – this desire does not prevent him from writing a screenplay based on his own experiences and the tales he has heard. It is a similar kind of contradiction that structures the series as a whole: Tony is a gangster undergoing psychotherapy (or, as Freud called it, "the talking cure"): a mob boss who has to talk to maintain his position. Nowhere is this contradiction more clearly staged than in the advertising for the show – which, at least at first, could be seen colonizing whole subway cars in New York – in which all the show's actors appeared with their mouths closed.

The contradiction between the need to talk and the imperative for silence can be seen as related to one that is more generally felt by inhabitants of postmodern (or late capitalist) societies. Tony is trying to sustain community solidarity and at the same time must relentlessly focus on the bottom line. Forced to inhabit a world in which the forces of commodification are such as to continually emphasize individualism and personal gratification at the expense of solidarity and communal pleasures, it is perhaps not surprising that Tony is insecure, to the point where he suffers from debilitating anxiety attacks. Nor is it surprising he reacts to events with a profound sense of nostalgia. In the pilot ("The Sopranos"/1001), Tony brings his daughter Meadow to the church his grandfather and great-uncle built. Meadow expresses disbelief: "Yeah, right. Two guys." "No," Tony replies, "they were two guys on a crew of, y'know, laborers. They didn't design it. But they knew how to build it." Tony's grandfather was engaged in a materially productive kind of labor that produced tangible, lasting results – a kind of productivity that no longer seems possible. "Go out now," Tony continues, "and try to find me two guys who can put decent grout around your bathtub." The work in which Tony and his contemporaries are involved is instead the more ephemeral production of the service and information economy: waste management and "pump and dump" stock schemes. The ephemerality of this production, of course, is again entirely symptomatic of the era of the "New Economy." With the recent collapse of "dot-com" stocks, it is not difficult to see Webistics (the stock that is pumped and dumped by Tony's crew in Season Two) as emblematic of the New Economy as a whole.

This is precisely the thrust of Jameson's argument: films about gangsters have served as an index of much broader changes in social relations. In the shift from Howard Hawks' Scarface to Coppola's Don Corleone to David Chase's Tony Soprano, what is being registered is a shift from the "rugged individualism" of early twentieth century laissez-faire capitalism, to the organizational imperative (with its corresponding "organization man") of the Keynesian economy of the post-war period, to the flexibility and ephemerality of the post-Fordist New Economy, whose analogue at the individual level remains only vaguely defined. Writing at a time when "organized capitalism" (Lash & Urry) was not yet at an end, Jameson notes a shift towards "organizational themes" detectable across a variety of film genres. But it is in gangster films that this shift fulfills a specific ideological function:

> When indeed we reflect on an organized conspiracy against the public, one which reaches into every corner of our daily lives and our political structures to exercise a wanton ecocidal and genocidal violence at the behest of distant decision-makers and in the name of an abstract conception of profit – surely it is not about the Mafia, but rather about American business itself that we are thinking, American capitalism in its most systematized and computerized, dehumanized, "multinational" and corporate form. . . . For genuinely political insights into the economic realities of late capitalism, the myth of the Mafia strategically substitutes the vision of what is seen to be a criminal aberration from the norm, rather than the norm itself. (31–2)

Extending Jameson's argument to the present, we see it is precisely this lack of an individual personality type corresponding to the demands of the particular structure of the contemporary economy that is so anxiety-inducing, and which leads Tony (but of course not only Tony) to his nostalgic longings. The dizzying pace of postmodern life, the demands of a globalized economy, where capital can literally traverse the globe at the speed of light, has rendered earlier coping strategies ineffective. When told by Dr. Melfi that Tony's condition has improved because of their therapy sessions, that "coming here, talking" is what is helping him, Tony demands: "Well who's got time for that?" But if on the one hand Tony seems to recognize that the hectic pace of contemporary life apparently renders more "modernist" adaptive strategies such as psychotherapy obsolete, this does not prevent him from *wishing* for regression in another sense. In an angry outburst when his kids' demands for autonomy overwhelm him, he bellows: "In this house, it's 1954!" ("Nobody Knows Anything"/1011). Tony's definitional (or identity) crisis leads him to long for the perceived certainties (the "solid ground") of an earlier era.

This desire to return to the 1950s (the decade that provides the setting for *The Godfather*) also manifests itself in a desire to reassert a particular form of racial segregation. Thus, when Meadow goes off to college, Tony's disgust finds a convenient target in Meadow's ultra-sensitive Californian Jewish African-American boyfriend, Noah Tannenbaum. Not, of course, that Tony admits to being a racist. As the opening episodes of *The Sopranos'* second season make clear, Tony is not above doing business with African-Americans. The anger that surfaces in his dealings with Noah arises, rather, from the fact that they are on a personal and not a business level (overdetermined, of course, by the fact that Noah is dating Tony's daughter). Given the fact that for Tony "business" and "family" are in some sense inextricably intertwined, and the corrosive effects commodification has on "the Family," Tony is forced to work extra hard in policing the boundaries between his business and personal life, and to continue to regard those immediately before him – like Morgan Freeman in *Se7en* – as invisible.

This desire for the 1950s, however, is not simply a desire for a moment when difference did not assert itself in such palpable form. It is also part of his attempt to identify himself as a stranger in a strange land, as the head of a collective who can rationalize his opportunistic tactics as an aspect of his cultural identity. Tony reaches for such a justification continually. The visit to Italy in "Commendatori" (2004) is a sustained exercise in showing how little the Soprano crew has in common with Italians. Indeed, Paulie (who, earlier, had shoplifted an espresso maker, outraged by the dominant culture's appropriation of "the gift of our cuisine" ["46 Long"/1002]) neither speaks nor understands a word of Italian. For Tony and his crew what is sought is not Italy but proof that it exists. The most revealing instance of Tony's invention of tradition occurs, of course, in Dr. Melfi's office. To Dr. Melfi Tony describes the Mafia as a collection of immigrants who, like American businessmen such as J. P. Morgan, simply want a better life and take extreme, sometimes brutal, steps in order to get it. Dr. Melfi's response is to ask: "But what do poor immigrants have to do with you?" ("From Where to Eternity"/2009). All Tony can do is repeat himself, and ask if Dr. Melfi has heard a word he has been saying. This is because he himself is already, in some senses, a repetition. A parodic version of what was once a radical insight.

Tony's racist attitudes, combined with the casual brutality his position entails, ensure he is not perceived in an entirely heroic or sympathetic light. Part of the reason for the show's resonance surely has to do with the fact that Tony's problems are symptomatic of a more generalized cultural anxiety, or a more widely felt insecurity generated by commodification and the decline of community. As James Gandolfini himself has suggested (responding to claims that the show is guilty of ethnic stereotyping): "This is a show about America, and anyone who watches with any degree of intelligence understands that right away" (quoted in Doyle 2001, R2). On the other hand, however, Tony's response to these anxieties surely generates some unease in many viewers. He is (like Louis-Napoleon) a "mediocre and grotesque" individual, both created and thrust into prominence by historical circumstance. By showing that brute force alone cannot solve all of Tony's problems, *The Sopranos* shows the limits of criminality as a response to contemporary problems, and does so more successfully than the more heavy-handed moralizing of earlier gangster films. On the other hand, while those earlier films were bound by Hays Code conventions (the Hays Office forced numerous changes to the original *Scarface* (1932) script, "scour[ing it] for any traces of amorality" [Remnick 43]), the only imperative for cable television at the end of the twentieth century is the bottom line: a demonstration of the pernicious consequences of a life of crime is hardly the point of this hit HBO "Original Series".

Rather, *The Sopranos* is in some sense about the exhaustion of the gangster *film*. Christopher asserts, while working on his screenplay, that "My cousin Gregory's girlfriend, Amy – the one who works for Tarantino – said Mob stories are always hot." But in an interview with Peter Bogdanovich after the show's first season, creator David Chase says precisely the opposite: that the genre has run its course. Tarantino's *Reservoir Dogs* (1992) signals this by cloaking the criminals in an anonymity that is preserved through the most literal means: ordered at the beginning not to use their real names, the characters refer to themselves only as Mr. Pink, Mr. Blue, Mr. White, and so on. In *The Sopranos*, the exhaustion of the genre is marked by the verisimilitude that the show manages to achieve. Freed from the constraints of the Hays Code, from the epic scale and star power of feature film production, and from the censors of network television, a cable series is at last capable of creating a fictional world that accurately reproduces the real one, to the point where FBI wiretaps document the praise heaped on the show by (alleged) genuine mobsters (Remnick 40).

But is this verisimilitude a signal of liberation? While cable television does provide for a certain authorial freedom, the form itself is also indicative of the closure of liberatory possibilities. In showing the quotidian anxieties of a Mob boss at the end of the twentieth century, *The Sopranos* allows us to demystify the myth that criminality might provide an escape from the pressures exerted by an economic system that we do not control. But the recognition that even those that seem to escape the imperative of the daily grind are trapped within it is hardly the same thing as a recognition that an alternative might be possible, even if it allows us to see that (in Marx's words) a "superstitious regard for the past" like Tony's is doomed to failure, and should be "slough[ed] off."

Jameson notes that gangster films (indeed all films) not only provide a symptomatic documentation of the society in which they are produced but also work to resolve the contradictions that structure that society through what Jameson calls the film's "utopian moment": "all contemporary works of art . . . have as their underlying impulse – albeit in what is often a distorted and repressed unconscious form – our deepest fantasies about the nature of social life, both as we live it now, and as we feel in our bones it ought rather to be lived" (34). But if the current moment is one in which alternatives to capitalism are scarcely even imaginable, then it is also a moment in which the capacity to provide some positive content to these utopian impulses is also to some extent lost. It is a world in which virtually all socialist governments have collapsed, and the past is either (as Tony Soprano's 1950s makes clear) shown to be brutal and ugly, or it is so Disneyfied (and hence commodified) as to be virtually indistinguishable from the present. In this world without a "ground floor" on which a utopian vision can be erected, the energies generated by society's contradictions can only be pushed into an amorphous future. And by continually deferring narrative closure, this is precisely what a television series succeeds in doing: the "utopian moment" of a television series is, in this sense, a moment that never arrives.

The gangster genre repeatedly stages the contradictions of capitalism – the tensions between needs satisfied through communal living and the alienating effects of the division of labor enforced by the profit motive – its latest incarnation presenting us with a mobster forced to talk in order to maintain a community based on a code of silence. Moreover, like its predecessors, *The Sopranos* shows us that criminality – anti-social behavior – cannot provide a satisfactory solution to the problems generated by our society's contradictions. At a certain level, we know that as long as things remain as they are, Tony Soprano – our postmodern, farcical Godfather – can no more resolve contemporary anxieties than Louis-Napoleon could those of his age. And yet the open-endedness of the series – what keeps us coming back week after week – is something that allows, or rather *insists* upon, a suspension of precisely this knowledge that might provide the ground for liberation.

The possibility (and impossibility) of thinking differently within the context of the increasingly diffuse production process that characterizes the postmodern condition should therefore also be linked to the relatively recent phenomena of the HBO "Original Series." Like the absence of advertisements, the idea of watching an Original Series allows us to believe we are in on the "ground floor." Indeed, the mass popularity of the show would seem to require, to some degree, a reformulation of theories of television that regard programming as a socially necessary but superfluous pretence for advertising. As Richard Dienst observes in *Still Life in Real Time*, such accounts have become antiquated:

> These accounts [which continue "to accept advertising as the primary economic mechanism of television"] stay close to the advertiser's own version of the story, which is part of every commercial's ideological protocol: the companies insist they just want to buy slots of time that they hope will be witnessed by a certain demographic slice. We, the audience, are supposed to understand, sympathize, play along. But with the multiplication of channels and the new attachment of VCRs this arrangement, this pact of complicity has become more obviously fragile. (61)

The Sopranos is on HBO. There are no censors. There are no commercials. Is it a television show, really? We think it is. *The Sopranos* is the exception that proves the rule: television has always been selling something other than what its advertisers have advertised themselves as selling. As Dienst goes on to argue:

> Television, in its fundamental commercial function, socializes time by sending images of quantifiable duration, range, and according to its own cultural coordinates. By generating a realm of collective, shared time, and by setting standards for the valorization of this time, television advances capitalism's temporal rule: everybody is free to spend time in their own way only because, on another level, that time is gathered elsewhere, no longer figured as individual. (61–2)

And this, of course, *is* what has been happening. Each Sunday, at nine, we take the phone off the hook and watch *The Sopranos*. We know the episode will be on again – in an "encore performance" (a label that, in its suggestion that the actors will act their parts a second time, that emphasizes the socialized time generated by the television) – on Wednesday, but it is important to see it there and then. Alone in our living rooms, and yet with everyone else. The next week, the same thing happens. We remain glued to our televisions, knowing that Tony's (and our) anxieties will not be resolved, until next week, or the week after that.

What, then, is the bottom line? Is it so simple: does one shut off *The Sopranos* in order to bring the revolution about? Probably not. Will the revolution take place while we are watching *The Sopranos*? Again, probably not. But even this, our concluding observation (which echoes an observation made by Gil Scott-Heron some three decades ago) – like the show itself, like so much in the show – echoes hollowly, like a parodic repetition of something once profound, something it was once possible to say, without irony. In Season Two ["House Arrest"/2011], as he prepares to leave the hospital, Uncle Junior has his leg bracelet reattached by a Federal Marshal named McLuhan. Junior sees the attendant nurse smiling and asks, "What's so funny?" "Nothing," replies the nurse, who then asks the Marshal if his name is indeed McLuhan. He tells her it is. She asks him again: "So that makes you Marshal McLuhan?" The Marshal nods, unsmilingly. But the real Marshall McLuhan, the Canadian intellectual who articulated a more politically motivated connection between the medium and the message, is long dead. The joke, which situates *The Sopranos* at a particular moment in history, is completely lost on the characters in the show. The show's audience, on the other hand, like the nurse, is doomed to repeat it.

EIGHTEEN

"THE BRUTALITY OF MEAT AND THE ABRUPTNESS OF SEAFOOD": FOOD, VIOLENCE, AND FAMILY IN *THE SOPRANOS*

Sara Lewis Dunne

Hence a cookery which is based on coatings and alibis, and is for ever trying to extenuate and even to disguise the primary nature of foodstuffs, the brutality of meat or the abruptness of seafood.

Roland Barthes, "Ornamental Cookery" in *Mythologies*

ANTEPASTO

The language of the popular HBO show *The Sopranos* has called attention to itself in a multitude of ways. Perhaps the most obvious linguistic marker of this contemporary Mafia narrative is the heavy use of obscenities and profanities. *Fuck* is used as an adjective, an adverb, a verb, a noun, as almost any conceivable grammatical unit, just as it is in modern American vernacular. Viewers have, more than likely, become immune to the impact. Other sexual terms abound as well (one character is nicknamed Pussy, another Paulie Walnuts), as do a multitude of Italian and Italian-American corruptions of sexual slang terms: *comare* and its various variations (*goomah, goomar, gomatta*) for mistress; *fanook* for homosexual; *Pucchiacha* for cunt; *puttana* for whore; *stugots* for testicles – and also the name of Tony's boat. There are numerous other examples of the language of the Mafia, so many that lexicons have been provided by the HBO.com *Sopranos* web site as well as in Allen Rucker's *The Sopranos: A Family History*. Learning the spoken language of the television show creates a community of insiders, as language is intended to do, but even beyond the slang of Italian-American gangsters, there is another, more subtle language that communicates on both verbal and non-verbal levels: the language of food.

The late French structuralist Roland Barthes declared in his *Elements of Semiology*, after a lengthy study of the science of signs, that food is a "signifying system . . . [an] alimentary language made of i) rules of exclusion, ii) signifying oppositions of units (sweet and sour or wet and dry, for example), iii) rules of association . . . ; iv) rituals of use which function . . . as a kind of alimentary rhetoric" (27–8). Food is language, and in Barthes' native France the "rules" of its rhetoric are determined by individual or large group practice rather than by "the action of a deciding group" (28). In the second edition of his collection of twenty-nine essays, *Mythologies* (1970), Barthes provides some examples of the language of food. We find an essay on "Wine and Milk" as binary opposites; another called "Operation Margarine," about the evil (in Barthes' estimation) and deceptive substitution of margarine for butter in popular French and American advertising; one about "Steak and Chips"; and an essay devoted to what he calls "Ornamental Cookery," based on his observation of photographs and texts in the French women's magazine *Elle*, which he declares to be "a real mythological treasure" (78). The "Ornamental Cookery" Barthes observes in *Elle* is, he says, "a cookery based on coatings and alibis . . . openly dream-like cookery . . . at once near and inaccessible" (78–9). The sauces, coatings, decorations, and glazes disguise "the brutality of meat or the abruptness of seafood" (78). The food in *The Sopranos* often celebrates, rather than disguises, the "brutality of meat and the abruptness of seafood," but that is only the beginning of the food language conveyed in this continuing narrative.

Sometimes the food of *The Sopranos* bespeaks "otherness" and underscores the difference between the characters' lifestyles and culture and that of most of the viewers. At other times the show's food bespeaks "us-ness," showing how much the crime family members are like us, the viewers. At still other times food bespeaks violence, betrayal, and sexual victimization. And, sometimes, the food they eat makes us envy their powerful and often glamorous lifestyle. Once in a while, food means what sentimental advertisers want it to mean: love, affection, family bonding, but those times are rare.

Tomato Sauce

Food does always signify something, and in America we often distinguish those "other" ethnic groups from our own by the foods they eat: Jews with lox, bagels, and chicken soup; Cajuns with crawfish; Irish with potatoes and cabbage; southerners with country ham and cornbread; Mexican-Americans with tortillas; Germans with sausage; African-Americans with various kinds of "soul food" – and the list could go on forever. Most Americans probably identify Italian-Americans with pizza, pasta, hoagies (sometimes called "grinders"), meatballs, but, most of all, with tomato sauce. Tomato sauce has become one of the clichés of Italian-American cooking, reinforced, according to Sylvia Lovgren in *Fashionable Food*, by prohibition and the rising popularity of speakeasies in the 1920s "with Mama doing the cooking and Papa making wine in the basement" (38). Lovgren cites a 1926 *Woman's Home Companion* menu suggestion for an Italian dinner party which features "Spaghetti with Tomato Sauce and Dried Porcini Mushrooms" as a second course (38). Interestingly, food historians credit America as the homeland of the tomato (Flandrin 357) and Naples – the region of the first Soprano immigrants – as the home of Italian tomato sauce for pasta (Harris 74). Shots of food with red sauce are common in many episodes of *The Sopranos*, and in addition to ethnic identity, tomato sauce becomes associated with, not surprisingly, maternal relations, family, and sexual feelings. This is a family show soaked not just in blood, but in what Louisiana Italians sometimes call "red gravy." Interestingly, a recent *New Yorker* article about *The Sopranos* features an illustration of Tony, the Mafia don, seated in a chair, being served spaghetti and tomato sauce by James Cagney, star of one of Tony's favorite gangster films, *Public Enemy* (1931) (Remnick 39).

Tony Soprano, the show's focal character, recounts a memory to his therapist, Dr. Jennifer Melfi, of his neurotic mother cooking her "gravy," or "red lead" as he calls it ("Down Neck"/1007). Livia stands at the stove with a fork in her hand, cooking the pork bones and veal for the tomato sauce. She is, as usual, screaming at Tony as a young boy for some minor offense and shouts "I could stick this fork in your eye!" Tony, accustomed even as a child to his mother's violent verbal abuse, is not traumatized by the memory. Later he will describe one of his neighbors, Dr. Cusamano, ("A Hit is a Hit"/1010) as a "Wonder Bread Wop" who "eats his Sunday gravy out of a jar" – both expressions Tony learned from his mobster father, Johnny Boy Soprano. Assimilated, suburban, non-Mafia Italian-Americans like Dr. Cusamano thus lack the emotional resonance of homemade tomato sauce.

Most of the show's episodes include at least one shot of the nuclear Soprano family (Tony, his wife Carmela, their teenage daughter Meadow and younger son AJ) eating dinner in their large, rather over-decorated suburban New Jersey home or scenes which take place at their extended-family Sunday dinners. In all of those shots of the dinner table, there is at least one dish that appears to feature tomato sauce. Similarly, when Tony eats dinner out with his family or his associates, they usually have a pasta dish with tomato sauce, and in the numerous interior shots of Pizzaland, a favored lunch spot and meeting place, there is no "gourmet" pizza featuring, perhaps, pesto as its base or olive paste or any other more recent pizza innovation. A "slice" here always reveals the "red lead" under the cheese (or other) topping.

When, in the second season of the show ("Commendatori"/2004), Tony, Paulie, and Christopher go to "the motherland" – to Naples – to cement a deal selling stolen American cars in Italy, Paulie, who has liked all the food and the women he has seen in Naples so far, looks askance at a dish of black pasta he is served at a large dinner in an exclusive Neapolitan restaurant and asks, through a translator, for macaroni and tomato sauce. One of the Italian gangsters comments in Italian to his friend, "And you thought the Germans were classless pieces of shit." (Paulie, of course, does not understand.) Perhaps his visit to his motherland has reminded Paulie of his American culinary roots. Like many Americans who "return" to their families' homelands, Paulie is reminded that he isn't Italian; he's American and, like most Americans, he misses the food of his actual motherland, not the Naples he has sentimentalized from his family's stories.

Because tomato sauce holds such an important place in the lives of the Sopranos and their friends, it is a feature of holiday dinners as well as everyday meals. The Thanksgiving episode of Season Three ("He is Risen"/3008) contains a scene in which Tony and friends describe their families' typical Italian-American Thanksgiving menus. Tony and Christopher tell Hesh Rabkin and Rev. James Jr., who will distribute hijacked turkeys to his poor parishioners, that they dread Thanksgiving dinner because it will include "major antepasto . . . then soup, meatballs . . . manicotta, then the bird." All present rub their bellies and groan sympathetically. The tomato sauce is a given of these meals, accompanying the meatballs, surely, and probably the manicotta. Christmas dinner, too, must include this sacramental food. In "To Save Us All From Satan's Power" (3010), when Janice hosts Christmas dinner, Carmela must contribute the lasagna and the sauce for this meal, necessitating that she will "have to transfer half the kitchen over there."

The non-Soprano Mafia characters, too, rely on tomato sauce as a basis of not just meals but family connectivity. In "The Telltale Moozadell" (3009), Ralph Cifaretto teaches Jackie Aprile Jr., his prospective step-son, the best way to combine tomato sauce and pasta, by adding some butter to the hot pasta so the tomato sauce absorbs more readily into the "macaroni." In a subsequent episode ("Amour Fou"/3012), Jackie Jr. and Dino Zerilli plan, while eating pasta with tomato sauce from a plastic refrigerator container, to rob a weekly "made guys'" card game. Later, Ralph will arrange to have Jackie Jr. assassinated for his disrespect and robbery of those same "made guys." On a lighter note in the same episode, which illustrates the pervasiveness of tomato sauce as a cultural signifier, Tony's fellow mobster Silvio jokes that Johnny Sack's wife Ginny is "so fat her blood type is Ragu."

Non-Mafia Italian characters on the show also have sentimental connections to tomato sauce. In "The Legend of Tennessee Moltisanti" (1008) Dr. Melfi is shown eating dinner with her parents, her son, and her ex-husband. Her son innocently refers to his grandmother's pasta sauce as "Ginzo gravy," and, although his grandmother is not offended by the ethnic epithet, Dr. Melfi and her ex-husband Richard, who works for the Italian Anti-Defamation league, do take umbrage at the term "Ginzo," a corruption of the term "Guinea," sometimes used to refer derogatorily to Italian-Americans.

Tomato sauce is also associated – albeit somewhat indirectly – with sexuality. In "College" (1005) Father Philip Intintola visits Carmela Soprano alone with Tony and Meadow away on college tours, and confesses to her: "I've got a Jones for your baked ziti." He stays to eat the ziti Carmela just happens to have in her refrigerator, and the two of them watch a DVD of *The Remains of the Day*, sitting on the floor drinking wine. Eventually, the good father passes out on the floor in Carmela's arms, having come uncomfortably close to kissing her, and spends the night at the Soprano house. They have not had sexual intercourse, but the ziti has perhaps served as a substitute for the obvious lust that the two of them have felt for one another. As Intintola agonizes over his near-lapse, Carmela reminds him that there's no commandment against eating ziti. The priest's sexual and culinary appetites appear again later, in the final episode of the first season ("I Dream of Jeannie Cusamano"/1013) when Carmela, unnoticed, sees her friend, the recently widowed Rosalie Aprile, give a dish of pasta to Father Intintola at the rectory and overhears their mildly flirtatious conversation as he eats the food and offers Rosalie a bite from his fork. Undetected, the obviously angry Carmela leaves the rectory and dumps the dish of sauce-covered ravioli she is carrying into a sidewalk garbage can. Near the end of the episode, when the priest drops in, admitting that he's something of a "shnorrer, a parasite," a chilly Carmela confronts him, summarizing one of this show's major points about food – especially food covered in tomato sauce – and sex. She says, "I think you have this M.O. where you manipulate spiritually thirsty women and I think a lot of it is tied up with food somehow as well as the sexual tension game."

Tony and his sister Janice have even more sexually and emotionally complex connections with tomato sauce. In the final show of Season Two, Janice has spent the day cooking her fiancé Richie Aprile's dinner and looking after her mother, the always-difficult Livia. They argue about Richie's son's interest in ballroom dancing, an activity that seems less than manly to the macho and sometimes savagely violent Richie. At the height of their argument, Richie smacks Janice in the mouth then shouts, "Put my fucking dinner on the table and keep your mouth shut!" He helps himself to a plate of pasta with tomato sauce, and Janice, being a true Soprano and not one to accept violence meekly, picks up a gun and shoots Richie twice in the chest and stomach, killing him. (This is at least the second time violence and tomato sauce have come together in this kitchen, the first being Livia's threat to put a cooking fork in Tony's eye in the episode cited earlier.) Janice, like Carmela and the priest, has added sex to this heady mix, perhaps catering to non-Italian-Americans' stereotypical views of Italian-Americans as fiery, sexy people who thrive on fiery, sexy, red food.

Viewers who have also seen the film *Big Night* (1996) might connect a chance remark of Tony's to *The Sopranos'* rather stereotypical use of red pasta sauce. In "Nobody Knows Anything" (1011) Tony declares to his family after a brief dinner table conversation about sex, "Out there it's the 1990s. In here it's 1954!" *Big Night* is Stanley Tucci's film about Jersey Shore Italian restaurateurs in the 1950s. Primo, the artistic Italian immigrant chef who wants to serve his customers dishes like shrimp risotto, is horrified when one of his diners insists that risotto isn't Italian food. To this New Jersey American in the 1950s, Italian food is spaghetti and meatballs in tomato sauce with extra cheese. Primo calls her "a philistine" and "a criminal." This woman's 1950s attitude seems to prevail among the characters in *The Sopranos* as well. Just as many non-Italian-Americans might identify Italian-Americans primarily – nay, solely – by tomato sauce, Tony, Paulie, Richie, *et al.* identify themselves with it. Instead of *Chicken Soup for the Soul*, Tony tells his mistress Irina, who is reading the popular self-help book, "Tomato sauce for your ass; that's the Italian version" ("The Knight in White Satin Armor"/2012). As if to illustrate the healing powers of tomato sauce, in Season Three's final episode ("Army of One"/3013), when Uncle Junior has "beaten cancer and beaten the can" (his house arrest for RICO offenses) we know that he is healthy again as he eats pasta at Nuovo Vesuvio after Jackie Aprile Jr.'s funeral, saying "good gravy tonight."

MEAT

Recalling Roland Barthes' comment about the "brutality of meat" (undisguised by tomato sauce), we turn to another aspect of Soprano food: Satriale's Pork Store. Among the opening sequence of shots in every *Sopranos* episode, the camera pans by Satriale's Pork Store in Newark. Part of the Sopranos' family history, as recorded in Allen Rucker's book, is the story of how Tony's father, Johnny Boy Soprano, came to own this business. In a fictional interview, the fictional Dr. Joseph Fusco recounts that after treating Johnny Boy in the Emergency Room of a Newark Hospital in the 1940s, he developed a friendship and a gambling connection with the elder Soprano: "Gambling was very important to me and Johnny ran the games. . . . It was shortly after we met that he maneuvered his way into Satriale's Pork Store over on Kearney Avenue because old man Satriale couldn't pay his gambling debts" (Chapter 2). In the next chapter, we learn from a fictional retired Newark police officer that "Johnny Boy's connection to the meat business led him, eventually, into 'buying into' the Pork Store over on Kearney Avenue, which could function as a legit enterprise. Buying in, of course, meant loaning the owner some money and then taking over the store when he couldn't pay up. A classic bust-out." The pork store, connected to a small café next door, provides places for Tony, his father's brother, Uncle Junior, and the other mob family members to meet. The store is decorated with large figures of a pig and a cow, and the camera often lingers on these carnal symbols when murder is being discussed.

The family eats the sausages made by the pork store, and at a family party where Tony is grilling a grossly intestinal-looking gray sausage, his younger sister Barbara comments that she loves to see men over a grill. Her jaded sister Janice smirks, "They're better over a spit" ("Guy Walks into a Psychiatrist's Office"/2001). Both women inadvertently remind the audience that even in the midst of a seemingly benign family gathering, the possibility of violence is always – sometimes just barely – beneath the surface. This hint at the connection between the pork business and gambling/murder/prostitution/drug/racketeering businesses is fully articulated in "The Knight in White Satin Armor" (2012) when Richie Aprile's corpse is taken to Satriale's in garbage bags, dismembered, and disposed of. At other times we have seen dressed pigs being carted in through the same doors where Richie's bagged corpse has been brought in. We see his blood splatter on the plastic divider curtains. Christopher, one of Tony's "soldiers" who is doing the dismembering and disposal with Furio, dryly remarks "It'll be a long time before I eat any Satriale's stuff again."

There are small random references to and shots of meat throughout the series. When Tony decides to fly to Naples on "business," Carmela, not happy to be left behind, takes a crown roast of pork out of the oven. She and Tony fume at one another a bit, and he stabs his large carving knife into the middle of the roast, displacing his anger "(Commendatori"/2004). In a different episode, Dr. Melfi sees Tony, Paulie, and Pussy in a restaurant after she has dropped Tony as one of her patients. She speaks politely to him and recommends the veal; in the next shot Pussy comments to Tony that Dr. Melfi has "good blow-job lips" ("Toodle-Fucking-oo"/2003). Janice, who, before her return to New Jersey from Seattle, had changed her name to Parvati, is, as we learn in the first episode in which we see her ("Guy Walks into a Psychiatrist's Office"/2001), a vegetarian. Tony complains about her soya milk and tofu in the refrigerator and the miso and seaweed soup he smells on the stove. Vegetarianism is anathema to Tony and the other Mafia captains and soldiers he commands. Meat is intimately connected to their survival, their livelihood, their ability to avoid the legal consequences of their actions, and to their sexuality. The frequent shots of the pig and cow icons at Satriale's and the panning shots of the store's window advertising sausage, veal, and suckling pigs remind us that even though we see Tony as a caring family man whose problems are much like our own and Christopher as an aspiring writer, they are still in the "meat" business and sometimes there is little difference between their brutal treatment of animal and of human bodies.

Tony's connection to the brutality of meat as both sexual and nonsexual violence is a running subtext in Season Three of *The Sopranos*. The FBI agents assigned to Tony's case are determined to find enough evidence on him through bugging his basement, necessary after Tony has killed their informer (and his old friend) Sal "Big Pussy" Bonpensiero for "wearing a wire" and "flipping" – turning informer against them. In "Mr. Ruggerio's Neighborhood" (3001), they refer to Tony's house as "the sausage factory." In the next episode the source of Tony's panic attacks and resultant anxiety attacks – the original cause of his seeking therapy with Dr. Melfi – begins to reveal itself. He is eating a slice of capicola, a meat that has always been provided by Satriale's, when he sees a picture of "Uncle Ben" on a box of rice and faints. ("Uncle Ben" is another ethnic signifier in this show, and Tony is concerned that Meadow is dating a young man whose ethnic background is partly African-American.)

The anxiety triggered by the capicola builds to a climax in "Fortunate Son" (3003). After his mother's death, Tony goes to her house to consult with the Russian caretaker he had hired to look after Livia. Looking for a snack, as he so often does, she tells him that his mother's usual meat order is in the refrigerator; the slice from her usual order of capicola provokes a vivid flashback to the same kitchen when Tony was eleven years old and suffered his first panic/fainting attack. That same day Tony witnessed his father and his Uncle Junior exact vengeance from old man Satriale, who owed them a gambling debt. He pays it with his "pinky" finger, which the two of them lop off with one of his meat cleavers. (Satriale has just begged for mercy and cried to Johnny Boy, "Your wife's weekly meat order is there, thirty dollars' worth of meat – capicola, chops, and a beautiful standing roast!") Satriale's hand is spread out on a butcher block table next to a hunk of raw beef, and the camera has played over large cuts of hanging meat, signs for various cuts of beef, pork, and veal, and their prices, and advertising posters for bacon, beef, and veal in the store. Later, at home, Livia remarks on the "beautiful cut of meat" Satriale sent, as she serves it up. She and Johnny Boy flirt in the kitchen as their children look on, Johnny Boy smirking, "You like it standing, with the bone in, huh?" Livia replies, as the meat is sliced, revealing its rareness, "Look at those juices!" and puts a bit of meat in Johnny's mouth. He begins to sing "All of Me" *à la* Frank Sinatra, and the two of them dance. Johnny squeezes Livia's buttocks and tells the children, "The lady loves her meat!" At this point, the sight of the rare red beef makes Tony faint, necessitating a trip to the doctor and four stitches in his forehead. "Ruined dinner," says Tony.

Upon hearing the above memory retold, Dr. Melfi is horrified and remarks that seeing his father chop off another man's little finger must have been quite a traumatic experience for Tony. He answers, "No, it was a rush." Whether Tony believes the sight traumatized him or not, Melfi does successfully tie all the pieces of narrative into a coherent explanation of Tony's panic attacks, telling him that meat, sexuality – both his parents' and his daughter's – and blood have triggered an overload of anxiety, especially for a pubescent boy. Tony does admit that his mother was made happy (and therefore kind to others) by meat, and he remembers that "When the meat delivery came, you could count on her being in a good mood." He muses that "Probably the only time the old man got laid" was meat-delivery day. Dr. Melfi, resorting to Freudian wordplay, wraps up this session by explaining that Tony, at age eleven, was overwhelmed with the idea that he, too, would someday have to "bring home the bacon, like [his] father." His tough-guy reply is, "All this from a slice of capicola?"

Tony brings home the bacon both literally and metaphorically not only to his wife, Carmela, but metaphorically (that is, sexually) to a series of casual partners and more serious mistresses, or *goomari*. In "Pine Barrens" (3011), after we have learned of Tony's meat/sex/violence connection, his mistress, Mercedes saleswoman Gloria Trillo, whom he has met in Dr. Melfi's waiting room, wants to make up after a fight by cooking London Broil for Tony, who has promised to show up for dinner at her house at nine that evening. He is late because of a family health crisis. Gloria, an unstable and neurotic young woman much like Tony's mother – a fact pointed out to him by Dr. Melfi – is drunk and angry by the time he gets there and ends their evening (and their fight) by throwing the London Broil at Tony as he leaves to rescue Paulie and Christopher, who are lost in the South Jersey Pine Barrens. When he tells Dr. Melfi in their next therapy session (in "Amour Fou"/3012) what has happened, she is amazed at Gloria's violent outburst and asks, dumbfounded, "Why would anybody hit you, of all people, with a side of beef?" Carmela, who knows nothing of Tony's affair with Gloria but has met her at the dealership where she works, casually mentions "mad cow disease." We learn exactly what a "mad cow" Gloria is when she lures Tony back to her house, fights with him again, and, as he straddles her supine body with his hands around her throat, begs him to kill her, echoing Livia's often-repeated wish that "the Lord would just take me now." He doesn't, but we know that Tony has reenacted the brutality of meat, sex, and violence again.

Seafood

The brutality of meat leads us to "the abruptness of seafood," another important "word" in *The Sopranos'* food language, and, again, a signifier of both sexuality and violence. The Latin root of *abrupt* is *abruptus*, or "broken off," and unlike beef or pork, fish is often served up whole, suggesting that it has just been "broken off" from its source, the sea, and undergone little if any mediating process, as, indeed, is the case with raw oysters, clams, and sushi. Let us first investigate the sexual imagery of seafood. As many of us know from numerous smutty jokes, female genitals are often compared to seafood in terms of "taste" and odor. Renowned food scholar Margaret Visser explains the semiotics of flesh in *Much Depends on Dinner* in less sexual or graphic terms, saying that "Meats themselves are placed on a ladder of power ranging from fish (the lowest rung and the most 'female' of meats), through poultry, to the 'strongest,' red meat" (151). Fish, she says, is so low on the meat scale that "it was commonly permitted in such religious strategies as Lenten abstinence or the Catholic institution of 'fish on Fridays.' Lowering one's sights from meat to fish was an exercise in humility" (151).

The association of fish, female genitals, and humility is made in the first season of *The Sopranos*, in an episode titled "Boca" (1009), a play on the word "mouth" and Uncle Junior's favorite Florida hangout, Boca Raton. When Junior takes his mistress, Roberta, to Boca Raton, we see them drinking champagne in bed and discussing their sex life together. Roberta shyly tells Junior that he's a "real artist" at "kissing down there," or cunnilingus. His reply is "pass me the red peppers," making it obvious that he does not care to discuss this secret and shameful practice. Roberta probes, asking, "Why the big secret about oral sex?" and Junior explains that in his circle of Italian-American men, "They think if you suck pussy you'll suck anything. It's a sign of weakness and possibly a sign that you're a *fanook* [homosexual]." Word does leak out, however, and when Tony finds out that Junior has been "whistling through the wheat field" and is a "bushman of the Kalahari," he teases him unmercifully, saying during a golf game with other Mafiosi, "Uncle Jun's in the muff," and "I thought you were a baccala [codfish] man, Uncle Jun. What are you doing eating sushi?" Junior's fears of ridicule by other men have, alas, been realized. He has, in Visser's terms, eaten the meat of humility, inconsistent with the macho posturing of his Mafia cohorts. Roberta's punishment suggests an important intertextual relation of this ongoing crime narrative to other tough-guy gangster films. Like Cagney in *Public Enemy* (1931), who rubs his doxy Kitty's face with a grapefruit half, Junior rubs a lemon meringue pie into Roberta's face, presumably restoring his status as boss of the Soprano family. Significantly, lemon juice is the common antidote for the smell of fish.

One of the intertextual connections we encounter throughout *The Sopranos* is Francis Ford Coppola's *Godfather* series, which the characters often mention and often enjoy imitating. In the first *Godfather* film, Luca Brazi has been killed and dumped in the ocean. This message is conveyed by a fish wrapped in newspaper, meaning "Luca Brazi sleeps with the fishes." This intertextual incident echoes throughout the show, signifying the offshore execution of Pussy Bonpensiero. Tony's growing suspicion of Pussy's betrayal is revealed to him through a dream-like vision Tony experiences in "Funhouse" (2013), an episode which features many eating scenes, some in an Indian restaurant where Tony and the owner collaborate on a phone card scam, some at Nuovo Vesuvio where Tony, Silvio, Furio and Pussy eat fried zucchini flowers and clams. In the Indian restaurant, we see a significant, lingering shot of a whole fish as it is carried by a waiter from the kitchen to a table. Later, Tony, suffering from food poisoning, hallucinates that he is at a fish market where one of the iced fish addresses him in the voice of Pussy, who confesses that he's a rat. The realization is part of Tony's violent physical illness, a reaction as much to his friend's betrayal as to the e. coli bacteria in the "fuckin' chicken vindaloo" from the Indian restaurant. After a long night of suffering, Tony, who finds Pussy's wire in a cigar box the next day, realizes what must be done. Tony, Pussy, and Silvio go out to sea in a borrowed boat, where Pussy makes jokes about "eating pussy," eventually confessing that he was driven to "flipping" for the FBI, before his execution and disposal. Pussy, who has joked about eating the meat of humility, becomes the "iced fish" of Tony's hallucination. Now, as his corpse is consumed by fish, he will *become* the meat of humility.

In Season Three, Tony is haunted by visions of fish, often in the form of the popular "Big Mouth Billy Bass" singing fish plaques so prevalent that season (2000–01). Because he has shared his vision of Pussy as an "iced fish" with no one else, the other characters continue unwittingly to remind Tony of his friend's betrayal and Tony's execution of him. When Georgie, one of the Bada Bing!'s bartenders, brings the "Big Mouth" fish to work ("Second Opinion"/3007), Tony is at first amused, then horrified, then enraged with Big Mouth's rendition of "Take me to the river/drop me in the water." His rage is such that he beats the hapless one-eyed barman over the head and shoulders with the plaque, screaming, "This is a place of business!" Later in that episode, Tony's guilt and anger surface again and he calls Angie, Pussy's widow, a "cunt." The singing fish reappears near the end of this episode after Paulie, Christopher's superior, has been "busting his balls" to remind him who's boss. (This exercise in humiliation has included Paulie's sniffing Christopher's fiancée's panties.) The singing fish this time sings the gay anthem "YMCA," again suggesting that fish is, in Margaret Visser's words, "the most 'female' of meats" (151). Finally, in the show's Christmas episode ("To Save Us All From Satan's Power"/3010), Meadow gives Tony one of the fish plaques as a Christmas gift, one he must accept with equanimity, having convinced his family that Pussy has been sent to the witness protection program.[1]

We cannot leave the topic of fish without mentioning another intertextual reference, Umberto's Clam House in New York's Little Italy, site of one of the many executions in *The Godfather*, a film which serves, in part, as godfather to this television series. Both because of the film and the restaurant itself, the Soprano Mafiosi grow misty-eyed when Umberto's is mentioned.

FINAL COURSE

There are other important and significant food episodes in *The Sopranos* which add to the narrative richness of the text. For example, AJ and his friends are identified as the vandals who trash their high school's swimming pool by their pizza order – "double meatball, pepperoni, extra mozzarella" ("The Telltale Moozadell"/3009); Carmela tries out Mario Batali's recipes on her family ("Fortunate Son"/3003); Carmela's mother, on hearing that Janice has taken the name Parvati, responds, "What? She's a cheese now?" ("Guy Walks into a Psychiatrist's Office"/2001); Artie Bucco serves the Soprano family (both the biological and Mafia members) special cheeses and other treats ("Amour Fou" /3012); their maid Lilliana steals a jar of imported Italian capers which the Soprano children refuse to eat ("Mr. Ruggerio's Neighborhood"/3001); a shot of Carmela's basement pantry shows numerous pasta boxes ("Mr. Ruggerio's Neighborhood"/3001); Tony jokingly threatens to shoot whipped cream down AJ's back ("Down Neck"/1007) and later takes him out for hot dogs after he proves his mettle on the football field ("Fortunate Son"/3003). Tony fantasizes that Dr. Melfi engages in fellatio with him and says how much she "loves [his] connolis" ("Pax Soprana"/1006); Paulie and Christopher are reduced to eating frozen ketchup and Tictacs when they are lost in the Jersey Pine Barrens ("Pine Barrens"/3011); earlier, Paulie has angrily wondered why Italians don't make more money from coffee businesses such as Starbucks ("46 Long"/1002).

These people seem, like so many Americans, to eat most of the time, and as we have seen, much of their food and their attitudes toward it mark them as stereotypical Italian-Americans. However, some of the incidental food shots and the placement of brand-name foods in those shots mark the Sopranos as part of the great salad mix of Americans. They drink Coke with their meals, dream of the Denny's Grand Slam breakfast, eat plain cheese pizza, or Popeye's Fried Chicken, or wish they had stopped by Roy Rogers' for lunch. Bobby Baccala, who takes care of Junior when he has cancer, loves White Castle hamburgers so much that he is called "Burger Boy." Jackie Aprile Jr. chases some Hispanic boys out of the Ooh-Fa Pizzeria and tells them to go to Taco Bell ("Amour Fou"/ 3003). Meadow, depressed over Jackie Jr.'s infidelity, answers the telephone with "Taco Bell" ("Army of One"/3013). Breakfast scenes show Tony, Carmela, AJ, and Meadow eating cereal (Capt. Crunch or Coco Puffs or Cheerios) or pouring Aunt Jemima syrup on their pancakes. In the third season, Tony and Carmela fight in the driveway over how much pulp is in the Tropicana orange juice ("Second Opinion"/3007), and the sometimes ruthlessly violent Ralph Cifaretto mixes up a mug of Swiss Miss with marshmallows to drink while he tells Jackie Aprile Jr. a story about his father's crime escapades ("Amour Fou"/3012). Such food is an important element of American popular culture and locates these characters in our lives more effectively than any dialogue could.

Familiar, brand-name foods emphasize, in part, the complexity of the characters and their lives and differentiate this narrative from its intertextual partners. The food of *The Godfather* films – Clemenza's tomato sauce, the erotic gnocchi-making scene, the poisoned connolis – and the elaborate cooking preparations of *GoodFellas*, where Anglo mobster-wannabe Henry Hill slices garlic with a razor blade and cooks pasta sauce while government helicopters roar overhead, reduce these characters to somewhat melodramatic ethnic stereotypes. While the food of *The Sopranos* sometimes does reinforce the stereotypes of the show's models, this show explores, through food, some larger cultural and literary issues. All of them, however, boil down to the issue of power, whereas the food of *The Godfather* films seems primarily just to signify their Italian ethnicity.[2] To the Soprano family men, too, eating is bound up with power, and when Uncle Junior is declared boss of the Soprano family, his arrogation of power is described as "eating alone." Junior's power is so absolute that, Raymond Curto says, "He don't even pass the salt" ("Pax Soprana"/1006). Tony reminds Junior that the Roman leader Octavian was well loved because "he never ate alone." This eating metaphor is sufficient for Junior to absorb its lesson. The Roman intertext begins, of course, with Livia, Tony's mother, the source of his first food. The Roman Livia was a famous poisoner, and Livia's power over Tony's life or death, even though her plot to have him murdered fails, never ceases until she dies.

The language of food in *The Sopranos* tells us that they are sometimes powerful, often powerless; that they have absorbed some of the lessons of history, that they are not like many of us, that they are exactly like many of us; that their lives, like the food they eat, are a mixture of values, traditions, economic forces, and uncountable other influences. The language of their food adds depth to the narrative and its characters and elevates this show's writing far beyond its generic formula.

THE SOPRANOS EPISODES: WRITERS AND DIRECTORS

By Season	Episode	Title	Written by	Directed By	Air Date
1001	1	Pilot: The Sopranos	David Chase	David Chase	01-10-99
1002	2	46 Long	David Chase	David Chase	01-17-99
1003	3	Denial, Anger, Acceptance	Mark Saraceni	Nick Gomez	01-24-99
1004	4	Meadowlands	Jason Cahill	John Patterson	01-31-99
1005	5	College	Jim Manos Jr. & David Chase	Allen Coulter	02-07-99
1006	6	Pax Soprana	Frank Renzulli	Alan Taylor	02-14-99
1007	7	Down Neck	Robin Green & Mitchell Burgess	Lorraine Senna	02-21-99
1008	8	The Legend of Tennessee Moltisanti	Frank Renzulli & David Chase	Tim Van Patten	02-28-99
1009	9	Boca	Jason Cahill, Robin Green, & Mitchell Burgess	Andy Wolk	03-07-99
1010	10	A Hit is a Hit	Joe Bosso & Frank Renzulli	Matthew Penn	03-14-99
1011	11	Nobody Knows Anything	Frank Renzulli	Henry J. Bronchtein	03-21-99
1012	12	Isabella	Robin Green	Allen Coulter	03-28-99
1013	13	I Dream of Jeannie Cusamano	David Chase	John Patterson	04-04-99
2001	14	Guy Walks into a Psychiatrist's Office	Jason Cahill	Allen Coulter	01-16-00
2002	15	Do Not Resuscitate	Robin Green, Mitchell Burgess, & Frank Renzulli	Martin Bruestle	01-23-00
2003	16	Toodle-Fucking-oo	Frank Renzulli	Lee Tamahori	01-30-00
2004	17	Commendatori	David Chase	Tim Van Patten	02-06-00
2005	18	Big Girls Don't Cry	Terence Winter	Tim Van Patten	02-13-00

By Season	Episode	Title	Written by	Directed By	Air Date
2006	19	The Happy Wanderer	Frank Renzulli	John Patterson	02-20-00
2007	20	D-Girl	Todd A. Kessler	Allen Coulter	02-27-00
2008	21	Full Leather Jacket	Robin Green &	Allen Coulter	03-05-00
2009	22	From Where to Eternity	Michael Imperioli	Henry J. Bronchtein	03-12-00
2010	23	Bust Out	Frank Renzulli, Robin Green, Mitchell Burgess, & David Chase	John Patterson	03-19-00
2011	24	House Arrest	Terence Winter	Tim Van Patten	03-26-00
2012	25	The Knight in White Satin Armor	Robin Green & Mitchell Burgess	Allen Coulter	04-02-00
2013	26	Funhouse	David Chase & Todd A. Kessler	John Patterson	04-09-00
3001	27	Mr. Ruggerio's Neighborhood	David Chase	Allen Coulter	03-04-01
3002	28	Proshai, Livushka	David Chase	Tim Van Patten	03-04-01
3003	29	Fortunate Son	Todd A. Kessler	Henry J. Bronchtein	03-11-01
3004	30	Employee of the Month	Robin Green & Mitchell Burgess	John Patterson	03-18-01
3005	31	Another Toothpick	Terence Winter	Jack Bender	03-25-01
3006	32	University	*	Allen Coulter	04-1-01
3007	33	Second Opinion	Lawrence Konner	Tim Van Patten	04-8-01
3008	34	He is Risen	Todd A. Kessler	Allen Coulter	04-15-01
3009	35	The Telltale Moozadell	Michael Imperioli	Daniel Attias	04-22-01
3010	36	To Save Us All From Satan's Power	Robin Green & Mitchell Burgess	Jack Bender	04-29-01
3011	37	Pine Barrens	Terence Winter	Steve Buscemi	05-6-01
3012	38	Amour Fou	Frank Renzulli	Tim Van Patten	05-13-01
3013	39	Army of One	David Chase & Lawrence Konner	John Patterson	05-20-01

* Teleplay by Terence Winter and Salvatore Stabile, Story by David Chase, Terence Winter, Todd A. Kessler, Robin Green, and Mitchell Burgess

The Sopranos Cast of Characters (A Selection)

This list does not presume to be comprehensive. Other cast lists are available online at HBO.com and Sopranoland.com.

Character	Actor/Actress	Identity
Jimmy Altieri	Joseph Badalucco Jr.	Capo, who wears a wire for the Feds; whacked by Silvio.
Giacomo (Jackie) Aprile	Michael Rispoli	Former North Jersey mob boss; dies from cancer.
Giacomo (Jackie) Aprile Jr.	Jason Cerbone	Incompetent aspiring mobser, son of Jackie Aprile Sr.; whacked by Vito Spatafore.
Richie Aprile	David Proval	Brother of Jackie Aprile; released from prison, he becomes a thorn in Tony's side; killed by Janice Soprano.
Rosalie Aprile	Sharon Angela	Wife/widow of Jackie Aprile; now the amour of Ralph Cifaretto, who had her son whacked.
Ariel	Ned Eisenberg	Owner/manager of the Flyway Motel, strong-armed by the Soprano crew into surrendering partial control of his establishment (after threat of castration).
Aaron Arkaway	Turk Pipkin	Janice's born-again narcoleptic boyfriend.
Bobby Baccilieri Jr.	Steven R. Schirripa	Junior Soprano's gentle, shy, seriously overweight assistant.
Bobby Baccilieri Sr.	Burt Young	Aging hitman, dying of lung cancer; dies in a car crash after whacking Mustang Sally.
Albert (Ally Boy) Barese	Richard Maldone	Larry Boy's ineffectual son.
Larry (Larry Boy) Barese	Tony Darrow	Capo, now in jail.
Dick Barone	Joe Lisi	Manager of Barone Sanitation.
Matt Bevilaqua	Lillo Brancato Jr.	Aspiring mobster; whacked by Tony and Big Pussy after trying to kill Christopher.
Angie Bonpensiaro	Toni Kalem	Wife of Big Pussy.

Salvatore (Big Pussy) Bonpensiero	Vincent Pastore	One of Tony's captains who becomes an informant for the Feds; whacked by Tony, Paulie, and Silvio, and dumped at sea.
Artie Bucco	John Ventimiglia	Restaurateur, childhood friend of Tony's. In love with Adriana LeCerva.
Charmaine Bucco	Kathrine Narducci	Wife of Artie Bucco.
Gigi Cestone	John Fiore	One of Tony's soliders, later a captain; dies of a constipation-induced heart attack.
Ralph Cifaretto	Joe Pantoliano	Loose canon North Jersey mobster, made a captain by Tony.
Agent Frank Cubitoso	Frank Pellegrino	FBI agent in charge of investigating Tony.
Raymond Curto	George Loros	Capo and FBI informant.
Dr. Bruce Cusamano	Robert Lupone	Tony's next door neighbor and family doctor.
Jeannie Cusamano	Saundra Santiago	Dr. Cusamano's wife.
Gabriella Dante	Maureen Van Zandt	Wife of Sylvio.
Silvio Dante	Steven Van Zandt	Tony's consigliere, manager of the Bada Bing!
Hugh DeAngelis	Tom Aldredge	Carmela's father.
Mary DeAngelis	Suzanne Sheperd	Carmela's mother.
Jon Favreau	Himself	Hollywood independent director and actor.
Brendan Filone	Anthony DeSando	Aspiring mobster, friend of Christopher; whacked by Mikey Palmice.
Dr. Ira Freid	Lewis J. Stadln	Local "prick doctor," specializing in penile implants, poker, and doing off-the-record medical work for Tony's crew.
Peter (Beansie) Gaeta	Paul Herman	Pizza parlor owner; paralyzed for life after Richie Aprile runs him over in a car.
Georgie	Frank Santorelli	Tattooed bartender in the Bada Bing!
Sean Gismonte	Chris Tardio	Aspiring mobster, killed by Christopher after he and Matt Bevilaqua try to kill him "on spec."
Furio Giunta	Federico Castelluccio	One of Tony's soldiers, imported from Italy.
Agent Harris	Matt Servitto	FBI agent investigating the Sopranos.
Don Hauser	Kevin O'Rourke	Verbum Dei soccer coach.
Father Phil Intintola	Paul Schulze	Catholic priest, infatuated with food, movies, and Carmela and other mob wives.
Mustang Sally Intile	Brian Tarantina	Low-life hood who puts an Aprile relative in a coma and is whacked by Bobby Baccilieri Sr.
Isabella	Maria Grazia Cucinotta	Fantasy Italian woman imagined by Tony.
Rev. Herman James Jr.	Gregalan Williams	Corrupt minister who appears to be following in the footsteps of his father but is in fact in cahoots with Tony.
Rev. Herman James Sr.	Bill Cobbs	An aging preacher and labor activist.
Dr. John Kennedy	Sam McMurray	Surgeon who operates on Uncle Junior and later shows concern for his chemotherapy after being threatened by Tony and Furio.
Svetlana Kirrilenko	Alla Kliouka	One-legged friend of Irina.
Dr. Elliot Kupferberg	Peter Bogdanovich	Dr. Melfi's psychiatrist.
Adriana La Cerva	Drew De Meteo	Christopher's girlfriend and fiancée.
Jason La Penna	Will McCormack	Dr. Melfi's college-age son; a student at Bard.
Dr. Richard La Penna	Richard Romanus	Dr. Melfi's ex, a psychiatrist.
Lilianna	Katalin Pota	The Sopranos' Polish maid.

Skip Lipari	Louis Lombardi	FBI agent working with Big Pussy.
Madam Debby	Karen Sillas	Owner of a North Jersey bordello.
Vin Makazian	John Heard	North Jersey cop in Tony's employ; jumps to his death off a bridge.
Slava Malesky	Frank Ciornei	Russian money launderer, through whom Tony is sending hundreds of thousands of dollars to international banks.
Massive Genius	Bokeem Woodbine	Gangster rapper who seeks reparations from Hesh.
Dr. Jennifer Melfi	Lorraine Bracco	Tony's psychiatrist.
Harold Melvoin	Richard Portnow	Uncle Junior's lawyer.
Neil Mink	David Margulies	Tony's lawyer.
Christopher Moltisanti	Michael Imperioli	Aspiring mobster, one of Tony's soldiers and now a made man.
Vic Musto	Joe Penny	Wallpaper hanger and almost lover of Carmela.
Joan O'Connell	Saundra Santiago	A prominent lawyer, twin sister of Jeannie Cusamano.
Mikey Palmice	Al Sapienza	Junior's right-hand man; whacked by Christopher and Paulie.
Patsy Parisi	Dan Grimaldi	Phil Parisi's twin brother, now part of Tony's crew.
Phil (Bones) Parisi	Dan Grimaldi	Junior's "piss boy"; whacked by Gigi Cestone.
Irina Peltsin	Oksana Babiy	Tony's Russian goomah.
Fabian (Febby) Petrullo (aka Fred Peters)	Tony Ray Rossi	Mob informant, whacked by Tony while in the witness protection program in Maine.
Herman (Hesh) Rabkin	Jerry Adler	Jewish friend and advisor of Tony.
Carlo Renzi	Louis Crugnali	Aspiring mobster, friend of Jackie Aprile Jr., killed (by Christopher) in failed Pontecorvo robbery.
Catherine Romano	Mary Louse Wilson	Neighbor of Junior, who befriends him during his house arrest.
Jesus Rossi	Mario Polit	Employee of the month who rapes Dr. Melfi.
Caitlin Rucker	Ari Gaynor	Meadow's Columbia University roommate.
Johnny (Johnny Sack) Sacramoni	Vincent Curatola	New York capo, now living in New Jersey.
Ginny Sacrimoni	Denise Borino	Johnny Sack's obese wife.
Amy Safir	Alicia Witt	Hollywood D[evelopment]-Girl.
Bobbi Sanfillipo	Robyn Peterson	Junior's former long-time girlfriend.
Richie Santini	Nick Fowler	Friend of Adriana's and lead singer of Visiting Day.
Francis Satriale	Lou Bonacki	Former owner of Satriale's Meats.
Hunter Scangarelo	Michele DeCesare	Friend of Meadow.
Davey Scatino	Robert Patrick	Childhood friend of Tony and former owner of a sporting goods store busted out by Tony and his crew.
Dr. Douglas Schreck	Matthew Sussman	Junior's doctor, whose office serves as a meeting place for business conversations.
Charles (Chucky) Signore	Sal Ruffino	One of Junior lieutenant's, whacked by Tony.
Frank Sinatra Jr.	Himself	Singer and regular participant in Soprano-sponsored "executive" card game.
Anthony (AJ) Soprano Jr.	Robert Iler	Tony and Carmela's teenage son.

Barbara Soprano Giglione	Nicole Burdette	Tony's sister.
Carmela Soprano	Edie Falco	Tony's wife.
Carrado (Uncle Junior) Soprano	Dominic Chianese	Tony's uncle.
Janice (Parvati) Soprano	Aida Turturro	Tony's sister.
John (Johnny Boy) Soprano	Joseph Siravo	Tony's late father.
Livia Soprano	Nancy Marchand	Tony's mother, who dies of a stroke in Season Three.
Meadow Soprano	Jamie-Lynn Sigler	Tony's daughter, now a student at Columbia.
Tony Soprano	James Gandolfini	North Jersey mob boss.
Vito Spatafore	Joseph R. Gannascoli	Portly Soprano family soldier, now in Ralph Cifaretto's crew.
Stasiu	Albert Makhtsier	The unhappy former engineer husband of Sopranos' maid Lilliana (back in Poland).
Sunshine	Paul Mazursky	Card shark regularly playing in Soprano-run games; killed in failed Pontecorvo robbery.
Noah Tannenbaum	Patrick Tully	Meadow's former African-American/Jewish boy friend.
Shlomo Teittleman	Chuck Low	Hasidic Jew who seeks Tony's help with his son-in-law.
Gloria Trillo	Annabella Sciorra	Mercedes saleswoman and former mistress of Tony.
Valery	Vitaly Baganov	Former Russian special forces hero, compatriot of Slava Malesky, who Paulie and Chris try to kill and dump in the Pine Barrens.
Paulie Walnuts	Tony Sirico	One of Tony's captains.
Jeffrey Wernick	Timothy Nolen	Mafia expert and frequent television talking head.
Leon Wilmore	Charles S. Dutton	North Jersey cop who tickets Tony for speeding.
State Assemblyman Zellman	Peter Reigert	A local politician in cahoots with Tony.
Dino Zerilli	Andrew Davoli	Aspiring mobster, killed by Christopher after the failed Pontecorvo robbery.
Annalisa Zucca	Sofia Milos	Daughter of Don Vittorio and real boss of the Italian mob with whom Tony must negotiate.

INTERTEXTUAL MOMENTS AND ALLUSIONS IN THE SOPRANOS

As film scholar Robert Stam has wittily observed, the first rule of sexually transmitted diseases – that an individual who has sex with another becomes heir to all of that other's sexual partners – applies to texts as well (202).[1] *The Sopranos* has definitely slept around and comes heavy with intertextuality and enough allusions to keep a team of annotators busy. A continuing, self-conscious – even hyperconscious – mob story, hybridized in the age of recombinant TV with a family drama ("Family – redefined" as HBO has it in one ad; "Either one family or the other will kill him," as another puts it), *The Sopranos* is, with the possible exception of the WB's (now UPN's) *Buffy the Vampire Slayer,* the most referential show on television. Intertextuality is central to its method. As Tanya Krzywinska observes (though she has *Buffy* in mind, she might well be thinking of *The Sopranos*), "jokes, as well as direct or indirect references to other shows [or novels] are part of a common cultural vocabulary that connects characters to a broader 'real' world culture. Such references lend the series a greater sense of meaningfulness, timeliness, and textual richness, further encouraging discussion between viewers and helping to interlace the [show's universe] with everyday life" (190).

A catalog of intertextual moments and allusions in *The Sopranos* follows:

Intertext/Allusion	Annotation
Albatross: Johnny Boy Soprano calls Livia a "fucking albicore around my neck" when she refuses to consider a move to Nevada.	In Coleridge's "Rhyme of the Ancient Mariner," a sailor kills an albatross, bringing a curse upon him and his ship.
***Anarchy, State and Utopia*:** Larry Arthur, a witness in Matt Bevilaqua's murder, sits in his living room reading *Anarchy, State and Utopia* just prior to learning that he will be testifying against a mob boss (and developing instant amnesia about what he saw) (2010).	Work of political philosophy by Robert Nozick, originally published in 1977.

Andretti, Mario: Tony calls AJ, playing a car-racing video game "Andretti" (1004).	(1940–). Famous race car driver, born in Italy.
Basic Instinct: Jackie Aprile Jr. and Dino Zerilli watch the notorious Sharon Stone interrogation scene from *Basic Instinct* while planning a soon-to-fail heist (3012).	1992 Paul Verhoeven film in which a detective (Michael Douglas) tracks a female serial killer (Stone).
Beatles: Father Phil and Carmela discuss Christ's teachings and the Beatles (1005).	British rock 'n' roll band whose music had a profound effect on cultural history.
Bernhard, Sandra: Christopher gives Janeane Garofalo and Sandra Bernhard obscene Italian dialogue advice (2007).	(1955–). Sardonic American comic and actress.
Beverly Hillbillies: In a flashback Livia refuses to move the family to Las Vegas, claiming "Oakies and misfits, that's who goes there. Losers, the Beverly hillbilly" (1007).	American television show (1962–71) about a poor, uneducated family from the Ozarks who become millionaires after discovering oil.
Birds, The: Tony wonders whether his watching of *The Birds* on TV influenced his dream of the birds making off with his penis (1001).	1963 film by Alfred Hitchcock.
Bogart, Humphrey: Humphrey Bogart's picture is on the wall in the pork store during Christopher's whack of Emil Kolar (1001).	(1899–1957). American movie star, who got his start in gangster films.
Boss, Hugo: Jackie Aprile Jr. tells Meadow, "You wanna know what I'm interested in? Men's fashion. Not the faggy part of it, but, like, to be Hugo Boss."	German designer of men's clothing.
Boyz II Men: After failing to whack Tony Soprano, two young African American hitmen are referred to as (1) "the Jamaican bobsled team" and (2) Boyz II Men (1012).	Popular 1990s African American R 'n' B boy group.
Brazelton, T. Berry: Tony expresses his anger about AJ's expulsion from Verbum Dei by telling Carmela that he's had enough of [T. Berry] Brazelton (3013).	Child psychologist, the Doctor Spock of Baby Boomers.
bris: Hesh advises Tony to "Make like a mohel. Finish his bris," in order to secure the agreement of motel owner Ariel (1003).	The Jewish ceremony of circumcision.

Bruno Magli: Paulie's improvised shoe (made of carpet and twine) causes Chris to proclaim "Bruno Magli here!" (3011).	Footprints left at the scene of the murder of Nicole Brown Simpson seemed to indicate a pair of Bruno Magli shoes owned by O.J. Simpson.
Brylcreem: "The federal marshalls are so far up my ass I can taste Brylcreem" (2003).	Grooming product, popular into the 1960s when longer hair styles made it passé.
Camus, Albert: See existentialists.	(1913–60). French writer and philosopher, author of books like *The Outsider* and *The Myth of Sisyphus*.
Canoe: When Livia asks Uncle Junior what cologne he is wearing (adding that he smells like a French prostitute), Junior answers that he is wearing Canoe.	Men's cologne, manufactured by Dana, available in the United States since the 1930s.
Carrey, Jim: Christopher speaks admiringly of the box office take of Jim Carrey in *The Grinch Who Stole Christmas* (2000) (3010).	(1962–). Popular 1990s comic and actor.
Casablanca: Carmela quotes *Casablanca* to Father Phil (1005).	1942 Michael Curtiz film starring Humphrey Bogart that has become one of the most popular movies of all time.
Casino: When asked what gangster films she and her friends like, Meadow mentions *Casino* (1005). See also Pesci, Joe.	1995 Martin Scorsese film about gambling and the mob in Las Vegas.
Castaneda, Carlos: Carlos Castaneda, quoted by Dr. Melfi, is mistaken for a boxer by Tony (2006). "Who the fuck listens to prize fighters?" Tony replies.	(1931–98). American anthropologist, author of books about his apprenticeship to a Yaqui Indian sorcerer.
Catskills: Ariel makes a joke when the gang has come to strong-arm him; Paulie asks "What is this, the Catskills? We got Shecky Greene here" (1003).	A range of the Appalachian Mountains and resort area in the state of New York, home to a variety of clubs where Jewish-American comedians honed their craft.
chemosabe: Brendan Filone describes Jackie Aprile as being "chemosabe" in his battle with cancer (1001).	On TV's *The Lone Ranger* (1949–57), Tonto frequently used "kemosabe" to refer to his partner, which apparently means "faithful friend" in the Potowatomie language.
Chicken Soup for the Soul: Tony's Russian goomah Irina reads *Chicken Soup for the Soul* (2012).	Jack Canfield's 1995 collection of feel-good stories that spawned an entire industry of similar books.

Churchill, Winston: Winston Churchill and Napoleon are both called to mind by Silvio (1012), seeking to explain Tony's depression to Christopher: "A lot of top guys have dark moods. That Winston Churchill, drank a quart of brandy before breakfast. Napoleon, he was a moody fuck too."	(1874–1965). British politician and writer, Prime Minister during World War II.
Cliffs Notes: Tony tells Melfi that he is familiar with *Prince Matchabelli* through Carmela's Cliffs Notes version (3006).	Academic study aids used by students since 1958.
Clooney, George: When a hospital orderly seeks to prevent Tony's verbal assault on his supposedly stroke-affected mother, he is called "George Clooney" and told to mind his own business (1013).	(1961–). American actor who rose to fame on the television program *ER* and went on to become a major film star.
Cobain, Kurt: The suicides of Kurt Cobain (1009) and Ernest Hemingway (1008) are evoked.	(1967–93). Lead singer of the Seattle Grunge band Nirvana, who committed suicide.
Cochran, Johnny: When one of the two boys who stole AJ's biology teacher's Saturn demands to see a lawyer, Big Pussy shoves a gun barrel in his mouth and says "I've got fuckin' Johnny Cochran right here" (1002).	Los Angeles criminal defense attorney, known for taking on racially-charged cases. Rose to national fame as O.J. Simpson's attorney.
Cooper, Gary: Tony laments to Dr. Melfi that there are no Gary Coopers anymore (1001).	(1901–61). Stoic American actor, best known for his heroic roles in westerns and other films.
Cops: Christopher watches (and comments skeptically on) Fox's *Cops*.	Fox Television docudrama that uses actual police documentary video footage.
Crater, Judge: Judge Crater is the punch-line of an Uncle Junior joke (2011).	Judge Joseph F. Crater mysteriously disappeared from New York in 1930, becoming one of the most famous missing persons of the century.
Crime and Punishment: Dr. Krakower recommends to Carmela that Tony read Dostoevsky's *Crime and Punishment* – in prison (3007).	1867 novel by the Russian writer Fyodor Dostoevsky (1821–81).
Crying Game, The: Christopher tells Jon Favreau and Amy Safir about a Mafioso's encounter with a transsexual, immediately reminding the d-girl of *Crying Game* (2007).	1992 film by Neil Jordan about a man who becomes involved with the IRA and falls for a beautiful transsexual.

Cuban Missile Crisis: See *Thirteen Days*.	1962 Cold War confrontation between the United States and the Soviet Union, precipitated by the latter's placement of missiles in Cuba.
Cuomo, Mario: Meadow uses the example of Mario Cuomo to refute her father's theory of discrimination against Italians as the socio-economic root of the Mafia: Tony: "There was a time, Mead, when the Italian people didn't have a lot of options." Meadow: "You mean like Mario Cuomo?" (1005).	(1932–). Former Governor of New York, often mentioned as a Presidential candidate.
Davis, Bette: Tony refers to his mother as a "fuckin' Bette Davis" (2006).	(1908–89). Beautiful, talented, but notoriously difficult Hollywood film actress.
Dementia 13: Noah Tannenbaum takes Meadow to see *Dementia 13* (3006).	The 1963 debut film of *Godfather* director Francis Ford Coppola (3006).
De Niro, Robert: Carmela and Father Phil discuss how Scorsese's *The Last Temptation of Christ* (1988) would have been very different with Robert De Niro in the lead instead of Willem Daffoe.	(1943–). Great American actor, best known for his work in a number of films with director Martin Scorsese and his portrayal of the young Vito Corleone in *The Godfather Part II*.
Devil's Advocate, The: Christopher cites the character arcs of Richard Kimble (*The Fugitive*) and the Keannu Reeves character (Kevin Lomax) in *The Devil's Advocate* as he wonders what his own arc is (1008).	1997 Taylor Hackford film starring Keannu Reeves.
Dickinson, Angie: Sex with Angie Dickinson (by Uncle Junior) is fantasized (1013).	(1931–). Beautiful but not very talented film and television actress.
Die Hard: See Rasputin.	1988 John McTiernan film in which Bruce Willis plays a resilient cop who thwarts a group of terrorists.
Donnie Brasco: A member of the posse of gangster rapper Massive Genius calls out to Christopher, "Yo, Donnie Brasco" (1010).	1997 Mike Newell film, starring Al Pacino and Johnny Depp, about an FBI agent who goes undercover with the mob.
Erin Brokovich: Carmela's parents disagree on whether *Erin Brokovich* is a a good movie (3006).	2000 Steven Soderbergh film starring Julia Roberts.

Evans, Dale: Sex with Dale Evans is fantasized (by Paulie Walnuts) (3011).	(1912–2001). American actress and singer, longtime wife and partner of cowboy star and singer Roy Rogers.
Existentialists: AJ becomes deeply depressed after reading the existentialists at school (Sartre, Kierkegaard, Camus, Heidegger are evoked, and of course the German philosopher "Nitch," and an English teacher, of course, is blamed – and the Internet) and learning that life is meaningless ("Death just shows the ultimate absurdity of life") (2007).	Philosophical and literary movement, originating in Europe and coming into prominence after World War II.
Fargo: "Pine Barrens" (3011), directed by Coen Brothers' veteran Steve Buscemi, evokes the winter landscapes of *Fargo*.	1996 film by the Coen Brothers.
Fatal Attraction: Tony's affair with Gloria Trillo (in Season Three) begins to imitate the plot of *Fatal Attraction*.	1987 film by Adrian Lyne starring Michael Douglas and Glenn Close about a married man's affair with a psychotic woman.
Father Knows Best: Asked by the soon-to-be-killed stripper Tracee whether he thinks she should have Ralph Cifaretto's baby and set up housekeeping, Tony sarcastically predicts a *Father Knows Best* future for them (3006).	American television show (1954–63) starring Robert Young.
Favreau, Jon: See *Crying Game, The*.	(1966). American independent film producer (*Swingers* [1996]) and actor.
Fields, W. C.: W. C. Fields fan Tony (1) uses his stolen DVD player to watch *The Bank Dick* (1002), (2) quotes a Fields line when playing golf with the Wonderbread Wops (1010), and (3) watches *It's a Gift* (1934) (3009).	(1880–1946). American comic actor and writer, first in vaudeville, then in film.
Francis, Connie: Tony brings his mother some CDs as a gift, including one by Connie Francis (1001). Dr. Melfi chides her ex-husband, "You devote your energies to the protection of the dignity of Connie Francis" (1008).	(1938–). American singer and actress of Italian ancestry.
Frankenstein: See Golem.	Name usually used for monster created by Dr. Frankenstein in Mary Shelley's 1818 novel and in all the films based upon it.

Fresh Prince of Bel Air: Tony calls Jackie Aprile Jr. "The Fresh Prince of New Jersey" (3006).	1990–96 television show that made Will Smith a star.
From Here to Eternity: The title of *From Here to Eternity* is echoed in the title of "From Where to Eternity" (2009).	1953 film by Fred Zinnemann, starring Frank Sinatra, based on a war novel by James Jones.
Fugitive, The: See *Devil's Advocate, The*.	1993 film by Andrew Davis, starring Harrison Ford.
Fuhrman, Mark: Christopher, unhappy with slow service in a mostly African American crowd in a restaurant, wonders aloud "What am I, Mark Fuhrman?" (1010).	Los Angeles police detective, one of the prime investigators in the murder of Nicole Brown Simpson, revealed during the trial to be a racist.
Full Metal Jacket: The title of *Full Metal Jacket* is echoed in the title "Full Leather Jacket" (2008).	1987 anti-war film by Stanley Kubrick.
Garofalo, Janeane: See Bernard, Sandra.	(1964–). American comic and actress.
Giuliani, Rudolf: Giuliani is considered (unfavorably) as a candidate for cloning (1002) and mentioned in 1004 as well.	(1944–). Mayor of New York City (1993–2002), known for his crackdown on crime, his conservative cultural politics, and his stewardship in the wake of the terrorist attack on the World Trade Center.
Gilligan's Island: Tony, suffering from food poisoning, mumbles the theme song to *Gilligan's Island*.	Silly American television series (1964–67) about a bunch of castaways.
Gladiator: Throughout Season Three, Ralphie Cifaretto obsessively quotes lines from *Gladiator*.	Oscar-winning 2000 film by Ridley Scott, starring Russell Crowe, about a former Roman general who seeks revenge against the emperor who betrayed him and killed his family.
Glass Menagerie, The: See *Rebel Without a Cause*.	1944 play by Tennessee Williams.
Godfather, The: *The Godfather* is referred to in numerous episodes. Paulie, for example, has a *Godfather*-themed car horn (1011). See David Pattie's essay in this volume.	Francis Ford Coppola's 1972 gangster film, starring Marlon Brando and Al Pacino.
Godfather Part II, The: Referred to in numerous episodes. See David Pattie's essay in this volume.	Francis Ford Coppola's 1974 sequel to *The Godfather*, starring Robert De Niro and Al Pacino.

Godfather Part III, The: Carmela tells Father Phil that Tony is no fan of *Godfather Part III*: "Three was like, what happened?" (1001). See also Pacino, Al and "Just when I thought I was out, they keep pulling me back in."	Francis Ford Coppola's long-delayed and largely unsuccessful 1990 sequel to *The Godfather*, starring Al Pacino and Andy Garcia.
Golem: Tony is compared to the Golem and then to Frankenstein by a Hasidic Jew who has sought his help and now wants nothing to do with him (1003). Tony refers to the bearded Shlomo Teittleman as "ZZ Top."	In Hebrew legend, an artificial man/monster made out of clay by a rabbi in Prague to be his servant.
GoodFellas: Father Phil asks Carmela what Tony thinks of *GoodFellas* (1001). The guests at a dinner party at the Cusamano house discuss it (1010). When asked what kind of films he wants to write, Christopher replies "*GoodFellas* and shit" (2005).	1990 Martin Scorsese gangster film starring Robert De Niro and Ray Liotta.
Goya, Francisco: Tony compares Gloria Trillo's beauty to a painting by "Goyim" (3012).	(1746–1828). Great Spanish painter, known for his portraits of royalty.
Greene, Shecky: See Catskills.	(1926–). Jewish stand-up comic and actor.
GQ: Tony refers to Mikey Palmice as "Mr. GQ" (1004).	*GQ* is a magazine offering "fashion, sports, women, journalism, fitness and more for the modern man" (from the magazine's website).
Grumpy Old Men: Tony offers to loan his DVD player to Uncle Junior so he can watch *Grumpy Old Men* (1002).	1993 film starring Jack Lemmon and Walter Matthau that gave rise to a sequel.
Grunge: Tony refers to Grunge in a discussion of Janice's years in Seattle (2001).	"A soulful hard-rock variant that was instrumental to alternative music's early-'90s move overground" (from alt.culture.com).
Gunga Din: Livia complains that the woman in the room next door in the Green Grove, "a regular Gunga Din," is always running water (1006).	Gunga Din was a character, an Indian boy serving as a water carrier for the British army, in a poem by Rudyard Kipling.
Hasidism/Hasidic. Tony and his crew come to the aid of Shlomo Teittleman, a Hasidic Jew, in securing a divorce for his daughter (1003).	A Jewish religious movement founded in the eighteenth century in Poland.

Hawthorne, Nathaniel: On the wall at Bowdoin College on a college visit with Meadow, Tony reads "No man can wear one face to himself and another to the multitude without finally getting bewildered as to which may be true" (1005).	From Chapter 20 of *The Scarlet Letter* (1850) by American fiction writer Nathaniel Hawthorne (1804–64), a Bowdoin graduate.
Heidegger, Martin: See existentialists.	(1889–1976). German existential philosopher, author of such books as *Being and Time* (1927).
Hemingway, Ernest: See Cobain, Kurt.	(1899–1961). American novelist, who took his own life with a shotgun.
Hockney, David: Irina has a painting (of a swimming pool) that reminds her of David Hockey (1003).	(1937–). Realistic British-American painter known for his pop-art depictions of subjects like swimming pools and lawns.
Hogan's Heroes: When Tony's crew heists a collection of German World War II memorabilia, Big Pussy, in uniform, does an imitation of Colonel Klink from *Hogan's Heroes* (2011).	Television sit com (1965–71) set in a World War II POW camp.
How the Grinch Stole Christmas: See Carrey, Jim.	2000 film by Ron Howard starring Jim Carrey.
Hunter, Catfish. Tony tries to convince Meadow that hating Coach Hauser should not prevent success by citing the difficult relationship of Catfish Hunter and Billy Martin.	Major league baseball pitcher with the Oakland Athletics and New York Yankees.
Hurston, Zora Neale: At Livia's first visit to Green Grove, we learn that Zora Neale Hurston's novels will be discussed in an upcoming presentation (1001).	(1903–60). African American writer, one of the major figures of the Harlem Renaissance.
Husserl, Edmund: See existentialists.	(1859–1938). Austrian-born German phenomenological philosopher.
I Dream of Jeannie: *I Dream of Jeannie* is echoed in the title "I Dream of Jeannie Cusamano" (1013).	American television series (1965–70) about a genie in service to an astronaut.
It's a Wonderful Life: Tony watches (unhappily) *It's a Wonderful Life* on television (3010).	1946 Frank Capra work, starring Jimmie Stewart, that has become a kind of holiday cult film.

Jamaican bobsled team: See Boyz II Men.	Unlikely participants in the 1988 Winter Olympics in Calgary.
Jewel: Christopher "masterminds" robbery of the box office of a benefit concert by Jewel at Rutgers University for Amnesty International (3003).	(1974–), Popular contemporary American folk/pop singer and poet.
Jughead, Monsignor: Tony refers to Father Phil as Monsignor Jughead (1005).	Jughead is a character in Archie comic books.
"Just when I thought I was out, they keep pulling me back in": Silvio Dante quotes this line on several occasions, including 1002 and 2001.	Al Pacino line (as Michael Corleone) in *The Godfather Part III.*
Kerouac, Jack: Janice Soprano plans to make a self-help video to be called *Lady Kerouac, or Packing for the Highway to a Woman's Self-Esteem* (2002).	(1922–69). American novelist and poet, one of the founders of the Beat Movement. His most famous novel was *On the Road.*
Key Largo: While snorting coke in the opening montage of Season Two, Christopher watches *Key Largo* on TV (2001).	1948 John Huston gangster film starring Edward G. Robinson and Humphrey Bogart.
Kierkegaard, Sören: See existentialists. Big Pussy's son tells AJ: "You should start at the beginning. Take a look at Kierkegaard" (2007).	(1813–55). Danish philosopher and theologian, the father of existentialism.
Kingsolver, Barbara: Carmela tells Meadow in her dorm room that she is reading "the new Barbara Kingsolver" (3007).	(1955–). Contemporary American novelist.
Kruggerands: Meadow recalls finding Kruggerands during an Easter egg hunt at the Soprano house (1005).	Gold coins issued by the nation of South Africa.
Kundun: When Christopher spots Scorsese at a movie theatre, he calls after him "*Kundun,* I liked it" (1002).	1997 film, a box office disaster, by Martin Scorsese about the Dalai Llama.
Lacan, Jacques: Melfi's son, Jason La Penna, takes a class on Lacan at Bard College (2011).	(1901–81). The French Freud, Parisian structuralist psychoanalyst.
Lancelot: Playing poker, Pussy laments that "I've eaten more queens than Lancelot!" (1006).	Arthurian knight who had an affair with Guinevere.

Last Temptation of Christ, The: Carmela and Father Phil discuss Scorsese's *The Last Temptation of Christ* (1988) (1005). See also De Niro, Robert.	Controversial 1988 film adaptation by Martin Scorsese of a Nikos Kazantzakis novel.
Lecter, Hannibal: Tony seeks to distinguish himself from "Hannibal Lecture" (1001).	Fictional serial killer, psychoanalyst, and cannibal, played by Anthony Hopkins in *Silence of the Lambs* (1991 – for which he won an Oscar) and *Hannibal* (2001).
Leopold and Loeb: Tony cites Leopold and Loeb as evidence that not all bad kids come from mob families (1007).	Chicago teenagers who committed a nationally famous vicious murder in the 1920s.
Lewis, Jerry: Tony asks Mikey Palmice why there is no Jerry Lewis telethon for "Fuckface-itis" (1002).	(1926–). American film comedian, known for his annual telethons on behalf of Muscular Dystrophy.
Livia: The name of Tony's mother echoes (alludes to?) an evil, scheming character in *I, Claudius*.	*I, Claudius* was a 1976 BBC mini-series basic on the novel by Robert Graves.
Lojack: When asked to find AJ's biology teacher's Saturn, Tony replies that he recently changed him name from "Lojack to Soprano" (1002).	A corporation that markets stolen vehicle recovery technology.
Machiavelli, Nicolo: Tony recalls (after reading Sun-tzu) his encounter (via Carmela's Cliff Notes version) with *"Prince Matchabelli"* (3006).	(1469–1527). Italian writer, statesman, and political theorist, author of *The Prince*.
Martin, Billy: See Hunter, Catfish.	(1928–89). Baseball player, mostly with the Yankees, and later New York's controversial manager.
Martin, Dean: Dean Martin's picture is on the wall in the pork store during Christopher's whack of Emil Kolar (1001).	(1917–95). Italian-American singer and actor.
Marx, Harpo: The FBI describes Tony (who they have been trying to catch on tape incriminating himself) as "quiet as Harpo Marx" (3001).	(1888–1964). Curly-haired, completely speechless member of the Marx Brothers comedy team.
Masada: Masada is evoked by Ariel, a Hasidic Jew whose bris is about to be finished by Tony's gang in order to insure his cooperation (1003).	Battle in which 900 Jews held off 15 thousand Roman soldiers for almost two years until their mass suicide by way of surrender in 73 A.D.

Matrix, The: AJ gives his mother a used copy of *The Matrix* on DVD for a birthday present (3009).	Blockbuster 1999 science fiction film by the Wachowski brothers.
McLuhan, Marshall: A federal marshal named "McLuhan" puts in an appearance (2011).	(1911–80). Canadian-born media theorist, author of *The Medium is the Message, The Gutenberg Galaxy,* and other books.
Menendez Brothers: Worrying about the implications of Tony seeing a psychiatrist, Junior tells Mikey Palmice: "Do you remember those two fuckin' Escobedo Brothers, or whoever the fuck, in California? They whacked their parents? The shrink was in the fuckin' witness chair" (1007).	Lyle and Erik Menendez mudered their parents and were convicted of first-degree murder in 1996.
Meucci, Antonio: Tony corrects AJ's assumption that Alexander Graham Bell invented the telephone. "You see? Antonio Meucci invented the telephone and he got robbed! Everybody knows that" (1008).	(1808–89). Italian inventor sometimes credited with inventing the basic technology of the telephone.
Memoirs of a Geisha: Carmela is seen reading *Memoirs of a Geisha* on several occasions.	1999 novel about pre-World War II Japan by Arthur L. Golden.
Men in Black: Tony mentions *Men in Black* as the perfect film to accompany his new DVD and some Orville Redenbacher.	1997 Barry Sonnenfield film starring Tommy Lee Jones and Will Smith.
Mickey Blue Eyes: Bad first weekend numbers for *Mickey Blue Eyes* result in a d-girl's sudden disinterest in the genre (2007).	1999 second-rate mob comedy starring Hugh Grant.
Millers Crossing: Evoked in "Pine Barrens" (3011), directed by Coen Brothers' veteran Steve Buscemi.	1990 gangster film by the Coen Brothers; in its most famous scene, a man is led into the woods at Miller's Crossing in order to be whacked.
Mister Rogers' Neighborhood: Echoed in the title "Mr. Ruggerio's Neighborhood" (3001).	PBS children's program that ran from 1966 to 2001.
Moe Green Special: Big Pussy and Paulie debate the mise en scene of the "Moe Green special" in "One."	In *The Godfather* (1972), Moe Green is murdered while getting a massage by a bullet in the eye.
Mohel: See bris.	In Judaism, an individual who performs the right of circumcision at a bris.

Morrison, Jim: See "People are Strange."	(1943–71). Charismatic lead singer of *The Doors*. He died of a drug-overdose in Paris.
Mummy, The: Richie Aprile and Junior discuss a pirated version of *The Mummy* (2008).	1999 Stephen Sommers film.
Napoleon: See Churchill, Winston.	(1769–1821). French military leader and emperor.
Nietzsche, Friedrich: See existentialists.	(1844–1900). Controversial German classical philologist and philosopher.
O'Keefe, Georgia: As Meadow watches a rerun of *The Howling III* on TV while making out with a Puerto Rican boyfriend, a horrid metamorphosis takes place on screen reminding her, as she announces, of "Georgia O'Keefe!" (1013).	(1887–1984). American painter, best known for her desert images of flowers and skulls.
One True Thing: Father Phil brings *One True Thing* to the Soprano house, hoping to watch it on Tony's DVD player with Carmela (1013).	1998 film by Carl Franklin.
O'Neil, Shaquille: When Tony recalls that Silvio has a bust of Frank Sinatra done by Fabian Petrullo, Christopher admits that he thought it was a likeness of Shaquille O'Neal.	(1972–). Huge, powerful professional basketball player, currently with the Los Angeles Lakers.
"Our true enemy has yet to reveal himself": Silvio Dante quotes this line on several occasions, including in 2013.	Al Pacino line (as Michael Corleone) in *The Godfather Part III*.
Ozzie and Harriet: "Oh, look at this" – Tony comments sarcastically when he first discovers his sister's co-habitation with Richie Aprile – "Ozzie and fuckin' Harriet here. That's beautiful" (2005).	*The Adventures of Ozzie & Harriet* (1952–66) was a corny, homey 1950s sit-com about the real-life Nelson family.
Pacino, Al: Silvio imitates (repeatedly) Al Pacino in *The Godfather* and *The Godfather Part III*.	(1940–). American actor, who starred in several gangster films, most famously as Michael Corleone in all three *Godfather* films.
Parcells, Bill. When Tony tells Uncle Junior he wants him to be the new boss, he flatters his strength and tells him he's going to call Parcells to get him a try-out (1004).	(1941–). At the time, coach of the New York Jets pro football team. Twice coached the New York Giants to Super Bowl titles (1987, 1991).

Passages: Sent to convince Irina that she should forget about her sugar daddy, Silvio cites Gail Sheehy's *Passages* to buttress his argument (2012).	1984 book by Gail Sheehy.
"People are Strange": Dr. Melfi's sometime boyfriend Randall says (after being beaten up by Detective Makazian) that he can't help thinking about The Doors' song "People are Strange" (1004). "Dead at 27 in a Paris bathtub," he continues, thinking of Jim Morrison.	Song by the rock group The Doors.
Penn and Teller: Adriana and Christopher, playing Truth or Dare, have a fight after she confesses (at his instigation) to having oral sex with Penn (3007).	American comical magic duo.
Pesci, Joe: Dr. Cusamano talks about the scene in *Casino* in which Pesci puts a man's head in a vice (1010). Christopher (Michael Imperioli) shoots the bakery counter boy in the foot (1008), revenge no doubt for what Tommy DeVito (Joe Pesci) did to Spider (also played by Michael Imperioli).	(1943–). American actor, who rose to fame in the films of Martin Scorsese, including roles as gangsters in *GoodFellas* and *Casino*.
Poe, Edgar Allan: Meadow finds an essay on Poe on the internet for boyfriend Jackie Aprile Jr., for which he receives an "A" (3009). When Jackie brags to Meadow's father about his good grade, Tony asks if Poe is not "the guy who did all the Vincent Price shit?"	(1809–49). American fiction writer and poet, best known for his tales of horror.
Pokémon: Christopher masterminds the heist of a truckload of Pokémon cards (2012).	"Pokémon is the general name given to the many creatures found in the Pokémon universe. These Pokémon are the stars of video games for Game Boy Color and Nintendo 64, trading card games and cartoons" (from the official Pokémon web site).
Poppin' Fresh: Christopher refers to the bakery shop clerk he shoots in the foot as "Poppin' Fresh" (1008).	The "real" name of the Pillsbury Dough Boy seen in numerous commercials.
Potsdam Conference: Tony cites the Potsdam conference as an example of the kind of history he has always been interested in (1005).	1945 meeting of the US, Great Britain, and the USSR to finalize the peace after World War II.

Price, Vincent: See Poe, Edgar Allan.	(1911–93). American film actor, best known for his horror films, including Roger Corman's versions of Poe.
Prince Matchabelli: See Machiavelli, Nicolo.	A brand of women's fragrances.
Princess Di: Princess Di is considered as a candidate for cloning. Silvio wonders if the Royal family had her rubbed out (1002).	(1961–97). Commoner who, as wife of Prince Charles, became Princess of Wales. Killed in a still mysterious high-speed auto accident in Paris.
Promise Keepers: Complaining about men to her sometime boyfriend Randall, Melfi laments "We tell you to be more sensitive, you join Promise Keepers" (1004).	Controversial, zealous Christian men's organization.
Raffi: A Globe Motors salesman seeks to swap schedules with Gloria Trillo so he can take his son to the Raffi concert (3013).	Popular Egyptian-born Canadian troubadour, known for his entertaining concerts for children.
Rasputin: The seemingly unkillable Valery, who escapes from Paulie and Christopher in the Pine Barrens, is deemed a "fuckin' Rasputin" (3011). (His several near-escapes from death provoke concern in Christopher that they are facing *"Die Hard* shit.")	(1872–1916). Enigmatic Russian faith healer and advisor to the Czar, killed, with great difficulty, by Russian nobility anxious to stop his influence.
Rebel Without a Cause: In an "Acting for Writers" class, Christopher becomes James Dean in a scene from *Rebel Without a Cause* after rejecting a part from *The Glass Menagerie* (2005).	1955 film by Nicholas Ray that made James Dean a star and teen idol.
Religions of Man: Father Phil gives Carmela a copy of *Religions of Man* and recommends the chapter on Buddhism (1005).	Book (originally published in 1958) by historian of religion Huston Smith that offers chapters on all the major world religions.
Remains of the Day: See *Last Temptation of Christ, The.*	1993 Merchant-Ivory film about the repressed private life of an English butler.
Remembrance of Things Past: Melfi tells Tony about Marcel Proust, Madeleines, and *The Remembrance of Things Past* (Tony responds that it "sounds very gay") (3003).	Long, seven-book novel by the French writer Marcel Proust (1871–1922).
Rent: A popular Broadway musical evaluated post-show by theatre critic Christopher Moltisanti: *"Rent.* Fucking Broadway	Popular Broadway musical, a kind of Americanized *La Boheme*, written by Jonathan Larson.

musicals. I mean we're supposed to get all fuckin' weepy-eyed cause they turned off the heat in some guy's loft" (1010).	
Rico: When Christopher turns down an evening with the gang to be with Adriana, Paulie laments "Mother of mercy. Could this be the end of Rico?" (1010).	Rico "Little Caesar" Bandelli (Edward G. Robinson) is a character in Mervyn Leroy's 1930 gangster film. Paulie quotes Little Caesar's last words.
Robinson, Edward G.: Edward G. Robinson's picture is on the wall in the pork store during Christopher's whack of Emil Kolar (1001).	(1893–1973). Romanian-born American film actor, famous for his portrayal of gangsters in films like *Little Caesar* and *Key Largo*.
Rockford Files: Tony's soldier Big Pussy tires to locate AJ's biology teacher's missing Saturn, lamenting that he feels "like Rockford here" (1002).	American television series (1974–80), created by Stephen J. Cannell. David Chase was one of its writers.
Rorschach test: Tony insists that the paintings in Dr. Melfi's outer office are some kind of "Gorschach test" (1003). AJ takes a Rorschach test at Verbum Dei (1007).	Psychological test that assesses emotional and intellectual states by requiring the subject to interpret a series of inkblots.
Saccho and Venzetti. In a dinner table discussion of discrimination against Italians, the case of Saccho and Venzetti is cited as a prime example (1008).	Two young Italian anarchists found guilty of murder and executed. Their case became a 1920s cause célèbre.
Salk, Jonas: Paulie talks about seeing a back specialist, "the Jonas Salk of backs" (1011).	(1914–95). American physician who discovered a vaccine against polio.
Sergeant Bilko: Tony, seeing AJ in his military school uniform, exclaims "Sergeant Bilko" (3013).	Army con-man, played by Phil Silvers, on American television's *The Phil Silvers Show* (1955–59).
Sartre, Jean-Paul: See existentialists.	(1905–80). French philosopher, dramatist, and novelist, a key figure in the movement known as existentialism.
Scorsese, Martin: Martin Scorsese is spotted at a movie theatre (1002).	(1942–). Major American film director, often working in the gangster genre.
Scream: When Christopher and his buddie hold up the Jewel concert, they wear *Scream* masks (3003).	1996 Wes Craven horror film which produced two sequels.
Scud Missile: When one of Christopher's earners tells him he gave his money to Junior's crew after being threatened,	Medium range missile used by Iraq in the Persian Gulf War to attack Israel.

Christopher replies "I don't care if they shove a Scud Missile up your ass" (1004).	
Shaft: Tony calls Officer Wilmore "Shaft" when he encounters him at a garden centre (3005).	1971 Gordon Parks film about a Black private detective, which led to several sequels and a remake.
Shoemaker, Willie: Paulie describes a prostitute at Madam Debby's as "riding better than Willie Shoemaker" (1011).	(1931–). Jockey, a legend of horse-racing.
Simple Plan, A: "Pine Barrens" (3011), directed by Coen Brothers' veteran Steve Buscemi, evokes *A Simple Plan*.	1998 film by Sam Raimi, which includes several chase scenes set against winter landscapes.
Simpson, Don: Don Simpson is evoked (sort of): after Gigi Cestone dies on the toilet (3008), Silvio recalls others who came to a similar ignominious end, including "Don, the producer of *The Simpsons*."	(1943–96). Late Hollywood producer, known for his blockbuster films co-produced with Jerry Bruckheimer.
Simpson, O. J.: The televised trial of O.J. Simpson makes several appearances: in "To Save Us All From Satan's Power" it is frequently on screen in the flashbacks to 1995.	(1947–). Former pro-football star whose televised trial for the brutal murder of his wife Nicole became a national spectacle in 1995.
Simpsons, The. See Simpson, Don.	Long-running satiric Fox Television cartoon sit com (1989–).
South Park: AJ, asked to respond to a Rorschach ink blot, replying that he sees someone "Watching TV, maybe. Maybe he's watching *South Park*. Number one is supposed to be on tonight. The one where Cartman gets abducted by aliens, and they give him an anal probe and makes him fart fire" (1007).	Comedy Central animated TV series (1997–) about a group of raunchy kids living in South Park, Colorado.
Spartacus: Ralphie Cifaretto is not impressed by *Spartacus*, recommended to him by movie-buff Christopher (3006).	1960 Stanley Kubrick film, starring Kirk Douglas, about the leader of a slave rebellion against the Romans.
Spice Girls: Big Pussy calls the two gays who stole AJ's biology teacher's car the "spice girls" (1002).	Manufactured 1990s British girl singing group, whose time in the media spotlight faded quickly.
Starbuck's: Big Pussy's assistant reports on AJ's teacher's missing Saturn: "My guys said that one of those goofballs had a	Popular 1990s chain of upscale coffee shops originating in Seattle.

uniform on from Buttfuck's. Whatever, the coffee shop" (1002).	
Stone, Sharon: See *Basic Instinct*.	(1958–). Popular American actress in films like *Basic Instinct* and *Casino*.
"Stopping by Woods on a Snowy Evening": Meadow explains Robert Frost's "Stopping by Woods on a Snowy Evening" to AJ (3002). AJ: "I thought black meant death?" Meadow (as she walks out of the room): "White too."	Famous, often taught, poem by Robert Frost (1874–1963).
Sun-tzu: Everybody reads Sun-tzu's *The Art of War*: Janice Soprano, Tony's sister, quotes it; Melfi recommends it to Tony, who later cites it with admiration.	Chinese warrior who authored the first systematic treatise on military strategy over 2,000 years ago.
***Survivor*:** Furio explaining how he would revise, mob style, *Survivor* (3002).	Phenomenally successful American reality TV series (2000–).
Talmud: When Shlomo Tittleman tries to give Tony some money for helping him with Ariel, he cites historical precedent – "As the Talmud says . . ." Tony is displeased and will have none of it: "I don't give a shit what he says" (1003).	The compilation of Jewish oral law with rabbinical commentaries.
Tarantino, Quentin: D-girl Amy Safir used to work for Quentin Tarantino (2007).	(1963–). American writer and director, one of the most important film-makers of the 1990s.
***Taxi Driver*:** Father Phil does his imitation of the famous "You talkin' to me" scene from *Taxi Driver* (1005) as if it were part of *The Last Temptation of Christ*.	1976 Martin Scorsese film, starring Robert De Niro.
***Thirteen Days*:** When Paulie recalls the Cuban Missile Crisis, Generation Xer Christopher replies in astonishment: "That was real? I saw that movie. I thought it was bullshit!" (he is thinking of *Thirteen Days* (2000) (3011).	Roger Donaldson's film about the Cuban Missile Crisis.
Thompson, Emma: Father Phil speaks of his admiration (partly sexual) of Emma Thompson (1005).	(1959–). British actress who appears in *The Remains of the Day* and many other films.
***Thorn Birds, The*:** Denying that anything happened between them when Father Phil spent the night at the	1983 mini-series (based on a best-selling novel by Colleen McCullough) about a woman who has an affair with a priest.

Soprano house, Carmela exclaims "Do I look like the friggin' thorn bird over here?" (1005).	
Tis: A Memoir: The mob wives book club discusses Frank McCourt's *Tis: A Memoir* (2011).	Memoir (published in 2000), sequel to the best-selling *Angela's Ashes*.
Ulrich, Skeet: Hunter tells of seeing Skeet Ulrich on her last trip to Aspen (1001).	(1969–). Young American film actor.
Valdez, Juan: "Juan Valdez has been separated from his donkey," Paulie Walnuts announces in a phone call to Tony – code for a successful robbery of some Columbian drug dealers (1010).	Quasi-racist icon of coffee-industry advertising, usually depicted with his burro in the mountains of Columbia.
Vishnu: Tony angrily accuses Janice of "ridin' into town like some Vishnu-come-lately and try to play the concerned daughter" (2003).	Hindu creator deity.
West Side Story: Tony claims one of the attractions of Gloria Trillo is having sex with his own kind, to which Dr. Melfi immediately responds, "What is this, *West Side Story*?" (3011).	1961 Robert Wise film, based on *Romeo and Juliet* (music by Leonard Bernstein) about rival New York street gangs.
Whiter Shade of Pale: At the breakfast table in "46 Long" (1002), Tony sings "Whiter Shade of Pale" while dancing with Carmela.	Popular 1960s song by the British group Procul Harem.
Williams, Tennessee: Christopher's illiterate attempts at a screenplay make him, in the eyes of Adriana, "a regular Tennessee Williams" (1008).	(1911–83). Major American dramatist, best known for *The Glass Menagerie* and *A Streetcar Named Desire*.
Wizard of Oz: In Dr. Melfi's bizarre dream, Tony dies in a horrible head-on collision with a huge truck to the tune of a munchkin song ("Out of the Woods") from *Wizard of Oz* (2003).	Classic 1939 film by Victor Fleming, starring Judy Garland.
Zellweger, Renée: See *Last Temptation of Christ, The*.	(1969–). American actress, who appeared in *One True Thing*.
ZZ Top: See Golem.	Hard-rocking, long-bearded rock 'n' roll duo.

APPENDIX D

THE SOPRANOS: A FAMILY HISTORY[1]

The text of *The Sopranos* does not stop at the television screen or with the video tapes, DVDs,[2] and comprehensive website HBO has made available. Last century John Fiske reminded us (in *Television Culture*) that TV series are "activated texts," generating much more than the individual episodes that constitute a series' actual on-air presence. Both secondary (criticism, publicity) and tertiary (discussion and commentary occurring at the fan level) texts, including unofficial websites like Sopranoland.com, follow in the wake of most TV shows, and the meaning and significance both kinds of texts generate are plowed back into the primary texts themselves, becoming part of how viewers "read" them. That *Entertainment Weekly* guide to *Seinfeld* deepened our appreciation of a show about nothing. That slash fanfiction we discovered on the internet, the one that imagines Kirk and Spock as lovers, lead us to see *Star Trek* in a radical new light. That book of "fantasy blueprints of classic TV homes" (Mark Bennett's *Television Sets*) enhanced our grasp of the textual geography of The Clampett mansion or Gilligan's island.

Contemporary television has likewise spun-off a wide variety of "commodity intertexts" (James Collins' coinage), secondary texts, both official and unofficial (this book is one), fiction and non-fiction, to satisfy the often cultic needs of television fans to know more – much more – and imagine more about their favorite programs. A decade ago, *Twin Peaks* produced not only *The Secret Diary of Laura Palmer* but *The Autobiography of F.B.I. Special Agent Dale Cooper: My Life, My Tapes,* and *Welcome to Twin Peaks: Access Guide to the Town* – all official *Twin Peaks* books. Over the last decade *The X-Files* industry has generated annual official guides to Chris Carter's series, now in its ninth season. *Buffy the Vampire Slayer* has inspired two *Watcher's Guides, The Monster Book,* and a score of popular paperbacks for those viewers who can't get enough of Sunnydale and its heroes and villains. *The Sopranos* has likewise produced an official companion, the brilliantly conceived and beautifully designed (by Dan Newman) *The Sopranos: A Family History.* Originally published in hardcover in 2000, between the second and third seasons, the book was reissued as a revised, updated paperback in the fall of 2001, between seasons three and four.

Purporting to be the by-product of author Allen Rucker's assignment to organize a massive archive on the Soprano family assembled by an expert on organized crime named Jeffrey Wernick, this coffee-table book presents itself as "little more than journalistic housecleaning" compared to "Wernick's Herculean efforts." At the outset we find a list of contributors: a group that includes all the people Wernick and Rucker supposedly spoke to, from ex-gangsters now in the witness protection program, to Tony Soprano's favorite teacher, to Livia Sopranos' briefly employed geriatric caregiver. Jeffrey Wernick, of course, is actually a character on *The Sopranos* (as are many of the other contributors), appearing on television in an episode like "The Legend of Tennessee Moltisanti" (1008), sharing his knowledge of the New Jersey mob with local media. One day, we are told, Wernick will tell all, but "the Sopranos story is a long way from over" (aka the series is still ongoing), and in the meantime we will have to make due with his assistant's pastiche assemblage of Sopraniana. False modesty is part of Rucker's fiction of course. The book offers all the givens of a TV companion volume: an interview with series creator David Chase (who, the official Sopranos website tells us, "was instrumental in developing the look and content of the book"), profiles of each of the major players, and an authoritative episode summary.[3] "As the Bible is to Western thought," Chase proclaims on the HBO website, "so is *The Sopranos: A Family History* to the field of companion books"!

In ten chapters – "The Sopranos," "A Soprano Family History," "Tony's Children," "The Soprano Crime Family," "Life with Livia," "Tony and Carmela," "Tony on the Couch," "The Business," "Growing Up Soprano," and "The Future" – Rucker presents us with deep background on the series in a variety of forms. We are privy to FBI e-mails detailing what is known about both of Tony Soprano's families; insights into New Jersey's immigrant population from a Newark Public Library expert; family photos (some from the old world); the crudely-conceived family trees of AJ; FBI surveillance transcripts; probation reports; a 1975 letter on Tony Soprano's behalf by an English teacher seeking to prevent him from being expelled; a college letter from Tony to Carmela; Johnny Boy Soprano's arrest record; a page from Christopher Moltisanti's awful unfinished screenplay, "You Bark, I Bite"; confidential reports on Livia Soprano (including complaints filed by fellow residents) from the Green Grove Retirement Home; a letter from Carmela to her interior decorator declining an offer to have her home featured in "New Jersey Today"; a list of materials found in Soprano trash; Carmela's ten favorite movies (from a contest at her video store); an "abridged dictionary of Northeastern regional mob patois"; a diagram of Soprano cashflow; a "body count" roster of those who have (allegedly) died at the hands of the Sopranos; transcripts of Meadow Soprano's visits to an online chatroom; Meadow's Discover Card bill; Joan O'Connell's equivocal letter of recommendation for Meadow to Georgetown (written as a result of Carmela's mob-mom encouragement) – and this is only a partial list.

The result of this polyphony of voices is a simulated oral history in which the series' already rich, multi-dimensional characters and its meticulously genuine milieu are realized even further. There is so much even a faithful watcher of the series would never have known: that Tony hates Bruce Springsteen (because the music of his fellow Jerseyite is too depressing), that Livia's father was a Eugene Debs-style socialist, that Tony subscribes to *Waste News*, that Livia had an annoying neighborhood dog whacked, that the yearly income of Paulie Walnuts is between $60,000 and $100,000 a year; that at Seton Hall Tony hired another student to write his English paper for him ("Symbolism in *Cat on a Hot Tin Roof*" – it received a B+); that Janice Soprano's estranged son Harpo may have changed his named to Hal after being beaten up on the playground . . .

In a classic essay on cult movies and "intertextual collage," Umberto Eco observes that one given of The Cult is its ability to "provide a completely furnished world so that its fans can quote characters and episodes as if they were aspects of the fan's private sectarian world, a world about which one can make up quizzes and play trivia games so that the adepts of the secret recognize through each other a shared experience" (*Travels in Hyperreality* 198). *The Sopranos: A Family History*, inspired by commercial motives but in its own way if not a "holy" text at least an essential Baedeker, will appeal most to cult followers of *The Sopranos* – to those always ready, despite the dangers, to drop in, at the next possible opportunity, to Northern New Jersey, a great place to visit, via the imagination, if not to live.

NOTES

1   Parts of this introduction originally appeared in the online journal *PopPolitics.com* (http://www.poppolitics.com/articles/2001-03-03-heavy.shtml) and appear here with permission.

2   In "The Telltale Moozadell" (3009) *Car Talk* is playing on the radio in the Soprano kitchen during a breakfast scene.

3   New *Sopranos* (aka Christmas) were late in coming because David Chase had asked HBO for more time to work on the scripts for the third season.

4   a) He tells us that Noah "beds" Meadow "except that they don't bother to use a bed" (they are on a bed); b) he speaks of the "semi-explicit emplacement of a condom" (in fact all we see is the condom in its wrapper, and Noah removes it off-camera); and c) he says that Tony "is angered by his lieutenant and hits him hard enough to cause his wrist to swell" (it is Ralphie's wrist, not Tony's, which begins to swell after beating Tracee to death). Is there a connection between misreading a television show (or a movie, or a book), accusing the audience of psychological depravity, and simply misremembering it?

5   Elaine Showalter has observed that Paglia's condemnation of *The Sopranos* is the product of "her current persona as a Giuliani-style Catholic populist."

6   See Appendix C, which provides a catalogue of *Sopranos* intertextual moments and allusions.

7   Tony is not always inarticulate. When he seeks to explain to Dr. Melfi that he is a soldier and not, therefore, evil, the History Channel fan readily finds exampes of the truly evil: Hitler and Pol Pot ("From Where to Eternity"/2009).

8   For Bakhtin, a "monological" text imposes a single, predetermined meaning on its audience; a "dialogical" text, on the other hand, articulates a polyphony of voices and presumes the reader's engagement in a dialogue.

9   Dostoevsky puts in an appearance in *The Sopranos*. In "Second Opinion" (3007), Dr. Krakower suggests to Carmela that Tony should read *Crime and Punishment* in prison while he repents his sins.

10   In a supremely self-conscious moment in "The Legend of Tennessee Moltisanti" (1008), for example, Dr. Melfi's father comments, in a discussion of Italian-defamation issues, gangster films, and westerns, that "You never saw the Scotch-Irish pissing and moaning about always being portrayed as rustlers and gunslingers."

ONE

1   This essay originally appeared in *The Nation*, 2 April 2001. It was written at the very beginning of Season Three of *The Sopranos*.

TWO

1   An earlier version of this essay originally appeared in *Television Quarterly* (Winter 2001): 34–8 and is reprinted with the permission of the author and the National Academy of Television Arts and Sciences.

THREE

1   Wolf, the creator of *Law & Order* (and its successors), tells James Longworth that, "My favorite hour show of all time is *The Rockford Files*. And David wrote probably 30 per cent of those episodes. He's got a unique voice, and he's one of the only people who can tell really good, self-contained stories that have good drama in them, but can also be hysterically funny. . . . He's an enormously talented writer" (18–19). Wolf, by the way, is evoked in the show when the entertainment lawyer father of Meadow's boyfriend Noah Tannenbaum name drops that he is having lunch with Wolf. Meadow does not know who he is ("University"/3006).

2   Fellini, Chase observes, inspired him to incorporate Italian themes into his stories (Rucker interview).

3   Chase virtually ignored TV in the 1960s and 1970s except for an addiction he calls "absurd" to *Medical Center* (1969–76) and an infatuation with *I Spy* (1965–68), a series whose writing (especially in its last two seasons) he greatly admired (Rucker interview).

4   Though we will not challenge here Chase's contention of primacy in "hour drama," we will point out, for the record, that he certainly should not aver that he was the first counterculture person in network television period. Ernie Kovacs, The Smothers Brothers, and Rowan and Martin would no doubt contest the broader claim.

5   For comprehensive versions, see the Rucker interview in *The Sopranos: A Family History* and the conversation with Bogdanovich on *The Sopranos* DVD.

6   See, for example, Chase's discussion of luck in the Rucker interview.

7   It is not hard to imagine Chase finding a passage like the following from Miller's book especially moving: "Children who are intelligent, alert, attentive, sensitive, and completely attuned to their mother's well being are entirely at her disposal. Transparent, clear, and reliable, they are easy to manipulate as long as their true self (their emotional world) remains in the cellar of the glass house in which they have to live – sometimes until puberty or until they come to therapy, and very often until they have become parents themselves" (22). For did not Chase tell Bogdanovich that he could not have made *The Sopranos* before becoming himself a father?

8   *The Sopranos* was not, of course, the only turn-of-the-century television series/movie to incorporate this startling premise. *Grosse Pointe Blank* (George Armitage 1997), *Analyze This!* (Harold Ramis 1999), and *Gun Shy* (Eric Blakeney 2000) all had Mafiosi/hit men in therapy, as did the unjustly ignored film *Panic* (2000), written and directed by Chase's friend and co-collaborator (on *I'll Fly Away* [1991–93]) Henry Bromell. In an interview with Michael Sragow, Bromell recalls that Chase "wrote *The Sopranos* pilot a little earlier than I wrote *Panic*, but we didn't know that. I was away in Baltimore and wrote mine and unbeknown to me he wrote his, and when I got back we were just trading stuff to show each other what we'd been writing. I read *The Sopranos* and he read *Panic*. And he went, 'How can this be?' Then, of course, there were others . . . all happening independently. So David and I just figured there must be a lot of writers in therapy!"

9   As Chase tells Bogdanovich, the ducks, like other "symbols" in the series, did not initially have fixed, intended significance. Only later were the writers forced, because of Tony's sessions with a psychoanalyst, to interpret retroactively the meaning of what they themselves had   created.

10   In a delightful self-referential moment (mise en scene by Fellini) at a Neapolitan outdoor café in "Commendatori" (2004), an episode which Chase himself wrote, Paulie Walnuts toasts a group of "natives" sitting at an adjoining table, declaiming "Commendatori" (commander). (When they ignore the uncouth American, he mutters "Cocksuckers" under his breath.) One of the toastees is a cigarette-smoking David Chase, *The Sopranos'* commander-in-chief, in a Hitchcockian cameo appearance.

11   "The Sopranos" (1001), "46 Long" (1002), "I Dream of Jeannie Cusamano" (1013), "Commendatori" (2004), "Funhouse" – with Todd A. Kessler (2013), "Mr. Ruggerio's Neighborhood" (3001), "Proshai, Livushka" (3002), and "The Army of One" – with Lawrence Konner (3013).

12   The first two: "The Sopranos" (the pilot) and "46 Long".

13   Frank Renzulli and the team of Robin Green/Mitchell Burgess have both written or co-written seven episodes. Among the directors, Allen Coulter with nine and Tim Van Patten with seven have been the most prominent.

14   New Zealand-born director Lee Tamahori (*Once Were Warriors* [1994], *Mulholland Falls* [1996], *The Edge* [1997], *Along Came a Spider* [2001]), and the next Bond film), who directed "Toodle-Fucking-oo" (2003) and Coen Brothers' regular and independent film actor and director Steve Buscemi (*Trees Lounge* [1996]), who helmed "Pine Barrens" (3011), are two examples.

15   In both the interviews with Peter Bogdanovich and Jim Lehrer ("Hit Man"), Chase discusses at some length his love affair with editing.

16   For a good discussion of *The Sopranos* as a "megamovie" see Vincent Canby's essay in *The New York Times* on *The Sopranos*. Canby suggests that *The Sopranos* should be compared to such works as Rainer Maria Fassbinder's *Berlin Alexanderplatz* (1980), which ran 930 minutes, and Dennis Potter & Jon Amiel's *The Singing Detective* (1986), 415 minutes. To date (at the end of Season Three) *The Sopranos'* total running time suprasses 2,000 minutes. For more on *The Sopranos* compared to *The Singing Detective*, see Creeber's essay in this volume.

17   Not surprisingly, given its penchant for intertextual relations, *Survivor* puts in an appearance on *The Sopranos*. In "Proshai, Livushka" (3002), at the dreadful wake for Livia Soprano, we find Furio explaining to Paulie and others his drug-inspired new money-making scheme: "This *Survivor* show. Somebody should find the winner, stick a pistol in his face, and say, 'You not going to survive unless you give me 25% of that fuckin' million dollars.'"

18   Chase told the British journalist Quentin Curtis: "All I know is that something has been lost. . . . Movies don't have the ability to mystify any more, to confound you, to sweep you up. So often there's a distance between you and them, and it's as if they're saying, 'love us, love me, love me,' always advertising their cuteness, or wonderfulness, or scariness. . . . The movies themselves used to aspire to something. They give the audience something to aspire to or an insight into an unfamiliar world."

19   Chase is not the only creative force in television caught on the horns of the television or the movies dilemma. Consider the similar case of the much younger Joss Whedon, creator of *Buffy the Vampire Slayer* and *Angel*, whose success in television has also made the jump to Hollywood possible. See my "The Genius of Joss Whedon," the afterword to *Fighting the Forces: What's at Stake in Buffy the Vampire Slayer*.

Five

1   All quoted material from: Canadian Broadcast Standards Council National Conventional Television Panel; CTV re *The Sopranos*; CBSC Decision 00/01-0139; Decided 8 March 2001; R. Cohen (Chair), M. Hogarth, E. Holmes, J. Levy, M. Lewis, H. Pawley. Available at: www.cbsc.ca/english/decision/010524.htm.

Six

1   Although HBO does still feature boxing, the sport with which it is most closely associated, most important championship matches are now pay-per-view events. In fact, HBO's subsidiary TVKO is one of the major players in the pay-per-view boxing world. Currently, live boxing (usually non-title matches between lesser known contenders) and replays of recent championship bouts appear on HBO's three boxing series, *HBO World Championship Boxing*, *Boxing After Dark*, and *KO Nation*. HBO's other major sporting event was Wimbledon. From 1975–1999, HBO broadcast the early rounds of the tennis tournament in partnership with NBC; in 2000, these rights went to TNT. Even so, HBO still has a sports presence. It produces a *60 Minutes*-style sports newsmagazine, *Real Sports With Bryant Gumbel*, an interview show hosted by Bob Costas, and a weekly NFL program during the football season. Sports-related themes also shows up in HBO's documentaries and original films (such as the 2001 film *61**).

2   For example, Tom Hanks and Steven Spielberg were signed as executive producers for the 2001 WWII mini-series *Band of Brothers*, a project that would have had trouble fitting in elsewhere. Although its own studio has carved out several successful niches (particularly in sports and African American films), HBO does not actually produce all of its "original" movies: HBO occasionally provides completion funds for promising independent film – and has also purchased distribution rights for many independent films that failed to get a theatrical release and would have otherwise headed straight to video.

3   Sheila Nevins, Vice President for Original Programming at HBO, has been in charge of the documentary division since 1979, when HBO began buying documentaries as it expanded from 8 to 12 hours of daily programming. Each year Nevins and her staff develop or purchase 12–15 documentaries, most of which end up on the *America Undercover* series (Lieberman). HBO's documentaries are divided between what might be termed prestige programming and less wholesome fare. The prestige projects have included acclaimed work such as *King Gimp*, winner of the 2001 Academy Award for Best Documentary Short Subject, and are either commissioned by HBO or purchased from independent filmmakers at festivals. The less prestigious projects (such as the ongoing *Real Sex*, a soft-core newsmagazine show, and *Taxicab Confessions*, in which cameras are concealed in the back of cabs while skilled actor/drivers engage passengers in revealing conversations) tend to focus on salacious content. These programs have historically done well in the ratings for HBO, despite the fact that the network does little to promote them.

4   During the 1980s and 1990s, the network was a major producer of stand-up comedy specials, but as the nation's interest in stand-up comedy waned, the number of these programs decreased. Specials and episodes of the *HBO Comedy Hour* featuring individual comedians were an important part of career-building for many popular television and film comedians (such as Ray Romano and Chris Rock), and the long-running *Def Comedy Jam* show gave exposure to many up and coming African American comedians. The network also featured sketch-based comedy programs such as the Canadian *Kids in the Hall* and the more recent *Mr. Show with Bob and David*. Stand-up comedy, though popular, did not distinguish HBO. At the height of the popularity of stand-up comedy, comedians could be seen on many cable and broadcast outlets. HBO did little other than offer comedians a chance to be more off-color than they could be on regular cable. It appears that HBO's latest programming strategy in the area of stand-up comedy is to develop star vehicles for performers like Chris Rock and Dennis Miller. These star vehicles seem more likely to become franchises that translate into brand equity than the traditional comedy showcase.

5   *The Hitchhiker* (1983–1987) was the network's first drama, but *Tales from the Crypt* (1989–1996) was more successful. Due to the participation of big names as executive producers (Joel Silver and Brian Giler) and A-List directors (Robert Zemeckis, Walter Hill, and Richard Donner) and a lingering fondness among many in Hollywood for the source material of 1950s horror comics, the program was able to attract top talent for its 93-episode run (Diehl 161–6). Although both programs exploited the freedom of pay cable to expand their level of grotesquery beyond standard

television fare, there was little distinctive about these shows – with minor editing, both became successful in off-network syndication on broadcast and basic cable schedules.

6   HBO is technically referred to as a "satellite cable network." This means that rather than have affiliates (like in the broadcast model), HBO acts as a wholesaler distributing its package of programming to a national "network" of cable operators. These cable operators then function as "retailers" who charge subscribers for the premium service. The monthly subscription fee for HBO is typically split 50/50 or 60/40 with the cable operator. Although HBO is widely known as a network, it does not have "affiliates" in the broadcast sense. It may indeed be more accurate to think of HBO not as a network, but as a packager of content.

7   In 1998, for example, the network had high hopes for *The High Life*, a comedy from David Letterman's Worldwide Pants production company. Despite a substantial marketing push and a prime slot after *The Larry Sanders Show*, *The High Life* failed miserably and quickly disappeared.

8   An official tie-in book, *The Sopranos: A Family History*, written by Allen Rucker, also facilitated *Sopranos* marketing even when the series was not on the air. For more on Rucker's book see Appendix D.

9   *Six Feet Under* was developed by Alan Ball, screenwriter of *American Beauty* (1999). In many ways, *Six Feet Under* exemplifies HBO's original programming strategy: hire quality talent to develop programs and give them the creative freedom and resources to make those programs distinctive enough to fuel the buzz of water cooler conversations and further enhance HBO's reputation as a purveyor of television worth paying for.

SEVEN

1   Again, Michael's veneration of his mother in *The Godfather Part II* provides a telling foil – the devoted son even puts off killing his brother while his mother is alive. What better proof of a son's love than that?

2   We might compare the way Annette Giancana knows and doesn't know about her luxurious upbringing as the daughter of Sam Giancana. In an interview on A & E's *Biography* (*Real Goodfellas: The Mobster Who Dreamed*) Annette Giancana spoke of "wonderful suits by Christian Dior, wonderful fur coats, some nice jewelry. Dancing, drinking, having a great time. It was almost like New Year's Eve everyday." A woman's naïveté, especially in the service of an economy of consumption, is a strategic pose for a "nice girl" to adopt. In response to an interviewer's question about whether the source of the money "soured" her experience, Annette Giancana asks ingenuously: "Why should I have thought where the money came from?"

EIGHT

1   While the number of overweight and obese bodies on *The Sopranos* far exceeds any other television series currently on the air, it must be noted that the corpulent body has received a great deal of attention on television over this past decade. Television series like *Roseanne*, *The Drew Carey Show*, *King of Queens*, *The Practice*, *The Steve Harvey Show*, *The Simpsons*, and *King of the Hill* have all featured overweight characters.

2   While this particular study examines fatness as it relates to the male body on *The Sopranos*, there is also a great deal of research that has been conducted into the role that weight management plays in conceptualizing the female body. Two of the texts used in this essay are primarily focused upon fatness as it pertains to women. These are Susan Bordo's *Unbearable Weight: Feminism, Western Culture, and the Body* and Peter N. Stearns' *Fat History: Bodies and Beauty in the Modern West*. Some other key texts include Stella Bruzzi's *Undressing Cinema: Clothing and Identity in the Movies*, Marcia Millman's *Such A Pretty Face: Being Fat in America*, Hillel Schwartz's *Never Satisfied: A Cultural History of Diets, Fantasies and Fat*, Yvonne Tasker's *Working Girls: Gender and Sexuality in Popular Cinema* and Susan McLeland's "Re-Shaping the Grotesque Body: *Roseanne*, Breast Reduction, and

Rhinoplasty." Many of these texts accurately describe the gendered power imbalance when it comes to the body that Western culture has imposed on women. While not the focus of this essay, a clear gendering of the body regularly occurs on *The Sopranos*, in which most of the female characters are forced to adhere to slender and fit cultural ideals, while male corpulence is celebrated. The only significantly female character on the show whose body type fails to live up to "idealized" standards is Janice Soprano, Tony's sister, and she is often presented as the most deviant and indulgent of the women characters on the show. Though critiques of male fatness have not been as explicit as those focusing on the female body, this essay hopes to demonstrate that the male body can also be understood in relation to culturally constructed codes concerning corpulence.

3   The case of Fatty Arbuckle reveals how quickly opinions about the innocence of fat people can change in Western culture. While his films often portrayed him as childlike and mischievous, when he was accused in real life of rape and murder, his corpulence was transformed into a signifier of his greed and over-indulgence.

4   "Childhood problems, difficulties at work, sexual hang-ups – all could combine to produce the immature response of gluttony, with its visible penalty in obesity" (Stearns 118).

5   According to Stearns, "the increasingly intense disapproval of fat, laced with moral and emotional overtones, divided middle-class humankind between the saved and the lost, the thin and the obese, with a host of anxious strugglers uncomfortably in between" (65).

6   "More than physical manhood, sports were celebrated for instilling moral virtue as well," Kimmel claims, "Sports developed 'courage, steadiness of nerve,' 'resourcefulness, self-knowledge, self reliance,' 'the ability to work with others' and 'readiness to subordinate selfish impulses, personal desires, and individual credit to a common end'" (33).

7   It is worth noting that on more than one occasion Satriale's has been used to carve up human flesh as if it were meat. In the pilot episode, Christopher and Pussy cut up Emil Kolar's body after Christopher has whacked him in the actual butcher shop. In season two, Christopher and Furio chop up Richie Aprile's body in a similar fashion after Janice has shot him while he was eating his dinner (and, of course, after he has struck her). The HBO online store even sells a Satriale's coffee mug bearing the inscription: "We grind our own."

NINE

1   A number of "quality" dramas from the American stable appear on British television, and *The Sopranos* falls into the camp of *ER, Homicide: Life on the Street, NYPD Blue*, and *The West Wing*.

2   Cultural capital, in Pierre Bourdieu's use of the term, refers to "the possession of knowledge, accomplishments, formal and informal qualifications by which an individual may gain entry and secure a position in particular social circles, professions and organizations" (Brooker 46). Individuals from different socio-economic groups have access to different kinds of cultural capital.

3   The British press have carried a few articles listing mob turns of phrase in a dictionary format.

TEN

1   For a discussion of Rucker's book, see Appendix D.

2   In this and other discussions of David Chase's intentions and the development of the series, I am guided primarily by the interviews with him in Allen Rucker's book and on the DVDs of the first season.

ELEVEN

1   In an interview that accompanied the film's video release, Tarantino (1992) argued that it was the sort of movie that would do well in video shops. "Having worked in a video store I know what

happens in there," he explained to his anonymous interviewer. "This is the sort of movie that, in particular, the young kids who work in the video store are going to like . . . so I think it's going to get a big in-store push . . ."

2   The TV series was later released on video in the UK (*Lock, Stock . . . the Television Series*: Ska/ Ginger Productions: 2000).

3   As an old-school Mafia don, Don Vito is disgusted by the modern spread of narcotics and refuses an invitation to get his "business" involved in dealing drugs. This refusal eventually leads to a Mafia war that results in his attempted assassination.

4   Curiously we never discover Tony's view of *GoodFellas* (1990). When Father Phil asks Carmela where her husband stands on the film, a suspected burglar immediately interrupts them. (Father Phil's shocked reaction to the gun that Carmela instantly acquires also offers a clear juxtaposition between his reaction to "screen" and "real" violence). Similarly, when Meadow tells Tony that her friends think that the Mafia is "cool," he seems shocked and surprised when she suggests the reason is *Casino*, apparently oblivious to *The Godfather*. Tony himself makes no comment ("College" /1005).

5   In the second episode of the third season of *The Sopranos* we see Tony watch *Public Enemy* (1931) on a number of occasions, clearly enthralled by this more "innocent" view of gangster life, particularly Tom Powers' (James Cagney) relationship with his mother.

6   This notion of intimacy appears in most early discussions of the medium. See, for instance, Ellis 132.

7   The movie Christopher visits is called *Female Suspects* and stars Janeane Garofalo and Sandra Bernhard, who both guest star as themselves in the episode.

8   Likewise, Sinatra's infamous association with the Mafia (the character of Johnny Fontane in *The Godfather* was rumored to be based on the singer and actor) further reminds the viewer of an earlier generic tradition – a world before the "amoral" onslaught on the new "brutalized" gangster movie, perhaps epitomized by the more contemporary rhythms of rock, pop and funk.

9   For example, critics have chastised *The Godfather* for implicitly mythologizing and glamorizing its portrayal of the Mob. In "Myth & Meaning: Francis Ford Coppola and Popular Response to the *Godfather* Trilogy," David Ray Papke has explained how the director was first amazed when people seemed to be *attracted* to many of the elements of the original movie. In particular, he was reported to be shocked that viewers thought he had intentionally "romanticized" Michael Corleone (Al Pacino). This was in stark contrast with his own belief that Michael was represented "as a monster" by the end of the movie (9). Ironically, the Mafia itself also seemed to be among some of the film's most enthusiastic supporters. As Papke points out, "According to anonymous reports, the old-fashioned and largely abandoned custom of kissing the hands of powerful Mafia leaders revived because of its portrayal in the film" (6). Indeed, according to the British journalist Ben Macintyre, recent transcripts of wire-tapped conversations from within the Mob show that *The Sopranos* itself is now similarly beginning to effect the behavior and discourse of the real Mafia, with Mobsters discussing the drama and repeating the characters' own hang-ups and concerns. According to Macintyre, "What these and other Mafia tapes show is not just that art mirrors life, but that the life of the mobster is in some ways controlled by art" (24).

10   Compare their portrayal, for example, with the psychiatry sessions in a movie like *Analyze This!* (1999), a film (often compared with *The Sopranos* because of its narrative similarities) where there is still a great deal of action and slapstick even in the meetings between patient and psychiatrist.

11   Although the series' own credit sequence employs both fast editing techniques and rock music (A3's "Woke Up This Morning"), it is frequently brought to a sudden halt when the drama itself begins, an inversion of Tarantino's familiar technique, where banal conversation usually precedes a dynamic opening credit sequence.

12   This is not the first time the series has been compared with *The Singing Detective*. "In its leisurely use of the form," Caryn James has argued, "it is strangely like *Brideshead Revisited, The Singing Detective* and *I Claudius*" (26). At the 2001 *Console-ing Passions: Television, Video, Feminism and New Media* conference, connections were also drawn by Roger Sorkin's "Murderous Matriarch: Liva Soprano."

13   Like Potter's Marlow, Tony's mother is clearly a powerful and domineering woman. Indeed, the similarities between the two women are significant, not least their strangely Oedipal relationship with their young sons (Livia even threatens to poke out Tony's eyes with a fork during one of the flashbacks to his childhood). Earlier, in episode four of the first season Tony dreams he is in Dr. Melfi's office, a woman he is sexually attracted to. After watching Silvio and a lap dancer have sex in the waiting room, he turns back to Melfi. However, as she turns around it is revealed to be his mother in the chair. (To make the connection with British television drama even more pronounced, Livia is also the name of the ruthless, scheming wife in *I, Claudius* [BBC 1976] – although it was also significantly the name of Chase's own mother). For a consideration of the role of the mother in *The Singing Detective*, see Creeber 166–78.

14   'Soprano' usually refers either to the highest adult female voice or the voice of a young boy before puberty. It is perhaps worth noting that both these television dramas refer to the act of singing in their titles. It is as if these quintessentially masculine genres (*film-noir* in the case of *The Singing Detective*) were being forced to take on board the more "feminine" characteristics traditionally associated with genres such as the soap opera or the confessional talk show. While "singing" is sometimes used as street-slang for the act of "grassing" to the police (or even, appropriately enough, *confession*), the surname Soprano refers to the female or adolescent section of a choir (an indication perhaps of the drama's own examination of a genre more commonly equated with the tenor or the mature male voice generally).

TWELVE

1   Other meanings that might be drawn from these texts are secondary ones. It is interesting to know that *The Tomb of Ligeia* is both a reference and a coded thank-you to Scorsese's former employer, and that Scorsese hero-worshipped John Ford, including *The Searchers* clip as an homage to the great American auteur; but it is not necessary to our understanding and enjoyment of the film.

2   For example, a sequence that parodies (almost shot for shot) the opening sequence of *2001* (1968) ends with an ape which looks suspiciously like Homer Simpson taking a nap against a jet-black monolith. The sequence ends on a parody of a famous image from the sequence (except that the symbolic conjunction of moon, sun, and monolith is joined by the rather less impressive image of a snoring, bald-headed ape).

3   Peter Biskind, in *Easy Riders, Raging Bulls*, reports that Mafia boss Joe Colombo threatened Robert Evans, the film's producer, with the comment (itself worthy of *The Godfather*'s script): "when we go after a fish, we cut off the head" (157).

4   *The Sopranos*' creator David Chase found that some mobsters had become TV critics: "[During] the first series in America, one of the few pieces of feedback Chase got from real-life mobsters went along the lines of 'It's a great show, but I'll tell you something, the boss don't wear shorts'" (Curtis).

5   "Taking to the mattresses," for those who don't speak Mafiosi, means living as if under seige (sleeping on mattresses brought in for the occasion) during a war with a rival clan or family.

THIRTEEN

1   "In Carmela, Tony has a loyal but ambivalent wife, repulsed by 'the business' yet all too happy to reap its material rewards" (Flaherty & Schilling 25).

THIS THING OF OURS

1   Source music (also known as diegetic music) is music that the characters are aware of – usually music from a radio or "live" band. Music scores, on the other hand, are only heard by the audience and are "extra-diegetic," i.e. not part of the film's "reality." Chase seems to have abandoned a strict adherence to this policy in the second and third seasons, however.

2   David Chase talks about his music-scoring decision in his interview with Peter Bogdanovich on the DVD release of the first season of *The Sopranos*.

3   The lyrics to "Core 'Ngrato" can be found at the end of this essay.

4   Though the Soprano family immigrated from Ariano di Puglia and Avellino, Italy, it is Naples that the Soprano crime family visits in order to establish new business. As "Core 'Ngrato" is a Neapolitan song, the "Naples connection" is clear.

5   The first season ended with Tony, Carmela, Meadow, and AJ at Artie Bucco's Nuovo Vesuvio restaurant. Not insignificantly, Silvio, Paulie, and Christopher are also enjoying a repast. Tony, in a reflective mood, toasts his family, reminding them, "Someday soon, you're going to have families of your own. And if you're lucky, you'll remember the little moments . . . like this . . . that were good. Cheers" ("I Dream of Jeannie Cusamano"/1013). The second season ended with scenes of Meadow's graduation party intercut with scenes that wrap up the stories in previous episodes. The seemingly normative scene of domestic bliss that both Soprano "families" display at the graduation party is undermined by the scenes of the various ways in which Tony's business activities have impacted several lives negatively. The sequence ends with a large amount of money, some of which will end up in Tony's pocket, at a card game. The camera returns to Tony, smoking a cigar and looking apprehensively towards the next season. With Uncle Junior still under house arrest and the ongoing police investigations, the happy gathering at the Soprano home is anything but "normal." The Rolling Stones song, "Thru and Thru" that accompanies the scene speaks to a similar sentiment of unrequited love that "Core 'Ngrato" articulates.

6   Like many of the scenes in *The Sopranos*, this dark moment also has its humorous elements. Christopher, who the audience knows is stoned on a combination of marijuana, cocaine, and alcohol, begins a long-winded monologue about death and the possibilities of identical personalities. The audience, aware of Christopher's debilitated state, laughs knowingly at his recursive monologue, while the other houseguests in the scene listen in bewilderment to his convoluted nonsequiturs.

7   As real-life convicted Mafia boss John Gotti stated in a Discovery Channel documentary, "Why do you think [the Gambino family] fell apart without me? Everyone became their own boss, set their own moral codes, set their own reasons, their own rhyme, and that's the end of it. . . . That's the end of the ballgame" (quoted in Hampson 3A).

8   In fact, music enters their conversation in "College" (1005). When Father Phil asserts, "You know what's remarkable . . . if you took everything Jesus ever said, add it up, it only amounts to two hours of talk." Carmela responds, "No . . . but wait, I heard the same thing about the Beatles. Except it was, if you add up all their songs it only comes up to ten hours." Her non-sequitur throws Father Phil slightly before he re-inserts religion back into the conversation, but it is an indication of the part music performs in the constellation of elements that comprise the Sopranos universe.

9   Carmela has maintained a series of flirtatious relationships with various men – notably Victor Musto, the "wallpaper artist" ("Bust Out"/2010), and her tennis teacher, Ed Rusticcio ("Mr. Ruggerio's Neighborhood"/3001), as well as Father Phil.

10   The Italian lyrics and English translation of "Con Te Partiro" can be found at the end of this essay.

11   See, for instance, the comments by Drea de Matteo, who plays Adriana, in Chris Heath's *Rolling Stone* article in the 29 March 2001 issue. Also, Ellen Willis argues in her article in this volume that Carmela is Tony's "emotional equal; she does what she likes, tells him off without hesitation and, unlike old-style mob wives, knows plenty about the business."

FIFTEEN

1   Dante's role is not entirely clear in the series, but he is referred to as an acting consigliere in Allen Rucker's *The Sopranos: A Family History*.

2   Ironically, Tony Soprano would probably not be a fan of Little Steven. In Rucker's *The Sopranos: A Family History*, the following quote is attributed to a "high school friend, name withheld": "he had a lot of records. Journey. Deep Purple. 'Hooked on a Feeling.' But not Springsteen. You'd think it'd be natural for a Jersey guy to like Springsteen, but Tony didn't. Fuckin' depressing, he would say." In this instance, Tony's psychopathology overrules his cultural geography. More to the point, Springsteen's songs force an identification with exactly the type of people who tend to be Tony's victims, an identification that has already driven him to seek psychoanalytic services at Dr. Melfi's Montclair office. Favoring the sentimentality of pop and the sensuality of heavy metal, Tony would also be comfortable with the self-satisfied crooning of Hoboken-born "friend of the family" Frank Sinatra; had they been born into the same generation, there no doubt would have been ongoing interaction between the Sopranos and the Sinatras.

3   The rest of the CD is uneven, but the inclusion of Bruce Springsteen's "State Trooper" is noteworthy, as the song is about the New Jersey Turnpike. Of course, much of Springsteen's music was made to be listened to while driving around New Jersey. "Woke Up This Morning (Chosen One Mix)" is also included on the second *Sopranos* soundtrack release, *The Sopranos Peppers and Eggs: Music from the HBO Original Series*, as a hidden bonus that comes on at the end of the CD's final track, "Dialogue from 'The Sopranos'." The version that appears on the A3 audio recording, *Exile on Coldharbour Lane*, simply titled "Woke Up This Morning," differs somewhat from the "Chosen One Mix," but I have tried it out and found it equally evocative when driving in New Jersey.

4   *Seinfeld* is also noteworthy in that it also has had an enormous impact on the cultural landscape, in this case of New York City. As a department chair at Fordham University in the Bronx, I have sat in on several meetings where administration officials have credited *Seinfeld* with increasing applications to the university by reversing New York's negative media image.

5   While my last name also ends in a vowel, I am Jewish, not Italian, and do not share the visceral reaction to *The Sopranos* that critics like Paglia have. I can sympathize with them, however, in that I have felt uncomfortable at the portrayal of Jewish-Americans in programs such as *Northern Exposure*, which David Chase also worked on. Jews play significant roles in *The Sopranos*, as business partners and advisors, but it is unlikely that we would protest our association with the mob on the series. Given the whining, Woody Allen-type wimps we are often portrayed as (on *Northern Exposure*, for example), Jewish wise guys make for a welcome countertype. Of course, if this were the early twentieth century, the sentiment might be altogether different, as Jews once had a strong connection to organized crime in the public mind, from Arnold Rothstein, the architect of the Chicago Blacksox scandals, to Dutch Schultz, Bugsy Siegal, and Meyer Lansky. I myself once worked for a company with organized crime connections (although I didn't realize it at the time), and the reality is hardly romantic. Jews and Italians often do business together (legitimate and otherwise) and live together, but they are probably more closely linked in the media, where the two groups are the most common symbols of ethnicity in general (as opposed to race), and where Jewish and Italian actors play Jewish and Italian characters interchangeably. And while Jews play a significant role in the public life of New Jersey, I believe that on *The Sopranos* they serve as a group that is a step higher in sociological status than the Italians, while the African-Americans, who also have a visible role in the series, represent a lower sociological status that the Italians left behind. Hence, the great confusion when, during the third season, Tony's daughter dates a mulatto whose father is Jewish.

6   Here too, there is a degree of ambiguity – compare the forthright redundancy of *New York, New York* to the oddity of *Jersey City, New Jersey*. And while it makes perfect sense for New York City to name its system of public colleges the *City University of New York*, when *Jersey City State College* recently changed their name, they inexplicably chose to call themselves *New Jersey City University*.

And this is not to mention the town of West New York, New Jersey!

7   In other words, we receive information about ourselves from foreign sources (New York and Philadelphia), not from domestic news media. This goes hand in hand with the tendency only to report accidents, natural disasters, and political scandals.

8   This chapter was written before the destruction of the World Trade Center on 11 September 2001, and I thank David Lavery for allowing me to add this footnote shortly after the disaster. The Twin Towers were visible from innumerable locations throughout North Jersey, and many felt that the best views of the skyscrapers could be found on our side of the Hudson River. David Chase's decision to include the World Trade Center as seen through Tony Soprano's rearview mirror in the opening credits has turned out to be prescient, for now the landmark exists only in the rearview mirror of memory and photography. Built by the Port Authority of New York and New Jersey, over half of the individuals who worked at the World Trade Center were from New Jersey, and as many as one third of the casualties came from the Garden State. It seems as if just about everyone living here in Northeastern New Jersey knows someone who was lost in the attack. Sopranoland will never be the same, and it is hard to imagine Chase not addressing this in the fourth season of *The Sopranos*.

9   See also the Weird NJ website (www.weirdnj.com).

10   Much like Poland during World War II, and Israel in the ancient world, New Jersey was a corridor through which competing powers moved their forces and engaged in combat. Much of the Revolutionary War was fought in New Jersey, including four major battles and ninety separate skirmishes, as the British and American forces moved up and down the state. South Jersey is known for Washington crossing the Delaware and the great victory at Trenton. Northeastern New Jersey is known for Washington's retreat route.

11   The Catskills included Italian resorts, as well as the famous Jewish borscht belt comedy circuit that strongly influenced early television programming, as detailed by David Marc.

12   That Chase knows about McLuhan is obvious from the second season episode "House Arrest" which includes a McLuhan reference. Uncle Junior is in the hospital for tests when an African-American man enters the room and introduces himself with "Mr. Soprano? I'm Michael McLuhan from the U.S. Marshal service. Here to reattach your bracelet." A nurse in the room then says, "Excuse me, your name's really McLuhan?" and when he answers affirmatively, she says, "So that makes you Marshal McLuhan." No one else seems to understand the significance of this, not even Michael McLuhan. The scene has no bearing on plot or character development, and so is clearly an insider reference indicating awareness of the electronic media ecology.

SIXTEEN

1   According to *Time*'s Mark Thompson, Capone's famous quotation has been taken up by President Bush's Defense Secretary Donald Rumsfeld, who believes that the gangster's emphasis on force over language is still "appropriate" to today's foreign relations if you "substitute 'ballistic missile' for the word gun – and put in the names of some regional Al Capones" (29).

2   "Cosa Nostra," in spite of its criminal connotations, also demonstrates a subtle use of linguistic ambiguity to convey a point. The term is literally translated as "Our Thing," which, in and of itself, does not suggest any kind of wrongdoing. Yet, for people familiar with the phrase, the implied meaning of the "thing" itself and all of the illegality that it entails, is perfectly clear.

3   Christopher takes part in essentially the same ritual when he is "made" at the beginning of the third season of *The Sopranos* ("Fortunate Son"/3003).

4   Even though Gravano turned his back on the mob by testifying against Gotti in court, his most recent arrests suggest that he has been unable to deny the allure of the criminal lifestyle or to abandon the use of Mafia intimidation techniques. After pleading guilty to running an "ecstasy" distribution ring in Arizona last May, Gravano, according to recently unsealed court documents, "adopted nonverbal communication skills [including winking and flexing his biceps] to keep his

underlings in line" (Francescani 23).

5   Uncle Junior's concerns about his sexuality also dovetail with Michel Foucault's discussion of language and sexuality and the development of sexual discourse in *The History of Sexuality: An Introduction* (Volume I). Within the Soprano family's more conservative sexual politics, Junior's behavior is rejected both as a sexual act and as a topic of public conversation. Yet, as Foucault explains, "if sex is repressed, that is condemned to prohibition, nonexistence, and silence, then the mere fact that one is speaking about it has the appearance of a deliberate transgression. A person who holds forth in such language places himself to a certain extent outside the reach of power; he upsets established law" (6). By speaking out, Tony and Junior's girlfriend Roberta both claim a power over him, a power that he attempts to take back by silencing them both, by having Tony killed and by pushing a "pie" in Roberta's face.

6   The robbery itself develops through an act of verbal manipulation, as Ralphie inspires Jackie Jr. by telling him about a similar incident that moved Tony up in the family.

7   As Tony mercilessly strangles the helpless Petrulio, he reminds him of the oath that he took. For Tony, Petrulio's violation of the code of silence more than justifies his vicious murder.

8   While Meadow tells Tony about her experience with speed in an "honest" moment during their trip, she also withholds information and deliberately avoids telling him that Christopher supplied her with the drug.

9   Even then, her safety is not always guaranteed. At the end of Season One and for the first half of Season Two, Dr. Melfi is forced to abandon her office and conduct therapy sessions from a motel room because rival mob members might be suspicious of what she knows.

10   As Tony explains to Carmela, if the "wrong people" found out about his therapy visits, he could wind up with "a steeljacket antidepressant in the back of the head" (1001). And Uncle Junior does put a hit out on Tony after he learns that his nephew is in counseling.

11   Celia Wren agrees that "what really gives [the show] a distinctive flavor is [this] atmosphere of subtle nostalgia" (20).

12   In spite of the disparate nature of their "callings," Dr. Melfi is ironically also bound by a "code of silence." Not only is she unable to talk about Tony with friends and family – when she runs into Tony at a restaurant, she must remind her date that she cannot tell him if Tony is her patient (1001) – but, her legal responsibility to report criminal activity also restricts Tony's ability to speak and adds to his language problems. (Dr. Melfi purposely prevents him from discussing his murderous plans for the soccer coach in "Boca" for this reason.)

13   The verbal roles that Tony and Dr. Melfi typically play in their therapy sessions are, interestingly enough, reversed in "Employee of the Month" (3004), when Dr. Melfi is brutally raped in a stairwell. Although she is strongly moved to tell him about the incident and even knows the identity of her attacker, she refrains because she knows what Tony's violent response will be and what her confession will mean for the rapist. (While she normally adheres to a professional and legal code of conduct her silence in this instance is based more on personal moral standards.)

Seventeen

1   The need to fuel a drug addiction might prove to be too powerful an incentive to disobey organizational imperatives, and the longer sentences imposed on drug offences, particularly after the War on Drugs was declared, gave prosecutors a dangerous amount of leverage. According to this line of reasoning, expressed by "former mob soldier turned author" Vincent Rizzo, who appears on television in "46 Long" (1002), it was the Mafia's eventual entry into the drug trade that was the cause of their decline.

Eighteen

1   Because it is the meat of humility and associated with female genitalia, fish is also dangerous

in its ability to make its consumers ill. When Tony suffers from food poisoning, he first blames the clams he ate at Nuovo Vesuvio, but the restaurant's owner, Artie Bucco, assures Tony that he inspected every clam by hand ("Funhouse"/2013). In the next season, Janice, Tony's new-age slattern of a sister, is not to be trusted in the Christmas episode with the Christmas Eve shellfish ("To Save Us All From Satan's Power"/3012). Her kitchen is a far cry from Carmela's spotless workplace.

2   *The Satires* of Juvenal also explore the food/power issue in some detail, particularly Satire V in which a wealthy Roman patron, Virro, serves a lesser client bad wine, tepid water, moldy bread, "half an egg/Stuffed with one prawn" (84–5), cabbage cooked in lamp oil, an eel that looks more like a river snake, a sewage-fed pike, and a rotten apple.

Appendix C

1   Our times are themselves clearly promiscuous. Whether we use the classification schemes of John Fiske – horizontal and vertical intertextuality – or Gerard Genette – paratextuality, architextuality, metatextuality, hypertextuality – it is quite apparent that many of television's most ingenious series, rife with intertextual reference, often humorous, to movies, to culture in general, to literature, to (self-referentially) themselves, come heavy as well. The predominance of the "already said," as Eco once observed, the inescapable contemporary realization of the antecedent, is, after all, one of postmodernism's signatures.

Appendix D

1   This appendix originally appeared in *Television Quarterly* (Winter 2001): 89–92 and is reprinted here with permission.

2   The box set of the first season of *The Sopranos* on DVD has sold over 500,000 copies despite its nearly $100 list price. The second season was likewise released on DVD in November 2001.

3   I did find five errors in the episode guide. (1) Tony is quoted as saying "Psychiatry and cunnilingus brought us to this" when the line is actually "Cunnilingus and psychiatry have brought us to this." (2) We are told that, after the Junior-ordered, unsuccessful hit (in "Isabella"/1012), Tony crashes "his Suburban into a tree," when in fact he smashes into some parked cars. (3) In "Guy Walks into a Psychiatrist's Office" (2001), Philly Parisi "runs into Gigi Cestone (working for Tony) at the airport and gets summarily whacked." In fact, Parisi had unwittingly gone to the airport specifically to pick his killer up. (4) Sandra Bernhard's name (she appears in "D-Girl"/2007) is spelled wrong (Bernhardt). (5) In the guest stars list (in the updated, paperback version), Dr. Freid is spelled *Dr. Fried*. Picky, picky? Perhaps, but this is, after all, an "official" companion.

BIBLIOGRAPHY

Allen, Robert C. *Speaking of Soap Operas*. Chapel Hill: U North Carolina P, 1985.

Anastasia, George. *GoodFella Tapes*. New York: Avon, 1998.

Andrew, Geoff. *Stranger than Paradise: Maverick Film-makers in Recent American Cinema*. New York: Limelight Editions, 1998.

Austen, Ian. "Culture between Commercials." Szuchewycz and Sloniowski. 74–82.

Austin, Thomas. "Gendered (dis) Pleasures: *Basic Instinct* and Female Viewers." *Journal of Popular British Cinema 2* (January 1999): 4–22.

Bakhtin, Mikhail. *The Dialogic Imagination*. Ed. Michael Holquist. Trans. Caryl Emerson and Michael Holquist. Austin: U Texas P, 1981.

Barthes, Roland. *Elements of Semiology*. Trans. Annette Lavers and Colin Smith. New York: Hill and Wang, 1967.

___ *Mythologies*. Trans. Annette Lavers. New York: Hill and Wang, 1972.

Baudrillard, Jean. *Simulations*. Trans. P. Foss, P. Patton & P. Beitchman. New York: Semiotext(e), 1983.

Behrens, S. "Technological Convergence: Toward a United State of Media." *Channels of Communication 1986 Field Guide*: 8–10.

Bellamy, Robert V., Jr. and Paul J. Traudt. "Television Branding as Promotion." *Research in Media Promotion*. Edited by Susan Eastman. Mahwah, NJ: Lawrence Erlbaum Assoc., 2000. 127–59.

Benjamin, Walter. "The Work of Art in the Age of Mechanical Reproduction." *Illuminations*. Edited Hannah Arendt. Trans. Harry Zohn. New York: Schocken Books, 1969. 217–52.

Berger, Warren. "At 25, Excellence and Big Budgets For a Late Bloomer." *The New York Times* 9 Nov. 1997, Late Ed.: Section 2, 23.

Bishop, David. *Bright Lights, Baked Ziti: An Unofficial and Unauthorized Guide*. London: Virgin Books, 2001.

Biskind, Peter. *Easy Riders, Raging Bulls: How the Sex-Drugs-and-Rock-'n'-roll Generation Saved Hollywood*. New York: Simon & Schuster, 1998.

Blackett, Tom. "Forward." *Brands: The New Wealth Creators*. Ed. Susannah Hart and John Murphy. New York: New York UP, 1998. xi.

Blimes, Alex. "*The Sopranos* Hit London." *GQ Magazine* July 2000: 162–70.

Blum, Howard. *Gangland: How the FBI Broke the Mob*. New York: Pocket, 1993.

Boorstin, Daniel J. *The Image: A Guide to Pseudo-Events in America*. New York: Atheneum, 1978.

Bordo, Susan. *The Male Body: A New Look at Men in Public and in Private*. New York: Farrar, Straus and Giroux, 1999.

___ *Unbearable Weight: Feminism, Western Culture, and the Body*. Berkeley: U California P, 1993.

Botting, Fred and Scott Wilson. *The Tarantinian Ethics*. London: Sage, 2001.

Bracco, Lorraine. "The Mobster and the Shrink." *Interview* (March 1999): 108–110.

"Brave New World in HBO's Sights: Cable Programmer to Explore Videocasette Distribution, Satellite Delivery, and Distribution of Major Theatricals." *ASAP* 19 Mar. 1984: 54.

Brioux, Bill. "CTV Gets Away with Murder: Uncensored Sopranos is a Huge Hit." *Toronto Sun* 29 September 2000.

___ "Sopranos Steal Gold in Ratings Race." *Toronto Sun* 22 September 2000.

Brooker, Peter. *A Concise Glossary of Cultural Theory*. London: Arnold, 1999.

Broughton, James. *Seeing the Light*. San Francisco: City Lights, 1977.

Browne, Nick, ed. *Francis Ford Coppola's The Godfather Trilogy*. Cambridge Film Handbooks. New York: Cambridge UP, 2000.

Bruzzi, Stella. *Undressing Cinema: Clothing and Identity in the Movies*. London: Routledge, 1998.

Buckley, William F., Jr. "On the Right – The Sopranos' Underside." *National Review* 30 April 2001: 58–9.

Burgess, Jacquelin and John R. Gold. *Georgraphy, Media, and Popular Culture*. London: Croom Helm, 1985.

Canadian Broadcast Standards Council. "CTV re *The Sopranos*." 8 March 2001. http://www.cbsc.ca/english/decision/010524.htm

Canby, Vincent. "From the Humble Mini-Series Comes the Magnificent Megamovie." *New York Times on The Sopranos*. 54–67.

Cannell, Stephen J. "Afterword: About David Chase." *New York Times on The Sopranos*. 147–55.

Carlson, Margaret. "Hit Women: Women in the Sopranos." *Vogue* v. 89, no. 12 (December 1999): 248–51.

Carpenter, Edmund. *Oh, What a Blow that Phantom Gave Me!* New York: Holt, Rinehart, and Winston, 1973.

Carter, Bill. "A Big 'Sopranos' Finale." *The New York Times* 23 May 2001: E7.

___ "He Engineered a Mob Hit, And Now It's Time To Pay Up." *The New York Times on The Sopranos*. 83–90.

Cathorpe, Peter and William Fulton. *The Regional City: Planning for the End of Sprawl*. Washington, D. C.: Island Press, 2001.

Clark, Kenneth R. "Thinking the Unthinkable: In 20 years, HBO has Gone from Polka Festivals to Blockbusters." *Chicago Tribune* 8 Nov. 1992: Tempo 3.

Clover, Carol. *Men, Women, and Chainsaws: Gender in the Modern Horror Film*. Princeton, NJ: Princeton UP, 1992.

Con Te Partiro" (lyrics). Con Te Partiro. Bocelli Online. 05 May 2001. http://www.bocellionline.com/Partiro.com.

Congreve, William. *The Complete Plays of William Congreve*. Edited by Herbert Davis. Chicago, U Chicago P, 1967.

Consentino, Mike. E-mail Interview. 17 August 2001.

"Core 'Ngrato" (lyrics). tenorissimo! lyrics from carmen, fanciulla, tosca, plus core 'ngrato, granada, federico's lament. Opera Resource. 18 June 2001. http://www.tenorissimo.com/domingo/Words/lyrics6.htm.

Cowie, Peter. *The Godfather Book*. Boston: Faber & Faber, 1997.

Creeber, Glen. *Dennis Potter: Between Two Worlds, A Critical Reassessment*. London: Macmillan, 1998.

Croft, Karen. "Made Women. *The Sopranos* Deals with Female Emotional and Sexual Desire Better than Any Other Show on TV." http://www.salon.com/sex/feature/2001/04/09/mob_women/index.html.

CTV Press Release. "Pass the cannoli . . . CTV announces full scheduling details for *The Sopranos*." 16 July 2001.

"Curse of 'The Sopranos': New Jersey Politics Returns to Dirty Past." *The Sunday Record* 22 April 2001: RO2

Curtis, Quentin. "The Very Model of a Modern Mobster Family." *The Daily Telegraph* 21 August 1999: 5.

Daly, Steve. "Bright Lights, Baked Ziti." *Entertainment Weekly* 7 January 2000: 20–7.

___ "David Chase." *Entertainment Weekly* 24 December 1999.

"David Chase: 'Hit' Man." Longworth: 20–6. [Referred to in the text as the Longworth Interview.]

Davis, Mike. *Prisoners of the American Dream: Politics and Economy in the History of the U.S. Working Class*. London: Verso, 1986.

DeCaro, Frank. "From Jersey with Love." *TV Guide* 17 March 2001: 18–22, 24–6, 28, 31.

___ "The Mob Squad." *TV Guide* 8 January 2000: 18–22, 24, 26, 29.

Diehl, Digby. *Tales from the Crypt: The Official Archives*. New York: St. Martin's Press, 1995.

Dienst, Richard. *Still Life in Real Time: Theory After Television*. Durham: Duke UP, 1994.

Dolan, Marc. "The Peaks and Valleys of Serial Creativity: What Happened to/on *Twin Peaks*." *Full of Secrets: Critical Approaches to Twin Peaks*. Ed. David Lavery. Detroit: Wayne State UP, 1994. 30-50.

Doyle, John. "Ethnic Stereotyping? Fuhgeddaboutit." *Globe & Mail* 9 April 2001: R2.

Ducey, Rick. "Co-branding Joint Ventures: Internet Age Business Strategies." Presentation slides available at the National Association of Broadcasters' web site: http://www.nab.org/Research/Reports/InternetBusinessStrategy/index.htm. Eizo Shuimbun Seminar, Las Vegas [Online], April 8, 1997.

Duffy, Robert. North Jersey 101. http://aolsvc.digitalcity.com/northjersey/aboutourcity/main.dci?page=main

Duncan, James and David Ley, eds. *Place/Culture/Representation*. London: Routledge, 1993.

Eco, Umberto. "Postscript." *The Name of the Rose*. Trans. William Weaver. New York: Harcourt Brace Jovanovich, 1983.

___ *Travels in Hyper-Reality*. London: Picador, 1986.

Edel, Raymond A. and Virginia Rohan. "Hits and Misses: A Weekly Guide to *The Sopranos*." *The Record* 18 March 2001, YT-2.

___ "Hits and Misses: A Weekly Guide to *The Sopranos*." *The Record* 22 April 2001, YT-2.

Ehrenreich, Barbara. "The Decline of Patriarchy." *Constructing Masculinity*. Ed. Maurice Berger. London: Routledge, 1995.

Einstein, Albert. *Relativity, the Special and the General Theory: A Popular Exposition*. Rev. ed. Trans. R.W. Lawson. London: Methuen, 1954.

Ellis, John. *Visible Fictions: Cinema, Television, Video*. London: Routledge, 1982.

Ellwood, Iain. *The Essential Brand Book: Over 100 Techniques to Increase Brand Value*. London: Kogan Page, 2000.

Ettedgui, Peter. *Cinematography: Screencraft*. East Sussex: England: RotoVision Books, 1998.

Faludi, Susan. *Stiffed: The Betrayal of the American Man*. New York: William Morrow, 1999.

Fejes, Fred. "Male Audiences and the Media, a Survey of Empirical Research." *Men, Masculinity and the Media*. Ed. Steve Craig. London: Sage, 1992.

Feuer, Jane. "Genre Study and Television." *Channels of Discourse, Reassembled: Television and Contemporary Criticism*. Ed. Robert C. Allen. Chapel Hill: U North Carolina P, 1992. 138–59.

___ "Melodrama, Serial Form and Television Today". *Screen* 25:1 (1984): 4–16.

Fiske, John. *Television Culture*. New York: Routledge, 1987.

Flaherty, Mike and Mary Kaye Schilling. "Family Reunion." *Entertainment Weekly* 11 June 1999: 24–9.

Flandrin, Jean-Louis and Massimo Montanari, eds. *Food: A Culinary History*. New York: Columbia UP, 1999.

Forkan, Jim. "What, No Bleepin' Role Models?" *Multichannel News* 24 January 2000: 6.

Foucault, Michel. *The History of Sexuality: An Introduction*. Volume I. Trans. Robert Hurley. New York: Vintage, 1990.

Francescani, Christopher. "Strong as a 'Bull.'" *New York Post* 17 August 2001: 23.

Fry, Katherine. *Constructing the Heartland: Television and Natural Disaster News*. Cresskill, NJ: Hampton Press, in press.

Gage, Nicholas. *The Mafia is Not an Equal Opportunity Employer*. New York: McGraw-Hill, 1971.

Genette, Gérard. *Palimpsests*. Trans. Channa Newman & Claude Doubinsky. Lincoln: U Nebraska P, 1997.

Genzlinger, Neil. "I Can't Take (It) Anymore." *The New York Times* Section 14, 1, March 18, 2001.

George Anastasia Interview. *Fresh Air*. Host Terry Gross. WHYY. 25 July 2001.

Gershon, Richard A. and Michael O. Wirth. "Home Box Office." *The Cable Networks Handbook*. Ed. Robert G. Picard. Riverside, CA: Carpelan Publishing Co., 1993: 114–22.

Golfman, Noreen. "Watch What You Wish For." Szuchewycz and Sloniowski: 100–3.

Goode, William J., *The Celebration of Heroes: Prestige as a Control System*. Berkeley: U California P, 1978.

Grillo, Jean Bergantini "What's up with Originals? For One Thing, Costs, as Networks Battle in a More Competitive Market." *Broadcasting and Cable* 28 May 2001: 18.

Grogan, Sarah. *Body Image: Understanding Body Dissatisfaction in Men, Women, and Children*. London: Routledge, 1999.

Gruber, Howard E. "And the Bush was Not Consumed": *The Evolving Systems Approach to Creativity. Towards a Theory of Psychological Development*. Ed. Sohan and Celia Modgil. Windsor, England: NFER, 1980. 269–99.

Hallam, Julia, with Margaret Marshment. *Realism and Popular Cinema*. Manchester: Manchester UP, 2000.

Hampson, Rick. "Curtains Descend on Gotti, Family." *USA Today* 25 July 2001. 3A.

Hardy, Phil, ed.. *The BFI Companion to Crime*. London: Cassell & BFI, 1997.

Harris, Valentina. *Regional Italian Cooking*. New York: Pantheon, 1986.

Harvey, David. *The Condition of Postmodernity: An Inquiry into the Origins of Cultural Change*. Oxford: Basil Blackwell, 1989.

Haskell, Ann. "The World of *The Godfather*: No Place for Women." *New York Times* vol. 146, section 2 (23 March 1997): H17.

Hawthorne, Nathaniel. *The Scarlet Letter*. Ed. Ross C. Murfin. Case Studies in Contemporary Criticism. Boston: Bedford Books of St. Martin's Press, 1991.

Heath, Chris. "Sopranos Stars Tell All!" *Rolling Stone* 29 March 2001. 42–51.

"Hit Man." Interview with David Chase. *The News Hour*. PBS. 8 August 2001: http://www.pbs.org/newshour/bb/entertainment/july-dec01/chase_8-8.html.

"Hit Man: *Sopranos* Creator David Chase Takes a Whack at Success a Second Time Around." *TV Guide* 8 January 2000: 20–1, 54.

Holden, Stephen. "*The Sopranos*: an Introduction." *The New York Times on The Sopranos*. xi–xix.

"How You Doin'? Some Italian-Americans Carp, but *The Sopranos* Still Pleases Its Fans." *People Weekly* 23 April 2001: 19.

Ianni, Francis A.J. "The Mafia and the Web of Kinship." *The Crime Society: Organized Crime and Corruption in America*. Ed. Francis A. J. Ianni and Elizabeth Reuss-Ianni. New York: New American Library, 1976. 42–59.

"An Interview with David Chase." *The Sopranos: A Family History*. Ed. Allen Rucker. New York: New American Library, 2000: n.p. [Referred to in the text as the Rucker interview.]

Interview with David Chase. Home Box Office (HBO). 03 May 2001. http://www.hbo.com/sopranos/insidersguide/interviews/davidchaseint.shtml.

Interview with David Chase, Museum of Television and Radio, BRAVO Television Network, 20 August 2000.

Jacobs, Jason. *The Intimate Screen: Early British Television Drama*. New York: Oxford UP, 2001.

Jagger, Mick and Keith Richards. "(I Can't Get No) Satisfaction." *Out of Our Heads* (1965). Lyrics downloaded from http://lyrics.rockmagic.net.

"James Gandolfini: Mixing Sangfroid with Gang Freud, He Gives us a Don with Demons." *People Weekly* 25 December 2000: 72.

James, Caryn. "Addicted to a Mob Family Potion." *The New York Times on The Sopranos*. 23–31.

Jameson, Fredric, *Postmodernism, or, The Cultural Logic of Late Capitalism*. Durham, NC: Duke UP, 1991.

___ "Reification and Utopia in Mass Culture." *Signatures of the Visible*. New York: Routledge, 1992. 9–34.

Johnston, Sheila. "Crossroads: Approaches to Popular Television Fiction." BFI Summer School, 1981.

Justin, Neal. "It's a Good Thing the Big Networks Refused *The Sopranos*." *Minneapolis Star Tribune* 14 January 2000: 1E.

Juvenal. *The Satires of Juvenal*. Trans. Peter Green. New York: Penguin, 1974.

Kelly, Audrey. "Made Man: Hit After Hit, David Chase Ushers *The Sopranos* into the Big Time." *Fade In*. http://www.fadeinmag.com/chase/interview/chase.html.

Kempton, Murray. *Rebellions, Perversities and Main Events*. New York: Random House, 1994.

Kimmel, Michael. "Consuming Manhood: The Feminization of American Culture and the Recreation of the Male Body, 1832–1920." *The Male Body: Features, Destinies, Exposures*. Ed. Laurence Goldstein. Ann Arbor: U Michigan P, 1994. 12–42.

Klinkenborg, Verlyn. "Why America Loves *The Sopranos*." *The New York Times* 16 January 2000: A16.

Kobler, John. *The Life and World of Al Capone*. New York: Da Capo Press, 1992.

Kolker, Rober. *A Cinema of Loneliness: Penn, Stone, Kubrick, Scorsese, Spielberg, Altman*. Third Edition. New York: Oxford UP, 2000.

Krzywinska, Tanya. "Hubble-Bubble, Herbs and Grimoires: Practical Magic and Witchcraft in *Buffy the Vampire Slayer*." Wilcox and Lavery: 178–94.

Lash, Scott and John Urry. *The End of Organized Capitalism*. Cambridge: Polity Press, 1987.

Lauzen, Martha. "Don't Forget the Brutalized Women behind *The Sopranos*." *Los Angeles Times* (16 April 2001). http://www.sicilianculture.com/news/sopranoswomen.htm.

Lavery, David. "Coming Heavy: Intertextuality, Genre, and *The Sopranos*." *PopPolitics.com* (March 2001): http://www.poppolitics.com/articles/2001-03-03-heavy.shtml.

___ "Creative Work: On the Method of Howard Gruber." *The Journal of Humanistic Psychology* 33 (1993): 101–21.

___ "The Genius of Joss Whedon." Wilcox and Lavery. 251–6.

___ Review Essay of *Buffy the Vampire Slayer: The Monster Book*, *Buffy the Vampire Slayer: The Watcher's Guide*, Vol. 2, and *The Sopranos: A Family History*. *Television Quarterly* 31.4 (Winter 2001): 89–92.

Le Carre, John. *Single and Single*. New York: Pocket Books, 1999.

Letters to the Editor. "Women in *The Sopranos* Are Living In the Real World." *Los Angeles Times* (April 23, 2001). http://www.calendarlive.com/top/1,1419,L-LATimes-Print-X!ArticleDetail-30060,00.html

Lieberman, Paul. "Confessions of an HBO Original; Sheila Nevins, Who Heads Documentary Projects at the Pay Channel, Balances the Crass with Crusading." *Los Angeles Times* 28 May 2000: 3.

Longworth, James L. *TV Creators: Conversations with America's Top Producers of Television Drama*. Syracuse: Syracuse UP, 2000.

Lovgren, Sylvia. *Fashionable Food: Seven Decades of Food Fads*. New York: MacMillan, 1995.

Lowry, Brian. "Prime-time TV Rankings; *Sopranos'* Season Finale a Big Hit." *Los Angeles Times* 23 May 2001: Calendar, 9.

Lupp, Robert. The Garden State and Other New Jersey State Nicknames. http://www.state.nj.us/njfacts/garden.htm

Macherey, Pierre. *The Theory of Literary Production.* Trans. Geoffrey Wall. London: Routledge, 1978.

Macintyre, Ben. "Godfathers Who Wish to Play the Starring Role." *The Times* 4/28/2001: 24.

Marc, David. *Bonfire of the Humanities: Television, Subliteracy, and Long-Term Memory Loss.* The Television Series. Syracuse: Syracuse UP, 1995.

___ and Robert J. Thompson. *Prime Time, Prime Movers: From I Love Lucy to L.A. Law – America's Greatest TV Shows and the People Who Created Them.* Syracuse: Syracuse UP, 1995.

Marx, Karl. "The Eighteenth Brumaire of Louis-Napoleon Bonaparte," *Karl Marx, Surveys from Exile: Political Writings Volume II.* Ed. David Fernbach. New York: Vintage, 1974: 143–249.

Mass, Peter. *Underboss: Sammy the Bull Gravano's Story of Life in the Mafia.* New York: HarperCollins, 1997.

McLeland, Susan. "Re-Shaping the Grotesque Body: Roseanne, *Roseanne*, Breast Reduction, and Rhinoplasty." *Spectator* 13.3 (1993): 21–7.

McLuhan, Marshall. "Canada: The Borderline Case." *The Canadian Imagination: Dimensions of a Literary Culture.* Ed. David Staines. Cambridge: Harvard UP, 1977. 226–48.

McDowell, W. and A. Batten. *Branding TV: Principles and Practices.* Washington, DC: National Association of Broadcasters, 1999.

McKegney, Margaret. "How *The Sopranos* Whacked Its Rivals." *AdAgeGlobal.* May 2001.

McLuhan, Marshall. *Understanding Media: The Extensions of Man.* New York: McGraw-Hill, 1964.

___ "Canada: The Borderline Case." *The Canadian Imagination: Dimensions of a Literary Culture.* Ed. David Staines. Cambridge: Harvard UP. 1977: 226–48.

McNeil, Alex. *Total Television.* New York: Penguin, 1996.

Meyrowitz, Joshua, J. *No Sense of Place.* New York: Oxford UP, 1985.

Miller, Alice. *The Drama of the Gifted Child: The Search for the True Self.* Trans. Ruth Ward. New York: Basic Books, 1997.

Miller, Toby. 'The Action Series.'" *The Television Genre Book.* Ed. Glen Creeber. London. BFI, 2001. 17–19.

Millman, Marcia. *Such a Pretty Face: Being Fat in America.* New York: W. W. Norton, 1980.

Molson Breweries. Advertisement. 1999.

Morgan, Thomas. "HBO Increasing Production of its Own Cable TV Films." *The New York Times* 1 Nov. 1986: Section 1, 50.

"Movies at Home Via Satellite." *The Economist* 25 Sep. 1976: 23.

"Moving Closer to a Pay-TV Payoff." *Business Week* 25 Aug. 1975: 24.

Newcomb, Horace. *TV: The Most Popular Art.* New York: Anchor Books, 1974.

The New York Times on The Sopranos, New York: ibooks, 2000.

Nienhaus, Brian Jacob. *Lost Causes: Mass Media Exposure's Empirical Meanings in Survey Research. A Critique and Introduction to Commodity Relations.* Unpublished dissertation, The University of Michigan, 1993.

O'Brien, Joseph F. and Andris Kurins. *Boss of Bosses – The Fall of the Godfather: The FBI and Paul Castellano.* New York: Simon and Schuster, 1991.

Ong, Walter J., *The Presence of the Word.* Minneapolis: U Minnesota P, 1967.

Orwell, George. "Politics and the English Language." *Shooting an Elephant and Other Essays.* New York: Harcourt, Brace, 1950. 77–92.

Paglia, Camille. "The Energy Mess and Fascist Fays." *Salon*, May 23, 2001. http://www.salon.com/people/col/pagl/2001/05/23/oil/index2.html.

___. "Feinstein for President, Buchanan for Emperor." http://www.salon.com/people/col/pagl/1999/10/27/paglia1027/index.html.

Papke, David Ray. "Myth & Meaning: Francis Ford Coppola and Popular Response to the *Godfather*

Trilogy."' *Legal Reelism: Movies as Legal Texts*. Ed. John Denvir. Urbana: U Illinois P, 1996. 1–22.

Paulson, Ken. "Don't Rub Out Uncle Junior's Right to Sing." *The Tennessean* 10 Sept. 2001: 13A.

"Pay Television in America: Feevee's Charge." *The Economist* 27 Sept. 1975: 76.

"Peter Bogdanovich Interviews David Chase." *The Sopranos: The Complete First Season*. DVD. NY: HBO-Time-Warner Prod., 2000.

Peyser, Marc. "HBO's Godfather: David Chase Created the Acclaimed *The Sopranos*. Now He Wants to Bump It off." *Newsweek* 5 March 2001: 54.

Pistone, Joseph. "David Chase: Showing That Even Hit Men Can Be Human, He Brings Humanity to the Screen." *Time* 9 July 2001: 74.

Poniewozik, James. "They Pull You Back In: David Chase's *Sopranos* Returns for Another Hit Job." *Time* 17 January 2000: 86–7.

Prince, Stephen. Savage *Cinema: Sam Peckinpah and the Rise of Ultraviolent Movies*. London: Athlone Press, 1998.

Pumphrey, Martin. "Why Do Cowboys Wear Hats in the Bath? Style Politics for the Older Man." *The Book of Westerns*. Ed. Ian Cameron and Douglas Pye. New York: Continuum, 1996. 50–62.

Putnam, Robert D. *Bowling Alone: The Collapse and Revival of American Community*. New York: Simon & Schuster, 2000.

Reeves, Jimmie L., Mark Rogers, and Michael Epstein. "Rewriting Popularity: The Cult Files." *"Deny All Knowledge": Reading The X Files*. Ed. David Lavery, Angela Hague, and Marla Cartwright. Syracuse: Syracuse UP, 1996. 22–35.

Reiss, Jeffrey C. "Premium Cable Programming." *Broadcast/Cable Programming: Strategies and Practices*. Fourth Ed. Ed. Susan Tyler Eastman. Belmont, CA: Wadsworth Publishing Co., 1993. 335–63.

Remnick, David, "Is this the End of RICO? With *The Sopranos* the Mob Genre is on the Brink." *New Yorker* 2 April 2001: 38–44.

Renoir, Jean. *Rules of the Game*. Classic Film Scripts. Trans. John McGrath and Maureen Teitelbaum. New York: Simon and Schuster, 1970.

Rohan, Virginia. "Class Guy from New York is Pure New Jersey." *The Record*, YT-1-YT-2, 16 March 2001.

Rucker, Allen. *The Sopranos: A Family History*. New York: New American Library, 2000. An expanded edition, covering all three seasons, was published in 2001.

Rudolph, Eric. "Mob Psychology." *American Cinematographer* 80: 10 (October 1999): 62–71.

Sacks, Arthur. "An Analysis of the Gangster Movies of the Early Thirties." *The Velvet Light Trap* 1 (1971): 5–11.

"Sam Giancana: The Gangster Who Dreamed." A & E Biography Special: Real GoodFellas.

Saunders, Dusty. "*Sopranos* Caps Season in Grand Fashion." *Rocky Mountain News* 23 May 2001: Entertainment, 2D.

Schatz, Thomas. *Hollywood Genres: Formulas, Filmmaking and the Studio System*. New York: Random House, 1981.

Schwartz, Hillel. *Never Satisfied: A Cultural History of Diets, Fantasies, and Fat*. New York: Anchor Books, 1986.

Seiter, Ellen. "Eco's TV guide – the soaps." *Tabloid*, 5 (Winter 1982): 2–14.

Seitz, Matt Zoller. "Location, Location, Location." *Star-Ledger* 16 January 2000. http://www.nj.com/sopranos/ledger/index.ssf?/sopranos/stories/location.html

Servadio, Gaia. *Mafioso: A History of the Mafia from its Origins to Present Day*. New York: Stein and Day, 1976.

Shadoian, Jack. *Dreams and Dead Ends*. Princeton: Princeton UP, 1983.

Showalter, Elaine. "Mob Scene." *The American Prospect* 28 February 28, 2000. Available online at http://www.prospect.org/print/V11/8/showalter-e.html.

Sierchio, Pat. "For He's a Jolly Goodfellas: From *Scarface* to *The Sopranos*. When Wiseguys Talk Wise

Writers Listen." *Written By* September 2000: 32–39.

Silverstone, Rodger. *Why Study the Media?* London: Sage, 1999.

Simpson, Philip L. "The Politics of Apocalypse in the Cinema of Serial Murder." *Mythologies of Violence in Postmodern Media.* Ed. Christopher Sharrett. Detroit: Wayne State UP, 1999. 119–44.

Smith, Anthony. *The Geopolitics of Information: How Western Culture Dominates the World.* New York: Oxford UP, 1980.

Smith, Sally Bedell. "HBO Altering its Plans After Year of Bad News." *The New York Times* 22 Jan. 1985: C18.

"Sopranos A-Z." *Entertainment Weekly* 11 June 1999: 30–31.

"*The Sopranos* Producer David Chase Named 'Hands Down' 1999 'Pasta-tute' of the Year by Italian-American One Voice Group Voters." http://members.aol.com/ItaliaAmOneVoice/pastatute99.html

The Sopranos Peppers and Eggs: Music from the HBO Original Series. Sony 2001.

The Sopranos: Music from the HBO Original Series. Sony 1999.

The Sopranos: The Complete First Season. HBO Home Video 2001.

Stearns, Peter N. *Fat History: Bodies and Beauty in the Modern West.* New York: New York UP, 1997.

Stevens, Elizabeth Lesly. "HBO's Challenge: To Keep the High-profile Programs Coming." *Business Week* 8 Dec. 1997: 77

Sragow, Michael. "Directors from B to Z." *Salon.com.* http://www.salon.com/ent/col/srag/2001/01/18/bromell_zemeckis/

Strum, Charles, "Even a Mobster Needs Someone to Talk To." *The New York Times on The Sopranos.* 101–10.

Szuchewycz, Bohdan and Jeannette Sloniowski, eds. *Canadian Communications: Issues in Contemporary Media and Culture.* 2nd edition. Scarborough: Pearson Education, 2002.

Tarantino, Quentin. *Reservoir Dogs* (CD featuring interview with Tarantino on the making of the movie). Dog Eat Dog Productions, Universal Pictures, UK, 1992.

Tasker, Yvonne. *Working Girls: Gender and Sexuality in Popular Cinema.* New York: Routledge, 1998.

Taubin, Amy. "The Men's Room." *Action/Spectacle Cinema: A Sight & Sound Reader.* Ed. José Arroyo. London: BFI, 2000.

Thompson, Mark. "Mr. Missile Shield." *Time* 8 Jan. 2001: 28–9.

Thompson, Robert J. *Television's Second Golden Age: From Hill Street Blues to ER.* New York: Continuum, 1996.

Thorburn, David. "Television as an Aesthetic Medium." *Critical Studies in Mass Communication* 4. 2 (June 1987): 161–73.

Tilley, Steve. "Singing the Praises of the Sopranos: Sex, Violence and Cussin' Integral to Series, Says CTV." *Edmonton Sun* 14 September 2000. http://www.canoe.ca/SunMediaArchives/home.html

___ "Wise Guys Will Love Sopranos: Gritty Series Has Top Acting, Writing." *Edmonton Sun* 15 Sept. 2000. http://www.canoe.ca/SunMediaArchives/home.html

Todreas, Timothy M. *Value Creation and Branding in Television's Digital Age.* London: Quorum Books, 1999.

Tommasini, Anthony. "A Forgotten Monument to Carousing and Clanging." *New York Times* 23 Nov. 2000, late ed.: E1+.

Tornquist, Cynthia. "'Hollywood Heavyweights'- Cable Genius Michael Fuchs." CNN Transcripts (*Showbiz Today*) 23 Dec. 1992: #198–6.

Tuan, Yi-Fu. *Space and Place: The Perspective of Experience.* Minneapolis: U Minnesota P, 1977.

Twitchell, James B. *Lead Us into Temptation: The Triumph of American Materialism.* New York: Columbia UP, 1999.

Vale, Allison. Telephone Interview. 17 August 2001.

Visser, Margaret. *Much Depends on Dinner*. New York: Grove, 1986.

Wallace, Bruce. "National Cultures in the Age of Globalization: The Case of Canada." *Communications Issues in Contemporary Media and Culture*. Toronto: Pearson, 2001: 55–8.

Warshow, Robert. "The Gangster as Tragic Hero." *The Immediate Experience:* 127–33.

___ *The Immediate Experience. Movies, Comics, Theatre and Other Aspects of Popular Culture*. New York: Doubleday and Co. Inc, 1962.

___ "Movie Chronicle: The Westerner." *The Immediate Experience*: 135–54.

Wasko, Janet. *Hollywood in the Information Age: Beyond the Silver Screen*. Cambridge: Polity Press, 1994.

Watzalwick, Paul, Janet Helmick Beavin, and Don D. Jackson. *Pragmatics of Human Communication: A Study of Interactional Patterns, Pathologies, and Paradoxes*. New York: W. W. Norton & Company, 1967.

Wernick, Jeffrey. "Introduction." *The Sopranos: A Family History*. Ed. Allen Rucker. New York: New American Library, 2000.

White, Rob. "Hitting the High Notes." *Sight and Sound* 1 (January 2001): 12–13.

Willis, Ellen. "Our Mobsters, Ourselves: Why The Sopranos is Therapeutic TV." *The Nation* 2 April 2001: 26–32.

"Why *The Sopranos* Sing: Nothing Else on TV Can Touch HBO's Mob Hit – and That's Got the Network Suits Watching Their Backs: Will *The Sopranos* Change the Face of Television?" *Newsweek* 2 April 2001: 48.

Wilcox, Rhonda V. and David Lavery, eds. *Fighting the Forces: What's at Stake in Buffy the Vampire Slayer*. Boulder, CO: Rowman and Littlefield, 2002.

Witchel, Alex. "The Son Who Created a Hit." *The New York Times on The Sopranos*. 42–53.

Wolcott, James. "HBO's Singular Sensation." *Vanity Fair* February 2000: 24–7.

Wolf, Naomi. *The Beauty Myth: How Images of Beauty are Used Against Women*. New York: William Morrow, 1991.

Wren, Celia. "Melancholy Mobsters: HBO's *The Sopranos*." *Commonwealth* 28 Jan. 2000: 20–1.

Wurtzel, Elizabeth. *Bitch: In Praise of Difficult Women*. New York: Doubleday, 1998.

INDEX

This thing of ours